THE PASSIONATE AMATEUR'S GUIDE TO ARCHAEOLOGY IN THE UNITED STATES

THE PASSIONATE AMATEUR'S

GUIDE TO ARCHAEOLOGY
IN THE UNITED STATES

JOSLEEN WILSON

COLLIER BOOKS
A Division of Macmillan Publishing Co., Inc.
New York

DEDICATION

To the People—the native Americans who stubbornly and with honor preserve their ancient heritage against almost insurmountable odds. Because of their pride and conscience, archaeologists have something more than pottery sherds and projectile points to help unravel the mysteries of ancient life in America; they can speak with living descendants of the first Americans, those who retain in their blood and their lives the art and religion and humanity of the old ones. To them, more than anyone else, this book is dedicated.

Macmillan Publishing Co., Inc.
866 Third Avenue, New York, N.Y. 10022
Collier Macmillan Canada, Ltd.

Library of Congress Cataloging in Publication Data
Wilson, Josleen.
The passionate amateur's guide to archaeology in the United States.
Bibliography: p.
Includes index.
1. Archaeological museums and collections—United States—Directories. 2. United States—Antiquities—Societies, etc.—Directories. 3. Indians of North America—Museums—Directories. 4. United States—Antiquities.
5. Indians of North America—Antiquities.
6. Excavations (Archaeology)—United States. I. Title.
E159.5.W55 930.1'025'73 80-18351
ISBN 0-02-098670-X

10 9 8 7 6 5 4 3 2 1

Printed in the United States of America

CONTENTS

ACKNOWLEDGMENTS

Archaeology is a science that exists not just in excavation trenches that pit the wilderness or in great monuments and fabulous artifacts, but in the minds and efforts of the men and women who serve it. These people believe, without exception, that a large part of their work belongs to the public. The unique aspect of archaeology in America is that it is everywhere open to visitors; it is faithfully developed and interpreted for the pleasure and education of the people as a whole.

Some archaeological sites are digs-in-progress located in remote corners of the wilderness, while others are fully staffed and offer fine museums as well as facilities for camping and picnicking. At even the smallest, everyone connected with the project goes to great lengths to provide the public with services. From the first, this investigation into archaeology for amateurs has been greeted warmly and helpfully by state archaeologists and other scientists, park service employees, university professors, and members of amateur groups across the United States.

I will not try to name everyone who contributed information for this book. Each site, museum, and organization described provided firsthand information about its programs. The following acknowledgments are to those who extended their help beyond courtesy and cooperation.

Instead of the usual perfunctory thanks to one's spouse, I place my husband, Neil Felshman, at the head of this list for many reasons, least among them patience and understanding. He is a big-city boy who thinks the turf of Manhattan is the only place to be, yet he scaled mountains, hiked into gullies, and hung from all sorts of precarious positions to take some of the pictures for this book. He also provided the most generous help one writer can give another when he read and critiqued this manuscript. I'm proud to be in his debt.

The character and shape of this work have been held together throughout its long and sometimes difficult passage by its editor, Joyce Jack. Her enthusiasm, absolute integrity, and skill kept the manuscript in focus; even more, all her editorial decisions were based first and last on what was best for the book.

There were many others who had no personal obligation yet volunteered help on every conceivable level, including lengthy correspondence, research, and even, on more than one occasion, provided dinner and overnight lodging. Special thanks to Michael and Rene Humphries of Maryland for putting me on the right track; Kate Quinn at the Thunderbird site; Jim Anderson and Bill Iseminger at Cahokia; Darrell Fulmer at Mitchell, South Dakota; and Kathy Schultz of Wyoming. Kathy and her husband, Jeff, are sheep ranchers who have had archaeologists camping in their backyard for several summers. Kathy didn't hesitate to leave a flock of baby lambs she was bottle-feeding to guide me across several miles of rough dirt track into the middle of nowhere to see George Frison and his team at work in Agate Basin.

Thanks also to the personnel at the national parks, monuments, and forests who protect many archaeological sites. Park rangers are the most knowledgeable and efficient people I have met anywhere. At no time did a letter go unanswered or was a request for information or photographs denied. Special thanks to John S. Mohlhenrich, chief park interpreter for the Natchez Trace; Don S. Squire, superintendent at Walnut Canyon; John K. Loleit at Navajo National Monument; Kathy Harlan at Tonto National Monument; Chris Judson at Bandelier; Lois Winter at Chaco Canyon; and Gerard Baker at Knife River.

At the state parks, staffers were friendly and informative, even when bombarded with endless questions. Invariably, any expression of appreciation met with the standard reply, "That's what we're here for."

Museum curators and staff archaeologists of institutions all around the country took the time to answer innumerable questions about their collections. Sharon Urban of the Arizona State Museum, Judith Furlong of the Stovall, Gregory Perrino of the Museum of the Red River, and county archaeologist Ruth D. Simpson of the San Bernardino County Museum went to great lengths to provide information on amateur archaeological programs in their states.

Many state archaeologists, university professors, and other scientists wrote or telephoned to offer information and assistance. The following people made invaluable contributions to the research: Douglas Reger, Alaska; Hester Davis and Charles R. McGimsey III, Arkansas; John W. Foster, California; Bruce Rippeteau, Colorado; Cara L. Wise, Delaware; Louis Larson, Georgia; Thomas J. Green, Idaho; Charles J. Bareis, Illinois; Dr. James H. Kellar, Indiana; Duane Anderson, Iowa; Thomas A. Witty, Kansas; Curtis R. Thompson and Joan K. Koch, Louisiana; Charles E. Bolian, Maine; Tyler Bastion, Maryland; John R. Halsey and David A. Armour, Michigan; Christy A. H. Caine, Elden Johnson, and Donn M. Coddington, Minnesota; Mary L. Kwas, Eleana C. Turner, and Charlotte Capers, Mississippi; Robert Bray, Missouri; Lorraine E. Williams, New Jersey; Stewart L. Peckham, Jack K. Boyer, and Jo Davidson Smith, New Mexico; Robert E. Funk, New York; Carol S. Spears and Gordon P. Watts, North Carolina; Nick G. Franke and Frederick Schneider, North Dakota; James L. Murphy, Ohio; Don Sychoff and Larry Neal, Oklahoma; Barry C. Kent, Fred Kinsey III, and Gustav A. Konitzky, Pennsylvania; William Turnbaugh, Rhode Island; Robert L. Stephenson, Alan B. Albright, and Daniel Ray Sigmon, South Carolina; Robert Alex,

South Dakota; Joseph L. Benthall, Tennessee; Joel Gunn, Virginia A. Wulfkuhle, and J. David Ing, Texas; David B. Madsen, Utah; Giovanna Neudorfer, Vermont; John Broadwater, Dennis J. Hartzell, and Polly Longworth, Virginia; Sheila Stump and Dr. Richard Daugherty, Washington; H. Michael Dorsey, West Virginia; Joan Freeman, Wisconsin; and George Frison, Wyoming.

I am especially indebted to the many amateur groups who described their programs and offered enthusiastic support for this project. Their spirit and sense of purpose are instrumental in preserving the archaeological record of America. All of the amateurs I spoke with were dedicated, knowledgeable, and generous with their time and help.

My personal thanks go to a trio of outstanding research assistants—Jennifer Shiley in California, and Jeanne Schuman and Tim Knowles in New York—who were irreplaceable. And special thanks to Carol Atkinson and Edna Gengerke for several all-night sieges at the typewriter. Also to Don Biglands, Jeffrey Felshman, David Vos, and Joe Feldman for research contributions. And to Len Shwartz and his people at Amity Datsun in New Haven, Connecticut, whose advice and help about transportation smoothed out many rugged roads on a long trip across the country.

NOTE TO READERS

You may notice that in this book, the word "archaeology" is sometimes spelled without the second *a* in the names of sites and organizations—e.g., Sussex Society for Archeology and History.

The reason for this variation is that the spelling of the word is slowly changing and, though most organizations have not yet adopted the newer spelling, some have done so.

Note: When this book went to press, the visiting days and hours for each listing were accurate. However, in preparing the information contained in this book, it became apparent that the visiting hours and days for sites, and particularly for museums, change frequently. **So to avoid disappointment and ensure your enjoyment, please take the added precaution, when planning a trip to any site, dig, or museum, of telephoning ahead to verify visiting times.**

INTRODUCTION

Like most kids of my generation I grew up with the movies, so very early I knew there were people called archaeologists. They wore odd helmets and were always defying some ancient curse—it was heady, romantic stuff. And while other children played cowboys and Indians, I longed for a shovel of my own. I wanted to be an archaeologist. Archaeologists were always digging in the desert, and to me the most mysterious and wonderful places in the world were the great American deserts of the Southwest.

We were Okies, although not exactly the kind John Steinbeck described. During the Depression my Sicilian grandparents fed their eight children and half their neighbors from four acres of rocky Oklahoma soil. But my mother followed her adventure-loving husband to California's promised land. Every summer my mother and I came back to Oklahoma. We headed east on the northern route, through towns like Reno ("the biggest little city in the world"), Salt Lake City, and Denver, hurrying to the small farm and what seemed like hundreds of cousins and aunts and uncles.

For me, the magic happened during the journey back to California. We would take the southern route on U.S. 66. In those days, the Southwest was even more desolate than it is today. We carried a canvas water bag slung across the nose of the Oldsmobile and stopped at every one-pump station posted "Last Chance" to fill up on Dr. Peppers and gasoline. Often we saw Indian families camped on the empty highway waiting for any passing car, holding up woven rugs and painted pottery for sale.

Sometimes we traveled all night and stopped only after the sun hovered on the horizon and cast long coppery rays across the cold landscape. Early desert mornings are chilly, even in summer. But as the sun rushes up into the cloudless sky, the heat begins to build up. Like the desert animals, we sought the shade. In places like the Big Chief Motel in towns like Winslow, Arizona, we slept through the worst of the heat.

But I was happy only back in the car, speeding along the blacktop. I knew that in this punishing desert there were lost cities set like jewels in the gold bluffs. I don't know why I was so certain; perhaps I had seen them in movies or read about them in books. Whenever the spare outline of a mesa appeared like a mirage out of the shimmering heat, I would beg my mother to stop the car. I knew the cliff palaces were made almost invisible by their rich protective coloring, as gold as the mesa itself. She would slow the car so I could peer, squint-eyed, at the distant rocks, but soon she would speed up again, to catch the elusive breeze. It was too hot to explore the desert, and my mother's dreams lay further west.

Every year we made the same trip and I scanned the hills, searching and wishing. But like Coronado seeking the seven cities of gold, I never saw the cliff dwellings. In fact, I had grown up and was living in a New York City cliff dwelling before I actually saw a prehistoric ruin in the Southwest. It was Hovenweep, a group of great square towers guarding an empty canyon along the Utah-Colorado border.

There is a germ of truth in the saying, "When you've seen one ruin you've seen them all." But today, after seeing hundreds of prehistoric ruins all over the United States, many larger and more impressive, I still find Hovenweep the most beautiful and mysterious of all.

I never became an archaeologist, but archaeology has remained a passion with me. And I've learned that I'm not alone in this; it seems that the childhood desire to dig in exotic places is almost as common as wanting to play cowboys and Indians. Perhaps there's a bit of the scientist in every child, and a little bit of child in every archaeologist.

Aside from its vital role in the discovery and interpretation of human history, archaeology is adventurous and romantic. I said as much to a professional archaeologist who was working like a mule one muggy ninety-nine-degree afternoon in southern Georgia. "You must be kidding," he said, sweat streaming down his dirt-smudged forehead and into his eyes. But he smiled as he said it.

Archaeologists insist that the work is hard and painstaking and often dismally unrewarding. True, but there's also no denying it: archaeology *is* fun. It's traveling to remote places and playing in the dirt. It's meeting interesting people, some of whom have been dead for centuries.

Out near what is called Agate Basin in eastern Wyoming—an area important to archaeologists since a distinctive sort of ancient projectile point was found there in 1943—is a sheep ranch sprawling over thousands of acres. On this chunk of empty land under heavy storm-filled skies, a small team of scientists scraped away at an excavation pit where, after weeks of patient work, a few bison bones had been uncovered.

Off to one side, John Steeger, a graduate student from the University of Iowa, kneaded mud in deep trays until the dirt washed through the sieved bottoms and left the tiny fragments of artifact and bone so dear to the heart of archaeologists. I stood snapping pictures, trying to keep my camera dry.

"Isn't the first thing that attracts people to archaeology the fun of playing in the dirt, John?"

"Certainly not," he said and waved a muddy hand at me for emphasis. "I hate this. It's disgusting."

I clicked off a few more pictures. "What I really like to do," he continued, gazing wistfully toward the excavation pit, "is dig in that big dirt hole over there with a shovel."

Archaeology may appeal to the child in all of us, but its greatest attraction is on a level that few scientists speak of but most, if asked, readily admit. Archaeology provides a personal, almost mystical experience. You needn't view the great gold baubles of Tutankhamen to experience its romance.

You may stand at the crest of a small, overgrown mound along the Mississippi River where not even a pottery sherd or piece of bone mark the long-dead civilization that once thrived there. Yet you can sense the presence of the people who came before. Those people watched the same dark, wandering sky and the motion of the hard-traveling river.

One spring afternoon on the banks of the Potomac, I talked with Michael Humphries, archaeologist for St. Mary's County in Maryland. He held in his hand an almost transparent projectile point about an inch long, its sharp edges flaked in dozens of delicate scallops. It was several thousand years old. As we talked about the special relationship between modern and ancient man, Mike fingered the tiny point and his voice blurred. "You know," he said, "an artist made this." And who could say that his presence was not felt in the tiny stone point by this other man, so far distant in time?

Archaeology in the United States is a living science. In many corners of the Southwest, modern Pueblo Indians are direct descendants of prehistoric people. Charles Lummis, who wrote extensively on the Southwest, said that Americans can "catch their archaeology alive."

Since modern Americans are, in the main, descendants of immigrants, we tend to look for our distant roots in the ancient cultures of Europe and the Middle East. But we are also people of this land, and so we are bound strongly to those who lived and died on this soil in centuries past. These ancient people are in a very real sense among our spiritual ancestors.

There has been an unfortunate tendency to try to place American archaeology in the same category as Old World archaeology—a feeling that a civilization is important only if it leaves behind magnificent ruins. In fact, the civilizations of North America were nothing like those of Europe or Egypt, and such formidable remains will probably never be unearthed here. These ancient Americans left behind something much more fragile than monuments and gold.

In America, archaeology is a branch of anthropology. It is the study of a single race of people—the native Americans—who explored and settled a vast continent extending from Alaska to Cape Horn. For this reason alone, the work of American archaeologists is vastly different from that of their Old World counterparts. No matter where American archaeologists dig, from the great mounds of the Mississippi Valley to the ancient cliff dwellings of the Southwest, from the shell heaps of Florida to the temples of Peru, they uncover the work of a single race.

Thousands of years before Columbus "discovered" this land, early Americans had traveled and settled throughout a continent that contained almost every conceivable kind of environment. They responded to all of nature's demands. A race of people emerged so closely tuned to nature that religion and art were one. They were a people in harmony with their gods and unrivaled in spiritual judgment and esthetic power.

America was a continent of loneliness and space, a grandiose masterpiece ruled only by natural phenomena, so nature itself was god. The geography was distinctly carved: great plains, vast deserts, and rocky mountain ranges that divided the land. Probably nowhere else in the world did the topography of a land so clearly influence the evolution of its various cultures.

In this timeless country, the ticking of seconds or the counting of days was incomprehensible. In his life the American Indian blended all the elements of usefulness and beauty, religion and art. His fervent spiritual life was rich in imagery, poetry, and symbolism—this was his extraordinary legacy. It is not a legacy found in books nor seen in fabulous monuments.

Sometime around the birth of Christ, there was an exuberance of building all over the American continent. From that time of constructive activity, we have the ruins of great ceremonial mounds and the wonderful cliff dwellings in the Southwest that were community apartments. But in the main we discover the story of early Americans in small things: finely made projectile points, hoes fashioned from shell, and some of the most beautiful pottery and baskets seen anywhere in the world.

In American archaeology all of the time before the first European contact is termed prehistoric. The history of North America after the Europeans arrived and introduced written language is a vast and fascinating panorama of colonization and growth, and the archaeology of that time to the present, called historic, is a large and separate study.

In this book the word *archaeology* is used synonymously with the prehistoric stage of the American peoples' development. But often the two stories overlap, and we find an historic site built on top of a prehistoric one. Early colonials often settled around existing Indian villages and occasionally moved into abandoned communities. So, it's not unusual for archaeologists digging on colonial sites to find signs that prehistoric peoples lived there first. This is one of the most interesting aspects of American archaeology. We can trace a whole people from the earliest time and follow the story through the overlapping influence of other cultures.

For this reason, archaeology in the tropical state of Hawaii is not included here. The Polynesian culture originated along the coasts and river valleys of southeast Asia. These people have always been at home on the high seas. For thousands of years, their culture developed in the Solomon Islands, the New Hebrides, Fiji, Tonga, and Samoa. Around the time of Christ, Polynesian explorers by chance or enterprise made the long leap eastward to the volcanic islands of Tahiti and the Marquesas. These archipelagoes became the staging ground to launch Polynesian boats to the remote outposts of Oceania: Easter Island, New Zealand, and Hawaii. The Polynesian discoverers of Hawaii probably reached the islands about two thousand years ago.

People reached the American continent, however, by an entirely different route: over the northernmost tip of Asia, from Siberia across the Bering Strait into Alaska. They came many thousands of years ago, and their ancestry is almost invisible.

To explore these two diverse and important cultural evolutions together and give a clear picture of both in a single volume would be a monumental task. *The Passionate Amateur's Guide to Archaeology in the United States* traces the life of those people who arrived on the uninhabited American continent sometime in the distant past, and still live here today—the American Indian.

ON THE TRAIL OF EARLY MAN IN AMERICA

The story of the early inhabitants of America is as full of holes as the surface of the moon and equally as fascinating. Until very recently, archaeologists believed people first began to live on the American continent two to three thousand year's ago. A few imaginative scientists and overeager newspaper reporters made claims of greater antiquity, but these couldn't be proved. In the early part of this century, William H. Holmes, a noted archaeologist, called such ideas "the jazz of American archaeology." Then the carefully constructed theory of the recent arrival of people in America tumbled like a house of cards when an unusual discovery was made.

On one of those hot dusty southwestern days, probably in 1908, a black cowboy named George McJunkin was chasing a cow down a dried-up arroyo in the northeast corner of New Mexico. The cow led him in and out of the cracked stream bed, and at one point McJunkin saw something big and round and naked-looking jutting out of the river bank. It was a bone—the biggest bone the cowhand had ever seen. With his pocket knife, McJunkin scraped away some of the hard mud and managed to chop out several oversized bones. He packed his discoveries away in his saddlebags and carried them back to the ranch house.

Without education or training, George McJunkin nevertheless had the natural curiosity of a born archaeologist. But no one at the ranch was even remotely interested in his bag full of old bones, and it wasn't until some years later, in 1926, that word of this unusual find reached a major scientific organization. J. D. Figgins, director of the Colorado Museum of Natural History in Denver (today the Denver Museum of Natural History), identified the bones as belonging to a bison species that had disappeared more than ten thousand years earlier.

The following summer Figgins excavated the site and found something more than bison bones—something that makes an archaeologist's heart beat faster: evidence of human life. Beneath the articulated bones of a bison skeleton were nineteen man-made projectile points. One point was still firmly lodged between the ribs of the bison. There was no doubt that the animal had been killed by ancient hunters.

Figgins named the spear points for the nearby town of Folsom. These projectile points had an average length of about two inches and a distinctive flute channeled up the center of both faces. The beautifully fluted points were the only evidence of man, but they were evidence enough. This electrifying discovery proved that people had been in North America much earlier than presumed and made the name Folsom famous around the country.

The Folsom site was made a state monument but the rush of spectators—all armed with picks and shovels—soon made the whole area look like Swiss cheese. To save the site for scientific excavation, authorities closed the monument to the public. Today the original Folsom point, still planted between the bison's ribs, can be seen in the Denver Museum of Natural History.

Even now, after many older artifacts have been found, the Folsom points remain a landmark in American archaeology because they set archaeologists on the trail of ancient people. The Folsom points were dated at 9000 B.C. A few years later, points fashioned in a different style were found at Clovis and Sandia, New Mexico, and the date of earliest human habitation in America was pushed back further. Archaeological evidence accumulated to show that people were living on this continent twelve thousand years ago.

This matched well with the geological evidence. It was believed impossible for people to pass through the great ice barrier that covered much of North America for most of the Ice Age before 10,000 B.C.

There was one peculiar piece of the puzzle, however, that did not fit. People did not learn how to make these beautiful points overnight. The projectile points were skillfully crafted by pressure flaking—chipping the edge with a sharp tool to create a finely chiseled ridge. This technique requires practice, control, and refinement. Further, while Clovis points have been found all over America, their like has never been found anywhere else, indicating that the art evolved on this continent. Where—and when—did people learn to make these stone points? Who were the earliest Americans?

ICE AGE PEOPLE

Scientists are almost certain that the first Americans were modern *Homo sapiens*, since no human skeletal traces from earlier stages of evolution have ever been found. And yet, human skeletons are fragile bones. Unlike the heavy fossilized chunks of animal bone found buried in mud and river silt, unburied human bones disintegrate and scatter in the wind. Most skeletons that archaeologists uncover in America are from a time after people began to practice careful burial methods.

It is, of course, possible that an earlier relative of modern human beings may have reached North America and left no visible trace. Whatever their stage of evolution, the earliest Americans probably came from Asia. This theory is based on two pieces of strong evidence.

Although they differ in many ways, Native Americans share some basic physical traits with Asians, including reddish-brown skin, dark eyes, and straight black hair. They have little facial or body hair. This similarity in appearance is the first reason to suspect that Asia was the original homeland of the first Americans. The second reason is geographical: Asia is the only place from which ancient people could have come to this continent without using long-range boats. Siberia and Alaska are separated by a scant fifty-six miles across the Bering Strait, and this short trip is broken by three island steps. For almost the entire journey land is in sight, and during the Ice Age the entire Bering Strait was probably dry land.

The Great Ice Age began about one and a half million years ago and ended only ten thousand years ago. Some scientists believe it is still happening—that we are presently "in between" glacial advances. During this Pleistocene geological epoch, the northern half of North America buckled under the weight of ice sheets two miles thick. There was no sign of life anywhere in this sterile, frigid whiteness. But the ice cover was not constant. There were several advances and retreats, and during the last great siege of ice, the story of the early Americans begins to unfold.

The last major glacial advance was called the Wisconsin. Water evaporated from the oceans, and more and more snow was deposited on the glacier's bulk as it crept down North America. As the Wisconsin continued to grow, the oceans shrank and the level of the world's seas dropped. Parts of the ocean floor became exposed, and what is now the Bering Strait was a land bridge more than one thousand miles wide. Since little moisture fell in this part of the Arctic, which is protected by mountain ranges on the north and south, the land bridge, Alaska, and the northern Yukon escaped the massive glaciers that buried the rest of the North. This ice-free sanctuary between Asia and America is called Beringia.

Coming from the Asian side, wooly mammoths, bison, and musk oxen lumbered over the flat tundra. Their natural enemies followed—lions, cheetahs, and saber-toothed tigers. And behind these four-legged predators trailed the weaker, slower hunters, humans.

For centuries, perhaps millennia, animals and people lived on this grassy plain bordered by glaciers. There was no suspicion that beyond the wall of ice that enveloped them, a new world waited.

How did people first make their way past the ice? We know from archaeological findings that before the Ice Age ended, human beings had already reached the tip of South America. There are several intriguing theories as to how they got there.

At its maximum, the Wisconsin was a solid sheet of ice. But this single ice cap was really formed from three separate lobes: two in the east merged to make the enormous Laurentide glacier that covered most of Canada, and in the west was the smaller Cordilleran. These masses came together at the foot of the Canadian Rockies, forming an ice barrier that sealed off Beringia from the rest of America.

Several times during the Wisconsin advance, temporary melts called interstadials created natural passages in the icy wall. During a melt, the

NORTH POLE
GREENLAND SEA
Siberia
ARCTIC OCEAN
Alaska
ATLANTIC OCEAN
HUDSON BAY
Labrador
NORTH
PACIFIC OCEAN
AMERICA
ATLANTIC OCEAN
GULF OF MEXICO
CARIBBEAN SEA
SOUTH AMERICA
Land bridge
Glaciers
Opening of southern corridor
Miles
Kilometers

two great lobes of ice would briefly break apart and a narrow corridor fifty to one hundred miles wide opened between them. Down this passageway people could follow game animals south onto the Great Plains where they had easy access to vast, ice-free lands all the way to South America.

When the two glaciers parted, the land bridge was submerged by melting ice, barring a return to Asia. As people moved south, the ice re-formed behind them, cutting the migrants off from the North. This southern passageway is seen by some scientists as a one-way valve, opening and closing at irregular intervals. Recent examination of animal and plant life around the Bering Strait now suggests another possibility: the land bridge may have been continuously exposed rather than intermittently flooded with water. Perhaps the one-way valve never existed.

Whether the corridor was permanently open, or whether it was passable only sporadically, the immigrants did not all come at the same time, nor were they even from the same group of Asians. Later arrivals seem to have remained in the far north and are probably the direct ancestors of today's Eskimos.

It also has been suggested that people might have skirted the ice by traveling down the West Coast along the continental shelf, that exposed ribbon of land that surrounds the continent and now lies just below sea level. Underwater archaeology on the Northwest Coast may eventually provide some new answers about the human habitation of America.

Given these possible entry points, the most provocative question in American archaeology is: *when* did people first penetrate the ice barrier?

The most widely accepted date for the first entry of people through the southern corridor is twelve thousand years ago, during an interstadial melt known as the Two Creeks. This coincides with a multitude of archaeological sites found in America. But recent geological evidence indicates that the date of the melt cannot be so precisely determined. Also, similar melts occurred throughout the middle and early Pleistocene epoch, so people might have traveled this passage several different times during the Ice Age. Some evidence suggests that the corridor was open more or less permanently, even during the worst sieges of ice. If this were the case, people could have reached the Great Plains at almost any time. Theoretically at least, people may have entered America thirty thousand, fifty thousand—even one hundred thousand years ago.

But archaeological proof—actual evidence of life—is scarce. The few

---

In the last siege of the Ice Age, the Wisconsin glacier covered a large portion of North America, exposing a land bridge across the Bering Strait. During an interstadial melt, the two lobes of the glacier began to separate, creating a passageway through the ice. Through this corridor, the first people entered the New World from Asia.

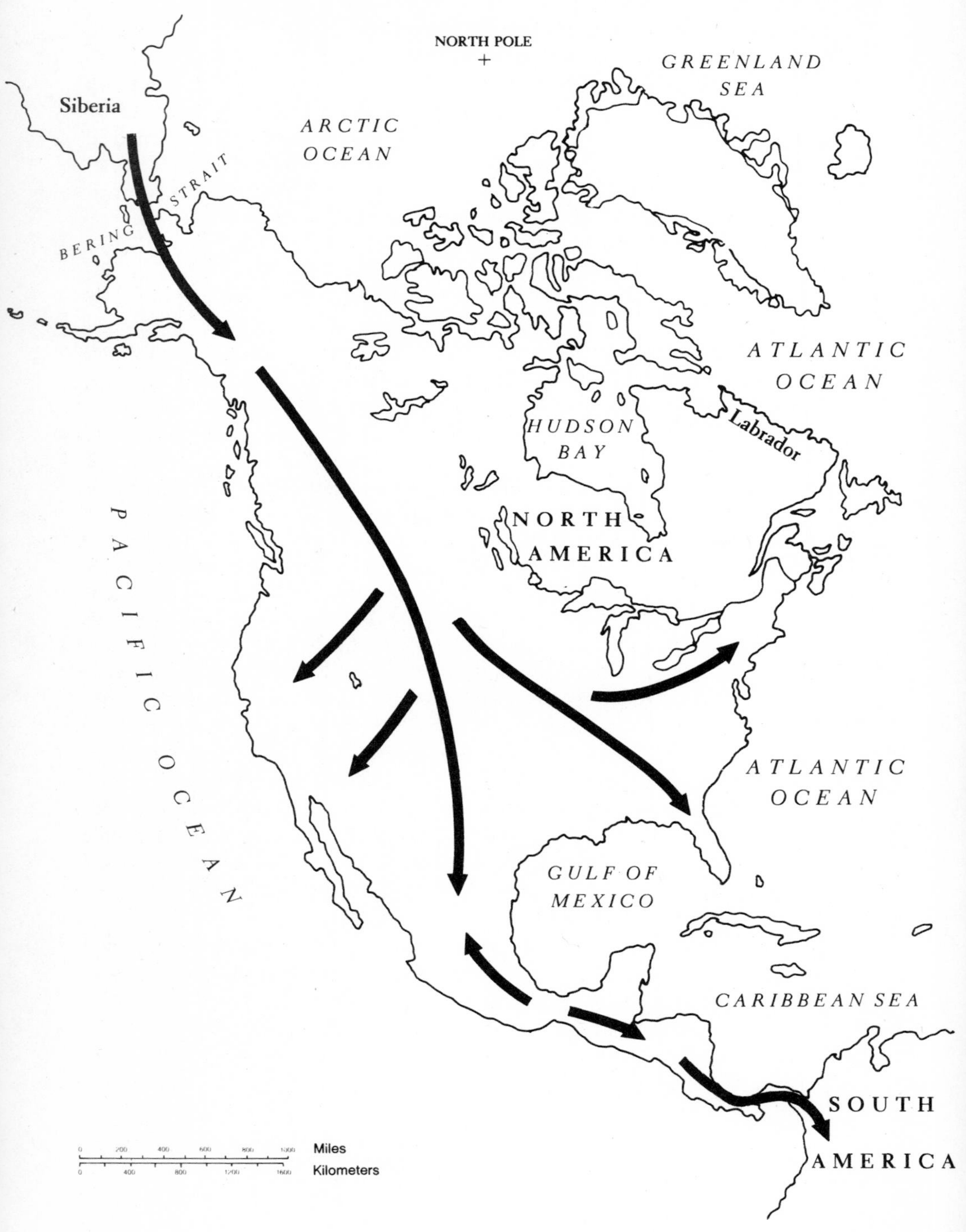
NORTH POLE
GREENLAND SEA
Siberia
ARCTIC OCEAN
BERING STRAIT
ATLANTIC OCEAN
HUDSON BAY
Labrador
NORTH AMERICA
PACIFIC OCEAN
ATLANTIC OCEAN
GULF OF MEXICO
CARIBBEAN SEA
SOUTH AMERICA
Miles
Kilometers

meager remains that have been unearthed tantalize scientists and laymen alike. If these early inhabitants of America existed at all, they left little to record their memory, perhaps no more than a broken rock with one sharp edge lying near a cold fire. Crude implements—simple tools fashioned by striking and chipping water-smoothed pebbles—have been found at scattered sites all over North and South America, often lying near dead hearths. Radiocarbon datings from these sites support the theory that humans warmed themselves by these campfires while a vast portion of the continent was still blanketed by glaciers.

Are these charred remains really campsites? The charcoal may be the result of natural fires and the tools may only be "geofacts," rocks fractured by the heat. But there is one important difference: these pebbles are chipped on one side only, and similar stones from the same period have been found in eastern Asia. Were these pebble-tool makers the first Americans? Evidence piling up almost daily strongly indicates they were.

Near the small town of Ayacucho in Peru, hidden in a hillside of volcanic rock, is Flea Cave. The cave is nearly 175 feet wide at its face and 80 feet deep. It is a perfect shelter, and archaeologist Richard S. MacNeish of the Peabody Foundation has proved that people have found it so for more than twenty thousand years.

From top to bottom, the cave floor revealed scores of stone tools together with bones of camels, horses, and big cats—all in a succession of animal bones and stone tools in well-stratified layers dating from 15,000 B.C. all the way back to 20,000 B.C. In the earliest and deepest zone of the cave floor, archaeologists found the remains of a giant sloth and four crude tools fashioned from volcanic tuff along with a few flakes struck from the tools. These flakes proved a vital clue, because one of them was a green stone that could only have come from outside the cave. These broken pebbles, which MacNeish calls "core tools," were not accidental geofacts.

Flea Cave contains some of the most conclusive evidence we have concerning early human life on the continent. But there is more. If people had made their way to South America by 20,000 B.C., they must have passed through North America much earlier. Controversial finds in California and Texas are keeping the trail of ancient man hot.

At the Calico Mountains site in the Mojave Desert, crudely fractured stones suggest that people lived there seventy thousand years ago. The exact location of ancient sites are closely guarded secrets, but the Calico site is one important Early Man location open to the public. Stone tools and bones of tiny dwarf elephants have been found on Santa Rosa Island, off the California coast. These remains may be forty thousand years old. And on a coastal

---

The first people filter onto the continent.

cliff, a human skull that scientists call Del Mar Man may prove to be forty-eight thousand years old.

In Friesenhahn Cave in central Texas, a large deposit of extinct animal bones was found together with crudely flaked tools. The bones and tools may date well back in the Wisconsin, perhaps even before the last stage of the Ice Age.

Other ancient sites have been discovered in Colorado and Pennsylvania. But it is in Alaska and the Yukon that archaeologists are focusing the most intense manhunt. Along the suspected pathways of ancient people, scientists are selecting potential sites around the Bering Strait and up and down the southern corridor.

So far, little evidence has turned up along the corridor itself. But in a few remote sites in the far north, new discoveries are creating excitement in scientific circles and stirring the imagination of Americans. In the ice-free corridor near Taber, Canada, the skeleton of an infant has been uncovered. The tiny bones suggest a possible age of fifty thousand years. And in the Yukon's Old Crow Basin—ice-free during even the most severe glacial periods—a serrated caribou bone shows unmistakable signs of human alteration. The bone is thirty thousand years old. Even today, some Eskimos use an almost identical tool to scrape animal hides. The many altered animal bones found at this site indicate that the first tools were made from bone rather than stone, a new insight into the life of the earliest Americans.

At the bottom of a thirty-foot gold mine in the Alaskan Yukon-Tanana uplands, a geologist found fossilized animal bones that have been securely dated to 29,700 years. The bones clearly showed chop and burn marks and spiral fractures, indicating the animals had been slaughtered by human beings.

These discoveries seem to prove without question that people lived in North America much earlier than twelve thousand years ago. Yet scientists disagree vehemently about the authenticity of these finds. The difficulty is in the probability of accidental dating inherent in the radiocarbon technique. Radiocarbon dating, called C-14, measures time by radioactive decomposition of material, usually charcoal, wood, bone, or shell. The technique can be used only on material that once lived, so stone tools can be dated only when found with organic remains such as bones or charcoal. To complicate matters, other elements can intrude on the material and contaminate the radioactive carbon, making the result of the test unreliable. A promising new dating technique known as amino acid racemization is based on the chemical changes that take place in bones and shell over time. But many scientists are still skeptical about the results from this process.

Even with these problems, archaeologists today continue their search for the earliest Americans; it is archaeology's most avid pursuit. How far back does their story go? We may never know. The footsteps grow more and more faint, until they disappear into the past.

Scientists today seem to favor one of three basic time frames for the entry of people into North America. The "early arrival" theory places people south of the ice sheets at least forty thousand years ago and perhaps one hundred thousand years ago. The "middle arrival" theory accepts a later date, perhaps thirty thousand years ago. And the "late arrival" theory—which is daily being challenged—accepts people in America no more than twelve thousand years ago.

Certainly we begin to trace early people with more authority around 10,000 B.C., when their skill in making weapons noticeably improved. This is the beginning of the Paleo-Indian Tradition, the days of the Big Game Hunters.

THE BIG GAME HUNTERS

A "tradition" is a broadly defined way of life practiced more or less in the same manner by different people at different times. The nomadic hunters of the Paleo-Indian Tradition are often grouped together and spoken of as a single culture living within a single time frame. But these Big Game Hunters lived all over North and South America. In a burgeoning population wave, they swept across ten thousand miles of raw frontier, from Alaska all the way to Tierra del Fuego. While it is true that all Paleo-Indians had the same goal—survival—and the same means—fire, spears, clothing—to hunt the giant game and tackle the elements, even in those days different clans adapted differently to the demands of their environment. As centuries and millennia passed, these adaptations would grow into very specific cultural traits.

In North America, the Big Game Hunters roamed over the Great Plains, the Eastern Woodlands, and the Southwest, following the Ice Age megafauna that fed on well-watered vegetation. The cold climate produced incredible beasts: sloths ten feet tall, beavers the size of grizzly bears, four species of mammoth, and three types of mastodons.

Although the hunters had no permanent homes, they undoubtedly returned to the same place over and over again. Bluff shelters, caves, and rude lean-tos were their dwellings. Clothed in skins and armed with stone weapons, they banded together with a few other families into small hunting parties. Eventually the hunters became more skilled and their tools and weapons more sophisticated.

Twelve thousand years ago, the Big Game Hunters dominated most of the continent save for small pockets in the West and Northwest, particularly the valleys of the Columbia River, where fishing and food gathering were all that was required to furnish the food supply. In these pockets a lifeway called the Old Cordilleran Tradition may have been contemporaneous with the Big Game Hunting Tradition.

Almost everywhere else people hunted the Ice Age giants: camels, tigers, horses, bison, and elephants. Three distinct projectile points —Sandia, Clovis, Folsom—are closely identified with the Big Game Hunters. Discovery of these points tells scientists where and when the hunters lived.

All stone points are generally called projectile points, meaning that they could have tipped different-size spears and darts. The wooden shafts of the spears have disintegrated, so we do not know the exact length of the spear to which each point was attached. But we do know that the early

Americans did not have bows and arrows, so these points are not called arrowheads.

Similar projectile points used by Big Game Hunters, which vary somewhat in size and shape, have been found throughout the country and carry the name of the first location where they were found. The most important fact about all of them is that they cannot be found on the Asian side of the Bering Strait.

THREE FAMOUS POINTS

A few years after J. D. Figgins identified the first Folsom points buried in or near the remains of an extinct bison, similar points were discovered among elephant bones near Clovis, New Mexico. But these projectile points were larger than the Folsom points, and the shallow fluting ran only halfway up the point. The Clovis points were eventually dated to 9500 B.C., slightly older than the Folsom points. The original Clovis point still lies among the bones of the mammoth foreleg in the Philadelphia Academy of Natural Science.

Folsom points have been found only in the high plains of the Southwest. Clovis points, on the other hand, have been discovered in every one of the mainland states, and many more in the East than the West. But eastern points are hard to date because they are found almost exclusively on the surface, turned up by the plow. Thanks to amateur archaeologists who have pinpointed and recorded their finds, we know that dense concentrations of Clovis points are centered in Kentucky, Tennessee, and Ohio. There is a wide geographical distribution of Clovis sites but all such projectile points apparently originated within the same narrow time span: from 9500 to 9000 B.C., although there is some evidence of earlier development.

The unusual fluting that marks both Clovis and Folsom points puzzles scientists. Why did the hunters go to such trouble to carve out a lengthwise channel on these points? Some suggest that the channel permitted a flow of blood from the hunted animal, others that it increased the velocity of the spear. Still others contend that the thinned base could be more easily inserted into the split end of a spear shaft. But the fluting also made the points fragile and difficult to make. We still don't know where the custom of fluting originated, nor why it was abandoned. But by 7000 B.C., the fluted points had disappeared.

Most Clovis points are discovered in campsites or sites where animals were killed. A campsite shows a wide variety of tools in addition to the fluted points. A kill site reveals only animal bones and points and sometimes a few butchering tools.

One famous kill site is near Dent, Colorado, where only three Clovis points were found among the remains of a dozen mammoths. How did the elephants die? By careful observation archaeologists re-created the scene of an ancient elephant hunt and solved the mystery.

All of the mammoth bones were concentrated in the bottom of a small gully, where a stream trickles out of a sandstone bluff into the South Platte River. On foot, hunters would maneuver the elephants toward the edge of the bluff and then stampede them over the side. Some animals were killed in the fall; others were wounded by falling rocks and killed with spear thrusts. Other kill sites verify that the Paleo-Indians were expert hunters, and their very efficiency eventually may have led to the demise of the giant herds of mammoths.

Clovis and Folsom points dominate the Paleo-Indian Tradition. But a third point has been discovered which may be even older. The Sandia point is slightly smaller than the Clovis point. It is not fluted, and one side of the stem bulges at the shoulder. The Sandia points have never been found in layers that can be precisely dated, and they may be older than or contemporary with the Clovis points. Only two sites have revealed Sandia points: a cave in Sandia, New Mexico, and a possible mammoth kill site found on the surface nearby. Sandia Man Cave in the Sandia Mountains east of Albuquerque is open to the public, and excavated material from the site can be seen at the Maxwell Museum of Anthropology in Albuquerque.

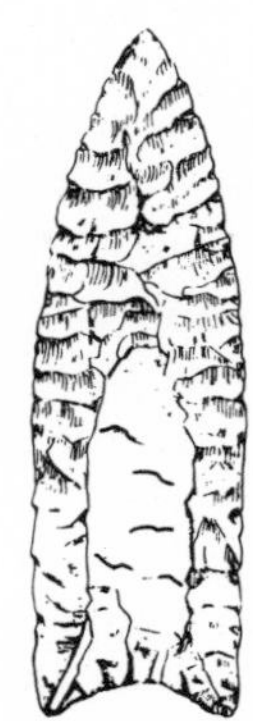

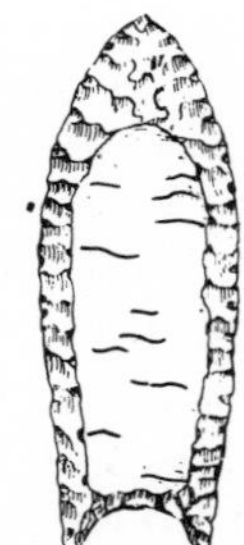

A. Sandia Point **B. Clovis Point** **C. Folsom Point**

A. Its one-sided bulge distinguishes the Sandia point. The points are between 2 and 4 inches long and usually crudely flaked.

B. Clovis points are more finely made than Sandia points. They are between 1½ and 5 inches long and usually have a flute that runs halfway up the face of both sides.

C. The leaf-shaped Folsom points are lighter and slightly smaller than Clovis points, between ¾ and 3 inches in length. They are marked by ear-like projections at the base, and the distinctive flute runs the full length of both sides.

THE ICE AGE ENDS

Nearly ten thousand years ago the great ice sheets began to melt, and as the ice receded, the giant animals faded into history. The mammoths and mastodons disappeared, as did the giant ground sloths and bison, the horses and camels. Lions and saber-toothed tigers vanished.

No one is sure about the reasons for their disappearance. Some scientists believe the animals could not adapt to the violent fluctuations in temperature which altered plant life. Others believe the Paleo-Indians were such accomplished hunters that they killed off the animals. Whatever the reason for this change, it brought about dramatic alterations in the life of the Big Game Hunters. The Paleo-Indian Tradition dwindled in different parts of the continent as the big game disappeared; it was slowly replaced by the Archaic Tradition.

EASTERN ARCHAIC TRADITION

The hunters turned gradually to depending on shellfish, plants, seeds and nuts, and smaller game for survival. They became gatherers of food and settled into more permanent campsites near streams and forests. Hunters of smaller game now used an atlatl, or spear thrower. (An atlatl is a stick of wood or bone, about 2 feet long, used to launch a dart. It has a hook at one end and a handhold or finger grip at the other. The notched dart shaft is fitted into the hook, and the hunter holds both the other end of the atlatl and the middle of the shaft in one hand. The atlatl is often weighted with a stone. When the hunter releases the dart, the atlatl has the effect of lengthening his arm and increases the velocity and distance of the dart.) The hunters also made delicate stone points and carved ornaments and beads from shell. In addition, they fashioned stone cooking and storage pots.

The human population continued to increase, and families began to live together and combine their efforts in small communities. It was common to change campsites with the seasons, returning to the same places summer and winter. This new stage of development is known as the Archaic Tradition.

The Archaic Tradition began as the ice melted and the big game disappeared. But it reached different parts of the country at different times, as distinct changes in the environment shaped the lives of the people. Even at this very early date in human life in America, distinct life styles began to evolve.

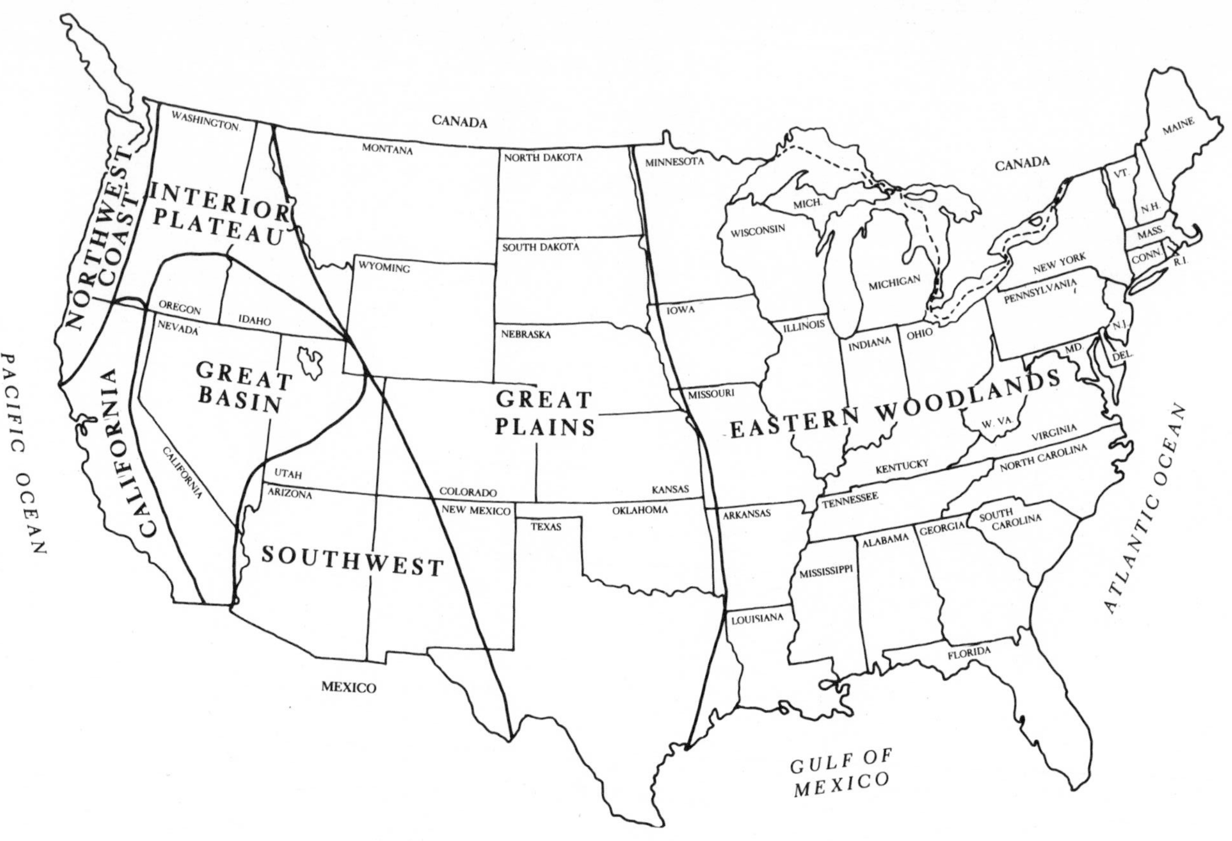

Ancient geographical regions of the United States.

The North American land area divided naturally along the Mississippi River on an east-west basis. Lush forests and rivers blanketed the East. Despite the loss of big game, Archaic families increased and the population thrived as people began to fish and gather plant food. Massive shell heaps along eastern rivers show that family groups stayed in one place for long periods of time. The eastern Archaic people ground and polished their stone tools, but they did little weaving or basketry.

The Archaic Tradition in the East began around 8000 B.C. and spanned the centuries until the introduction of farming around 1000 B.C. It is difficult to imagine such a long stretch of time in our present society, where anything that happened two hundred years ago is considered ancient history. But life over these millennia was peaceful and unhampered by wars or major migrations. It remained virtually unchanged until farming, probably introduced through a trade network from the Southwest via Mexico, was adopted. Agriculture ushered in a new tradition whose trademarks were pottery, farming, and the use of the bow and arrow. This was the Woodland Tradition.

WOODLAND TRADITION

Geographically, all of the United States east of the Mississippi is called the Eastern Woodlands. But "Woodland" is also an archaeological term used to describe a life style that followed the Archaic Tradition in the East.

In the far Northeast, the land was rocky and heavily wooded, and the people clung to a hunting and gathering life. But further west and in the regions to the south, crude cultivation of plant food was a new and valuable addition to the life of the Woodland people. Permanent villages sprang up, and hundreds of communities dotted the bluffs overlooking the planted fields in the river bottoms. Most of the prehistoric excavations on the eastern seaboard today involve Woodland sites, for that was the first time people began to live together in large groups and leave behind unique artifacts.

Specific cultures also developed, within the Woodland Tradition. In Minnesota, Wisconsin, and northern Michigan, people began to shape pure native copper into tools and ornaments. These people of the Old Copper Culture were the first Americans to use metal. There was a distinct style of pottery and burial practices throughout the region. In the Midwest and some northern regions, the unusual custom of burying red ochre in graves gave rise to the name of the Red Ochre people.

The most outstanding trait of the Woodland people was mound building. The construction of earthen burial mounds over graves and tombs flourished all over the eastern United States, but the various builders were not necessarily related nor did they exist in the same time.

To the north effigy mounds in the shape of birds and animals covered the hillsides of Wisconsin, Illinois, Minnesota, and Iowa. Some are seen as far south as southern Ohio. And there is a strange mound of white pebbles shaped like an eagle in Georgia; its wingspan is 120 feet.

Two extraordinary cultures that influenced communities all over the Eastern Woodlands evolved in the Ohio Valley. These are known as the Adena and Hopewell cultures. Some anthropologists believe the Adena and Hopewell people were actually members of a religious cult whose ideas spread among many different cultures. These two famous mound-building cultures are invariably discussed together but they were, in fact, different cultures or cults that thrived at different times.

The Adena people lived earlier and disappeared sooner than the Hopewellians. Their culture radiated from its center at Chillicothe, Ohio, and covered the Ohio River Valley and some parts of West Virginia and Kentucky. Its influence spread up the Ohio River and perhaps as far east as Chesapeake Bay. The Hopewell culture overlapped the Adena and spread over a much larger area, including Illinois, Michigan, Iowa, Missouri, and northeastern Oklahoma. Its influence was felt as far east as New York and south to the Gulf of Mexico.

These people were never full-fledged farmers. They cultivated some plants but continued to hunt and gather food. Resources must have been plentiful and easily obtained because both cultures emphasized art and religion, practices that they developed to magnificent proportions and that are sure signs of affluence in any society. They made extraordinary pottery and imported copper from the north to make bracelets, rings, and beads. They are best known, however, for their burial mounds and the lavish art forms associated with these mounds.

The Adena people built conical mounds, while the Hopewellians constructed mounds that are round and low to the earth. The Hopewell surrounded their mounds with precise earthworks in geometric shapes of squares, circles, and octagons. The dirt walls were as much as twelve feet high and fifty feet wide at the base. One of these complexes at Newark, Ohio, covers four square miles.

The Adena and Hopewellians also differed from each other physically, indicating that they came from different parts of the country. The Adena people were round headed and the Hopewellians had long heads. Both groups, however, practiced cranial deformation, flattening the back of the head and slanting the forehead.

The burial practices of both cults were religious in connotation and were the bases for high artistic development in both cultures. Adena mounds grew larger over the years as more bodies were added and covered with earth. Grave offerings that honored the dead often seem to identify their lifetime occupations. All these centuries later, we can recognize artisans because of the flint, stone, and projectile points buried with them. And yet just as often, the grave goods are puzzling. Usually a single pipe was placed with each burial. But what of the thirty-two pipes arranged around one body? Was this individual a pipe maker or a highly revered member of the cult?

Many other puzzles are also unsolved. What was the purpose of the incised stone tablets recovered from several Adena mounds, especially the tablet bearing strange hieroglyphics recovered from Grave Creek Mound in West Virginia, the largest of all Adena mounds? The use of these tablets is unclear. Here also appears for the first time the famous Adena bird of prey, a highly stylized raptorial bird repeated on many other artifacts. And what was the purpose of the most conspicuous and famous of all American mounds—the Great Serpent Mound? No artifacts have ever been found within its rotund twists, but a nearby burial mound has yielded Adena artifacts. The Great Serpent Mound, located in central Ohio, is a quarter of a mile long and the largest serpent effigy in the world. Today it is preserved in a state park, and an observation tower permits a full view of all of its 1254 feet.

There are still many unsolved mysteries about the Adena people, but the most pressing questions may never be answered. How and where did the Adena culture originate? Were the Adena people absorbed or pushed out by the Hopewellians? If there was no contact, where did the Adena

Serpent Mound, Jackson, Ohio. (Photo courtesy of the Museum of the American Indian, Heye Foundation.)

people go? All we know is that as suddenly as they came, the Adena people vanished from the Ohio Valley at the beginning of the Christian era.

For another seven hundred years after that, the Hopewellians extended their influence over large areas and diverse cultures of the United States. They raised art to even greater heights. Buried within their mounds are found evidence of an accomplished and cultured people: copper headdresses, fresh-water pearls worked into beautiful patterns, knives of polished black obsidian, translucent pink drinking cups made from shell, and thin mirrors of mica cut into exotic shapes. There are also carved stone statues, pipes shaped like birds and men, and other opulent gifts that paid honor to the dead. Some of the art is highly abstract and some so closely representative that the precise genus and species of animal is easily identified.

Some suggest the Hopewell originated in Mexico and came up the Mississippi, pushing the Adena people out. But no sites have been found between Mexico and Ohio that trace the suggested migration. Others are sure the Hopewell spread east from Illinois to Ohio. There are many signs that the Hopewell people depended on a vast network of trade threading its way up and down the rivers to supply them with raw materials for their artworks and a link to other religious groups.

Then suddenly the Hopewellians, too, were gone. No one knows why, but their influential and widespread cult collapsed. Its decline was swift and final; drought and plague are probable causes. The Hopewellian decline may have been related domino-fashion to the collapse of the great city of Teotihuacán in the Valley of Mexico, the largest pre-Columbian city in the New World.

Mexico was the source of the new agriculture, for corn and beans were first cultivated there. The Valley of Mexico became the central influence both north and south along the riverways. But something drastic happened there around A.D. 700. Warring villages may have interrupted the trade network and cut off supplies. However, lurking in the background is an idea that a mysterious invasion from a powerful enemy was the cause of Teotihuacán's destruction. It remains another of the great mysteries to be solved by future archaeologists.

Both the Adena and Hopewell cultures reached their climax without making the transition to a fully agricultural society. With their demise craftsmanship deteriorated and mound building became a crude shadow of its earlier magnificence.

MISSISSIPPIAN TRADITION

The disappearance of the Hopewellians around A.D. 700 marked the end of the Woodland Tradition in the East. The people of the Mississippi followed the river north and south searching for bottom land to farm. They began to develop an intensive form of cultivation that for the first time included maize. They cleared land and cultivated crops. Large towns grew up, and the population expanded again into a new, purely agricultural tradition called Mississippian. The Mississippian Tradition flourished over great regions of the East, especially in the lower and central Mississippi River Valley and the Southeast. This farming tradition was less dominant in the North and Northeast.

The affluence of the new farm communities supported higher art forms. Artists during these years worked on skins and fibers that have long since decayed. But they also worked in shell, stone, bone, copper, and clay. Some of the most unusual and beautiful pottery from this period is at Mound State Monument in Alabama. Here the Mississippian Tradition is seen in its purest form, and the artifacts recovered from the mounds are unique.

By the time the Mississippian Tradition reached full bloom, a sophisticated religious and governmental system had evolved. The construction of large flat-topped mounds, which we call the great temple mounds, was part of the system.

It is not yet known where these mound builders learned their craft. There were mound-building societies all over Mexico, but there is no positive way to know if the practice spread from north to south, or vice versa. Speculation is that refugees from the Valley of Mexico migrated north and established colonies along the river, but there is no sign that they came as far north as Illinois, where the greatest Mississippian city grew up.

Whatever their inspiration, the Mississippian mounds were never used for burials. They were exclusively religious or ceremonial in purpose and design. Their broad, flat summits supported large ceremonial buildings or temples. Thatched houses sprang up around the temple mounds, and the dead were buried in cemeteries usually outside the main compound. Some mounds are the size of playing fields, and archaeologists believe that ceremonial games were held here. A few are so large that other mounds are built on their level summits.

The greatest mound north of the Rio Grande was built at this time. The fabulous Monks Mound at Cahokia in Illinois is one hundred feet high, sixteen acres at its base, and packed with twenty-two million cubic feet of soil. The task of building this mound by hand is almost inconceivable, because for all of their achievements the prehistoric people of the New World did not have the wheel. Hundreds of thousands of individual baskets of soil were carried to the mound and deposited there. Some of the borrow pits, left from where the soil was dug, are so large that they are today permanent lakes. Most scientists feel that everyone in the community participated in the mound building. Construction of this colossus shows great organization, but there is no evidence of a subjugated society forced into slave labor to a ruling class.

As its zenith Cahokia was one of the most densely populated areas in prehistory, surpassed only by the great cities of the Valley of Mexico. Cahokians traded salt, tools, jewelry, and ceremonial goods throughout the country for the raw materials needed for their crafts. This extraordinary city flourished between A.D. 900 and 1300. No larger city existed in the United States until Philadelphia grew to more than thirty thousand people in 1800.

Unlike the earlier Woodland cultures, the people of the Mississippian Tradition had many ties with Mexico and Central America. One unusual cult that seemed strongly influenced by people from further south arose during the later phases of the Mississippian. This cult, seen mainly in the Southeast, was preoccupied with symbols of death. Traces of its fanaticism are seen as far west as Spiro, Oklahoma, and as far east as Etowah, Georgia. The so-called Death Cult (also called the Southern Cult) is identified by certain bizarre designs engraved on polished black pottery, carved on shell, or embossed on thin copper pendants: horned rattlesnakes, swastikas, human

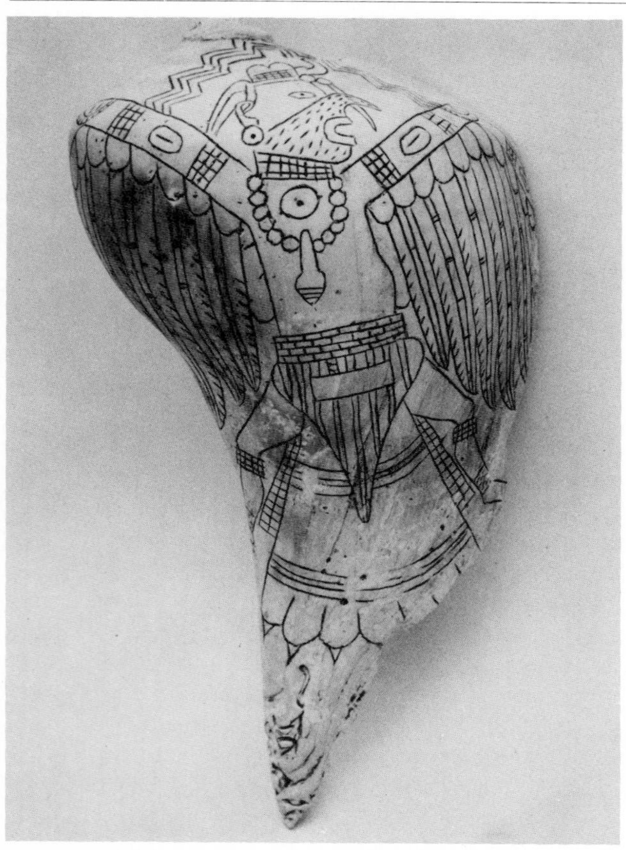

A conch shell etched with the famous Eagle-Man design recovered from Spiro Mound in Oklahoma. (Photo courtesy of the Museum of the American Indian, Heye Foundation.)

skulls, hearts and severed arms, and a hand with an eye inscribed on the palm.

Some scientists believe the cult's symbols could have been expressions of vitality and suggest they are associated with harvest and life renewal rather than death. The origin and true purpose of the cult has never been discovered nor has the reason for its meteoric rise and fall. It had completely disappeared by the time of European contact.

Remnants of the Mississippian Tradition survived into the historic period, but most of their grandeur had faded by the time the first Europeans came. Cahokia's heyday was long past when the French passed through in the sixteenth century and the explorers found only overgrown mounds.

As they penetrated the deeper recesses of the continent, the Europeans found a widely settled land where many civilizations had already risen and declined. As they probed the remote rivers and valleys of North America, these invaders could not fail to notice the great mounds, although the mound builders themselves had all but disappeared.

As English colonials pushed westward during the eighteenth century, they began to circulate the myth that the great mounds and their wonderful treasures were products of a lost civilization of white settlers who had been overwhelmed by the Indians. These stories had more than a shade of righteousness and self-interest about them. They all sought to justify the whites' confiscation of the land and life of the American aboriginals. The myths grew in proportion to the incursion until the Smithsonian Institution finally launched a large-scale investigation in 1880 and ten years later proclaimed in an eight-hundred-page report that the rugged and majestic mounds were built by no one else but the ancestors of the present American Indians.

WEST OF THE MISSISSIPPI

From as early as the time of the Paleo-Indians, the people in the western part of the continent lived in a manner quite unlike the easterners. For a while the climate was warm and humid, but as the Ice Age ended the landscape grew dry. Big game hunting ended early in the West, and the people adopted an Archaic life style, which reflected their arid environment. They depended on hunting small game, gathering seeds and plant food, and fishing along the coastal regions. In most of the West, the Archaic Tradition persisted in various forms into historic times.

THE GREAT PLAINS

At the end of the Ice Age, that great swath of country extending south from Canada all the way to Texas called the Great Plains was almost deserted. But as the climate improved, lush grasses drew a new kind of game. Herds of hairy, humpback animals related to the bison ranged freely over the plains. And man, the hunter, was not far behind. Now he used a bow and arrow resembling those used by eastern Archaic peoples and his prey was buffalo.

As agriculture reached the East, some Woodland people spilled over into the grass steppes and began to farm the river bottoms. Hundreds of farming towns lined the rivers of the Great Plains and some lasted into historic times.

But game was so abundant and easy to kill that most of the Plains people abandoned farming and devoted themselves once more to hunting. These Indians of the plains are probably the only prehistoric people to give up agriculture as a major means of survival once it had been acquired. Further west on the plains, the climate was too dry for farming ever to take hold.

NORTHWEST COAST AND INTERIOR PLATEAU

On the Northwest Coast and Interior Plateau a tradition sometimes called the Old Cordilleran blended with the Paleo-Indian Tradition. Little is known about the origin of this lifeway that is often identified by a leaf-shaped projectile point. The Old Cordilleran Tradition takes its name from the giant glacier that covered this part of the country during the Ice Age.

In the Pacific mountains and all along the coast, the Old Cordilleran

Tradition was parent to an exclusively northwestern culture that began around 5000 B.C. and remained largely unchanged into historic times. This country west of the Rockies was isolated from other developing cultures, and the people here settled along river rapids and created a highly specialized culture that thrived on fishing and gathering. Their unique and luxurious arts and religious practices evolved into modern times and identify them even today.

The Interior Plateau is a geographic pocket that includes Idaho and part of Washington and Oregon. The people who lived in the region led a harder life than their neighbors on the coast and barely survived on small game and wild plants. None of the peoples of the Northwest Coast or Interior Plateau ever practiced farming or developed pottery.

DESERT TRADITION

In southern areas of the West, the land became arid as the Ice Age ended, and plants and animals adapted themselves to a new environment. Once again the way of life altered to suit the environment. These westerners developed a mode of living completely different from those who lived anywhere else in the country. The Big Game Hunters were here, but the western Archaic very early on overlapped the Paleo-Indian Tradition and evolved into what is sometimes called the Desert Tradition. This Desert Tradition extended all the way from southern Oregon into Mexico.

THE GREAT BASIN

The Great Basin is that sunken piece of geography that lies between the Rockies and Sierras. It includes southern portions of Oregon and Idaho, the California deserts, a big part of Utah, and all of Nevada. It is a land of little rainfall, but great lakes formed here as glaciers melted off the mountain ranges into the geological sinks. The Great Salt Lake is such a place.

Some Paleo-Indians settled on the fringes of these early lakes to fish and hunt deer and antelope. As the climate grew drier, they had to depend on smaller animals and even insects for survival. Meat was scarce and wild seeds were important. These people of the desert made special tools to grind seeds ten thousand years ago—at least two thousand years before millstones and manos appeared in the Old World. These westerners also invented the first baskets seen anywhere in the world for holding seeds. They used the atlatl (spear thrower), made finely woven netting, and perfected smaller bone tools. This way of life waxed and waned with shifts in the climate and continued almost unchanged into historic times.

California, in addition to being a state of mind, is an archaeological designation that takes up most of the California coastline but none of its deserts. Those who lived on the coast enjoyed an abundant food supply and a perfect climate. Further inland the Old Cordilleran blended with the Desert Tradition of the Great Basin. Californians used millingstones and hand stones to grind seeds and nuts, and you can still see hundreds of thousands of pits worn into flat rock throughout the state. California is the center of much archaeological activity and speculation, since scientists are not at all sure when people first entered the region nor where they came from.

THE SOUTHWEST

The people of the Southwest followed a Desert pattern similar to the people of the Great Basin. They had been Big Game Hunters and very early on began to hunt small game and gather seeds. But whereas the Desert Tradition of the Great Basin remained almost unchanged, that of the Southwest formed the basis for one of the most extraordinary cultural displays of prehistory. Here the western Archaic developed into a basic culture called Cochise, which followed a life style very similar to that of the Great Basin dwellers. Out of this Cochise culture grew the three great desert traditions known as the Mogollon, Hohokam, and Anasazi—the famous cliff dwellers.

The skill and art of these great cultures were reflected in the everyday life of the people. Their agriculture showed enormous sophistication, and today you can still trace the paths of their water control systems, which included both irrigation canals and flood farming. Those who lived near rivers and streams, where the water supply was more or less constant, dug irrigation canals. Others built systems of dikes that caught seasonal rains and released the water when needed. They watered the desert and grew squash, corn, beans, and cotton.

Although they built no temples or pyramids, they developed a highly organized religious life based on climate, weather, and close observation of all the elements of nature. Unlike the mound builders, their skill in architecture is reflected in the houses they built for everyday living.

The Mogollon, oldest of the great southwestern traditions, centered in the southern mountain valleys between Arizona and New Mexico. The Mogollon were the first people outside of Mexico to grow maize. But today they are best remembered for their highly stylized pottery called Mimbres. The fantastic black and white Mimbres designs are so beautiful and unique that they are recognized all over the world.

During the time of the Mogollon, another southwestern culture called Patayan briefly flourished along the Colorado River Valley near the Arizona-

California border. Almost nothing remains to speak of the life and times of the Patayan people. Although they apparently never developed a major culture, archaeologists are intrigued by these farming people whose ruined houses and other remains may lie beneath layers of silt washed down by the river. The people of the modern Yuman tribes may be descendants of the Patayan.

Southwestern Arizona was the home of the Hohokam, a people at least partially contemporary with the Mogollon. Across the dry lowland desert of the Gila and Salt river basins, the Hohokam spun a network of irrigation canals that forced vast tracts of inhospitable land into burgeoning fields of cotton and corn. In prehistoric times, between 200 and 250 miles of canals may have criss-crossed the desert around present-day Phoenix. The modern Pima and Papago Indians are the direct descendants of the ancient Hohokam gardeners. *Hohokam* is the Pima word for "those who have gone."

The Anasazi came later and probably absorbed the Mogollon people. They lived all over the Four Corners area where today Utah, Colorado, New Mexico, and Arizona join. Of all the great southwestern cultures, the Anasazi are the best remembered, for they are the builders of the magnificent jewellike cliff dwellings. In our own century the glowing backdrops of Anasazi country has lent beauty and romance to countless Hollywood films. Today the Navajo Reservation occupies most of the old Anasazi territory, although the Navajo are unrelated to these "ancient ones."

Before A.D. 400 the Anasazi followed a traditional Archaic life style. These future builders of apartment complexes lived in pit houses dug beneath the ground. But along with a new sophistication in farming came new ideas in architecture.

When they first used adobe bricks, the Anasazi built houses of every shape, size, and variety. Out of this flurry of invention came the beautiful system of many rooms attached to each other and stacked several stories high to form a compact village. They built these rambling apartment buildings on open mesas and tablelands. All the rooms are almost exactly the same size, indicating that there was no superior or ruling class.

The sprawling ruin of Chaco Canyon is a remarkable example of this kind of building. Discovered in 1849 by an expedition of U.S. soldiers, Chaco, in the northwest corner of New Mexico, had eight hundred rooms and thirty-two underground ceremonial centers called kivas. It was the largest apartment building anywhere in the world until the twentieth century, and it was built in A.D. 1100.

Around A.D. 1200 the Anasazi retired to natural caves in cliffsides, probably as a defense against marauding tribes. They built even more beautiful apartments into the cliffsides. All over the Southwest, impossibly straight, sheer walls and extremely beautiful masonry mark the presence of these master architects.

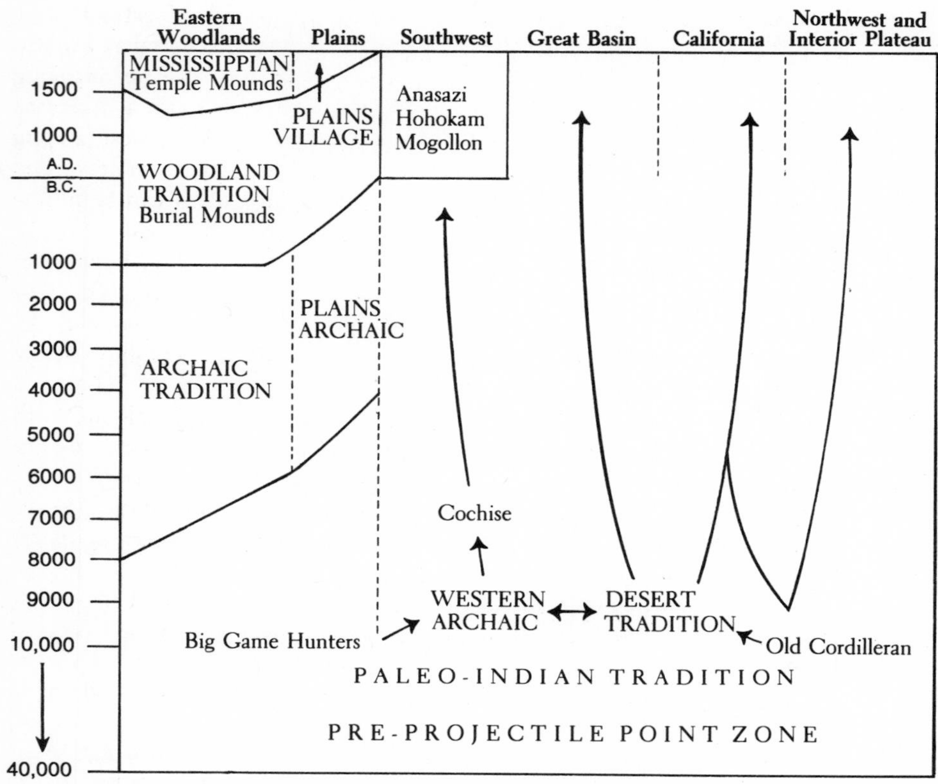

Where various cultures developed in the New World.

Today hundreds of Anasazi communities dot the Four Corners, some now protected by the modern Indians whose reservations enwrap them. In addition to Chaco Canyon, the greatest Anasazi centers of population are at Mesa Verde, Kayenta (today set aside as Navajo National Monument), and nearby Canyon de Chelly.

The drought of 1276 signaled the end of these great farming communities. As they weakened in their struggle against the elements, they were easy prey for the roving bands of desert marauders who lived off the more stable farmers. The great Anasazi disappeared—vanished into the emptiness of the desert. Some believe a few of the great clan drifted south, where today their blood flows in the veins of the modern Hopi and Pueblo Indians.

These Anasazi cities were undoubtedly the legendary cities of gold sought by Coronado. But the Europeans found no gold when the secret cities were finally discovered—only magnificent moldering ruins, all the more precious for the life that once throbbed there and vanished.

As you travel the roads of America today, two kinds of extraordinary prehistoric ruins are visible in the landscape. All across the central and southern United States, the great flat-topped temple mounds rise up, breaking the flat horizon of the Mississippi and Ohio valleys as far south as Alabama and Georgia, east to Virginia, and north to Minnesota. To the west, among the deep red and gold canyons of the Southwest, whole cities crumble, ragged walls framing empty deserts. In the sand dried-up irrigation canals outline the tracts of ancient farmlands.

Most of what are now ruins were built in a construction boom that affected the whole continent in the first few centuries after A.D. 1000. This epic run of building took place for several centuries and then suddenly declined sometime before the European invasion. The cause of the decline remains a great mystery in American archaeology.

This is the outline that frames the story of prehistoric people in North America. These are the broadest possible strokes, and you will fill in thousands of details as you visit the many archaeological sites around the country.

In California you will see where the ancestors of the present-day Mewoc wore thousands of holes into rock as they patiently ground acorn seeds for their staple food.

At Cahokia in Illinois, you can stand on top of the greatest mound of all and look out on a modern city. Nipping at the flanks of Monks Mound today are do-it-yourself car washes and fast-food restaurants. But not even the golden arches can diminish the ragged magnificence of this incredible construction.

In the languid South, you can visit an open burial mound where silent tombs are protected from the damp climate by hermetically sealed doors. The grave goods of the honored dead still lie in place at the sides of their skeletons.

At Mammoth Cave in Kentucky you can still see a worn-out sandal abandoned by an ancient miner on a ledge inside this prehistoric gypsum mine.

At Chaco Canyon you will see the remains of one of the world's most beautiful civilizations. And down a seldom traveled river, through a canyon that one enters with only a backpack, you can visit a jewellike dwelling fashioned from pink Navajo sandstone.

These are only a few. They are part of a fascinating story, one that is in a constant state of flux. For in archaeology today's news is tomorrow's castoff theory. The goal of science is to discover the unknown, and the relationship of knowledge to mystery is always changing.

This is why we search: not for pottery and points, not for cities and palaces, but to learn about people. That is the beauty of American archaeology . . . it is a living, breathing science. The ancients are visible to us in the form of their descendants. In the faces of American Indians we see the

The art of stone masonry reached its height at Chaco Canyon. Chaco was occupied from about A.D. *1 until 1200, more than a thousand years. At one of the three great Anasazi centers, twelve hundred people once lived in Pueblo Bonito, an eight-hundred-room apartment house. Fifteen hundred smaller sites are scattered throughout the Canyon, but best known are Pueblo Bonito and the Great Kiva at Casa Rinconada. (Photo courtesy of the National Park Service.)*

faces of the men and women who founded a race and settled the American continent. It is their heritage we seek, yet it is our own also, because the past is still infinite. And somewhere as we travel backward, we are joined in the family of man.

EUROPEAN CONTACT BEFORE COLUMBUS

For decades the battle has raged among historians over the first European contact with this continent. No one has given an inch, even when confronted with almost incontrovertible proof. "Columbus discovered America," his backers cry, even though it was obviously here and occupied before 1492. "The Vikings were the first," say some others, and they seem to have evidence of landings, at least, in the northern part of this continent. But the Japanese may have been here even earlier, or the Celts. And Thor Heyerdahl, who set out westward on a raft from the Mediterranean, proved that early Egyptians *could* have crossed the Atlantic to the New World.

It is almost certain that there were landings on the continent as far back as 3000 B.C. Granted, these were few, and probably accidental. After water poured over the Bering Strait land bridge, small groups began to reach various parts of the New World by sea. Larger seagoing craft encouraged sailors to venture further across unknown oceans, and often they wandered far off course, forced by storms and currents to land on strange shores.

The boats of lost Japanese fishermen may have washed up on the Pacific shores of South America, and it's possible that pottery was introduced to the New World by one of these accidental encounters. Prehistoric Japanese pottery called Jōmon closely resembles pottery found on the coast of Ecuador. But it is now thought this resemblance is coincidental.

There's an idea that certain plants such as cotton were brought from other continents, but more likely, these plants were native to North America. The stories of Norsemen or Vikings landing on North America are legion, and undoubtedly there was intermittent contact with European and Scandinavian sailors over the centuries before Columbus.

There is avid interest in these brief encounters, and a few archaeological sites open to the public may have been the scene of early contact: Mystery Hill in New Hampshire claims to be the site of a Celtic settlement, and the Heavener Runestone in Oklahoma may be a Viking artifact. In both of these instances, scientific evaluation is controversial, but these finds have generated much interest and publicity. L'anse aux Meadows National Historic Park on the tip of the great northern peninsula in Newfoundland claims to be a Viking settlement of A.D. 1000, in the time of Leif Ericsson. Dighton Rock in Massachusetts was inscribed by Portuguese explorers in A.D. 1511. And some research suggests that Portuguese navigators may have visited the rock two decades *before* Columbus.

The Phoenicians and Vikings from the East and sailors from the Pacific islands in the West all may have touched the shores of the Americas. But with the possible exception of the Japanese contact, none of these encounters seemed to have changed the pattern of life in prehistoric America.

THE PASSIONATE AMATEUR'S GUIDE

Archaeology is an interpretive science. Practically artistic in scope, it demands a solid understanding of both the whims of nature and the characteristics of man. All stages of human life are material for study, and many sciences contribute pieces to the archaeological puzzle: geology, zoology, and botany are all vital parts of the overall picture.

Much of the story of early Americans' struggle for survival has been erased. The surface soil of the United States has been plowed, dug, mined, and blasted. Some prehistoric sites have been mauled deliberately and their treasures stolen by the unskilled hands of the pothunter. Only artifacts in their original context are valuable to archaeologists. By analyzing the layers of soil, bits of charcoal, and even traces of pollen that surround the artifacts, they can determine when—and by whom—the site was occupied. If the surface is disturbed by plow or by hand, the story is lost forever.

Once archaeologists have done their work, the site itself has no further meaning for them. It may be covered over, bulldozed, or—in some lucky instances—prepared for the public. But the careful research yields up stories and often the meaning of daily life many generations before and places them in the large picture of the ancient people of America.

To get some idea of the size of that job, consider that our history since Columbus covers only five hundred years. Written records give us some dim idea of the complex nature of this relatively recent time, but other civilizations rose and declined in North America for at least twelve thousand years before that—and people may have lived on the continent for as long as fifty thousand or even one hundred thousand years. Each individual, each society, each civilization has left a history of its events buried somewhere in the earth. The only way we can trace these centuries of life is through archaeology.

With our rapid rate of growth, it's surprising that there are any ancient sites left untouched in the United States. But there are and they are many, for the prehistoric civilizations that occupied our country before Columbus were numerous and widespread. Sites are still being uncovered that archaeologists hope will reveal just when humans entered North America.

Prehistoric people lived in so many places that some sites must wait for excavation. Many known sites are purposely left untouched for a later day—a day when anticipated new technology can glean better information. These sites are similar to other locations already excavated. If scientists dig now, they believe the information gained would be merely repetitive, and archaeological sites reveal their story only once. So, the refuse heap, called a midden, hidden beneath an ancient cliff dwelling will remain undisturbed (except for notation in a scientist's report) for another twenty years or more, until archaeologists have new tools to trace its story.

Developing technology is one reason to keep some sites on a "hold" basis. There is another: with the available people and funds, it is impossible to explore every known prehistoric site, so sites are excavated on a priority basis. Much of today's archaeology centers around "contract" work: scientists racing against time to record ancient stories etched in the earth before they are obliterated by highways and dams. These sites cannot be preserved and most will be flooded or blown up. In this race between the future and the past, some scientists have had to trade their hand trowels for bulldozers and it's not unusual to find an archaeologist running a big Cat. Sites located out of harm's way are temporarily held aside while this other pressing work goes on.

There is one more reason that excavation may be held in check. Digging is only part of the job. Before digging any more, many scientists believe that excavated material already stored in laboratories around the country should be analyzed.

Above all, archaeology is a science of human beings. It is the men and women of today striving to understand the lives of those who have gone before. It is a great endeavor where willing hands and heads are needed.

In most states a strong alliance has sprung up between amateur and professional archaeologists. There are some exceptions. For years pothunters have used archaeological sites as storehouses to be raided at will, often selling pottery and other artifacts for large sums of money. This is still going on, and many scientists tend to look at all nonprofessionals with suspicion.

But there is an enormous difference between an amateur and a pothunter, and in most parts of the country amateurs take an active part in archaeological work. The demands of this science are so many and varied that the great adventure of archaeology can be shared by passionate amateurs everywhere. Many states now grant certification to amateurs who complete courses and field work. This is like gaining a diploma; the holder is qualified to fill an important post on digs and in the laboratory.

Many skills are helpful in archaeology: photography, map making, research, drawing, laboratory analysis, diving, and cataloging. Experience in any one of these fields makes the amateur a valuable member of the archaeological team. Those without skills can also contribute a fundamental service: painstaking labor in the field.

Sometimes experienced or certified amateurs are paid for their work. Most often, amateurs volunteer their services free of charge and pay their own expenses of travel, food, and lodging. Sometimes they pay an additional fee in the form of tuition. For their money, amateurs are educated in the field and participate fully in a scientific adventure. In turn, their money helps support the dig.

There are many ways to experience archaeology without actually going on a dig. You can visit museums and sites that have been prepared for the public. Here, interpretation is the point, and one can learn more about archaeology and early life in America by visiting actual ruins and museums than any place else. It's also possible to visit excavations-in-progress and observe how archaeologists do their work. Visitors make an important contribution: the person who travels and sees this exciting work firsthand gains a new awareness of the meaning of archaeology.

In following chapters you will find information on every prehistoric site in the country open to the public and museums that have prehistoric holdings. You will also learn how to visit excavations in progress and which state offices and organizations to call to keep abreast of current excavations in the field.

My evaluation of sites is, by and large, a personal one. I have tried to indicate which sites were most valuable in unfolding the story of human life in America and also give you some idea of what you will see when you travel to a site.

Permanent sites prepared for the public are usually open year round. These include places like Cahokia and Walnut Canyon. Excavations normally take place only in summer months, both because the weather is better and because excavators usually are college students and professors. If the work is not completed by the end of the digging season, the excavation is backfilled—covered with dirt—until the following year when it is reopened.

Sometimes excavations last one summer, sometimes several years—depending on funds and the extent of the site. Once it is closed down, unless some provision is made for a permanent exhibit, the site cannot be visited.

Digs or field schools that accept amateur volunteers run anywhere from two weeks to three months. Most teams prefer volunteers to remain for the life of the dig because it takes time for an amateur to become familiar with his or her job.

ABOUT VISITING SITES

The motto at all archaeological sites across the country open to the public is: "Take nothing but photographs; leave nothing but footprints."

There's little to add to that. Most archaeological sites are fragile and constantly threatened by destruction. Every year, severe winters and rushing, rainy springs wash away a little more of our prehistoric heritage. Many sites are located along rivers that periodically overrun their banks and carry away parts of the site. At Mitchell, South Dakota, a small lake laps away ominously at the edge of a prehistoric earth-lodge village, each day washing out and burying valuable features of the site.

Sites are also threatened by large numbers of visitors. Sometimes people climb on delicate stone walls and pick up pieces of shell or stone to take home as souvenirs. This not only erodes the site but is often dangerous, since the ancient walls can begin to crumble. The result of people erosion can be the closing of the site to the public.

Most people visit archaeological sites during summer vacations when the weather is good. The well-known sites can be crowded in the summer—not as crowded as Coney Island, not actually *teeming* with people, but often too crowded to allow the privacy and space needed to fully appreciate the site.

I think the best time to visit sites is off-season, during the late spring or fall. If you are willing to overcome some difficulties, winter can offer a completely different perspective on prehistoric life. And in the South and Southwest, winter weather presents only a minor difficulty, if any. Probably the best all-around months to visit sites are May, September, October, and November.

If summer is the time you must go, the best time of day to visit any site is very early in the morning or late in the afternoon. The shadows and light make the site more interesting and there are fewer people around. Rainy days can be wonderful, too, if you are not traveling on dirt roads. These kinds of days allow you to experience the prehistoric setting under different conditions, and wet shadows play on the imagination. If you plan to visit under other than optimum weather conditions, keep your boots and a rain poncho in your car.

Sites in the North and Southeast are usually located in well-manicured parks. The mound sites in particular are very civilized, with neat stairways up and down the mounds and paved paths weaving through them. (But watch those steep stairways in hot weather.) The further west you go, the rougher the terrain. Most sites in the country can be reached by regular automobile, but in a few instances four-wheel drive is a must and a few trips require horses. Information about access is given for each site.

Traveling in the Southwest, you can expect to encounter dirt and gravel roads. Generally these roads are well traveled and maintained, but they can be hazardous in wet weather. Make sure to read the notes on traveling in the Southwest that precede the section.

ABOUT VISITING EXCAVATIONS-IN-PROGRESS

During the summer it is possible to visit many excavations in the field. Some are located near related museums, and many provide a guide to explain the history of the site and discuss how the archaeologists work.

When visiting an excavation-in-progress, keep these guidelines in mind: (1) Stay outside any boundary that protects the site, and don't step on the planks or ground covers that are used to cover the site at night. These might be lying over a big hole in the ground. (2) Don't disturb any equipment or artifacts. (3) Ask permission before taking photographs. (4) Don't remove anything you find at or near the site, including bits of pottery, bones, or even rocks. (5) Wear boots or sturdy walking shoes and plan to get a little dirty. (6) Don't carry too much paraphernalia.

If the site is open but there are no guides, use your good judgment about talking to the archaeologists. Most excavating teams are on short and demanding schedules, and too many visitors can interrupt their work. But visitors who are genuinely interested and are low on nuisance value are generally welcome. If you hang around a dig long enough, someone will probably put you to work.

Almost all in-progress sites ask that you contact the excavation team in advance for an appointment for admission. Some long-term excavations are listed by state in this book. Other excavations, however, last only a year or two and then are backfilled. A list of current summer excavations is published every year in the May/June issue of *Archaeology* magazine. Information about excavations that receive visitors can also be gotten from the office of the state archaeologist in your state.

GETTING THE MOST FROM MUSEUMS

Some people actually don't like to dig. Digs are rough and dirty, and usually you have to camp out in the field. If this does not appeal to you, other skills are needed in the laboratories and museums. Museums always need good volunteers to do everything from manning the information desks to cataloging material or helping with displays. Many museums offer training programs, and if you have any skills or training in creating exhibits, they can use you. Lab work requires experience, but it is absorbing and interesting work.

The great finds of American archaeology are housed in the exhibit halls and sometimes the basements of its museums. Museums are the backbone of archaeology, for not only do they interpret and exhibit findings from excavations, they sponsor research and fieldwork, and their libraries are home to scholars. Many archaeological holdings never put on display offer unparalleled opportunities to study prehistoric life in America. Often the libraries and sometimes the stored collections can be used and studied by serious amateurs.

Museums can be as vast as the Smithsonian—a city in itself—or as unique as Kolomoki, where the museum is built right over the entrance to a burial mound. When you pass through its doors, you literally enter the core of the mound.

In the museum listings for this book, I have tried to give some idea of the museum's philosophy and the extent of its prehistoric exhibits. Some otherwise fabulous museums have only minor archaeological exhibits, while other specialized institutions are devoted to prehistoric material.

Museums have both permanent and temporary exhibits. I have listed only those exhibits that are considered permanent. Unfortunately, this does not guarantee that the exhibit will be up when you get there. On the other hand, the museum may have some fine temporary exhibit that coincides with your visit. You can never be sure just what will be showing. But if a museum is known for its prehistoric holdings, it is likely that at least some of them will be on display most of the time. If you are interested in one particular exhibit, call ahead to make sure it is up.

Museums frequently change their hours and days off, as well as their admission fees, so it's a good idea to call ahead in any case. Phone numbers are provided for each listing. Museums also are good sources of local information. If any new sites or exhibits in the area have been developed for the public, the museum will know about them. So, don't hesitate to ask for information.

ABOUT ORGANIZATIONS

If museums are the backbone of American archaeology, then amateur societies are its heartbeat. Amateur societies research, survey, inventory sites, and work closely with professional groups on various levels: local, state, and national. Groups of amateurs often intervene to save threatened sites and protect them for future research or public development. The state or city historic society, the conservation commission, universities and museums, and the professional societies are all enhanced by the services of amateur groups. They publish reports, newsletters and bulletins. They organize field schools and in many states offer training programs and certifications so that their members can be of real value on excavations.

Many people who join amateur societies begin as enthusiastic hobbyists and go on to earn credit in university field schools, take classes, and earn degrees in anthropology. Eventually they wind up in career jobs.

Most societies do not have permanent offices and change their addresses as they change presidents. In place of the current address, I have tried to give a central location to call for up-to-date information, either a university department that works closely with the organization or a museum with which it is affiliated. If you have any trouble reaching an organization, call the anthropology department of the nearest college or the office of your state archaeologist and ask for help. Some states have one major organization with several chapters, while others have several independent organizations.

The office of the state archaeologist can usually put you in touch with organizations active in your area at any given time.

ABOUT FIELDWORK

If a "dig" is what you're after, there are many ways to go. Amateur societies often excavate, and there are several commercial expeditions (see last chapter) where amateurs can work with professionals in faraway exotic places . . . for a price. The best way to receive good training and experience, as well as adventure at a price most people can afford, is to join a university summer field school.

Schools vary in their approach to amateurs. Some take only students registered at the university, while others accept nonmatriculated volunteers. The only way to know is to check with the local anthropology department at a school near you. I have tried to list some field schools in each state.

Adult education programs also sponsor digs. If a call to the anthropology department is unproductive, call the department of informal studies, continuing education, or adult education (all terms for the same thing: noncredit programs for nonmatriculated students). Many of these ongoing education programs now offer field schools in archaeology as part of their summer curriculum, and they are open to everyone.

IF YOU FIND A SITE

If you think you have stumbled across an archaeological site—either by accident or design—report it immediately. There are several ways to do this. If you belong to a society, report to an officer and he or she will pass the information on to the proper authority.

If your site does not receive the attention you think it deserves, you can move to protect it yourself. Report your find to the local historic commission or conservation commission or call the office of the state archaeologist (listed in this book at the end of each state). Most of these people will send someone out to look at your discovery and will file a report on the site. Many important sites have been set aside and protected through the efforts of determined amateurs.

This book helps you reach out to the past. It sets out the broad paths to travel and opens doors that lead you closer to the science of archaeology. This is not a textbook, and the strokes that describe the lives of the ancient peoples of America are necessarily broad. They are an outline of the United States in prehistoric times. As you move through time and across ancient trails, you can fill in the details for yourself.

Although *The Passionate Amateur's Guide to Archaeology in the United States* is designed for travelers, you needn't go any further than a corner of your own state. Whether you're on the road or on a city bus, an exciting adventure in archaeology is nearby.

Note: Wherever possible, prehistoric cultures are matched with modern state lines. But some cultures do not fall neatly into place with modern geography. To aid the traveler, I have left the states in one piece and fractured the cultural boundaries. All sites are listed according to present-day state lines, with the exception of the Four Corners region—that geographical sandwich dense with Anasazi ruins. I have treated this area separately because to visit the many sites found here, you must continually cross back and forth across state lines. Much of the time the traveler in this region is on Indian reservations and doesn't know—or care—whether he is in Utah, Colorado, New Mexico, or Arizona.

THE NORTHEAST

Connecticut

Delaware

District of Columbia

Maine

Maryland

Massachusetts

New Hampshire

New Jersey

New York

Pennsylvania

Rhode Island

Vermont

Virginia

THE NORTHEAST

The two best ways to catch archaeology alive in the Northeast are to visit museums and to join in the activities of the amateur archaeological societies. While archaeologists excavate all over the Northeast, few sites are prepared for the public because of the prevailing weather conditions. The damp woodsy climate and highly acidic soil rapidly decay any exposed ruins or artifacts. Once an excavation is exposed and researched, it is covered up again.

However, many field expeditions welcome serious visitors during summer excavations. When you visit these sites, you get a new perspective on archaeology. You begin to look for the small things—the tiny bits of pottery and shell—that tell a large story. Visiting these sites develops an awareness of what the science of archaeology is about in America.

The three major traditions of the Northeast are the Paleo-Indian (10,000 B.C.–8000 B.C.), the Archaic (8000 B.C.–1000 B.C.), and the Woodland (1000 B.C.–historic). The early people of the Northeast built their houses of wood and made their clothes from skins and woven grasses. All that is left to tell their story are some fragments of pottery, heaps of shells and animal bones, and bits of seed that describe their diet and some of their customs. But if the climate destroyed what they might have left behind, it also prepared them for a way of life different from any other on the continent.

At the end of the Ice Age, trees began to grow on the more southerly fringes of the glaciers, and the forest gradually spread northward into Canada as the ice melted. Soon the whole of the Northeast was covered with trees and that green, wooded blanket determined the Paleo-Indian way of life in the whole region. Hunting, fishing, shell gathering, and plant collecting were the modes of survival; these formed a basic pattern that distinguished the people of the northeastern Woodlands from their neighbors to the south and west for thousands of years.

The subsequent Archaic Tradition hit its full stride around 500 B.C. and lasted for about four thousand years. The people ground and polished their stone tools and ornaments, and they used large, broad projectile points for hunting. Fish trapping along the coast became an advanced skill. Construction workers digging the foundation for a new building in Boston recently uncovered sixty-five thousand wooden stakes driven into clay. There were indications that branches had been woven between the stakes to trap fish. This sophisticated obstacle course for fish was constructed between 4000 B.C. and 2000 B.C. and today lies beneath the New England Mutual Life Insurance Building on Boylston Street.

The Archaic people who lived further inland were no less inventive. They designed a clever device to overcome the deep snowfalls that confined them to cave shelters for long winter months. With the new snowshoes strapped to their feet, hunters traveled across soft, snowy surfaces faster than the game they pursued.

The rivers became their highways, and hunters began to travel great distances in canoes. They camped along river banks all over Pennsylvania, New York, and New Jersey. The Archaic people made their first cooking pots from stretched hides, into which they dropped hot stones to make the water boil. Later they carved big bulky pots from a soft stone called steatite—the first carved cooking utensils.

About 1000 B.C. a strong new pattern emerged in the Northeast: the Woodland Tradition. The distinctive trademark of the Woodland Tradition is cord- or fabric-marked pottery. Crude pottery had been introduced some years earlier, but these new vessels set a more advanced style: before firing the soft clay, the potter patted the vessel with a cord- or fabric-wrapped wooden paddle. The finished design is unmistakable, and the clumsy steatite pots were replaced by the lighter and more compact baked clay vessels.

Also, for the first time, the Woodland food gatherers began to cultivate wild plants. Gardens of sunflowers and Jerusalem artichokes were the first signs of farming in the East. Soon afterward, the Woodland people cleared land along the river bottoms and began to grow maize and beans. The new farming seemed to spread out of Ohio, Mississippi, and lower Missouri into the eastern river valleys and westward onto the plains. In the Northeast agriculture became an important way of life from Virginia to Canada.

The Woodland Tradition continued to expand, and large villages began to replace the individual farms. In New York State, the Hopewell influence was marked by small burial mounds and distinctive copper jewelry and effigy platform pipes. In western Pennsylvania the Monongahela culture arose, and in New York the Owasco culture was predecessor to the later Iroquois-speaking peoples.

Among the Iroquois related families lived together in long houses that were concentrated in large, fortified villages. The Iroquois villagers cleared and cultivated hundreds of acres of land and continued to live together into historic times, when the Iroquois-speaking tribes formed an alliance. They fought on the side of the British in the French and Indian War. Later, the tribes divided and took different sides in the American Revolution, from which the great Iroquois league never recovered.

Throughout their development the prehistoric people of the Northeast never built the great cities seen in other parts of the country, nor did they develop high forms of art. But they were fearless and independent and had enormous influence on the European colonists who first settled in America.

There are many things about the early northeastern Americans that we will never know because much of their story is lost in the soil. They are best recalled in the culture of modern tribes that trace their ancestry directly to these early people and still preserve their traditions.

Amateur archaeologists in the Northeast are among the nation's busiest. They are deeply involved in temporarily restraining the wave of industrialization that threatens prehistoric sites. I have tried to list all of the organizations open to membership in each state, but new groups are being formed all the time. When you attend the meeting of any archaeological society, you will soon learn about all the other activities in the state.

CONNECTICUT

Anyone visiting Connecticut who is interested in archaeology or prehistoric Indian life should go at once to the American Indian Archaeological Institute in Washington, Conn. This is about the only place in the country where museum exhibits, research programs, fieldwork, and training programs are all open to the public, operating under one roof. The AIAI is the center of archaeology in this state, and it is situated in one of the prettiest towns in Connecticut. Western Connecticut is a picturesque region of small towns, wooded hillsides, and rolling rivers.

Connecticut also sports several outstanding museums, including the great Peabody and two excellent children's museums, the New Britain Youth Museum and the Children's Museum of Hartford.

At this time there are no permanent archaeological sites open to the public in Connecticut, but the state has several active archaeological societies that sponsor fieldwork, and there is some digging going on in the state every year. As in all parts of the Northeast, the biggest concern is protection of threatened sites.

MUSEUMS

Canton

• *Roaring Brook Nature Center*
(See listing under West Hartford)

New Britain

• *New Britain Youth Museum*
30 High Street (P.O. Box 111)
New Britain, Connecticut 06051 *(203) 225-3020*

This busy children's museum is always looking for new and interesting ways to entertain and teach young people. Their prehistoric Indian collections are not always out, but some material is usually on exhibit along with a nice collection of kachina dolls from the Southwest. The collection is always available to teachers, amateur archaeologists, and other people who show interest and request permission to see it. The museum staff continously develops new programs for children, so make sure to ask them about current projects. The museum also has a collection of circus memorabilia and some marine and animal life exhibits.

HOURS: Monday–Friday: 1:00 P.M.–5:00 P.M.
Saturday: 10:00 A.M.–4:00 P.M. (Labor Day–June 15)
Sunday: 1:00 P.M.–5:00 P.M.
Closed Saturdays and Sundays in the summer; closed major holidays.
ADMISSION: Free.

New Haven

• *Peabody Museum of Natural History*
Yale University
170 Whitney Avenue
New Haven, Connecticut 06520 *(203) 436-0850*

The Peabody, one of the world's finest natural history museums, is home to a vast archaeological storehouse. Permanent and changing exhibits of prehistoric life in Connecticut are profuse, and you are sure to see something remarkable at any time you choose to visit. Artifacts, drawings, and photographs of prehistoric lifeways in Connecticut all contribute to the marvelous atmosphere of this museum. The Peabody also lends special programs to schools for study and classroom presentations.

The museum also holds the world's largest natural history murals, one on the Age of Reptiles and the other on the Age of Mammals. Be sure to see the famous Hall of Dinosaurs with its seventy-foot brontosaurus skeleton. Mineralogy, astronomy, geology, and zoology are the themes of other displays.

Many other beautiful eighteenth-century buildings on the Yale campus are open to the public: The **Beinecke Rare Book and Manuscript Library** at High and Wall streets; the **Sterling Memorial Library** on High Street; the fine **Yale University Art Gallery** at 1111 Chapel Street; and the **Yale Collection of Muscial Instruments** at 15 Hillhouse Avenue. If you are visiting the Peabody, make a day of it and stop in and visit these other valuable collection.

HOURS (PEABODY MUSEUM): Monday–Saturday: 9:00 A.M.–4:50 P.M.
Sunday: 1:00 P.M.–4:50 P.M.
Closed July 4, Thanksgiving, Christmas, New Year's.
ADMISSION: Tuesday, Thursday, Saturday, Sunday: Adults 75¢, children 25¢. Monday, Wednesday, Friday: Free.

Stamford

• *Stamford Museum and Nature Center*
39 Scofieldtown Road
Stamford, Connecticut 06903 *(203) 322-1646*

There are exhibits depicting the lifeways of the Woodland Indians; other exhibits describe the life of prehistoric people in the Southeast, on the plains, and in the Southwest and Northwest. The museum also features a dairy farm, zoo, planetarium, weather station, art gallery, observatory, and nature trails. This outing can be a lot of fun, especially for children, and it requires several hours to see everything. Planetarium shows are on Sunday afternoons at 3:00 P.M.

DIRECTIONS: The museum is at High Ridge and Scofieldtown roads on SR 137; go ¾ mile north of Merritt Parkway exit 35.
HOURS: Monday–Saturday: 9:00 A.M.–5:00 P.M.
Sunday and holidays: 1:00 P.M.–5:00 P.M.
Closed Thanksgiving, Christmas, New Year's.
ADMISSION: Adults $2, children under sixteen and senior citizens 75¢, not to exceed $5 per car.

Washington

• *American Indian Archaeological Institute*
Curtis Road (Box 260)
Washington, Connecticut 06793 *(203) 868-0518*

In this quiet woodland setting, it is easy to imagine life as it was in the past. On these lovely hillsides and river banks, people have lived for more than ten thousand years. Everyone is welcome at this remarkable center, from the smallest child to the most serious amateur and professional scientist.

The American Indian Archaeological Institute is the only regional center of its kind on the East Coast, and its multitudinous projects extend to all parts of the Northeast. The AIAI is involved in all phases of archaeology. Its aims are discovery, preservation, and public information, and it actively pursues all of these goals with the cooperation and services of both professionals and amateurs.

In 1977, AIAI archaeologists were part of an Earthwatch-sponsored field school that discovered the earliest site ever excavated in New England, dating to 10,190 years ago. Many of the Paleo-Indian artifacts recovered from this dig in the Shepaug Valley are part of the institute's enormous collection, and several pieces are on display in the museum.

The AIAI is a chapter of the Archaeological Society of Connecticut.

It has an excellent small museum and a remarkable range of activities. It also owns the only mastodon skeleton that exists in the state.

The Museum: Many museums in the state have loaned or donated prehistoric collections to the AIAI, and its holdings and displays continue to grow as newly excavated material comes in from the institute's own excavations. The life of northeastern people is traced from Paleo times through the Archaic and Woodland periods, all the way to historic contact. A long house reconstructs the home of a Woodland family. And a simulated dig shows how archaeologists perform in the field.

Just off the museum hall are a reference library (by appointment to members) and a laboratory. Laboratory researchers identify, clean, and catalog artifacts fresh from field excavations. These are later stored or used in displays.

The Museum Shop carries many original publications and a good selection of books on archaeology and anthropology. Original Indian crafts and jewelry are for sale.

Outside the main building is the **Quinnetukut Habitat Trail,** where you can walk through a time zone into the past and enjoy a fine view of how Woodland Indians lived in their environment. The habitat trail also shows how the environment changed as the Ice Age receded. Native plants believed to have grown in the region during the ten-thousand-year span are now growing along the habitat trail; dried samples are preserved in the herbarium. A prehistoric camp is re-created along the trail, and a farm demonstrates past and present Indian life. The quarter-mile trail is open year round and is a fine hike in any kind of weather. You can pick up a trail guide at the Museum Shop.

Educational services at the AIAI are many and range all the way from adult university courses for credit to third-grade school tours. Staff members give programs and teach classes by appointment; loan kits and classroom displays are available to schools. Craft workshops, adult lecture programs, field training sessions, and independent study for high-school students are only a few of the special educational programs offered.

The AIAI sponsors excavations in many parts of the state and amateurs at all levels of experience can apply to do **fieldwork.** The institute conducts surveys of ancient villages and campsites and sponsors controlled digs.

Volunteers are used on digs, on the museum staff, and in the laboratory. Everyone is welcome and those wishing to volunteer their services in any of these areas should apply to the museum research department.

The best way to keep up with the many activities of the AIAI is to become a member. Dues are minimal and members receive the newsletter *Artifacts,* which describes all the opportunities for amateurs in the area.

It's difficult to describe the scope and achievement of this archaeological center. If you haven't guessed, it is *the* place for amateurs in Connecticut and the whole of the Northeast.

DIRECTIONS: The institute is just west of Route 199 in Washington, Connecticut.

HOURS: Monday–Saturday: 10:00 A.M.–4:30 P.M.
Sunday: 1:30 P.M.–4:30 P.M.
Closed Easter, Thanksgiving, Christmas, New Year's.

ADMISSION: Adults $1, children 50¢, tours $2, members free.

West Hartford

- *Children's Museum of Hartford*
950 Trout Brook Drive
West Hartford, Connecticut 06119 *(203) 236-2961*
- *Roaring Brook Nature Center*
70 Gracey Road
Canton, Connecticut 06019 *(203) 693-0263*

Children from all over Connecticut, Massachusetts, and New York come to visit this outstanding museum and nature center. It is one of the country's oldest museums dedicated to children, but you needn't be a child to enjoy it. In addition to one of the finest native American collections anywhere, the Children's Museum has a small saltwater aquarium, a live animal collection, and a fine planetarium.

In the *American Indian Room,* displays are continually changing. Four permanent dioramas depict northeastern coastal groups, a southeastern Woodland group, the Plains Indians, and the eastern Woodland Indians. Travel, fishing, farming, and cooking displays show how the prehistoric people of the Northeast exploited their environment in every season. This room is a beautifully prepared introduction to native Americans and one that all children should see.

Among the fascinating stars and planet shows offered in the Planetarium is a very simple program called "The People," stories of the creation of the heavens and earth as told by native Americans.

In the Doll Room, a Mirror Image of Man shows how early people used dolls as a replica of the human form. The famous Hopi kachina dolls are included along with many other ancient dolls from all over the world.

The Museum Shop has a large collection of books, minerals, shells, slides, and charts for sale.

Just twenty minutes away, the **Roaring Brook Nature Center** is an outdoor laboratory of the Children's Museum. Six miles of trails and 115 acres of woods show the relationship of people to nature and traces the ecology of the region through the four seasons. You can walk the interpreted trails on your own, and on weekend afternoons and evenings naturalists lead special guided tours. Call the center for the current schedule of these guided walks. The trails are open year round, and in deep winter the center provides the snowshoes.

Both the museum and the center offer outstanding special programs for school classes and other children's groups. Teachers and naturalists at both places conduct classes, show films, and offer demonstrations. Staff members also travel to different schools and bring the museum program along with them. An extensive loan program is available to teachers. All of these special programs require reservations. Call the museum for their program catalog.

A good full day's outing begins at the museum in the morning and continues to the nature center. There is no cafeteria in either facility, but the nature center has some limited picnicking.

DIRECTIONS: *The Children's Museum:* From Hartford drive west on I-84 to exit 43. Then go right on Park Road and left on Trout Brook Drive.
Roaring Brook Nature Center: From Hartford drive west on Route 44 to Canton. Then go right on Lawton Road (across from Route 177) and follow the signs.

HOURS: Monday–Saturday: 10:00 A.M.–5:00 P.M.
Sunday: 1:00 P.M.–5:00 P.M. Closed major holidays.

ADMISSION: Adults $2, children $1. Planetarium additional fee.
Special rates for schools and groups. The Nature Center is free, but donations are accepted.

STATE OFFICE

Douglas F. Jordan
State Archaeologist
University of Connecticut*
Storrs, Connecticut 06268 (202) 486-2119

OPPORTUNITIES FOR AMATEURS

The office of the state archaeologist sponsors an annual field school in conjunction with the anthropology department of the University of Connecticut. The excavation team is made up of undergraduate students, but local amateurs are sometimes accepted.

* During the school year, there is a good archaeology exhibit open to the public in the lower level of the Jorgenson Auditorium on campus.

If you think you have located a prehistoric or historic site in the state of Connecticut, file a report with:

Connecticut Historical Commission
595 Prospect Street
Hartford, Connecticut 06106 (203) 566-3116

ORGANIZATIONS TO JOIN

Archaeological Society of Connecticut
c/o Central Connecticut State College
1615 Stanley Street
New Britain, Connecticut 06055

This lay-professional society has several independent chapters throughout the state. The Archaeological Society is primarily concerned with location and preservation of threatened sites, and members do considerable fieldwork. Meetings attract many well-known speakers, and the society publishes a quarterly newsletter and an annual bulletin.

DELAWARE

Delaware is a small state of unusual variety. Its topography today is probably similar to the way it looked in prehistoric times. Dense forests teem with game along the northern rivers. Scattered ponds lie along the peninsular backbone, and short streams flow to the sea. There are remote and lonely marshes on the coastline and great stretches of bare sand dunes. The southern part of the state is level and well suited for farming. This terrain offered a great variety of resources to the prehistoric people who lived here.

The Leni-Lanape people ("real men") lived here and in many parts of Pennsylvania, New Jersey, and New York. Their descendants greeted Henry Hudson when he sailed up Delaware Bay in 1609 and claimed the land for the Dutch. But the Leni-Lanape fiercely resisted European settlement and wiped out more than one Dutch and Swedish colony before they finally established a fur-trading relationship with the invaders. Delaware's history after European settlement is rich with pirates, sunken treasure, and the colors of many foreign flags.

While there are many historical archaeological sites in the state, there is only one major prehistoric excavation open to the public: the Island Field site near Bowers Beach on Delaware Bay. This major site was occupied by different groups for more than three thousand years and has led to many important discoveries, including a village and burial ground. The people of Island Field were hunters and fishermen; they traded up and down Delaware's finely spun network of rivers. There is a museum on the site, and an archaeological dig in progress. This is one of the most important sites in the Northeast and one of the few open to the public.

SITES AND MUSEUMS

South Bowers

- *Island Field Site and Museum*
South Bowers Beach, Delaware *(302) 335-5395*

Stop first at the Island Field Museum at South Bowers Beach. Exhibits and a slide show explore the history of the first Americans who lived in Delaware. There are guided tours to the site itself.

This land between the Murderkill and Mispillion rivers had abundant game and vegetation during the Woodland period. All kinds of shellfish made the diet of the Delaware people unusually varied, and they traded their shells for other valued materials such as mica and stone from as far away as the Great Lakes.

There is a large cemetery and village site at Island Field. Exhibits at the site include a partially excavated Indian cemetery with grave offerings left in place exactly as they were found. Other artifacts—bone tools, harpoons, carved stone pipes, and ornaments recovered from the site—can be seen in the museum. The museum building also houses an archaeological study collection and a library on regional prehistory.

Archaeology teams are digging there through most of the summer months, and Island Field provides an excellent opportunity to watch a major dig in progress.

DIRECTIONS: *From the south (Milford):* Drive 2 miles north on Route 113, and right (east) on Route 19 (Bowers-Thompsonville Road); then follow the signs to the museum.
From the north (Dover): Drive 12 miles south on Route 113; cross the Murderkill River on the Frederica Bypass. Take the first road to the left (Route 120) and follow signs to the museum. Note: this is the only approach from the north. There is no bridge between Bowers and South Bowers (see map).

HOURS: March 1–November 30*
Tuesday–Saturday: 10:00 A.M.–4:30 P.M.
1:30 P.M.–4:30 P.M.

ADMISSION: Free.

* Other times by appointment. Groups tours should be arranged in advance. Call (302) 335-5395

STATE OFFICE

Bureau of Archaeology and Historic Preservation
Division of Historical and Cultural Affairs
P.O. Box 1401
Dover, Delaware 19901 (302) 679-5314

OPPORTUNITIES FOR AMATEURS

The state of Delaware uses volunteers from time to time on excavations. To apply, contact:

Bureau of Archaeology and Historic Preservation
c/o Dr. Daniel R. Griffith, Administrator
Hall of Records
Dover, Delaware 19901

ORGANIZATIONS TO JOIN

There are two good archaeological societies in the state. Both are primarily involved in locating and preserving threatened sites, although they do some fieldwork. Both of these organizations file their reports with the Bureau of Archaeology, publish newsletters, and have regular meetings. The Sussex Society is a particularly active amateur group. For information, write:

Archaeological Society of Delaware
P.O. Box 301
Wilmington, Delaware 19899

Sussex Society for Archeology and History
c/o Mr. William L. Pedersen
R.D. #3, Box 190
Laurel, Delaware 19956

DISTRICT OF COLUMBIA

The nation's capital has some of the finest museums in the world, and at least two of them have magnificent archaeological exhibit halls. The first is in the northwestern quadrant of the city, and the second is part of the Smithsonian complex. Both museums are open to membership, and anyone seriously interested in archaeology benefits enormously from the many activities and publications offered to members only.

• *Explorers Hall*
National Geographic Society
17th and M Streets NW
Washington, D.C. 20036 *(202) 296-7500*

Fabulous and dramatic exhibits illustrate the society's explorations all over the world. Since the turn of the century, the National Geographic Society has undertaken many dangerous and exciting expeditions into remote areas of the United States to discover some of the great archaeological finds of America. The permanent and changing exhibits reflect many of their excavations. Especially beautiful is the exhibit of the cliff dwellers of the Southwest—don't miss it. The large research library is open to the public on the premises. There is a reading room, and National Geographic publications are for sale. By all means, get the museum guidebook before starting out.

HOURS: Monday–Friday: 9:00 A.M.–6:00 P.M.
Saturday: 9:00 A.M.–5:00 P.M.
Sunday: 10:00 A.M.–5:00 P.M.
Closed Christmas.
ADMISSION: Free.

• *National Museum of Natural History*
Smithsonian Institution
10th Street and Constitution Avenue NW
Washington, D.C. 20560 *(202) 381-5954*

It takes weeks to see all of the Smithsonian. You can begin at the National Museum of Natural History and explore the great halls of archaeology. Archaeologists and anthropologists have spent lifetimes developing these extensive, almost limitless exhibition halls to tell the story of all the cultures of America from earliest prehistoric times to modern days. There are exhibits on population development, the biology of the American Indian, their geographic areas and culture groups, food supplies and environmental studies, and prehistoric art from all over the country. All the different cultures and traditions are traced independently and then related to the whole.

In a purely scientific sense, any education in archaeology is incomplete without time spent in this magnificent museum. In addition to the halls of anthropology and archaeology, there are enormous exhibits of gems and minerals, a naturalist's center, geological exhibits, and a live insect zoo. Plan to spend the day. There are museum shops, a restaurant, and a bookstore in the building.

HOURS: Winter: 10:00 A.M.–5:30 P.M. daily.
Extended spring and summer hours determined yearly.
Closed Christmas.
ADMISSION: Free.

MAINE

Before the English came the French were here, and before the French, the Vikings touched the state's rough coast. Thousands of years before the Vikings, native Americans lived along the shores and camped in the forests of Maine. Today, many old French forts are open to visitors, but there are few places where the remains of prehistoric people can be seen. Yet their presence is felt everywhere in this territorial masterpiece.

On Indian Island, a few miles north of Bangor, the Penobscot Indians are building a new museum. Here artifacts of prehistoric peoples have passed directly into the hands of their descendants. Surprisingly, this is almost unique in archaeology. Most Indian tribes do not possess the material excavated from prehistoric sites. Visitors are welcomed to the Penobscot Reservation, which occupies this charming island, and can meet and visit with the people whose earliest ancestors were the first Americans.

SITES

Damariscotta

The few prehistoric sites in Maine open to the public center around Damariscotta. This area is one of the state's prime resort areas, and there are many points of interest as well as quiet inns, sporting camps, and hotels. For full information about visiting this area, call, write, or stop in at one of the two information bureaus: Business Route #1, Damariscotta; or U.S. Route #1, Newcastle. The telephone number of the former is (207) 563-3176.

● *Damariscotta River Shell Mounds*
Damariscotta, Maine 14543

Several oyster-shell mounds were slowly built up over the centuries from the refuse of Maine's famous Red Paint people. These heaps can be clearly distinguished from across the Damariscotta River and can be visited with permission. Make your request at the Damariscotta Information Bureau.

MUSEUMS

Augusta

● *Maine State Museum*
Capitol Complex
Augusta, Maine 04333 *(207) 289-2301*

Small interpretive exhibits illustrate the life of prehistoric Indians in Maine from ten thousand years ago into the historic period. Artifacts on display include stone tools, beads, and copper vessels. The museum plans to expand these exhibits over the next two years to show off more of its large collection. Other exhibits in this major, newly expanded complex are devoted to Maine wildlife, minerals, geology, and history. There is a museum shop and a research library open for use on the premises.

HOURS: Monday–Friday: 9:00 A.M.–4:00 P.M.
Saturday and Sunday: 1:00 P.M.–4:00 P.M.
Open Tuesday and Thursday evenings till 8:00 P.M.
ADMISSION: Free.

Castine

• *Wilson Museum*
Perkins Street
Castine, Maine 04421

Castine is a small town south of Bangor facing Penobscot Bay. This natural history museum holds prehistoric Indian material from all over North and Central America in its collections. Exhibits change frequently, and if the material you are interested in is not on display, information is available on the premises. During the summer there are demonstrations of blacksmith work, the making of silver flatware, spinning, weaving, forging, and casting.

HOURS: Summer only, May 27–September 15.
Tuesday–Sunday: 2:00 P.M.–5:00 P.M.
Closed Mondays.
ADMISSION: Free.

Indian Island

• *Indian Island National Historical Society*
Box 313
Old Town, Maine 04468 *(207) 827-2240*

In the spring of 1980 the Penobscot Indian tribe will open a new museum on its reservation, the three-and-one-half-mile-long Indian Island. This log-cabin structure in the shape of a thunderbird will devote one section to exhibits and artifacts of the tribe's early ancestors. Collections of artifacts originally owned by the Penobscot have been donated back to the tribe by museums all over the state.

The Penobscot people welcome visitors and are knowledgeable and friendly. This is more than a museum—Indian Island itself is living history and a wonderful example of the way native Americans have preserved their heritage for the benefit of all. Over the next few years, facilities will be expanded to make this museum a center for Indian material in the state.

A museum shop will offer original Penobscot crafts for sale, and a research library can be used on the premises.

DIRECTIONS: Indian Island is 12 miles north of Bangor on Route 2 and is reached via a one-lane bridge. The museum is located next to the new municipal building.
HOURS: Spring–August 31: 1:00 P.M.–6:00 P.M. daily.
The museum is open to schools and groups by appointment the rest of year.

Orono

• *Anthropology Museum*
Department of Anthropology
University of Maine
Orono, Maine 14473 *(207) 581-7102*

This anthropology museum holds collections from all over the world and particularly from the northeastern United States. Changing exhibits reflect fieldwork from Maine excavations. The University of Maine is a center for archaeology in this state and works closely with the Maine Archaeological Society. Orono is near Indian Island, and the university is donating part of its Penobscot material to the new museum.

HOURS: Monday–Friday: 8:00 A.M.–4:30 P.M.
Closed Easter, Christmas, and during university recesses.
ADMISSION: Free

STATE OFFICE

Maine does not have a state archaeologist. The department of archaeology at the University of Maine in Orono acts as a central clearinghouse for archaeological activities in the state. You may telephone (207) 581-1110.

ORGANIZATIONS TO JOIN

The **Maine Archaeological Society** is a statewide lay-professional organization devoted to research, investigation, and preservation of threatened sites. The society does very little fieldwork. Its twice-yearly bulletin includes articles by professionals and amateurs, and many members are from out of state. The society works closely with the University of Maine; official address is:

Maine Archaeological Society
Anthropology Department
University of Maine
Orono, Maine 14473

MARYLAND

One of the few archaeological parks in the country is on a small peninsula on the western shore of Chesapeake Bay. An archaeological park is a large site set aside for long-term excavation. A major part of its purpose is to interpret the excavation for the public and act as a learning center for everyone interested in archaeology.

Maryland, like most of the eastern states, is primarily concerned with its colonial history. But the Potomac Archaeological Park and its museum trace prehistoric Indian life in the area from 7000 B.C. through colonial times. When the British first arrived in Maryland, they moved into settled Indian villages. Because of the resultant overlapping of prehistoric and historic cultures, this archaeological park is an ideal place to trace a long, uninterrupted study of early human life here. The early colonial remains such as glazed European pottery, buttons, and hooks are interposed on such late Woodland material as projectile points and pottery sherds.

The Indian material reflects backward and forward: it traces the ancient cultures that preceded the European contact and then shows how these cultures were altered by European conquest. The archaeological park also compares the growth of culture here with that in Europe and other parts of America.

This task is seldom attempted, but it is the most fascinating aspect of archaeology. How did the life of the Woodland Indians compare with the life of the European serfs who lived at the same time in history? The scientists working here are trying to add yet another dimension to the large picture of human existence. For this reason alone, the Potomac Archaeological Park is a rare experience.

Nearby, a major historical restoration project is under way at Old St. Mary's City. Both sites are in St. Mary's County, beautiful country free from the great onslaught of tourism.

SITES

Colton Point

- *St. Clement's Island–Potomac Museum*
Potomac Archaeological Park
Colton Point, Maryland 20620 *(301) 769-2222*

Stop first at the small Potomac Museum housed in an old-fashioned, white clapboard house. From its waterfront porch you can look across the river to St. Clement's Island, the site of the third English colony in the New World. Settlers led by Leonard Calvert landed here on March 4, 1634,

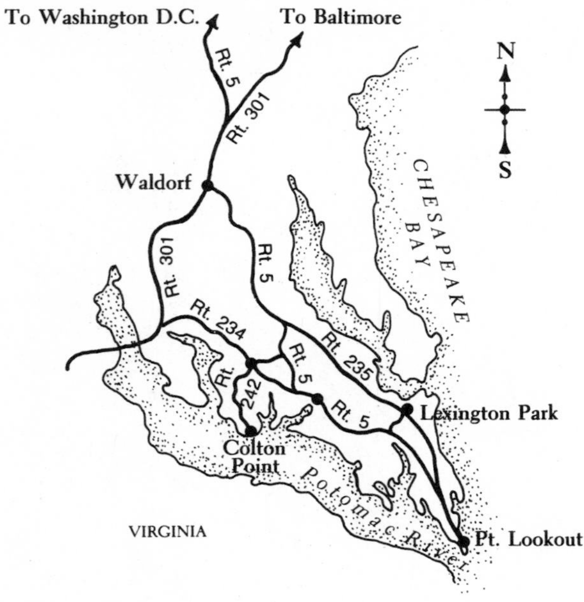

Map locating St. Clement's Island—Potomac Museum at Colton Point, Maryland. (Courtesy of St. Clement's Island—Potomac Museum.)

and took possession of Maryland in the name of Lord Baltimore. Only two weeks later, they moved inland to what is now St. Mary's City. Today, only a commemorative cross marks their stay.

St. Clement's Island is a wildlife sanctuary under the protection of the Conservation Commission. During fine weather the museum staff will treat you to a boat ride to the island. There is room for a few overnight campers on the island, and you can request a camping permit at the museum.

The Potomac Museum is intimate and charming; it is built directly over the site of a prehistoric Indian village. Exhibits tell the history of the island from the Archaic period through late Woodland and Algonquin periods. Museum displays also show many fine seventeenth-, eighteenth-, and nineteenth-century colonial artifacts. Almost every visitor receives a personal tour by one of the staff.

The museum is constantly changing and growing in its efforts to bring the story of archaeology to the people. There are special tactile exhibits for the blind, and the building is easily accessible to the handicapped. Museum collections not on display can be seen on request, and learning kits are available to schools. The museum is open year round. If you call ahead members of the staff will also help you make reservations at campgrounds and motels in the area.

Potomac Archaeological Park is about 20 minutes from the museum, off State Route 5. The park, situated on a bluff overlooking historic Breton Bay, has revealed Indian remains more than seven thousand years old. On top of the prehistoric site, colonials settled in the seventeenth century. This is one of those fascinating views of ancient history that takes one from the dim past into the historical period, all within a scant few acres of ground.

The site is fringed by a freshwater marsh that played a major role in the settlement of the area. Specially prepared displays show how an entire hillside six feet high was created by discarded oyster shells and how archaeologists date excavated material; a small garden demonstrates how the colonials learned from the Indians to cultivate tobacco, corn, squash, and gourds. As new exhibits are added, this archaeological park will be growing every year and should become one of the major interpretive centers for archaeology in the East.

The park site was originally on private land later donated by the owner for archaeological exploration—another example of how the public enters into archaeology and can help scientists. Visitors of all ages are welcome here, but as with all active digs in progress, you are asked not to touch or pick up anything from the site, even rocks or pebbles. You can spend as long as you want visiting the museum and park. Everyone is welcome, and the park tries to provide enough staff to give you as much information as you want.

DIRECTIONS: Colton Point is about 2 hours from Baltimore and 1 1/2 hours from Washington, D.C. Follow SR 301 south until you reach the small town of Waldorf, Maryland (about 45 miles south of Baltimore). Turn left onto SR 5 and continue south. Follow SR 5 to SR 242, and continue all the way to the end of SR 242, where the museum building sits right on the banks of the Potomac River. If you get lost, give the museum a call and they'll set you right. Members of the museum staff will also direct you to the archaeological park, which is about 15 miles southeast.

HOURS: The museum is open year round, 8:30 A.M.–4:30 P.M., daily.
The archaeological park is open summer and fall.
During the summer it is a good idea to call a day ahead and let them know you'll be visiting.
May–September: 9:00 A.M.–4:00 P.M. daily.
October–November: 10:00 A.M.–4:00 P.M. weekends.

ADMISSION: *Museum:* Contributions accepted. *Park:* Adults $1, children 50¢.

Note: When you visit the Potomac Archaeological Park, by all means call the information office at St. Mary's City and find out what's open to the public while you are there. Group and individual tours can be arranged by calling the information center at (301) 994-2943 or dropping into the 1676 Maryland State House.

MUSEUMS

Several museums in Maryland have small exhibits of prehistoric artifacts. If you are in the vicinity, be sure to visit some of those listed below.

Catonsville

- *Catonsville Community College*
  800 South Rolling Road
  Catonsville, Maryland 21228 — *(301) 455-4316*

On the second floor of the Science-Planetarium Building are exhibits of prehistoric and historic artifacts recovered from local excavations.

HOURS: Monday–Saturday: 8:30 A.M.–4:30 P.M.
ADMISSION: Free.

- *University of Maryland*
  Baltimore County
  5401 Wilkens Avenue
  Catonsville, Maryland 21228 — *(301) 455-2232*

A model and large map of a prehistoric site located directly beneath the site of the present-day campus are on exhibit on the second floor of the library. The model shows excavations in progress with artifacts in place.

HOURS: Monday–Thursday: 8:00 A.M.–11:00 A.M.
Friday: 8:00 A.M.–5:00 P.M.
Saturday: 10:00 A.M.–4:00 P.M.
Sunday: 1:00 P.M.–5:00 P.M.
ADMISSION: Free.

Salisbury

- *City Hall Museum and Cultural Center*
  West Church Street at Route 50
  Salisbury, Maryland 21801 — *(301) 546-9007*

This museum exhibits prehistoric and historic artifacts recovered from the lower eastern shore of Maryland. Dioramas trace the history of all the major cultural periods.

DIRECTIONS: The museum is on West Church Street at Route 50 between the Wicomico River bridge and the Route 13 intersection.
HOURS: Monday–Friday: 9:00 A.M.–4:00 P.M.
Saturday: 10:00 A.M.–2:00 P.M.
ADMISSION: Contributions accepted.

STATE OFFICE

Tyler Bastion
State Archeologist
Division of Archeology
Maryland Geological Survey
Latrobe Hall, Johns Hopkins University
Baltimore, Maryland 21218 (301) 235-0771

Anyone who would like to help in the many field and laboratory projects in Maryland is invited to register with the Division of Archeology.

The best way to report archaeological finds in Maryland is to contact either the Division of Archeology or the Maryland Historical Trust (21 State Circle, Annapolis, Maryland 21401, (301) 269-2438).

The Division of Archeology will send you a Maryland Archeological Site Survey form and a detailed map of the area you describe. You are asked to complete the form, mark the site location on the map, include photographs or sketches, and send the package back to them.

OPPORTUNITIES FOR AMATEURS

The **Potomac Archaeological Park** sponsors weekend digs twice a year that are open to the public, one in the spring and a second in the fall. There are seminars and fieldwork; the fee is twenty dollars for a full day. Call the museum number to register. The museum also takes a field trip for tombstone rubbing four times a year.

Every summer, in cooperation with George Washington University, excavations are conducted at the park. Amateurs can sign up as volunteers if they live in the county; out-of-county volunteers can audit the dig for $150 for an eight-week session. On-site camping is available.

The **Maryland Geological Survey** also sponsors an annual dig every year in conjunction with the **Archeological Society of Maryland.** The dig lasts for at least twelve days, and volunteers from Maryland and out of state can apply to the state archaeologist. They also sponsor several projects throughout the year in lab- and fieldwork. Tyler Bastion, state archeologist for Maryland, suggests that anyone wishing to volunteer for these special projects should join the Archeological Society of Maryland.

George Washington University sponsors an eight-week summer field school that is open to graduate and undergraduate students, qualified high-school seniors, and noncredit students. Apply to:

Department of Anthropology
George Washington University
Washington, D.C. 20052 (202) 676-6075

ORGANIZATIONS TO JOIN

Members of the **Archeological Society of Maryland** are up to date on all important archaeological programs in the Northeast. There is an annual meeting in October, and leading scientists lecture at a spring symposium. Members participate in the annual field session in conjunction with the state archaeologist. A monthly newsletter and biannual journal *Maryland Archeology* are published by the society. The state archaeologist recommends that anyone wishing to participate fully in the many archaeological activities in Maryland should join:

Archeological Society of Maryland, Inc.
17 East Branch Lane
Baltimore, Maryland 21202

MASSACHUSETTS

When the Pilgrims landed at Plymouth in 1620, the Wampanoag Indians were there to greet them. For several thousand years the Wampanoags had hunted and fished all over Massachusetts and even today their campsites and artifacts can still be found at some places along the shoreline.

From the most ancient times Massachusetts has been a pivotal center. Archaeologists have uncovered some of the country's most unusual prehistoric sites here, although none are open to the public. But recovered artifacts can be seen in the Commonwealth's great museums. Material from the famous Boylston Street Fish Weir site in Boston and the Early Man site at Bull Brook are on display at the Peabody museums in Andover and Salem.

SITES

South Wellfleet

- *Cape Cod National Seashore*
  South Wellfleet, Massachusetts 02663 *(617) 255-3421*

All of Cape Cod is rich in Indian lore. Eastham, on the bay side of Cape Cod, is where the Mayflower shore party first met the Indians. The Wampanoag Indians camped and fished all along this shore, and there are still many unexcavated shell heaps and campsites buried in its sands.

The museum at the Visitors' Center has small displays of prehistoric artifacts, and exhibits show how implements were used. At the museum, ask directions to **Indian Rock** at **Skiff Hall.** Here on this twenty-ton boulder you can see the deep grooves where ancient fishermen sharpened their harpoons and fishhooks.

If you are planning to visit Cape Cod, the **Cape Cod Chamber of Commerce,** Hyannis, Massachusetts 02601, lists current events and other places of interest. Call them at (617) 362-3225. The park superintendent's office is in Wellfleet.

DIRECTIONS: The Salt Pond Visitors' Center is located in Eastham.
HOURS: Summer: 8:00 A.M.–6:00 P.M. daily.
Winter: 10:00 A.M.–4:00 P.M. Friday–Tuesday.

MUSEUMS

Andover

• *Robert S. Peabody Foundation for Archaeology*
Phillips and Main Streets
Andover, Massachusetts 01810 *(617) 475-0248*

This major archaeological museum draws on its vast collections to interpret the lives of prehistoric people who lived all over North America and Mexico. Exhibits include material excavated from closed sites such as the Boylston Street Fish Weir and the Bull Brook site. The Paleo and Archaic traditions are represented, as well as the burial cult of the Adena and Hopewell people. Artifacts recovered from major sites around the country are shown, including Etowah in Georgia and Moundville in Alabama. The research library on archaeology and anthropology can be used on request. This museum also sponsors research in Peru and Central America. It is one of the important museums in Massachusetts and not to be missed by anyone seriously interested in archaeology.

HOURS: Monday–Friday: 9:00 A.M.–4:00 P.M.
Closed holidays.
ADMISSION: Free.

Attleboro

• *Bronson Museum*
8 North Main Street Building
Attleboro, Massachusetts 02703 *(617) 222-5470*

This charming, well-interpreted museum plays an important role in Massachusetts archaeology. It is among other things the headquarters for the prestigious

Massachusetts Archaeological Society, and its director, Dr. Maurice Robbins (former state archaeologist), has been a leading figure in archaeology in the Northeast for many years.

The Bronson concentrates on the life of prehistoric people in Massachusetts from Paleo through colonial times, and many of its exhibits show material recovered from sites excavated by members of the society. The Bronson is especially recommended for children, since its fine interpretive displays offer a superb introduction to the story of archaeology and the early peoples of America.

HOURS: Monday–Friday: 9:00 A.M.–4:00 P.M. (October–May)
Monday, Wednesday: 9:00 A.M.–4:00 P.M. (June–September)
ADMISSION: Free.

Cambridge

• *Peabody Museum of Archaeology and Ethnology*
Harvard University
11 Divinity Avenue
Cambridge, Massachusetts 02138 *(617) 495-2248*

Although a world-famous university, Harvard is also the weather-worn brick and ivy that denote the quintessential American college. The **Peabody Museum of Archaeology and Ethnology** is part of a museum complex that includes the **Geological and Mineralogical Museum, Botanical Museum,** and the **Museum of Comparative Zoology.** All four museums are housed on a square formed by Oxford Street and Divinity Avenue.

The Peabody is one of the world's finest archaeological museums, and exhibits trace the story of different cultures and their periods of development from all over North America. The Hopewell, Hohokam, Owasco, Nodena, Caddoan, Adena, Fremont, Mimbres, and Old Copper cultures are all represented. Artifacts are shown from the Great Serpent Mount in Ohio, Tonto and Montezuma Well in Arizona, and Moundville in Alabama. The Peabody also displays rare material excavated from important sites that have never been open to the public: Stallings Island in Georgia, Weeden Island in Florida, and Hueco Mountains in Texas are only a few.

In addition to all this, the Peabody holds what may be the world's finest collections of Mayan artifacts, and other collections from the Pacific islands, Africa, and South America are also on display. There is an outstanding Iron Age exhibit from central Europe and a Neanderthal skull found in Palestine.

Take time to visit the other three museums in this complex, then stop in at the **Fogg Art Museum** at 32 Quincy Street and the **Busch-Reisinger Museum** at 29 Kirkland Street and Divinity Avenue.

Tours of the campus take you by the aging, rosy brick buildings that date from 1720. In summer, tours leave the Information Center at 1350 Massachusetts Avenue (mid-June–September 1). During the school year (September 2–June 14), tours leave from the Information Center in Radcliffe Yard. Tours leave several times a day and are free.

HOURS (PEABODY): Monday–Saturday: 9:00 A.M.–4:30 P.M.
Sunday: 1:00 P.M.–4:30 P.M.
Closed July 4, Thanksgiving, Christmas, New Year's.
ADMISSION: Adults $1, children under fifteen 50¢.

Dartmouth

• *Children's Museum, Inc.*
Russells Mills Road
Box 98
Dartmouth, Massachusetts 02714 *(617) 993-3361*

A children's museum is usually as much fun for adults as it is for children. This museum in the southeast portion of Massachusetts has both an indoor and outdoor facility. The indoor museum features historic bows, arrowheads, baskets, jewelry, and other artifacts from the Great Plains and Southwest as well as local prehistoric Wampanoag artifacts. Indian exhibits change periodically and are not always on display. Also in the indoor museum are hands-on displays for children of all ages, live animals, and electric game boards. Other exhibits include antique toys, a doll collection, fossils, and a large collection of stuffed birds that was mounted in 1904. The museum teaches school classes throughout the school year.

Three miles down the road are five acres of wooded nature trails called the **Museum Outdoors.** Every year in March, museum staffers do maple sugaring for the public free of charge. Trails are open year round and are especially beautiful in the spring when tulips, daffodils, scilla, and tiny blue chionodoxa carpet the paths. The Museum Outdoors is free. The two museums together make a fine day's outing for children and adults.

HOURS (CHILDREN'S MUSEUM): Wednesday: 2:00 P.M.–5:00 P.M.
During the school year
Saturday: 10:00 A.M.–5:00 P.M.
Sunday: 2:00 P.M.–4:00 P.M.
Summers
Tuesday–Saturday: 10:00 A.M.–5:00 P.M.
Sunday: 2:00 P.M.–4:00 P.M.
Closed Mondays.
ADMISSION: Children 25¢, adults 50¢.

Deerfield

• *Memorial Hall Museum*
Main Street
Deerfield, Massachusetts 01342 *(413) 773-8929*

Deerfield, a town with a violent past, has one of the most beautiful streets in America, a mile-long avenue of colonial houses dating from the seventeenth century called Old Deerfield Street. Originally a slapdash frontier outpost, the town was twice destroyed in Indian battles in the 1600s. It survived to become nationally famous for its boarding schools, which include the Deerfield Academy founded in 1797.

The Memorial Hall Museum has small but interesting exhibits of prehistoric artifacts from the Connecticut River Valley. There are Paleo points and tools, points used by early Archaic caribou hunters, late Archaic stone bowls, and a pottery and agricultural exhibit from the Woodland-historic period. Also on display are a skeleton and artifacts from an Algonquin gravesite excavated at Deerfield. In addition to its Indian exhibits, the museum has three floors of fine eighteenth-century historical items and period rooms.

There are a dozen other buildings of historic interest in Deerfield, including a tavern, printing shop, silversmith, and the Indian House Memorial. Stop in at the Information Center at Hall Tavern on Main Street (open year round) to purchase reduced-rate combination tickets. The phone number there is (413) 773-5401.

DIRECTIONS: Deerfield is just off I-95, between Northampton and Greenfield. Definitely worth the side trip.
HOURS (MUSEUM): Monday–Saturday: 10:00 A.M.–4:30 P.M.
Sunday: 12:30 P.M.–4:30 P.M.
Closed November to April.
ADMISSION: Adults $1.50, children 50¢, students $1, families $3.50.

Holyoke

• *Wistariahurst Museum*
238 Cabot Street
Holyoke, Massachusetts 01040 *(413) 536-6771*

This museum in the bustling Connecticut River Valley is especially suited to young people. The **Youth Museum** in the carriage house has many special science and natural history features. Exhibits trace the story of prehistoric Indians of the valley, but most artifacts are comparatively recent. Slide and film programs on early Indian lore are available to groups by appointment. There is an art museum in the **Mansion** and many changing exhibits and dioramas.

HOURS: Tuesday–Saturday: 1:00 P.M.–5:00 P.M.
Closed Sundays, Mondays, and holidays.
ADMISSION: Free.

Salem

- *Peabody Museum of Salem*
  161 Essex Street — *(617) 745-9500 for hours*
  Salem, Massachusetts 01970 — *(617) 745-1876 other*

The Peabody owns extensive archaeological material from all over the Northeast, and it is preparing a new gallery devoted to native American cultures over the 10,500 years of known human occupation in New England. Particular emphasis will be given to the Paleo-Indian material recovered from the famous Bull Brook site in Ipswich, which has never been open to the public. Bull Brook is one of the earliest and most important Early Man sites in the Northeast.

There are many changing exhibits on Indians of the Northeast, and this museum also specializes in maritime history, marine art, and wildlife. The research library is available for use on the premises and scholars, amateurs, and professionals may make appointments to see special collections.

Salem is one of the oldest and most famous of New England seaports, and its stories of witchcraft have been told over and over again in fact and fiction. There are many houses and museums open to the public. Stop in the Visitors' Center in the **Customs House** on Derby Street opposite the wharf for information.

HOURS (MUSEUM): Monday–Saturday: 9:00 A.M.–5:00 P.M.
Sunday and holidays: 1:00 P.M.–5 P.M.
Closed Thanksgiving, Christmas, New Year's.

ADMISSION: Adults $1.50; students, senior citizens, and children six to sixteen 75¢; under six free.

STATE OFFICE

Valerie Talmadge
State Archaeologist
Massachusetts Historical Commission
294 Washington Street
Boston, Massachusetts 02108 — (617) 727-8470

OPPORTUNITIES FOR AMATEURS

State Archaeologist Valerie Talmadge believes the most important archaeological task in the East is to preserve threatened sites—"catch them before the bulldozer gets to them." Massachusetts, like all of the East Coast, is up against the pressure of development.

Amateurs can help by locating sites and reporting them to their local historical commission or local conservation commission. Almost every town in Massachusetts has such a group. These local bodies are concerned with preservation and site survey and have the power to hold sites or ensure that they are properly surveyed and excavated before modern industry obliterates them. Amateurs in Massachusetts belong to the Massachusetts Archaeological Society, one of the oldest and most prestigious archaeological societies in the country (see below).

Underwater Archaeology. State Geologist Joseph A. Sinnott awards licenses to skin divers to perform archaeological work on wrecks over one hundred years old and with an estimated value in excess of five thousand dollars. All work is done on an individual basis. For information write:

Joseph A. Sinnott
State Geologist
Department of Environmental Quality Engineering
Division of Waterways, Room 532
100 Nashua Street
Boston, Massachusetts 02114

ORGANIZATIONS TO JOIN

The **Massachusetts Archaeological Society** publishes an outstanding bulletin and is involved in site survey and digs all over Massachusetts and other states in the Northeast. Scientists come from all over the United States to speak at its meetings. Headquarters for the Massachusetts Archaeological Society is:

Bronson Museum
8 North Main Street
Attleboro, Massachusetts 02703 (617) 222-5470

NEW HAMPSHIRE

Tens of thousands of years ago, Pleistocene glaciers cut through the weak zones of the granite White Mountains that stretch diagonally across New Hampshire and left a series of rugged notches for which the state is famous. New Hampshire today is probably very much like it was when the ice sheets finally melted away, leaving hundreds of lakes and streams in mountain pockets. Forests grew up and eventually covered almost 90 percent of the state. The mountainous, well-watered country rolls down to a strip of Atlantic coast.

From the time people first entered North America, hunters lived in

New Hampshire. Later, ancient people supplemented their hunting and fishing and began to cultivate the valleys between the many mountain ridges, just as farmers do today.

SITES

Many sites in New Hampshire are open to the public in the summer, but these vary from year to year, as they are actually excavations-in-progress. They usually last one season, and another site is excavated the following year. Anyone interested in visiting a dig in the field should call or write:

Department of Sociology and Anthropology
University of New Hampshire
Durham, New Hampshire 03824 (603) 862-1547

The university also welcomes amateurs on digs (see "Opportunities for Amateurs" below).

North Salem

• *Mystery Hill*
North Salem, New Hampshire 03073 *(603) 893-8300*

Mystery Hill is the only permanent site in the state, and it is surrounded by controversy. It is privately owned and purports to be the four-thousand-year-old site of a Celtic settlement. It is definitely the location of several historic occupations from the eighteenth century on. Several stone artifacts found on the site indicate prehistoric carbon-14 dates.

The New England Antiquities Research Association (NEARA), under the directorship of site owner Robert Stone, has a large membership dedicated to proving that Mystery Hill is genuine. But many leading scientists are convinced that claims for prehistoric antiquity are unsupported and caution that the genuine eighteenth-century material may be mixed with unproved prehistoric artifacts.

It costs three dollars to visit this site, which takes approximately one hour. Skeptics and advocates alike can visit the site daily from April 1 through December 1.

DIRECTIONS: From I-93, take exit 3. Follow the signs east on Route 111 for 5 miles.
HOURS: Spring and fall: 10:00 A.M.–4:30 P.M.
Summer: 9:00 A.M.–5:30 P.M.
ADMISSION: Adults $3; teen-age students, military personnel, and senior citizens $2.50; children six to twelve $1. Group rates available; appointment necessary.

MUSEUMS

Dover

• *Woodman Institute*
182–192 Central Avenue
Dover, New Hampshire 03820 *(603) 742-1038*

In 1915 Mrs. Annie E. Woodman left a sum of money for the creation of a museum devoted to local history and natural history. Over the years, the Woodman Institute has built several outstanding collections, all carefully displayed and labeled. The entrance to the museum is through the front door of Annie Woodman's home, built in 1818. One room has a large showing of Indian artifacts, including pieces from the Madbury people, who lived in New Hampshire from three to six thousand years ago, and also an exhibit on the famous Red Paint Indian culture of Maine. There are further displays of artifacts from all over North America, and one cabinet shows Inca artifacts from South America.

HOURS: Tuesday–Sunday: 2:00 P.M.–5:00 P.M.
ADMISSION: Contributions accepted.

Hanover

• *Dartmouth College Museum and Galleries*
East Wheelock Street
Hanover, New Hampshire 03755 *(603) 646-2348*

Wilson Hall has permanent displays that describe the life of different Indian cultures around the country. College students prepare temporary exhibits that reflect ongoing excavations and studies in anthropology. There is always something new here and often excellent temporary exhibits drawn from the museum's large collection of prehistoric materials.

HOURS: Monday–Friday: 9:00 A.M.–5:00 P.M.
Saturday and Sunday: 12:00 M.–4:00 P.M.
ADMISSION: Free.

Manchester

• *Manchester Historic Association*
129 Amherst Street
Manchester, New Hampshire 03104 *(603) 622–7531*

The small permanent exhibit has displays of artifacts from the Manchester area dating back to the time of the Big Game Hunters ten thousand years ago. By appointment, you can view the museum collections that include artifacts recovered from Amoskeag Falls, a fishing and hunting region that attracted prehistoric people from all over the Northeast. The collection also includes local finds donated by amateurs and professionals and stone artifacts from New York and western states. The library is open for use on the premises and includes the Peter McLame Indian collection.

HOURS: Tuesday–Friday: 11:00 A.M.–4:00 P.M.
Saturday: 10:00 A.M.–4:00 P.M.
Closed Sundays and Mondays and major holidays.
If a holiday falls on Monday, the museum is also closed Tuesday.
ADMISSION: Free.

OPPORTUNITIES FOR AMATEURS

The hub of archaeological research in New Hampshire is the **University of New Hampshire.** The department of sociology and anthropology sponsors field schools for amateurs and welcomes amateur participation on all of its excavations. For information, write or call:

Department of Sociology and Anthropology
University of New Hampshire
Durham, New Hampshire 03824 (603) 862-1547

ORGANIZATIONS TO JOIN

The leading lay-professional organization in the state is the **New Hampshire Archaeological Society.** Members are involved in survey and protection of threatened sites. They cooperate with various state organizations and hold a summer field school in association with the University of New Hampshire. This is a statewide organization, and headquarters change as new officers are elected. The society can always be reached at the University of New Hampshire at the above address.

The **New England Antiquities Research Association** is primarily concerned with research into European and Asian contact before Columbus. This is an interesting area of archaeology, and many amateurs in New Hampshire belong both to the Archaeological Society and to the NEARA. Other members come from all over the U.S. and many foreign countries. NEARA sponsors two field trips each year; members receive the quarterly *NEARA Journal.* For information, write:

Alex Manaila
292 Lake View Avenue
Apt. A8
Patterson, New Jersey 07503

NEW JERSEY

Beyond the clogged industrial thoroughfares that choke the state's eastern border on the Hudson River, New Jersey is as rustic and mellow as any New England countryside. The Lanape Indians made their home among these gentle slopes and rivers, and although there are no archaeological sites open to the public, there are several good museums and a very active archaeological association.

MUSEUMS

Morristown

• *Morris Museum of Arts and Sciences*
Normandy Heights and Columbia Roads
Morristown, New Jersey 07961 *(201) 538-0454*

This museum has something for everyone: galleries devoted to Indians of North America, small live animals, earth science displays, rocks and minerals, a model railroad, dinosaurs, fossils, and mounted birds and animals. There are also art galleries and a Five Senses Learning Center. Special exhibits illustrate the life of New Jersey Indians, as well as Indians from the Great Plains, Southwest, and Northwest Coast. A research library can be used on the premises, and there is a gift shop.

DIRECTIONS: The museum is just off I-287 in Morristown.
HOURS: Monday–Saturday: 10:00 A.M.–5:00 P.M.
Sunday: 2:00 P.M.–5:00 P.M.
July and August
Tuesday–Saturday: 10:00 A.M.–4:00 P.M.
Closed holidays.
ADMISSION: Adults $1, students and senior citizens 50¢, children three to twelve 25¢, under three, free; special group rates.

Newton

• *Sussex County Historical Society*
82 Main Street
Newton, New Jersey 07860 *(201) 383-6010*

Many local finds are displayed here and artifacts on exhibit date from the Archaic through the Woodland periods. Life-size dioramas show a rock-shelter habitation. This is primarily a historical museum and focuses on local genealogy. A research library is available for use on the premises. The museum publishes a newsletter as well as several pamphlets written by members.

HOURS: The museum is open Friday: 9:00 A.M.–12:00 M., 1:00 P.M.–4:00 P.M.
Also open the last Tuesday in each month: 1:00 P.M.–4:00 P.M.
ADMISSION: Free.

Princeton

• *Museum of Natural History*
Princeton University
Guyot Hall
Princeton, New Jersey 08544 *(609) 452-4102*

This natural history museum is world renowned for its vertebrate fossil collection. It also has outstanding archaeology exhibits from the Cody Complex in Wyoming, artifacts recovered from excavations on the Northwest Coast, and many local finds.

You can tour the many historic buildings on the Princeton campus by contacting the office at Stanhope Hall and requesting a campus guide. Please call a few days ahead at (201) 452-3603. Tours are free.

HOURS (MUSEUM): Monday–Saturday: 9:00 A.M.–5:00 P.M.
Sunday and holidays: 2:00 P.M.–5:00 P.M.
ADMISSION: Free.

Trenton

• *New Jersey State Museum*
205 West State Street
Trenton, New Jersey 08625 *(609) 292-6300*

Three floors of exhibits explore archaeology, geology, and biology. This museum has an extensive collection of local archaeological artifacts and holds the material excavated from New Jersey's famous Abbott Farm site, which is now closed to the public. In the new Hall of Cultural History, exhibits illustrate the story of the Indians of the Southwest, Great Plains, Alaska, Northwest Coast, and California.

The Planetarium has special space exhibits. Children under seven are not admitted there except for special programs held on Friday mornings during the summer. There is a gift shop and solar observatory in the building. Dr. Lorraine Williams, New Jersey state archaeologist, is the curator of archaeology and ethnology, and the museum works closely with the Archaeological Association of New Jersey.

HOURS: Monday–Friday: 9:00 A.M.–4:30 P.M.
Saturday, Sunday, and holidays: 1:00 P.M.–5:00 P.M.
Closed July 4, Thanksgiving, Christmas, New Year's.
ADMISSION: Free.

STATE OFFICE

Lorraine E. Williams
State Archaeologist
New Jersey State Museum
Department of Education
205 West State Street
P.O. Box 1868
Trenton, New Jersey 08625

ORGANIZATIONS TO JOIN

The address of the **Archaeological Association of New Jersey** changes when new officers are elected. You can always reach the organization through the New Jersey State Museum at the above address.

This is a lay-professional statewide organization, and some of New Jersey's leading scientists have been its officers. Members participate in fieldwork through the Archaeological Research Center at Seton Hall University, hold regular meetings, and publish a newsletter and bulletin. This is the preeminent archaeological society in the state for both professionals and amateurs.

NEW YORK

The Lamoka was the earliest known Archaic culture in New York State. Later, in the Woodland period, the Owasco culture became prominent. The famous Iroquois-speaking tribes that had such a major effect on the fate of the British colonials were direct descendants of that culture.

For most of the eighteenth century, the Iroquois-speaking tribes were the strongest native power in North America. Yet they never numbered over 12,000, and only 2200 of these were fighting men. Even so, the Five Nations of the Iroquois—the Onondaga, Mohawk, Oneida, Cayuga and Seneca—decimated all of their surrounding enemies. They overwhelmed their traditional Algonkian-speaking enemies and even crushed the Iroquois tribes that did not belong to their confederacy.

Historian Francis Parkman spoke of the Iroquois as the "Romans of the New World." Sometime in the fifteenth century, the Iroquois established the pattern of ritual torture and cannibalism that was familiar throughout historic times. But for all their warlike nature, they conceived a League of Peace that protected the tribes of their confederacy, and they settled large farming communities without fear of outside invaders.

The prehistoric period of the Iroquois lasted till late in the sixteenth century, when they began to receive European trade goods. But they did not make direct contact with the Europeans until French missionaries reached them in the middle of the seventeenth century. By that time the Iroquois held sway from the Illinois River in the West to the Kennebec in the East, and from the Tennessee River all the way north to Ottawa. When the Tuscarora Indians were expelled from North Carolina by the British, they moved north to join the Oneidas, increasing the confederacy from five to six tribes.

While the tribes of the confederacy lived peacefully together, their tradition of warfare and human sacrifice continued. All of the league sided with the British against the French and Algonkians in the French and Indian War. But in the Revolution each tribe was allowed to make its own choice. Only the Oneidas and Tuscaroras helped the Americans. The rest of the confederacy, led by the powerful Onondagas, sided with the British. The Revolution led to their destruction, for the triumphant Americans launched punitive campaigns against them in 1779 and almost wiped out the tribes. The few remaining Onondagas moved to a reservation near Buffalo and later to a parcel of land near Syracuse, where their home is today. The Oneidas and Tuscaroras moved to Wisconsin, and the Mohawk and Cayuga tribes followed the British to Canada.

New York is a big state. Some of the world's great museums are in New York City, but there are dozens of smaller museums located in small towns all over the Empire State. Almost all of them have some special Iroquois artifacts, and the fine science museum in Rochester holds the world's largest collection of Iroquois material. Because there are so many museums in the state, they have been numbered and keyed onto a state map.

MUSEUMS AND SITES

Albany

● *New York State Museum*
Cultural Education Center
Empire State Plaza
Albany, New York 12224 *(518) 474-5877*

This important museum is undergoing extensive renovation. When complete, its several divisions all will emphasize human interaction with nature. A major gallery showing the geological base of the Adirondacks and extinct animals has just opened, and a prehistoric mastodon model is on display. The prehistoric Indian exhibits will be called "Upstate Region," and they will interpret how the early Indians adapted to their environment in the

Map of New York state showing location of sites.

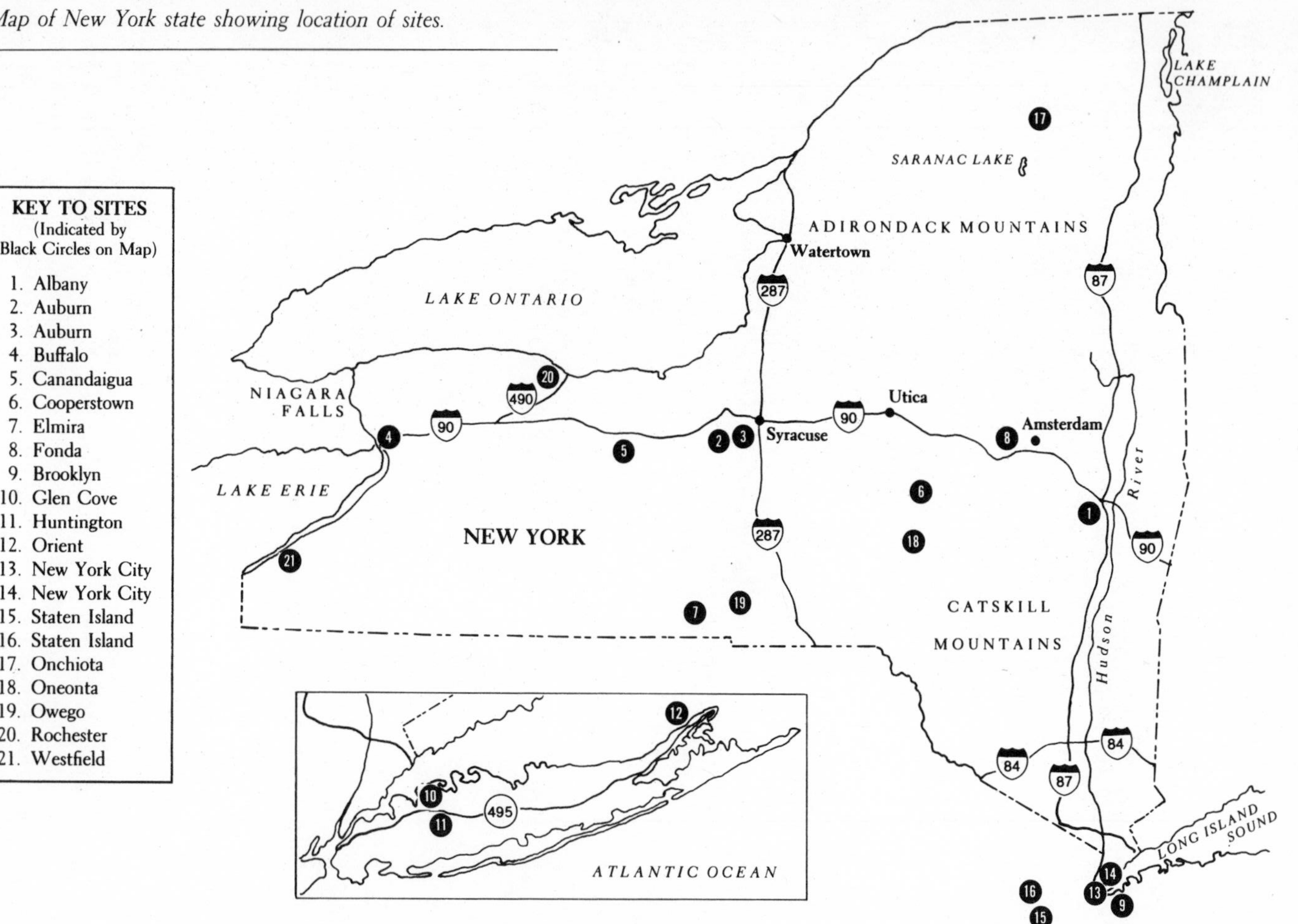

face of natural phenomena. The museum holds a large collection of artifacts, and the emphasis is on interpretation. The renovation is largely completed as of this writing, but the museum will not be in full swing until the summer of 1981.

The museum has an extensive research library for use on the premises, and the Museum Shop sells rocks, minerals, shells, and decorative art items.

HOURS: 10:00 A.M.–5:00 P.M. daily and holidays.
Closed Thanksgiving, Christmas, New Year's.
ADMISSION: Free.

Auburn

• *Cayuga Museum of History and Art*
203 Genesee Street
Auburn, New York 13021 *(315) 253-8051*

This small museum is devoted to the Indians of the Northeast, especially the prehistoric people of the Owasco culture. The Indian Room also has samples of early stone work and artifacts from all over North and South America. The museum is parent to the **Owasco Stockaded Indian Village,** and after you have seen the interpretive collections at the museum, take the time to go out to the village, which is about three miles south of town. The Cayuga Museum is also the headquarters for the **Archaeological Society of Central New York,** one of the outstanding amateur-professional organizations in the state. Museum Director Professor Walker K. Long can give you information on the society.

The museum is open to the public only during the summer months of July and August, but special tours for schools and groups can be arranged throughout the year.

DIRECTIONS: Auburn is southwest of Syracuse, off I-90.
HOURS: July–August only
Tuesday–Friday: 1:00 P.M.–5:00 P.M.
Saturday: 9:00 A.M.–12:00 M., 1:00 P.M.–5:00 P.M.
Sunday: 2:00 P.M.–5:00 P.M.
ADMISSION: Adults 50¢, children 25¢.

• *Owasco Stockaded Indian Village*
Emerson Park
Auburn, New York 13021 *(315) 253-8051*

Emerson Park is near Owasco Lake where the Owasco Indians lived, and two long houses have been scientifically reconstructed. Closely related families lived in a long house, which often measured twenty-five feet wide by several hundred feet long. Exhibits inside the long houses show the daily life of the people in A.D. 1150—their pottery and hunting weapons, their gardens and hearths.

Special tours for groups and schoolchildren can be arranged by calling the Cayuga Museum. The village is normally open to the public in conjunction with the museum, but recent funding problems may force the village adjunct to close. If you would like to visit the village, ask at the museum or give them a call.

DIRECTIONS: The village is at the foot of Owasco Lake, 3 miles south of Auburn.

Buffalo

- *Buffalo Museum of Science*
  Humboldt Parkway
  Buffalo, New York 14211 *(716) 896-5200*

This science museum has lively exhibits on anthropology, geology, zoology, botany, and astronomy. From extensive prehistoric holdings, museum curators are continually fashioning new exhibits and the emphasis is on the early Iroquois. Other exhibits usually include material from the Northwest Coast and Southwest Indians. A new anthropology section will open within the next year, and a research library is available for use on the premises Monday through Friday.

HOURS: Daily: 10:00 A.M.–5:00 P.M.
Holidays: 1:30 P.M.–5:30 P.M.
ADMISSION: Free.

- *Buffalo Historical Museum*
  25 Nottingham Court
  Buffalo, New York 14216 *(716) 873-9644*

Outstanding exhibits are presented of Iroquois life just before European contact: large dioramas, beadwork, baskets, pottery, clothing, plus extensive interpretation. The historical section of the museum has period rooms and shops. Other exhibits of pioneer crafts and an 1890 pilothouse evoke the era of the Niagara frontier in the eighteenth and nineteenth centuries.

HOURS: Monday–Friday: 10:00 A.M.–5:00 P.M.
Saturday and Sunday: 12:00 M.–5:00 P.M.
ADMISSION: Free.

Canandaigua

- *Ontario County Historical Society*
  55 North Main Street
  Canandaigua, New York 14424 *(716) 394-4975*

As this book goes to press, the museum is undergoing a major renovation. Different sections will be opening and closing through the year. Permanent exhibits follow the occupation of the North American continent from the Ice Age to the present. The society's large collection of Indian artifacts is presently in storage but can be seen by appointment.

DIRECTIONS: Canandaigua is halfway between Rochester and Syracuse off the New York State Thruway.
HOURS: Tuesday–Saturday: 1:00 P.M.–5:00 P.M.
Closed Sundays, Mondays, and holidays.
ADMISSION: Free.

Cooperstown

- *Cooperstown Indian Museum*
  1 Pioneer Street
  Cooperstown, New York 13326 *(607) 547-9531*

Today, Cooperstown is probably most famous for its National Baseball Hall of Fame and Museum, since it is the place where General Abner Doubleday invented the game in 1839. But Cooperstown was famous long before it or anyone else ever saw a baseball. The town was founded in 1786 by Judge William Cooper, father of James Fenimore Cooper, who made the whole region world famous when he wrote *The Last of the Mohicans.*

The Indian Museum has archaeological dioramas and exhibits arranged in cultural sequence. Most of the artifacts come from within fifty miles of Cooperstown and represent cultures from the Paleo-Indian Period through the late Woodland Period. These are outstanding exhibits of Indian life in New York State and many Iroquois artifacts—altogether a wonderful museum day.

There are at least six other museums in town, all of them interesting, fun, and worthwhile. You can purchase a combination ticket to visit three of them: the **Farmers' Museum, Fenimore House,** and the **Baseball Hall of Fame.**

HOURS (MUSEUM): May 15–October 15: 1:00 P.M.–5:00 P.M. daily.
ADMISSION: Adults 90¢, children 40¢, special group rates.

Elmira

- *Chemung County Historical Society, Inc.*
  Historical Center
  304 Williams Street
  Elmira, New York 14901 *(607) 737-2900*

The society's comprehensive collection features New York State and leans heavily toward archaeological exhibits that encompass the Archaic through contemporary periods. It is noted for its collection from Lamoka Lake, and this and many other outstanding collections can be reviewed by qualified researchers on request.* An excellent three-thousand-volume library of rare books is available for use on the premises.

In the fall of 1980, the society moves to new quarters in a historical bank building. The new address is:

415 Water Street
Elmira, New York 14901

The society hopes to expand its daily hours after the move. Call to check the new hours.

CURRENT HOURS: Tuesday, Wednesday, Friday: 1:00 P.M.–4:30 P.M.
RESEARCH LIBRARY: Monday-Friday: 9:00 A.M.–5:00 P.M.
ADMISSION: Free.

Fonda

- *The Mohawk-Caughnawaga Museum*
  State Route 5
  Fonda, New York 12068 *(518) 853-3646*

This indoor-outdoor museum directed by the Franciscan Fathers is on the site of a completely excavated and staked-out Iroquois village. The museum proper has outstanding Iroquois exhibits and artifacts. There's a nature trail, picnicking, and a gift shop.

HOURS: May 15–October 15
Tuesday–Sunday: 10:00 A.M.–4:00 P.M.
Closed during the winter.

* There's some confusion regarding the definition of "qualified researcher." In some museums the term means only full-fledged professional scientists. For the Chemung County Historical Society "qualified" means anyone with a letter of reference: writers, researchers, schoolteachers, college professors—even a high-school student writing a paper for class.

Note: **Fort Johnson** is only a few miles down the road, and the two museums are easily seen together in a single day's outing. Fort Johnson stands virtually as it was in 1774; the original house is now a museum of colonial and Indian artifacts, some of them fashioned by the earliest Indians who lived in the valley. Phone number is (518) 842-0683.

DIRECTIONS: Fort Johnson is 3 miles west of Amsterdam on Route 5 connecting with the Thruway.
HOURS: May–June, September–October: 1:00 P.M.–5:00 P.M. daily. July and August: Tuesday–Saturday: 10:00 A.M.–5:00 P.M. Sunday, holidays, and Monday: 1:00 P.M.–5:00 P.M. Closed during the winter.
ADMISSION: Adults $1, children free if accompanied by adults.

NEW YORK CITY AND VICINITY

Brooklyn

- *Brooklyn Children's Museum*
145 Brooklyn Avenue
Brooklyn, New York 11213 *(212) 735-4400*

Prehistoric stone tools and other artifacts are used in changing exhibits of American Indian life styles. Students are welcome to make appointments with the curator to study the large American Indian collections held by the museum. Art and science are emphasized here, and a bulletin lists current children's activities offered by the museum. A children's lending library, an outdoor theater, and an indoor greenhouse are all part of the facilities.

HOURS: Wednesday–Monday: 1:00 P.M.–5:00 P.M. Closed Tuesdays. Classes by appointment.
ADMISSION: Free.

Long Island

- *Garvies Point Museum and Preserve*
Barry Drive
Glen Cove, New York 11542 *(516) 671-0300*

Garvies Point is the leading center for archaeological research on Long Island. Museum exhibits are devoted to the special geology and archaeology of the island environment. The story begins with the migration of people from Asia and traces their cultural evolution through prehistoric times. The life of the early Indians of Long Island is portrayed in a series of beautiful dioramas and includes many fine artifacts. Other exhibits pinpoint the first European contact and the subsequent demise of the Indian culture. There is a model of an archaeological dig, and visitors can look through a plate glass window in the exhibit hall to observe the archaeological laboratory.

Outside the museum sixty-two wooded acres make up the Preserve. Trails meander through woods and meadows all the way to the high cliffs along the shoreline. All variety of birds and wildlife are protected here, and hundreds of different species live in the Preserve.

The museum, under the directorship of Dan Kaplan, is heavily involved in ongoing research in Long Island archaeology. Members of the staff survey and test dig in an attempt to locate and preserve valuable sites. Anyone wishing to help can apply directly to the museum. This is also the headquarters for the **Nassau County Archaeological Association.**

DIRECTIONS: From the Long Island Expressway, Northern State, or Meadowbrook Parkway, exit on Glen Cove Road northbound. Continue on Glen Cove Bypass (keep left at fork) to the last traffic light at Glen Cove Firehouse. Follow the signs to the museum. (The museum is *not* on Garvies Point Road.)
HOURS (MUSEUM): 9:00 A.M.–5:00 P.M. daily.
Closed major holidays.
ADMISSION: Free.
HOURS (PRESERVE): Monday–Friday: 8:00 A.M.–as posted.
Saturday: 9:00 A.M.–as posted.
Closed major holidays.

Note: No dogs or other pets are allowed on the Preserve, and no rock collecting is permitted on the beach.

Huntington

- *Suffolk County Indian and Archaeological Museum*
Huntington, New York *(516) 261-6612*

The only drawback to this museum is that it's open only one day a week. The indoor-outdoor exhibits here are particularly fine for young people and children. Dioramas and displays of projectile points, stone and bone tools, pottery, and ax heads make up just a few of the exhibits and special emphasis is placed on how the archaeologist works in the field.

The museum teaches a college-level course on the Indians of Long Island and also offers a variety of programs on both archaeology and Indian life. A circulating and research library on American Indians and archaeology is open to the public. A special collection of rare, out-of-print books is available for use by appointment. Books and Indian crafts are for sale in the Museum Shop.

HOURS: Sunday: 2:00 P.M.–5:00 P.M.
Other times by appointment for groups and school classes.
Closed Easter, July 4, Christmas.
ADMISSION: 25¢.

Orient

• *Oysterponds Historical Society, Inc.*
Village Lane
Orient, New York 11957 *(516) 323-2480*

The old fishing village of Orient is on the less-traveled shore of Long Island, and a drive out to Orient Point takes you through many beautiful, old shore towns. The history of whaling and fishing is the highlight of the society's exhibits. But many ancient, local Indian artifacts are on display, including a Clovis point.

A large research library on local history is available, but books are for use only on the premises. Souvenirs and antiques are for sale in the Museum Shop.

HOURS: July and August
Tuesday, Thursday, Saturday, and Sunday: 2:00 P.M.–5:00 P.M.
ADMISSION: Adults $1, children 50¢.

Note: Orient is at least three hours' drive from New York City and worth every minute of the trip, but you should plan to stay overnight.

Manhattan

• *American Museum of Natural History*
Central Park West at 79th Street
New York, New York 10024 *(212) 873-1300*

It takes days to see all of the great halls and exhibits in one of the world's great science museums. Everything is here—mammals and birds of the world, insects, amphibians and reptiles, fishes and fossils, galleries of minerals and rare gems, great constructions of dinosaurs, and even a dinosaur factory where life-size duplicates are molded and sent to museums around the world. The vast anthropology halls are almost endless: the Eskimo and Northwest Coast exhibits are outstanding, as are the galleries devoted to the Indians of the Northeast, Southeast, and Great Plains. And a special archaeological exhibit is tucked away on the fourth floor.

The library and rare book room are open for research on the premises.

There is a cafeteria, a sales counter for children, and an excellent museum shop that sells fine reproductions of rare artifacts.

The museum can be overwhelming. The lighting in the great halls tends to be somewhat theatrical—that is, dim. I've seen adults startled in their tracks when stuffed bears and totem poles suddenly loom up out of the shadowy depths of the long galleries. I suggest you take a child, or at least a friend, along for company. Children run cheerfully up and down the slightly spooky corridors and gallantly confront all manner of beast and oddity without turning a hair.

If you wish to take in the whole museum in one grand sweep, join one of the guided tours that leave regularly from the main lobby. If you prefer to concentrate on the anthropology and archaeological exhibits, ask directions to the various displays at the Information Desk on the main floor.

HOURS (MUSEUM): Monday–Saturday: 10:00 A.M.–4:45 P.M.
Wednesday: 10:00 A.M.–9:00 P.M.
Sunday and holidays: 11:00 A.M.–5:00 P.M.
Closed Thanksgiving, Christmas.
HOURS (LIBRARY): Monday–Friday: 11:00 A.M.–4:00 P.M.
ADMISSION: Suggested: Adults $1.50, children 75¢.

Note: As if all this isn't enough, the world-famous **Hayden Planetarium** is in the same building, complete with a sky theater, the Guggenheim Space Theater, the Hall of the Sun, classrooms, and a library of books on astronomy. The Hayden is open on weekday afternoons from 1:00 P.M. to 5:00 P.M., Saturdays from 10:00 A.M. to 6:00 P.M., and Sundays from 12:00 M. to 6:00 P.M. It is closed Thanksgiving and Christmas.

• *Museum of the American Indian, Heye Foundation*
Broadway at West 155th Street
New York, New York 10032 *(212) 283-2420*

All the way uptown, the world's largest collection of American Indian material is on display at this outstanding museum. Collections from North, South, and Central America show how different cultures wandered back and forth and up and down the American continent. You can get a good grasp of why some cultures became important and influential and others remained isolated.

The whole story of prehistoric America is here, told in well-interpreted exhibits that relate both time periods and cultures. Many rare artifacts on display are from sites that have never been open to the public. The quality of this material is outstanding, and no finer examples can be found anywhere. The Museum Shop sells authentic Indian-made products. This museum should be seen by everyone interested in the life of the American Indians.

It's the best of its kind. The museum's research library devoted to the American Indian is in the Bronx and available for use by appointment. Call (212) 829-7770.

HOURS: Tuesday–Saturday: 10:00 A.M.–5:00 P.M.
Sunday: 1:00 P.M.–5:00 P.M.
Closed Mondays and major holidays.
ADMISSION: Adults $1, students and senior citizens 50¢, under seven free.

Note: The museum is part of a group that includes four other museums on the same block: the **American Academy of Arts and Letters** (368-5900), the **American Geographical Society** (234-8100), the **American Numismatic Society** (234-3130), and the **Hispanic Society of America** (690-0743). Hours vary for these museums, and it's best to call ahead if you wish to be sure they're open when you travel uptown.

Staten Island

• *Staten Island Institute of Arts and Sciences*
75 Stuyvesant Place
Staten Island, New York 10301 *(212) 727-1135*

Visitors and residents of New York City love to sail across New York Harbor on the Staten Island ferry. Lots of people take the round-trip ferry ride and never set foot on Staten Island proper. Yet just two blocks away from the ferry slip on the Staten Island side is the enterprising and absorbing Institute of Arts and Sciences. Exhibits here are based on environmental themes and Indian archaeology. Permanent and temporary exhibits concentrate on Staten Island plant and animal life, geology, marine life, and archaeology. There are many special programs for children, a nature center, and children's gifts for sale. A thirty-thousand-volume library of books on history, art, and science can be used by appointment.

DIRECTIONS: The institute is located at 75 Stuyvesant Place and Wall Street in St. George, two blocks from the ferry.
HOURS: Tuesday–Saturday: 10:00 A.M.–5:00 P.M.
Sunday and holidays: 2:00–5:00 P.M.
Closed July 4, Labor Day, Thanksgiving, Christmas, New Year's.
ADMISSION: Free. Nature lectures: Adults $1, students 50¢.

• *Museum of Archaeology at Staten Island*
631 Howard Avenue
Staten Island, New York 10301 *(212) 273-3300*

This privately operated archaeology museum is on the campus of Wagner College. Collections from all over the world can be seen in this small museum dedicated to archaeology: Rome, Africa, Egypt, Greece, and South America are all prominently represented. Some changing exhibits focus on the prehistoric Indians of Staten Island.

A research library on world history and archaeology is available for use by appointment. Books, stationery, and reproductions of Egyptian scarabs are for sale at the sales counter.

DIRECTIONS: The museum is located on Grymes Hill on the campus of Wagner College. From the ferry take the #6, 106, 111, or 112 bus to the college (a ten-minute trip). A shuttle bus takes you up steep Grymes Hill. By car take the Verrazano Bridge. Follow Bay Street to Victory Boulevard and turn right. At Clove Road turn left to Howard, and left again up Grymes Hill.

HOURS: Tuesday, Wednesday, Thursday: 10:00 A.M.–4:30 P.M.
Sunday: 1:00 P.M.–4:30 P.M.
Closed month of August.
Closed July 4, Christmas, New Year's.

ADMISSION: Free.

Onchiota

- *Six Nations Indian Museum*
Onchiota, New York 12968 *(518) 891-0769*

This museum is devoted to the Iroquois culture. Almost all of its extensive collection is from the historic period of the Six Nations, but it has a few prehistoric exhibits "going way back," probably from settlements around Lake Champlain.

DIRECTIONS: The museum is near Saranac Lake, just off Route 3, one mile out of Onchiota.

HOURS: May 31–Labor Day: 9:30 A.M.–6:00 P.M. daily.
Other times by appointment.

ADMISSION: Adults 75¢, children 40¢.

Oneonta

- *Yager Museum of Hartwick College*
Library-Museum Building
Oneonta, New York 13820 *(607) 432-4200*

Collections of artifacts from the upper Susquehanna River are used in displays that trace the Archaic and Woodland periods in New York State. Other exhibits show special collections from Central and South America. The museum is involved in excavations in the upper Susquehanna region, and material not on display may be seen by appointment. A research library on the American Indian is on the premises.

HOURS: Monday–Friday: 10:00 A.M.–4:00 P.M.
Closed weekends and holidays.
ADMISSION: Free.

Owego

- *Tioga County Historical Society Museum*
110–112 Front Street
Owego, New York 13827 *(607) 687-2460*

A whole room is devoted to prehistoric Owasco exhibits: pottery, tools, and projectile points (including a Clovis point) found in the vicinity. Other artifacts are from the Lamoka Lake, early Iroquois, and Susquehannock cultures. The rest of the museum is devoted to the historic pioneer period of Tioga County with displays of farm tools, primitive paintings, and furnishings.

DIRECTIONS: Owego is near Binghamton, and just off I-390.
HOURS: 1:30 P.M.–4:30 P.M. daily.
Tuesday–Friday mornings: 10:00 A.M.–12:00 M.
Wednesday night: 7:00 P.M.–9:00 P.M.
Closed major holidays.
ADMISSION: Free.

Rochester

- *Rochester Museum and Science Center*
657 East Avenue
Rochester, New York 14603 *(716) 271-4320*

Recent acquisitions have made this important anthropology museum the owner of the world's largest collection of Iroquois artifacts. Rare Seneca and Iroquois material is finely displayed in a variety of exhibits. The influence of the Adena and Hopewell cultures is also reflected in displays that trace life in New York State from the Archaic to the historic period. Other exhibits focus on prehistoric lifeways all over North America.

The museum is headquarters of the **New York State Archaeological Association.** It also has a nature center and planetarium, and its extensive research library is open to the public by appointment. The museum also offers gift shops, guided tours, and many member activities.

The **Cumming Nature Center** in the Bristol Hills is part of the museum and has been designated a national environmental study area by the U.S.

Department of the Interior. Trails are open year round (and you should bring your own snowshoes or skis in the winter). There are demonstrations of maple sugaring, log harvesting, and open-hearth cooking at appropriate times of the year.

HOURS: Monday–Saturday: 9:00 A.M.–5:00 P.M.
Sunday and holidays: 1:00 P.M.–5:00 P.M.
Closed Christmas.
ADMISSION: Adults $1, children and senior citizens 50¢, preschoolers and members free.

Westfield

- *Chautauqua County Historical Society*
Main and Portage Streets
Westfield, New York 14787 *(716) 326-2977*

Projectile points, arrowheads, and pottery left by the early people who settled around the fringe of Lake Erie are displayed here. Prehistoric and historic artifacts from the Iroquois and Algonkian peoples are also shown.

DIRECTIONS: Westfield is right on Lake Erie near Chautauqua Lake.
HOURS: April 15–October
Tuesday–Saturday: 10:00 A.M.–12:00 M., 1:00 P.M.–4:00 P.M.
Closed rest of year and holidays.
ADMISSION: 50¢, children 10¢.

ONGOING EXCAVATIONS

Archaeologists dig with a purpose all over upstate New York in the summertime, and a few digs are open to visitors. The **New York Institute of Anthropology** has been excavating around the **Valhalla Rocks Site,** and digs will probably continue here for some years. Digs can only be visited with a guide, and there is a small on-site museum. This is a working excavation, but visitors with a genuine interest in archaeology are welcome. The institute is open to membership, and special member tours are arranged during the summer months. For information in New York, write:

Edward J. Platt, Director
New York Institute of Anthropology
34–15 94th Street
Jackson Heights, New York 11372

In the summer call (518) 827-5942 for an appointment.

STATE OFFICE

Dr. Robert Funk
State Archaeologist
New York State Museum
Buffalo, New York 12222 (518) 474-5813

OPPORTUNITIES FOR AMATEURS

There are no formal programs to train amateurs in New York State. But Dr. Robert Funk says that amateurs are welcome to visit his summer digs if you write first for permission (see above).

The Suffolk Archaeological Association, along with the State University at Stony Brook, has organized an original amateur program called **Saturday Archaeology.** This weekend field school is open to talented people of all ages from schoolchildren to senior citizens. It runs weekends for ten-week sessions in the spring and fall. Saturday Archaeology attracts all sorts of interesting people, and it's an inventive idea for public education. If you are interested, call the informal studies department of the State University at Stony Brook at (516) 246-5000.

ORGANIZATIONS TO JOIN

New York State Archaeological Association
Rochester Museum and Science Center
657 East Avenue
Rochester, New York 14603 *(716) 271-4320*

The NYSAA is primarily an amateur association involved in research and preservation of threatened sites. There are twelve local chapters throughout the state, and some individual chapters have training programs and sponsor local fieldwork. Activities range from excavation to frequent meetings, informative lectures, museum displays, research, and historic and prehistoric site conservation. The main publication of the NYSAA is the *Bulletin* published four times a year, and an annual conference brings all chapters together.

Archaeological Society of Central New York
Cayuga Museum of History and Art
203 Genesee Street
Auburn, New York 13021 *(315) 253-8051*

Leading archaeologists from all over the United States have been guest speakers at the society's special lecture programs. Amateur and professional members are closely involved in preservation of threatened local sites and also sponsor excavations. The organization was founded in 1947 by Professor

Walter Long, director of the Cayuga Museum, and its members were the first to document the early Owasco culture.

Suffolk Archaeological Association
P.O. Drawer AR
Stony Brook, New York 11790

Members of this enormously vigorous association intervene between threatened archaeological sites and bulldozers. They are involved in every aspect of archaeology on Long Island, including inventorying sites and encouraging exploration of sites threatened by new construction. The association is a center of archaeological consciousness raising on Long Island, and anyone who knows of a site that needs protection should get in touch with its members.

The association has a network of contacts among state offices and is instrumental in getting sites on the National Register.

Nassau County Archaeological Association
Garvies Point Museum
Barry Drive
Glen Cove, New York 11542 *(516) 671-0300*

The Nassau County Archaeological Association is the second independent amateur group on Long Island. Its newsletter is widely distributed in Long Island, and members offer their services for lab and field work to the Garvies Point Museum.

PENNSYLVANIA

Archaeologists find a little bit of everything in prehistoric Pennsylvania; it appears to have been a merging point for many diverse cultures and ideas. Some of the oldest well-dated evidence of the presence of human life in North America has been discovered in a sandstone outcrop just forty miles southwest of Pittsburgh. Recent excavations by archaeologists from the University of Pittsburgh reveal that a small group of people lived almost at the edge of the great Laurentide glacier. In a rockshelter, they cooked their game and sharpened their tools. Radiocarbon dating indicates that these campsites are between seventeen thousand and nineteen thousand years old.

About seventy-five miles north, work continues at the State Road Ripple site, where deep layers of stratigraphy show that people first began to camp here along the Clarion River twelve thousand years ago. There are no permanent sites in Pennsylvania open to the public, but the ongoing excavations at the Ripple site can be visited during the summer through the courtesy of Clarion State College, and digs sponsored by the University of Pittsburgh are also open to visitors.

SITES

- *State Road Ripple Site*
  Clarion State College
  Clarion, Pennsylvania 16214 *(814) 226-2513*

In this V-shaped valley, the river is shallow and runs swiftly over a gravel-filled bed. Off to the northwest, an old Indian trail can be seen on the valley slope. Over the years all sorts of artifacts have turned up along the Clarion River, where the river flattens out over an almost level strip of ground.

Beginning in the spring of 1970, the archaeology lab of Clarion State College, along with a small group of high-school students, began to excavate here. Summer digs over the last nine years have traced the occupation of the river site from the nineteenth-century lumbermen back through the entire Woodland sequence, further back into the Archaic Period, and deeper still down to the first stratum, which rests directly on the Pleistocene gravel sheet. Here two ancient hearths were uncovered. Bits of charcoal yielded a carbon-14 date of 11,385 ± 15.

From the bottom to the top, the deeply stratified site gives up clear evidence of each cultural period: stone points with forked bases, broad projectile points, knives, fragments of steatite vessels, stone tools, and camp debris. In the historic layer, glass beads, brass projectile points, metal fishhooks, and other trade items from the early eighteenth-century fur trade were found. And just below the plow zone was evidence of military camps and lumbermen: ox shoes, nails and spikes, bottles and tools.

The absence of ceramics and building in the early strata indicates the site was a seasonal trail camp, and no evidence has been found of winter occupation during prehistoric times. The style of the recovered artifacts shows that the prehistoric people who lived here were influenced by their neighbors to the east and west. The unusual blend of traits suggests that this spot where the Indian trail and the river converge may have been a kind of "shatter zone," where diverse cultures mingled.

Geographically, the area around the Ripple site has been little explored by archaeologists, and the ongoing dig is contributing valuable information on Pennsylvania's prehistory. Major training programs have been established at Clarion College to keep up with the excavation. High-school and college students and any interested amateur can participate (see "Opportunities for Amateurs" below).

The Ripple site is open to visitors during field schools, usually from the end of June to the middle of August. There is no entrance fee for visitors, and no special permission is required to visit the site. Take a slicker or raincoat along, because wet weather comes on fast in the valley. The site is located nine miles from the campus on a dirt road. The field director requests that visitors stop in at the archaeology lab at the college for directions.

DIRECTIONS: Clarion College is located in Clarion, just off I-80, in the western part of the state.

OTHER SITES: The University of Pittsburgh usually conducts a regular schedule of tours to its summer excavations. For up-to-date information about current digs open to the public, call the public relations office at (412) 624-4238, or the Carnegie Institute at (412) 622-3328. To inquire by mail, write:

Cathedral of Learning
University of Pittsburgh
Pittsburgh, Pennsylvania 15260

MUSEUMS

Airville

- *Indian Steps Museum*
R.D. 1
Airville, Pennsylvania 17302 *(717) 862-3948*

Several rooms of exhibits portray the lives of the Susquehannock Indians. Exhibits include many artifacts found in the area, and other prehistoric material has been donated from around the United States. This is a lovingly prepared Indian museum, and the building itself is located on the west bank of the Susquehanna River on the site of an old Indian village.

DIRECTIONS: Airville is southeast of York, going toward the Maryland border. From York, follow PA 74 to the intersection of PA 425 in Airville, then take a local road east to the museum, which is right on the river.

HOURS: April 1–October 31
Tuesday–Friday: 10:00 A.M.–4:00 P.M.
Saturday and Sunday: 11:00 A.M.–6:00 P.M.

ADMISSION: Contributions accepted.

Athens

- *Tioga Point Museum*
724 South Main Street
Athens, Pennsylvania 18810 *(717) 882-7225*

Some artifacts in the museum, including a Clovis point from Ohio, are ten thousand years old. Exhibits illustrate three important excavations from Murray Garden, Spanish Hill, and Abbe-Brennan sites, which were occupied from the Woodland period to historic times. Other science exhibits are wide ranging and valuable, including western prehistoric artifacts from Oklahoma and the Great Plains. This museum has been called a miniature Smithsonian in its broad range and solid interpretation.

HOURS: Wednesday and Saturday: 2:00 P.M.–5:00 P.M.
Monday: 7:00 P.M.–9:00 P.M.
Individual and group tours by appointment other days.
ADMISSION: Free.

Harrisburg

• *William Penn Memorial Museum*
3rd and North Streets
Harrisburg, Pennsylvania 17120 *(717) 787-4980*

This six-story circular building has an authentic country store, period rooms, a planetarium, a collection of antique automobiles, one of the world's largest framed paintings (Rothermel's *The Battle of Gettysburg*), and a nature museum. It also has wonderful Indian life exhibits in its Hall of Archaeology that cover the story of the Pennsylvania Indians from Paleo through historic times. A series of dioramas show the development of the Delaware culture, and other exhibits are devoted to archaeological techniques and fieldwork in the Northeast. The office of the state archaeologist, Barry Kent, is in this museum.

DIRECTIONS: The museum is adjacent to the state capitol.
HOURS (MUSEUM): Monday–Saturday: 9:00 A.M.–5:00 P.M.
Sunday: 12:00 M.–5:00 P.M.
Closed holidays.
HOURS (PLANETARIUM): Shows at 1:30 P.M. and 3:00 P.M., Saturday and Sunday only.
ADMISSION: Free.

Lancaster

Lancaster is in the heart of the famous Pennsylvania Dutch country, and there are many picturesque points of interest in the area. Stop in at the Visitors' Information Center, U.S. 30 at Hempstead Road, for a brief orientation film, and pick up free brochures and maps.

• *North Museum*
Franklin and Marshall College
College and Buchanan Avenues
Lancaster, Pennsylvania 17604 *(717) 291-3941*

One whole section of this large natural history museum is devoted to all the cultural periods of the prehistoric Indians from all over the Northeast.

Dioramas and displays tell the story of early Americans from Paleo times through the Archaic and Woodland periods. Special exhibits are devoted to pottery making and highlight artifacts recovered from local sites at Shenk's Ferry village and the Susquehannock culture. Many curatorial posts at the North Museum are staffed by volunteer amateur archaeologists, and the anthropology department of the college sponsors local summer work in the field.

HOURS: Wednesday–Saturday: 9:00 A.M.–5:00 P.M.
Sunday: 1:30 P.M.–5:00 P.M.
July and August
Saturday and Sunday only: 1:30 P.M.–5:00 P.M.
ADMISSION: Free.

Philadelphia

• *University Museum*
University of Pennsylvania
Spruce and 33rd Streets
Philadelphia, Pennsylvania 19174 *(215) 243-4000*

This important museum has prehistoric material from all over the world: North America, China, Africa, and the Pacific islands. The European and Middle East collections begin in prehistoric times and continue through the fall of Rome. The museum is outstanding in its study of ancient and primitive peoples, and its archaeological exhibits are skillfully prepared and interpreted. The University Museum has been involved in excavations all over the East, and exhibits reflect many of its important finds. Films, lectures, recitals, and special programs for children are offered throughout the year.

HOURS: Tuesday–Saturday: 10:00 A.M.–5:00 P.M.
Open Sunday during the winter: 1:00 P.M.–5:00 P.M.
ADMISSION: Contributions accepted.

Pittsburgh

• *Carnegie Museum of Natural History*
4400 Forbes Avenue
Pittsburgh, Pennsylvania 15213 *(412) 622-3243*

The Carnegie is world renowned for its Dinosaur Hall, natural science exhibits, Egyptian artifacts, and American Indian displays. Archaeological exhibits depict various cultures across North America, and the Monongahela culture of Pennsylvania is detailed. This is a lavish museum in every respect and not to be missed. Stop first in the Orientation Center, where a push-button audiovisual program introduces the major sections of the museum. There is an important research library available to qualified students and research workers, and the Museum Shop has natural history items for sale.

HOURS: Tuesday–Saturday: 10:00 A.M.–5:00 P.M.
Sunday: 1:00 P.M.–6:00 P.M.
Closed Mondays and national holidays.
ADMISSION: Adults $1, students 50¢. No charge on Saturdays.

Wilkes-Barre

• *Wyoming Historical and Geological Society Museum*
49 South Franklin Street
Wilkes-Barre, Pennsylvania 18701 *(717) 823-6244*

This important, small museum holds some extensive collections from turn-of-the-century archaeological digs in the area: projectile points, bone needles, ax heads, and soapstone vessels from Paleo through Archaic times. It has a good collection of Late Woodland material and some outsized pots and jars. Over the years the society has published reports on local excavations, and a few of these rare old pamphlets can be purchased at the museum.

The museum is at 69 South Franklin Street, and the Wyoming Historical Research Library is housed in the building next door. The library is open to nonmembers for a nominal reading fee. Group tours and school programs are available by appointment.

Currently the museum building is open only three days a week, but the society would welcome volunteer staff to help extend its services and hours.

HOURS (MUSEUM): Wednesday and Friday: 1:00 P.M.–4:00 P.M.
Saturday: 10:00 A.M.–4:00 P.M.
Summer only: Thursday 11:00 A.M.–5:00 P.M.
Closed Saturdays during the summer.
HOURS (LIBRARY AND OFFICE): Tuesday–Friday: 10:00 A.M.–5:00 P.M.
Saturday: 10:00 A.M.–4:00 P.M.
Closed Sundays and Mondays.
ADMISSION: Free.

STATE OFFICE

Barry C. Kent
State Archaeologist
William Penn Memorial Museum
Box 1024
Harrisburg, Pennsylvania 17120

OPPORTUNITIES FOR AMATEURS

The **North Museum,** under the directorship of Dr. W. Fred Kinsey, works with amateurs in connection with digs, laboratory work and analysis, report writing, and museum posts. He suggests that amateurs sharpen their skills by registering for university classes and field schools. The North Museum accepts volunteers, and if you are interested in applying, call or write:

North Museum
Franklin and Marshall College
College and Buchanan Avenue
Lancaster, Pennsylvania 17604 (717) 291-3941

The **University of Pittsburgh** has been excavating at two Rocky Dell rock shelters just outside of Pittsburgh. The university has excellent field schools and training programs every year in conjunction with the Carnegie Museum of Natural History. Both undergraduate and graduate students registered for the university summer school can apply, and preference is given those with special skills or previous experience in the field. Sometimes special tours can be arranged to visit the excavations during fieldwork. Contact:

University of Pittsburgh
Summer Archaeology Field Program
Department of Anthropology
Pittsburgh, Pennsylvania 15260

The **Clarion State College Archaeology Laboratory** is responsible for the work at the State Road Ripple site, located nine miles from the campus. The project began with high-school students, and now there also are field schools for college students; nonregistered adults can join through the School of Continuing Education. Although each group has its own program, the various crews work together under the directorship of Dr. Gustav A. Konitsky.

No college credit is given for the adult workshops, and there are three one-week sessions every summer. The workshops are sponsored by the School of Continuing Education, and anyone interested can sign up for one or more sessions. There are no prerequisites. The cost of the workshops is nominal and includes transportation to and from the excavation site, meals, and bunking in the campus dorms, as well as professional training in the field.

Both Pennsylvania and out-of-state undergraduate students are welcome to the eight-week, college-credit field school. And qualified high-school students have a special program of their own—a seven-week session divided into three weeks of classroom lectures and laboratory work and four weeks in the field.

Everyone applies to:

Archaeology Laboratory
Clarion State College
Clarion, Pennsylvania 16214 (814) 226-2513

ORGANIZATIONS TO JOIN

Society for Pennsylvania Archaeology, Inc.
University of Pennsylvania
Philadelphia, Pennsylvania 19104

This lay-professional society was founded in 1929 to encourage scientific exploration, reporting, and cataloging, and to release the information to the public. Its quarterly bulletin, the *Pennsylvania Archaeologist*, is one of the best journals of its kind in the East, and it publishes reports by professionals and amateurs.

There are thirteen local chapters, and a two-day, statewide annual meeting is generally held the last weekend in April at alternating ends of the state. Both nonprofessionals and professionals are welcome to join.

RHODE ISLAND

When the glaciers retreated from Rhode Island, they left rugged hills in the northwest sliding gently toward the southeast. But the coast of this tiny state is so deeply indented and zigzagged that its shoreline is four hundred miles long. Prehistoric Indians lived on the many islands in Narragansett Bay, all around the state's sparkling lakes and everywhere that fish and game abounded. Europeans did not penetrate Rhode Island until William Blackstone rejected Puritanism in Massachusetts and moved north in 1635. He was followed a year later by Roger Williams, who made the first white settlement at Providence. The new settlers were at peace with the Indian population until King Philip's War in 1675, in which the great Indian chief of that name was killed.

There are many Indian sites in the state, but excavations are normally short-term and none are open to the public. The Narragansett Archaeological Society presents a fine opportunity for amateurs to get involved in science and the Haffenreffer Museum in Bristol has one of the few Arctic collections in the country.

MUSEUMS

Bristol

The Wampanoag Indian chief, King Philip, made his stronghold in the swampy foothills of Mount Hope just east of Bristol. His war began in 1675 and ended with his death here one year later. Longfellow's poem "The Skeleton in Armor" was inspired by an armored skeleton discovered at Mount Hope.

• *Haffenreffer Museum*
Mount Hope Grant
Bristol, Rhode Island 02809 *(401) 253-8388*

Arctic exhibits reflect expeditions made by Brown University scientists into the Far North. The Alaskan Indians, Eskimo and Denbigh cultures, and the Red Paint culture are all explained in well-interpreted displays. Harpoon heads, slender blades, carved figurines, masks, and many other artifacts are used in the displays.

There are numerous artifacts from South America and exhibits representing the Archaic cultures of California and the West. Other anthropological exhibits include tribal arts displays from the Pacific islands and Africa. A research library is available to students for use on the premises.

HOURS: June 1–August 31
Tuesday–Sunday: 1:00 P.M.–5:00 P.M.
April–May, September–October
Weekends only.
Closed during the winter.
ADMISSION: Adults 50¢, children 25¢.

Providence

• *Roger Williams Park Museum and Planetarium*
Roger Williams Park
Providence, Rhode Island 02905 *(401) 941-5640*

This natural history museum traces the chronology of the earliest Americans from the time they first crossed the Bering Strait. Exhibits compare different regions and cultures and also show the way agriculture developed in different parts of the country.

The museum is located in a beautiful 430-acre park with a dozen lakes and many flower gardens. There are concerts and outdoor productions in a natural amphitheater, a zoo with an aviary, and tropical greenhouses.

HOURS (MUSEUM): Monday–Saturday: 8:30 A.M.–4:15 P.M.
Sunday and holidays: 1:00 P.M.–5:00 P.M.
ADMISSION: Free.

STATE OFFICE

There is no state archaeologist in Rhode Island. If you wish to report an archaeological site, get in touch with:

Public Archaeology Laboratory
Brown University
Providence, Rhode Island 02912

This laboratory is primarily concerned with locating and preserving threatened sites, and it will send someone out to investigate immediately.

OPPORTUNITIES FOR AMATEURS

For serious training in the field, Rhode Island archaeologists suggest that amateurs apply to the several summer field schools conducted by the various colleges in the state, including:

Brown University
Anthropology Department
Providence, Rhode Island 02912 (401) 863-3251

Rhode Island College
Department of Anthropology and Geography
Providence, Rhode Island 02908 (401) 456-8005

University of Rhode Island
Department of Anthropology and Sociology
Kingston, Rhode Island 02881 (401) 792-1000

ORGANIZATIONS TO JOIN

Narragansett Archaeological Society of Rhode Island
277 Brook Street
Providence, Rhode Island 02906

This is an excellent amateur society that takes its work seriously and contributes valuable information concerning archaeology in Rhode Island. The society sponsors many weekend digs throughout the year under its research director. Members excavate according to professional standards, write and publish site reports. Special guest lecturers speak at regularly scheduled meetings.

VERMONT

The Ice Age glaciers tamed most of the New England mountains into gentle rolling hills. But the granite backbone of Vermont resisted the glacial onslaught and when the ice retreated, the Green Mountains still ridged the state from south to north. Lake Champlain, the largest freshwater lake east of the Great Lakes, is in Vermont.

From the time the ice disappeared and the forests began to grow, the Vermont Indians followed an Archaic life style that persisted into historic times. One of the places they hunted and fished was Isle La Motte in Lake Champlain, and their campsites and artifacts have been found all over this island and many smaller islands that stud the lake.

There are no permanent archaeological sites open to the public in Vermont. Digs in the state are usually small, since the Vermont Indians built no large communities, and there are no long-term excavations. But the state Division for Historic Preservation is working to develop workshops and field schools for amateurs, and the Vermont Archeological Society records and reports sites and helps in the effort to preserve threatened sites.

MUSEUMS

Burlington

• *Robert Hull Fleming Museum*
University of Vermont
61 Colchester Avenue
Burlington, Vermont 05401 *(802) 656-2090*

This museum is primarily a teaching facility for the University of Vermont and other schools in the state. Exhibits focus on art and ethnology, and local finds and other artifacts of the Eastern Woodlands are displayed. Other displays show baskets and pottery of the Southwest and Northwest. By appointment visitors can study the hands-on Indian collection in the education room. A research library and sales desks are in the building.

HOURS: Monday–Friday: 9:00 A.M.–5:00 P.M.
Saturday and Sunday: 1:00 P.M.–5:00 P.M.
Closed holidays.
ADMISSION: Free.

Montpelier

• *Vermont Museum*
Pavilion Building
109 State Street
Montpelier, Vermont 05602 *(802) 828–2291*

The Indian exhibits show artifacts recovered from the Archaic site on Isle La Motte in northern Vermont. The museum also features paintings, antiques, and costumes from the colonial period. A large genealogical collection is available for use on the premises.

HOURS: September–June
Monday–Friday: 8:00 A.M.–4:30 P.M.
July–August
Saturday and Sunday: 10:00 A.M.–5:00 P.M.
ADMISSION: Contributions accepted.

STATE OFFICE

Giovanna Neudorfer
State Archaeologist
Division for Historic Preservation
Pavilion Building
Montpelier, Vermont 05602 (802) 828-3226

OPPORTUNITIES FOR AMATEURS

The Division for Historic Preservation is developing a new program for amateurs that will include workshops and small field schools. There is ample opportunity for amateurs to join summer digs in Vermont. If you would like to participate, contact State Archaeologist Giovanna Neudorfer at the above address, or write:

Dr. Peter Thomas
Director of Cultural Resources Program
Williams Science Hall
Department of Anthropology
University of Vermont
Burlington, Vermont 05401

ORGANIZATIONS TO JOIN

The **Vermont Archaeological Society** publishes an excellent quarterly newsletter and sponsors various public education programs. The society is doing no fieldwork at present, but members volunteer their services to the office of the state archaeologist. Write:

Vermont Archaeological Society
P.O. Box 601
Burlington, Vermont 05402

VIRGINIA

With Virginia's great colonial heritage, it is small wonder that archaeologists in this state concentrate on historical work. People have roamed the mountains and valleys of Virginia since the Ice Age, but there is only one archaeological site in Virginia devoted to prehistoric research. This is the Thunderbird Early Man site near Front Royal.

At many colonial excavations, however, archaeologists have found prehistoric sites under historic villages and plantations. At the Hatch site in Spring Grove, archaeologists excavating a colonial village found that the site had been continuously occupied for at least nine thousand years. This offers an ideal opportunity to learn how the native Americans lived before the arrival of the colonists and how the English influenced the later Indian culture. The Hatch site is near Williamsburg, and all of the Williamsburg area is rich in history and archaeology.

Virginia offers outstanding opportunities for amateurs to observe excavations and volunteer their services in the field and in the laboratory. Enthusiastic amateurs come here from all over the country for training and they are welcome in almost every capacity.

SITES AND MUSEUMS

Alexandria

• *Alexandria Community Archaeology Center*
Union and King Streets
Alexandria, Virginia 22313 *(703) 750-6200*

This new interpretive center is closely associated with the Alexandria Archaeology Research Center and is a giant step forward in lay-professional community relationships.

The research center excavates exclusively in the city of Alexandria, and its findings date from the eighteenth century right up to the present day. Even though it has no prehistoric holdings, its work here is so interesting to the amateur archaeologist that we include it here.

The research center does the excavating; the community center displays and interprets the excavated material and describes the archaeological process.

The community center has a much larger theme than mere exhibits. It is a changing, visible, and accessible community service. The center holds regular tours for schoolchildren and adults and presents educational programs on topics such as urban history and preservation.

The community center is also headquarters for archaeological activity.

Visitors and members of the community can call the center to find out where current excavations are going on, make appointments to observe the dig, or volunteer their services. Senior citizens, young people, students—everyone who is interested in the art and science of archaeology is welcome here.

DIRECTIONS: The community center is located on the second floor of the Torpedo Factory Art Center* in Old Town Alexandria. Entrance is on the corner of Union and King streets.
HOURS: Friday–Sunday: 10:00 A.M.–3:00 P.M.
After April 1, the center will be expanding its hours. Please call for additional information.
ADMISSION: Free.

Bedford

- *Peaks of Otter Visitors' Center*
Milepost 86, Blue Ridge Parkway
Bedford, Virginia 24523

The Visitors' Center has many artifacts recovered from prehistoric campsites in the Blue Ridge Mountains and one particular site nearby. Other displays feature wildlife. This is a nice place to stop on the long Blue Ridge drive. An adjacent lodge and restaurant are open year round, but the Visitors' Center is open only in the summer. Telephone for the lodge is (703) 586–1081.

DIRECTIONS: Follow the Blue Ridge Parkway to Milepost 86.
HOURS: June–October: 9:00 A.M.–6:00 P.M. daily.
Closed rest of year.
ADMISSION: Free.

Front Royal

- *Thunderbird Museum and Archeological Park*
Route 1, Box 212D
Front Royal, Virginia 22630 *(703) 635-7337*

This peaceful stretch along the Blue Ridge Mountains is at the entrance to one of the country's loveliest national parks. The Thunderbird Archaeological Park has a wonderful interpretive museum with wall-to-wall windows that look out over the Shenandoah Valley. A slide show and well-interpreted exhibits explain the twelve thousand years of human prehistory in the valley.

The Thunderbird site is located at a jasper quarry that attracted hunters

* The Torpedo Factory is a busy arts center and houses many artists' studios and exhibit rooms.

from Paleo times all the way through the Woodland period. The jasper was highly prized for making projectile points, and many Clovis points have been found here. The archaeological teams work all summer in this specially reserved park, which is a National Historic Landmark. Visitors are welcome at the dig sites and amateurs can volunteer their services. The trails to the digs are relatively flat and easy to walk.

The archaeologists are in the field only during the summer, but in the spring and fall you can walk the beautiful trails where the Blue Ridge Mountains fall away to the Shenandoah Valley and where ancient people lived from earliest times.

The museum has local crafts from the Shenandoah area for sale, and special group tours can be arranged through the staff.

DIRECTIONS: The museum is on Route 340, 6 miles south of Front Royal.
HOURS: 10:00 A.M.–6:00 P.M. daily.
ADMISSION: Adults $1.50, children $1, eight and under free.

Richmond

- *Valentine Museum*
1015 East Clay Street
Richmond, Virginia 23219 *(804) 649-0711*

In the Junior Center, the Valentine Museum has simulated an archaeological dig for children. Dioramas tell the story of early Virginia Indians before colonial settlement, and there are special programs on cultural history. Their enormous Indian collection can be seen by appointment. Permanent exhibits depict the life and history of Richmond and include an extensive costume collection.

HOURS: Tuesday–Saturday: 10:00 A.M.–4:45 P.M.
Sunday: 1:30 P.M.–5:00 P.M.
Closed Mondays and major holidays.
ADMISSION: Adults $1, students 50¢, military personnel and children under five free. Admission does not exceed $2.50 for families.

Spring Grove

- *The Hatch Site*
Route 1, Box 185
Spring Grove, Virginia 23881 *(804) 866-8542*

Archaeologists believe that Hatch is the site of the Weyanoke Old Town described in early colonial records. After researching these documents, survey teams searched out the location of the site, tracing Weyanoke Old Town to this location on the east bank of Powells Creek. The site, which is near Williamsburg, has been occupied for nine thousand years or more. Archaeologists have found bone tools, projectile points, choppers, stone axe heads, and several Indian house patterns and burial pits. Vast quantities of pottery and stone artifacts suggest the Weyanoke Indians had a large trade network.

On top of this ancient site, there is evidence of three colonial structures built as early as 1612. Muskets, lead shot, knife blades, forks, English ceramics, and sword hangers have been recovered. The main purpose of the project at Hatch is to study the early Indian village prior to and after European contact.

Visitors are welcome at all times during regular work hours. Members of the archaeological team describe the site's history and talk about the work they are doing. There is no admission fee, but the work here is privately funded and visitors are asked to contribute at least $5 toward the expense of operating the site. This money pays the salaries of the employees, buys equipment used in excavation, and makes it possible to keep the site open to the public.

To make arrangements to visit the Hatch site, write or telephone:

L. B. Gregory
Director of the Hatch Site
Route 1, Box 185
Spring Grove, Virginia 23881 (804) 866-8542

DIRECTIONS: The site is located approximately 8 miles from the Benjamin Harrison Memorial Bridge and 12 miles from Hopewell, Virginia.

Note: If you would like to participate in field or laboratory work at Hatch, see "Opportunities for Amateurs" below.

OPPORTUNITIES FOR AMATEURS

Virginia is bursting with opportunities for amateurs to become involved in both field and laboratory work. Almost all of the sites described here use volunteers in a variety of jobs.

Alexandria Community Archaeology Center
Union & King Streets
Alexandria, Virginia 22313 *(703) 750-6200*

Visitors and members of the community can volunteer time to both the center itself and to urban excavations.

Thunderbird Museum and Archaeological Park
Route 1, Box 22D
Front Royal, Virginia 22630 *(703) 635-7337*

Amateurs can participate in summer digs, usually through university field schools. The Catholic University of America runs a field school for college and high-school credit. For information, write:

Director of Summer Session
Catholic University of America
Washington, D.C. 20064

Hatch Site
Route 1, Box 185
Spring Grove, Virginia 23881 *(804) 866-8542*

One of the major goals of the Hatch expedition is to involve the general public in excavation and teach professional archaeological methods and techniques to amateur archaeologists. Amateurs are trained in field survey and recording, grid orientation, artifact recognition and identification, excavation techniques, laboratory procedures, and field osteology.

Volunteers can work with the team either in the field in the summer or in the laboratory in the winter. The Hatch team believes in public involvement and is especially willing to work with the aspiring amateur archaeologist.

This is a good opportunity for amateurs to receive professional training in the field and laboratory. If you are interested, write or call (see above).

STATE OFFICE

Virginia Historic Landmarks Commission
Research Center for Archaeology
Wren Kitchen
College of William and Mary
Williamsburg, Virginia 23186

ORGANIZATIONS TO JOIN

Two archaeological associations are open to membership:

Archaeological Society of Virginia
Rossmore Road
Richmond, Virginia 23225

Chesopiean Archaeological Association
Ms. D. Painter
7507 Pennington Road
Norfolk, Virginia 23500

The **Archaeological Society of Virginia** works in both historic and prehistoric Virginia archaeology. The society sponsors several excavations each year in various parts of the state and publishes a quarterly newsletter and bulletin.

THE SOUTHEAST

Alabama

Arkansas

Florida

Georgia

Louisiana

Mississippi

North Carolina/South Carolina

Tennessee

THE SOUTHEAST

During the Pleistocene epoch, the ice never reached the Southeast. In Paleo times, the camels, elephants, and giant ground sloths luxuriated in a damp, rainy climate. Early hunters roamed all over the southern region, and their Clovis points have been found in almost every state in the South.

When the big game disappeared, the hunters' lives took a new turn as they began to rely on the rivers and oceans for their food. Great heaps of discarded shells dot the banks of the southern rivers and the Atlantic and Gulf shores. In Florida the preserved shell heap at Turtle Mound is almost fifty feet high. Thousands of these trash heaps were discovered everywhere in the Southeast, but in recent years most of them have been crushed and used to build modern highways.

In some parts of the South, the Archaic life style persisted with little variation into historic times. But in other parts, crude grass-tempered pottery appeared very early, and introduced the Woodland period. And soon another dramatic change occurred, when people first began to bury their dead in mounds. These early mounds were simply piles of earth covering the bodies or cremated remains of the dead. They were small and cone-shaped. The mounds grew bigger as more burials were added.

The Hopewell people in Illinois and Ohio probably introduced the idea of burial mounds into the South. The Hopewellians traded along the river network, and their ideas about mound building seem to have journeyed along the same route. Shells, tools, mica, pipes, and religious concepts all traveled up and down the river together.

The people who built the burial mounds were part-time farmers. And when the Hopewell culture died out, the mound-building societies in the Southeast also dwindled. But a new, radically different, and highly sophisticated civilization arose in their shadow. By A.D. 1000 agriculture was practiced on a large scale. Enormous tracts of land in the South came under cultivation, the population expanded, and large communities developed everywhere. Lavish religious and ceremonial practices were centered around colossal handbuilt pyramidal mounds. Since the temple mound idea spread along the Mississippi River, its culture and art are called Mississippian.

The earthen temple mound is similar in design to the stone-faced pyramids of Mexico and Central America. The most formidable groups of earthen mounds are in Illinois. But some small temple-mound sites on the Gulf Coast are older than those in Illinois. One theory is that an early temple-mound culture was introduced into the South from Mexico. The idea spread up the Mississippi River Valley, where it developed into a high art in Illinois, then returned to the South in a more vigorous form. Certainly Moundville, Alabama, is one of the most spectacular of these ceremonial centers, but it was built after Cahokia in Illinois.

As the Mississippian culture rose to pre-eminence, art became sublime. The fanatical Southern Cult was a high point of Mississippian times. The cult left behind objects carved from hard stone, copper beaten onto wooden carvings of people and birds, human bones and skulls engraved on pottery or etched on stone disks. Feathered serpents and raptorial birds with tearing beaks were other common motifs. Moundville was a great Southern Cult center and a pure expression of the Mississippian culture.

As suddenly as this rich, thriving culture arose, it disappeared. Its demise is one of the great mysteries of archaeology. When De Soto launched his army into Florida and Georgia all the way west to Arkansas, some mound-building communities may still have been in existence. But they were in rapid decline. Whatever vitality remained was quickly extinguished by the

Bynum Mounds in Mississippi under excavation in January 1948. (Photo courtesy of the National Park Service.)

Spanish troops, who killed and enslaved thousands of Indians, raided their food supplies, and spread diseases to which the Indians had no immunity. The mound builders were so thoroughly decimated that historic tribes were never able to trace their links with the people of the Mississippian culture.

The Southeast region of the United States today offers outstanding opportunities to visit the great ruins of the burial and temple-mound builders. Archaeologists have recovered thousands of exquisite artworks from the mounds, and this material, along with extensive interpretive displays, is on exhibit in the large on-site museums. Every state in the Southeast offers fine archaeological parks, museums, and active amateur societies.

ALABAMA

Three outstanding archaeological sites in Alabama reflect the whole pattern of prehistoric life in the Southeast from the earliest Archaic times through the historic occupation by the French and British. Russell Cave in the northeast corner of the state was the home of prehistoric people for eight thousand years through the Archaic and Woodland periods. After A.D. 500 the cave was seldom used, since most nomadic people then settled around the large farming communities that grew up during the great Mississippian period.

The story of the Southeast continues at Mound State Monument in Moundville, where the finest examples of Mississippian temple-mound building can still be seen. By the middle of the sixteenth century, Moundville, too, was abandoned. But the site at Fort Toulouse picks up the threads of the historic period and traces the French, British, and finally American military life of this region.

All three sites are open to the public, and Moundville and Russell Cave offer extensive exhibits and interpretation. Fort Toulouse is still undergoing excavation and reconstruction, and it should be fully interpreted within the next few years. Archaeologists continue to dig at this site, and it offers an exciting opportunity to watch work in the field and also to observe the painstaking job of reconstruction.

SITES

Bridgeport

- *Russell Cave National Monument*
  Route 1, Box 175
  Bridgeport, Alabama 35740 *(205) 495-2672*

In 1953 four amateur archaeologists from the Tennessee Archaeological Society came upon a cave on the edge of the Tennessee River in northeastern

Alabama. For some time people had been picking up projectile points and other bits of stone tools from the fields around the cave. Now the amateur sleuths located a deposit just inside the mouth of the cave that contained numerous flint chips, projectile points, pottery sherds, animal bones, and freshwater shells. They systematically began to excavate the cave floor, carefully cataloging and reporting their findings each step of the way.

The four men found the site productive, but they believed it went much deeper than their surface excavation. The amateurs were quite sure that the site required a major dig, and they reported their findings to the Smithsonian Institution. The Smithsonian, with the cooperation of the National Geographic Society, launched a major archaeological exploration. Later, the National Park Service added its support, and from this combined work force came the knowledge that people had found shelter in Russell Cave for thousands of years. This rock shelter, tucked into the side of a gray limestone hill where the Tennessee River passes through the Cumberland Plateau, attracted nationwide attention in the press. So, more than nine thousand years after prehistoric people first stumbled onto this shelter, Russell Cave became a world-famous monument.

Its earliest inhabitants probably used the cave for protection against rainy winter weather. Their campfires and spear points were found twelve feet below the present floor of the cave. Charcoal from the hearths dates their arrival at about 7000 B.C. Every fall and winter, small groups of Archaic hunters from the region came to live in the great main room of the cave. It was a perfect haven. A clear, spring-fed pool of water flowed into a sinkhole just outside the entrance to the cave. The surrounding forests yielded game and a full crop of nuts and seeds through the winter months. When spring came, the people moved out of the cave and camped along the banks of the Tennessee River a few miles away.

All through the Archaic Period, the families who lived here pursued a hunting and gathering life. Their life style changed only slightly when the rest of the region entered the Woodland period. Great quantities of pottery and arrowheads have been found in the upper strata of the cave floor. The workmanship on the bone tools is more refined, and the people of that time made a variety of bone and shell ornaments.

While the great burial-mound cultures flourished elsewhere in the Southeast, life in the vicinity of Russell Cave continued almost unchanged. But later, with the rise of the lavish Mississippian culture, Russell Cave fell into disuse. Occasionally small parties of hunters still came to the cave and left a scattering of tools and points, and these were found almost on the surface of the cave floor. But for the most part, people all over the region now lived in permanent villages near the rich river bottoms, where they raised fields of corn.

In historic times the Cherokee Indians and the white settlers who occupied this part of the Tennessee Valley sometimes visited the cave and left a few odd objects behind. These were the last people to use the cave.

In 1961 the National Geographic Society donated an area of 310 acres to protect Russell Cave and its surroundings for the people of the United States, and the cave was established as a national monument.

Visiting Russell Cave: A steep, well-marked hiking trail leads to the mouth of the cave. Hidden drop-offs and sinkholes make any off-trail hiking dangerous.

Immediately outside the entrance to the cave, several large boulders lie on top of an unexcavated fill. The cave is one hundred feet wide at its face, and its arched roof rises twenty-five feet above the floor. The main room is nearly 150 feet deep, with a gradually down-slanting roof. Russell Cave is part of a much larger cavern that stretches at least a mile into the side of the hill. The excavation site in the main room has been prepared for the public, but the deeper recesses of the cave are closed.

Archaeological exhibits at the site show how the cave was used for eight thousand years. Sometimes the guides grind corn, chip flint points, use the atlatl (or spear thrower), and show visitors how to cook by heat transfer.

All the artifacts recovered from the layers of the cave floor are either on exhibit in the cave itself or in the Visitors' Center. There is no camping in the park, but the town of Bridgeport is only eight miles away.

DIRECTIONS: Drive from Bridgeport on U.S. 72, west on County 91 and north on County 75 to the monument's entrance.
HOURS: 8:00 A.M.–5:00 P.M. daily.
ADMISSION: Free.

Haleyville

- *Kinlock Knob Petroglyphs*
Bankhead National Forest
P.O. Box 339
Haleyville, Alabama 35565 *(205) 486–2424*

Bankhead National Forest is comprised of 180,000 acres of lakes, limestone gorges, a natural bridge, and a wildlife management area. Only ardent observers of Indian rock art would want to make a special trip just to see the small group of petroglyphs at Kinlock Knob. But if you are camping in the forest or enjoying its recreational facilities, you might want to search out the pictures.

Rangers at the Forest Service Office in Haleyville will direct you to the petroglyphs if you call or check in with them.

DIRECTIONS: Haleyville is on the western edge of Bankhead National Forest. The Forest Service Office is on Highway 195E, a few blocks east of downtown.

Moundville

• *Mound State Monument*
Moundville, Alabama 35474 *(205) 371–2572*

The first thing you notice at Moundville is the heat—and then the big mound. The rough-hewn stairway up the grassy slope looks easy enough, but after the first few steps you are panting heavily. The southern humidity is like wet flannel.

A small thatched house sits a few yards away across the flat mound top. It's called a temple but doesn't look impressive by classical Greek standards. Inside, life-sized mannequins stolidly perform a ritual ceremony.

Outside again, the faint shape of tiny huts can be seen in the hazy distance. Smaller mounds are scattered all around the flanks of the big chunk on which you stand. Far away, the Black Warrior River pushes its way between muddy banks and outlines the boundaries of what was once the finest and largest prehistoric community in the South. If you stand for a moment under the canopy of heat and dampness, you are transported back in time.

Here was the flower of the prehistoric South—the high center of Missis-

The Temple Mound at Moundville, Alabama. (Photo: JW.)

sippian life and art and religion, and nowhere was the culture more purely expressed.

These were people who believed in a fire-sun deity, farmers and artists joined by the bond of religion. Much of what we know of their life is based on the Natchez people, who survived into historic and modern times. Every year in deep summer, they celebrate the Busk, or Green Corn, ceremony as thanks for the new harvest. The Busk climaxed the ceremonial year for these agriculturalists. In prehistoric days the elaborate ceremonies stimulated the construction of the massive earthen pyramids, which in turn led to the crafting of more and more ritual art objects.

Old fires were extinguished and new fires were taken from the temple's sacred hearth to light the individual camps of the villagers. Warriors drank a black drink made from local plants to purify themselves. Grownups danced to the music of drums and flutes, and young men played a game that was a combination of bowling and hockey. They rolled highly polished "chunkey" stones down a long lane, and other contestants tried to hit the small concave disc with spears.

Religious concepts, notions about rank, and certain ceremonial practices such as human sacrifice might have come from the traveling Aztec pochteca, a group of aggressive, aristocratic merchants from Mesoamerica who made long-ranging trading forays into North America.

Whatever its origin, the complicated system of the Mississippian culture centered on a chief who was both a political leader and a powerful religious figure. Whenever a chief died, the temple and houses on top of the great mound were burned and covered with new layers of earth. Sometimes his retainers and kinsmen mutilated themselves or committed suicide on his grave. Sometimes they were sacrificially slain by other members of the community. Over the centuries the temple was burned and covered over many times, and each time the mound grew larger.

Mississippian families lived in small huts modeled on the same design as the temple itself. Houses were grouped together around the main compound, and the great temple mound also served several outlying villages. The people worked in the fields, hunted in the forests, fished in the rivers, and crafted the most elegant artworks ever seen in prehistoric times. Some motif designs were in abstract form, but clay models and stone carvings of animals and humans could also be completely naturalistic. Artists imported copper, marine shells, and galena from long distances to make all manner of ornaments. A few of their artworks carved from wood were preserved in the inner mounds: rattles shaped like animals and red cedar masks inlaid with shell. Cloth was woven from plant fibers and rabbit hair, and ceremonial garments often were laced with a brilliant surface of feathers.

Moundville was abandoned before De Soto explored the region in 1540. No one really knows what happened to the thriving communities of the

Mississippian cultures. Early Spanish records show that a group of people called the Napochi may have been living on the Black Warrior River during the middle of the sixteenth century. But the connection is faint and was completely obliterated when the Creeks and Spanish went up against the remaining Napochi and wiped them out in 1650. The fate of the Moundville people themselves has never been discovered.

Today it is difficult to imagine this neatly mowed park as a thriving hub of activity. The grounds are peaceful and quiet and saturated with a kind of honorable respectability. Paved roads curve around the mounds and swing out to a little village of five reconstructed houses. Inside the huts models re-create the daily life and chores of the ancient people.

The best of Moundville is indoors. The museum at Moundville is one of the finest on-site museums anywhere. The building itself is directly over two excavated burial grounds. In one wing more than fifty skeletons have been uncovered and left in place with their treasures at their sides, exactly as they were found by the archaeologists. Each skeleton lies on its own small, raised dais formed by the careful spading of the scientists.

A push-button audio-visual program lends an eerie electronic atmosphere for the ghosts of these ancient people. Many modern Indian tribes have taken exception to displays of ancestral bones and have insisted that exposed burials be shrouded from public view. This is one of very few such exhibits still remaining in the United States. If you are not superstitious, and if you don't mind a touch of the macabre, pass through the hermetically sealed doors into the final resting place of the Moundville people.

Fortunately for me the skeletons are only a part of the museum. The art of the Moundville people is unmatched in prehistory, and other sections of the museum are devoted to the finest collections of Mississippian artifacts found anywhere in the country.

There are bowls and jars shaped like humans and birds, some burnished a shimmering black, others painted a distinctive red and white. There are shell trumpets, gorgets, beads, and pottery—all incised or engraved with fanciful or symbolic motifs. A long-nosed god mask cut from a sheet of copper resembles an Aztec god, and it hints at still another link with Mesoamerica.

Visiting Moundville: (The museum building has no wheelchair ramp but the short flight of wide steps should not be difficult for a handicapped person to negotiate.) The park grounds at Moundville are spacious, and the paved roads are broad and easy to drive around. Nature trails go out to some of the smaller mounds. All the temple mounds and burial grounds were excavated forty years ago, but there is usually some digging on the smaller mounds during the summer. Visitors are welcome to observe and talk to the archaeologists.

Only the major temple Mound B can be climbed. The slope is mislead-

Inside the North Cemetery at Moundville, skeletons lie on their excavation platforms as they were uncovered by archaeologists. (Photo: JW.)

ingly gentle looking, and a hike to the top requires either extreme youth, good physical condition, or a lot of optimism.

Spring and summer are the busiest times of year for the park, and it is least crowded in the fall and winter. Since Alabama has a good year-round climate, off-season is probably the best time to visit.

You can camp in the park for four dollars per night, and there are motels in nearby Tuscaloosa. Groups can arrange to stay in a dormitory building in the park where there is also a conference room for group meetings. A souvenir shop sells gift items and books for children.

DIRECTIONS: Moundville is located 13 miles south of Tuscaloosa on Route 69.
HOURS: 9:00 A.M.–4:30 P.M. daily. Closed Christmas.
ADMISSION: Adults $2, students $1, five and under free. Group rates for fifteen or more, 50¢ each.

Note: Moundville is maintained by the University of Alabama Museum of Natural History. More exhibits recovered from the excavation are on display in the main museum in Tuscaloosa (see listing below).

Wetumpka (Montgomery)

- *Fort Toulouse Park*
  Route 6, Box 6
  Wetumpka, Alabama 36092 *(205) 567–3002*

Because of its highly strategic position at the confluence of the Coosa and Tallapoosa rivers, this spot just north of modern Montgomery was the scene of many important events in the life of North America. Archaeologists digging at the site learned that nomadic hunters had camped here in prehistoric times. These early people were followed by the mound builders, who used the site as a permanent hunting base and built several large temple mounds in the vicinity, although only one remains today. When De Soto reached the area in 1540, he found a thriving Creek Indian community.

Today most of the archaeological activity at Fort Toulouse is centered around its French inhabitants, who built a fort here in the heart of the Creek Confederacy at the beginning of the eighteenth century. The fifty men who manned the garrison were surrounded by the Cherokees, the Choctaws, and the Chickasaws. They made friends with the Indians and traded glass, beads, and guns for furs and deerskins. But their life at the fort was lonely and often the food supply was short. Mutinies contributed to a generally tense, unruly atmosphere and the quality of life deteriorated. The fort grew shabby and rundown. The French, however, placed great value on the strategic position of the fort and threw considerable resources into rebuilding the outpost in 1751—to little avail. After nearly fifty years of occupation, the French lost possession of Fort Toulouse to the British, who later abandoned it. The fort fell into ruins, and by 1796 only the old moats and cannon could be seen beneath a tangle of overgrowth. The Indians came back to live within the fort's abandoned walls.

But that wasn't the end of the story of Fort Toulouse. During the Creek Indian War, Andrew Jackson rebuilt the fort and renamed it Fort Jackson. But by the end of 1817, Fort Jackson also was abandoned and the settlement moved downstream to what later became Montgomery.

When archaeologists began to excavate the area in 1971, they found traces of the old Fort Toulouse. Today the scientists are building a reconstruction of the old fort based on the original outline and remnants of buried log walls. The reconstruction will include the commander's quarters, a chapel, storehouse, barracks, and powder magazine.

There is a visitors' center on the working site and an archaeology lab where students work with archaeologists. The thousands of artifacts excavated from the site include military buttons, bottles, beads, pottery, and weapons. Archaeological work continues year round at Fort Toulouse, and the opportunity exists for amateurs to volunteer their services through the **Alabama Archaeological Society.**

The Fort Toulouse site is set aside in a 180-acre game and wildlife sanctuary in the foothills of the Appalachian Mountains. No digging or collecting is permitted, but the park offers a variety of facilities for visitors. Picnicking, nature walks, camping, fishing, swimming, and boat ramps are all available within the park. Write ahead or call on weekdays for camping reservations. An arboretum with wooden walkways that meander through woods and fields of wildflowers has been especially designed for the enjoyment of the elderly and handicapped.

The ancient temple mound and all of the excavated historic sites are open to visitors, and for the next few years you can watch the reconstruction in progress.

DIRECTIONS: The site is located 12 miles northeast of Montgomery off U.S. 231 North (3 miles south of Wetumpka).
HOURS: 8:00 A.M.–5:00 P.M. daily.
May–August: 8:00 A.M.–6:00 P.M.
Closed Christmas, New Year's.
ADMISSION: Free.

MUSEUMS

Birmingham

• *Birmingham Museum of Art*
2000 Eighth Avenue North
Birmingham, Alabama 35203 *(205) 254–2565*

Exhibits change frequently at this fine arts museums. Art collections from all over the world are on display, and American Indian and pre-Columbian artworks are permanently featured. Several galleries are devoted to fine ceramics from Asia, seventeenth- to nineteenth-century paintings and porcelains, and a highly prized collection of Remington bronzes. There is a fairly small but good collection of pottery from Moundville and a famous painted deerskin by Nachihe. Costumes from the Plains Indians, California Indian baskets, masks from the Northwest Coast Indians, and Navajo blankets are also on display. An art history library is open for use on the premises and there is a gift shop.

HOURS: Monday–Saturday: 10:00 A.M.–5:00 P.M. (Thursday till 9:00 P.M.)
Sunday: 2:00 P.M.–6:00 P.M.
Closed Christmas and New Year's.
ADMISSION: Free.

• *Red Mountain Museum*
2330 15th Avenue South
Birmingham, Alabama 35205 *(205) 254–2757*

This is an outstanding new museum in the Southeast. The museum is on the site where an interstate highway cut through Red Mountain and revealed geological strata from three hundred million years ago to the present. The new museum emphasizes the geology and physical sciences of Red Mountain. Other important displays trace the four major periods of human life in this area of the New World from the Paleo through Mississippian traditions, and many artifacts and dioramas focus on the regional flavor of the Southeast. Still other exhibits show stone and bone tools from the most ancient times of human life on other continents.

HOURS: Monday–Friday: 8:30 A.M.–4:30 P.M.
Saturday: 10:30 A.M.–4:30 P.M.
Sunday: 12:30 P.M.–4:30 P.M.
Closed major holidays.
ADMISSION: Free.

Montgomery

• *Alabama Department of Archives and History*
624 Washington Avenue
Montgomery, Alabama 36130 *(205) 832–6510*

This museum is part of the capitol complex where Jefferson Davis was inaugurated as president of the Confederate States of America in 1861. The museum features fine arts, the Alabama Hall of Fame, Civil War relics, and many other historical items. In the Indian Room are displays of pottery, projectile points, trade silver, and local archaeological finds. There is little in the way of interpretation here, but the museum as a whole is interesting and fun to visit.

HOURS: 8:00 A.M.–5:00 P.M. daily.
Saturday and Sunday: closed between 11:30 A.M. and 12:30 P.M.
Closed Thanksgiving, Christmas, New Year's.
ADMISSION: Free.

University (Tuscaloosa)

• *Alabama Museum of Natural History*
Smith Hall on Sixth Avenue
P.O. Box 5897
University, Alabama 35486 *(205) 348–7550*

The museum, located on the University of Alabama campus, is responsible for the exhibits at **Mound State Monument.** The exhibits here are extended to include material from all over the United States and South America.

HOURS: Monday–Friday: 8:00 A.M.–4:30 P.M.
Closed weekends and university holidays.
ADMISSION: Free.

STATE OFFICES

Alabama Historical Commission
725 Monroe Street
Montgomery, Alabama 36130 (205) 567–8431

Office of Archaeological Research
University of Alabama
Box BA
University, Alabama 35486 (205) 348–7774

OPPORTUNITIES FOR AMATEURS

The ongoing excavations at **Fort Toulouse** use some amateur volunteers. To apply, contact the Alabama Archaeological Society (see below).

ORGANIZATIONS TO JOIN

The Alabama Archaeological Society works closely with the Office of Archaeological Research and the Alabama Historical Commission. The main purpose of the society is to locate and conserve historical artifacts and sites. The society offers scholarships to students and funds worthwhile projects with special grants. Members are primarily involved with conservation and public information and generally do not do much excavating. The society publishes a monthly newsletter and two journals. Both professionals and amateurs from all over the United States belong to this society, and it has five active chapters across the state. For information, contact:

Alabama Archaeological Society
c/o Betty Henson
7608 Teal Drive Southwest
Huntsville, Alabama 35802

ARKANSAS

Arkansas leads the way in bringing amateur and professional archaeologists together in the interest of scientific goals. It was the first state to offer certification programs where amateurs could formally train in various aspects of archaeology and receive recognition for their contributions. Members of the Arkansas Archaeological Society participate in excavations all over the state and work closely with the Arkansas Archaeological Survey.

The state of Arkansas is presently developing several important prehistoric sites for the public. Given the state's remarkable background in public information, you can expect these interpretive sites to be among the country's finest. Toltec State Park near Little Rock will be the first to open in the spring of 1980. Various other sites will be opening in the state over the next few years. A phone call to the Arkansas Archaeological Survey will give you up-to-date information.

SITES

England (North Little Rock)

• *Toltec Indian Mound State Park*
Route 1, Box 154A
England, Arkansas 72046 *(501) 961–9442*

This is the first professional archaeological site in Arkansas to be opened to the public, and over the next few years it will be developed into a major interpretive center. The site is a large village and multiple-mound complex on the edge of a lake. Today, three large mounds are still visible, although most of the others have been leveled by plowing.

Trails lead across the site and past the major earthworks. A boardwalk along the edge of the lake has several outdoor exhibits that interpret the relationship between the environment and the people who lived here about fifteen hundred years ago. Excavations will continue here for several summers and visitors are welcome to observe.

The Visitors' Center exhibits material excavated from the site and interprets the findings with displays, graphics, and an audio-visual program. The on-site laboratory has a viewing section for visitors. The long-range research here is under the direction of the Arkansas Archaeological Survey and the overall interpretation on this site should be outstanding.

DIRECTIONS: The site is 15 miles southeast of North Little Rock on Arkansas 130, then ½ mile west on AR 386.
HOURS: 8:00 A.M.–6:00 P.M. daily in summer; till 4:30 P.M. in winter. Tours daily from 10:00 A.M. until 1 hour before closing. Closed Thanksgiving, Christmas, New Year's.
ADMISSION: Free.

MUSEUMS

Fayetteville

• *University of Arkansas Museum*
338 Hotz Hall
University of Arkansas
Fayetteville, Arkansas 72701 *(501) 575–3555*

The strong point of this museum is its research collections. In one room prehistoric artifacts describe the Indians of Arkansas, with representative displays of four major periods in Arkansas prehistory: Paleo, Archaic, burial mound, and temple mound. There is also a Plains Indian exhibit of Sioux, Blackfoot, and Apache artifacts and relics.

The museum is the center for archaeological activity in the state and is headquarters for the **Arkansas Archaeological Survey,** the **state archaeologist,** and the **Arkansas Archaeological Society.**

HOURS: Monday–Saturday: 9:00 A.M.–5:00 P.M.
Sunday: 1:00 P.M.–5:00 P.M.
Closed Christmas.
ADMISSION: Free.

Jonesboro

• *Arkansas State University Museum*
Campus
Jonesboro, Arkansas 72401 *(501) 972-2074*

This is one of the top archaeological interpretive museums in Arkansas. A new building will offer lavish exhibits tracing prehistoric life in Arkansas from the Archaic period up to the present.

DIRECTIONS: The campus is on the east edge of town on AR 1.
HOURS: Monday–Friday: 1:00 P.M.–5:00 P.M.
ADMISSION: Free.

Little Rock

- *Museum of Science and History*
  MacArthur Park
  500 East 9th Street
  Little Rock, Arkansas 72202 *(501) 376-4321*

General Douglas MacArthur was born in this museum's arsenal building when it was the quarters of army officers and their wives. Today the museum displays many archaeological and Indian collections from the mound-building and Woodland cultures of the Southeast, and it also has exhibits from the Great Plains and Southwest. There are extensive collections of birds and minerals as well. Rocks, crafts, and reproductions are for sale in the Museum Shop.

HOURS: Monday–Saturday: 9:00 A.M.–5:00 P.M.
Sunday: 1:00 P.M.–5:00 P.M.
Closed Thanksgiving, Christmas, New Year's.
ADMISSION: Free.

Wilson

- *Hampson State Museum*
  P.O. Box 32
  Wilson, Arkansas 72395 *(501) 655-8622*

In the early 1920s, Dr. James Hampson began to practice medicine in southern Arkansas near the plantation where he had grown up. Dr. Hampson was an ardent amateur archaeologist, and he and his family began to study the remains of an early aboriginal population that had lived in the county. Their discoveries led to the excavation of the **Nodena site,** a fifteen-acre palisaded village. Further excavations by the University of Arkansas and the Alabama Museum of Natural History uncovered a central plaza and two connecting pyramidal ceremonial mounds.

The Nodena people were farmers who cultivated corn, beans, and squash. They supplemented their agriculture by hunting and fishing and gathering local plants. They used local back-swamp clays to make elaborate vessels as well as utilitarian pottery. Stone for tools was imported through the north from a complex trade network that also provided shells from the Gulf of Mexico and salt from Missouri.

Everything in the museum today is from the Nodena plantation. There are exhibits on archaeological techniques, the study of bones, Mississippian trade water routes, and displays of red and white Nodena pottery. Other displays trace the Paleo, Archaic, Woodland, and Mississippian cultures. A newly completed renovation has attractive graphics that explore the life styles of the farming civilizations that inhabited this area from A.D. 1350 to 1700.

The museum today is part of a state park. There are four acres for picnicking and a playground for children.

DIRECTIONS: Wilson is on the Mississippi River north of Memphis, Tennessee. The museum is off Highway 61, less than 1 mile from Wilson.

HOURS: Monday–Saturday: 9:00 A.M.–5:00 P.M.
Sunday: 1:00 P.M.–5:00 P.M.
Closed Thanksgiving, Christmas, New Year's.

ADMISSION: Free.

STATE OFFICE

Hester Davis
State Archaeologist
Arkansas Archaeological Survey
University of Arkansas
Fayetteville, Arkansas 72701

OPPORTUNITIES FOR AMATEURS AND ORGANIZATIONS TO JOIN

Arkansas pioneered training programs for avocational archaeologists in the United States. The Arkansas Archaeological Survey offers both field training programs and certification programs in cooperation with the Arkansas Archaeological Society. The **field training program** provides lay archaeologists with experience in excavation and laboratory analysis under professional supervision. Field schools are held at different sites throughout the state during the summer and provide amateurs with various digging problems and experiences. Evening lectures on a variety of topics fill out the training program.

The **certification program** offers society members formal and extended training in specific aspects of archaeology and awards certification when they complete the course. Those in the certification program participate in the field training sessions and also work in other excavations and laboratories throughout the year. Participants in either program must be members of the Archaeological Society.

The **Arkansas Archaeological Society** is largely an association of amateurs, but officers and journal editors are professionals. A coordinating office guarantees a close working relationship between the Arkansas Archaeological Survey and the society. Dr. Charles McGimsey III, director of the survey, works closely with members of the society and together they locate, report, and excavate sites.

The **Arkansas Archaeological Survey** has eight research stations that cover the state. Central headquarters is in Fayetteville.

If you have a site to report, call the survey at (501) 575-3555, and you will be directed to the nearest research station.

Headquarters for both the Arkansas Archaeological Survey and the Arkansas Archaeological Society is:

University of Arkansas Museum
Fayetteville, Arkansas 72701

FLORIDA

Much of Florida was nearly desert during the Ice Age. Paleo-Indians hunted in at least one part of this region. An underwater archaeological site on a lake bottom near Sarasota has yielded artifacts twelve thousand years old. After the Ice Age, early Americans found Florida a lush and desirable dwelling place. There are many different mound sites all over Florida, and the most interesting concentration is around Tampa Bay, a subtropical region on the eastern coast of the state.

The fine natural history museums in Florida are especially interesting because, in addition to prehistoric Indian material, they often have wonderful marine life and sunken treasure exhibits from the Caribbean.

Several French and Spanish forts still stand in the state. While these are not prehistoric sites in the strictest sense of the word, they are the points where the Spanish and French met American Indians for the first time. These forts were the scene of many bloody encounters between Europeans and Indians, and frequently among Europeans themselves.

SITES

Bradenton (Tampa Bay)

• *Madira Bickel Mound State Archaeological Site*

For sixteen hundred years following the birth of Christ, this area at the southern edge of Tampa Bay was inhabited continuously. As in many areas in Florida, the climate, lush foliage, and abundant shellfish supported life and the development of culture over a long period of time.

The earliest recorded materials from this site are relatively simple tools, but after about A.D. 700, the pottery and other items are more elaborate and closely resemble the artifacts from the nearby Weeden Island cultures. Another change occurred around A.D. 1400, when the people here began

At Madira Bickel Mound in Florida, palm trees and lush foliage overgrow a prehistoric Indian village. (Photo: Neil Felshman.)

to farm with new methods and built an elaborate ceremonial mound and temple.

A narrow twisting road follows the coastline to the Madira Bickel Mound. On the left, clear green water rolls gently onto the grassy shore. The site is about two miles down the road; a small white frame house is its next-door neighbor. Forming a barrier between the two is a line of modest swells: small burial mounds. The large mound itself is heavily wooded, but a path that tours the mound is clear and well marked. The presence of the site is almost casual, noted only by a small arrow and marker. There is no information center or other amenities, but the site is always open to the public and admission is free.

DIRECTIONS: To get to the Madira Bickel Mound site, exit west off Route 41 at the marker 6 miles north of Bradenton, and then continue 2 miles to the site.

Note: The South Florida Museum is in Bradenton (see listing below).

Crystal River (Tampa Bay)

● *Crystal River State Archaeological Site*
Route 3, Box 457-E
Crystal River, Florida 32629 *(904) 795-3817*

Where the Crystal River meets the Gulf of Mexico, less than a hundred miles north of Tampa Bay, early Florida Indians lived for more than sixteen hundred years. The Crystal River site was an important ceremonial and cultural center continuously inhabited from about 200 B.C. to A.D. 1400.

The Indians who lived here built a solar observatory, which they used both to mark the passing of time and to worship the sun. A huge calendar was constructed from sand and shell and stone.

Excavation of burial and refuse mounds that began in 1903 has shown that these people traded and had contact with other people from hundreds of miles north and west and from as far south as the Yucatan peninsula. This site is the only place north of Mexico where the large, engraved ceremonial stones called *stelae* have been found. More than 450 burials have been explored here, and an exhibition of the discovered artifacts in the site's museum show the many cultural changes that occurred during the hundreds of years that people lived in the area.

The Crystal River State Archaeological Site and Museum is in a parklike setting at the end of a residential road. There are seven distinct mounds at the site. One temple mound stretches 235 feet in length and another is 30 feet high. One of the burial mounds has been cut to reveal an open crypt that has been treated and encased in glass. From the modern white and glass museum, trails go out over the site, winding through thick, neatly trimmed grass cover. The site is not overgrown, but palms and other tall trees shade the entire area. A long wooden stairway up one side of the tallest temple mound leads to a platform and a view of the site and the Crystal River. The sides of the mound that face the river are heavy with plant life.

The paths throughout the site are well marked, and the various mounds and stelae are marked and explained. The museum has a collection of artifacts excavated at the site, including pottery from different periods of habitation and various projectile points.

There are many motels and resorts in the area surrounding Crystal River and a full range of leisure activities.

DIRECTIONS: The Crystal River Archaeological Site is 1½ miles north of the town of Crystal River off Routes 98 and 19. A small directional sign points the way, west on State Park Road, directly to the site.

HOURS: 9:00 A.M.–5:00 P.M. daily.

ADMISSION: 25¢

Fort Walton Beach (Gulf Coast)

• *Indian Temple Mound Museum*
P.O. Box 1449
139 Miraclestrip Parkway S.E.
Fort Walton Beach, Florida 32548 *(904) 243-6521*

This ancient temple is reconstructed under a modern shelter on its original site. On-site museum displays trace ten thousand years of Gulf Coast living from St. Andrews to Mobile Bay. After depicting the earliest migrations onto the continent, several exhibits concentrate on the spiritual and artistic development of the Gulf Coast people. From crude ceramics to exotic painted pottery, the whole story is here. The pottery of the Fort Walton culture is unique in the Southeast and shows a strong influence from Central and South America. Also on display are artifacts from the Weeden Island culture. Other exhibits extend into the historic period and include early European trade items such as beads and sixteenth-century coins recovered from burial and village sites.

DIRECTIONS: The site is in Fort Walton Beach at the intersection of U.S. 98 and FL 85.
HOURS: Tuesday–Saturday: 11:00 A.M.–4:00 P.M.
Sunday: 1:00 P.M.–4:00 P.M.
Special tours by appointment.
Closed Mondays, Christmas, New Year's.
ADMISSION: Adults 50¢, children ten and under free.

Note: Fort Walton Beach is near several museums in Pensacola, and Gulf Island National Seashore is only a few miles further down the coast.

New Smyrna Beach (Daytona region)

• *Turtle Mound State Archaeological Site*
New Smyrna Beach, Florida 32069

The site is on a spit of land practically surrounded by water. To the left as you enter is a graveled parking area, and there are picnic tables on the grass overlooking a quiet lagoon. To the right a path leads into the mound, which is densely overgrown with palms, shrubs, and flowers. There is a stand at the entrance that holds leaflets describing the history and topography of the archaeological site.

Trails crisscross the mound and lead to lookout stations that provide good views of both the mound itself and the surrounding area. All of the trails are lushly covered by green overgrowth, and in some places you have to stoop to get through.

This shell mound is almost fifty feet high, higher than many temple mounds in the South. Crumbled shell covers the top, and the discarded shells of thousands of years slope and dip like a hilly ravine. Turtle Mound is as yet largely unexcavated, but it is preserved under the protection of the state park, thanks to the efforts of local citizens.

DIRECTIONS: Exit from U.S. 95 at FL 44. Head east following the signs to New Smyrna Beach. Go through New Smyrna Beach, east across the bridge to the last road before the beach, South Atlantic Street. This is Routh A1A, but it is marked only sporadically. Head south on A1A, almost nine miles from New Smyrna Beach. The area is built up with new houses and condominiums lining the way. Approximately 50 yards before the road comes to a dead end, a right-hand turnoff is marked with a small sign to Turtle Mound State Archaeological Site.

HOURS: 8:00 A.M.–5:00 P.M. daily.

ADMISSION: Free

Safety Harbor (Tampa Bay)

● *Safety Harbor Site*
Safety Harbor, Florida 33572

The Safety Harbor site is along the calm, rounded shore of Old Tampa Bay. Here is a ceremonial mound, about 150 feet across and 25 feet high. This was part of the main village of the Tocobago Indians. The site was first occupied during the late prehistoric period, and artifacts discovered belong to what is now called the "Safety Harbor Period," which lasted three hundred years, from A.D. 1400 to 1700. Just a few yards southwest of the mound, Count Odet Philippe settled and built his home in 1834.

The mound is crossed by footpaths, and plant and grass growth is minimal. Clambering up and down on the mound is a relatively simple exercise, and many people use the top as a vantage point in the park.

There is no on-site museum, but Safety Harbor has a small historical society museum at 106 Main Street.

DIRECTIONS: To get to the Safety Harbor site, take Route 60, Courtney Campbell Causeway, which runs east and west between Tampa and Clearwater, and exit north on local Route 593. Turn right off 593 onto 590 to Philippe Park just past Safety Harbor.

Once in the park, directions to the mound are not marked. Take the first turnoff to the left off the main park road, and follow this road to the right past two marked recreation areas to its end at the parking area. The mound is straight ahead.

HOURS: 7:00 A.M.–dark.

ADMISSION: Free.

Tallahassee (Gulf Coast)

- *Lake Jackson Mounds*
  State Archaeological Site
  1313 Crowder Road
  Tallahassee, Florida 32303 *(904) 385-7071*

This was an important mound complex in northern Florida built between A.D. 1200 and 1500. Two large temple mounds served as a religious center for several villages, and the complete complex consisted of six temple mounds and possibly one burial mound.

The two largest mounds and at least part of the village are within the present boundaries of the site. There were probably several stages of development for the largest mound, which measures 278 by 312 feet at its base and is approximately 36 feet high. After one stage was completed, a thin layer of clay was applied to the surface to form a foundation for a building. At various times the temple building was burned and covered over, and the mound grew larger.

There is evidence that the Lake Jackson Indians were part of the Southern Cult. Quantities of pottery and stone tools have been recovered from the site along with many elaborate objects: copper breastplates embossed with ritual figures, copper badges and axes, and shell beads worked into necklaces, bracelets, and anklets. All of these artifacts indicate religious ties with the other large, prehistoric ceremonial centers in the Southeast, especially Etowah in Georgia, Moundville in Alabama, and Spiro in Oklahoma.

At present there is no interpretation at the site, and all the visitor can see are two nice grassy mounds. But you are welcome to bring your lunch and contemplate the past.

DIRECTIONS: The site is 8 miles north of the capitol building, on U.S. 27N.
HOURS: 8:00 A.M.–sundown daily.
ADMISSION: Free.

MUSEUMS

Bradenton

- *South Florida Museum and Bishop Planetarium*
  201 10th Street West
  Bradenton, Florida 33505 *(813) 746-4131*

Exhibits trace the history of Florida from the Stone Age to the Space Age and focus on the mound-building society. Life-sized dioramas depict the prehistoric Indian life and burials of early Florida and include a great variety of artifacts of southwestern Florida. Other exhibits include minerals, fossils, shells, wildlife, birds, and fish. And period rooms show the way of life in the Spanish homes of the early conquistador days.

Children come especially to visit a sea cow named Snooty who performs gracefully at feeding time in the Aquarium Room.

DIRECTIONS: Bradenton is on Florida's western coast on the south end of Tampa Bay. The museum is very near the Madira Bickel Mound site and it is convenient to visit the two locations together.

HOURS: Tuesday–Friday: 10:00 A.M.–5:00 P.M.
Saturday and Sunday: 1:00 P.M.–5:00 P.M.
Planetarium shows daily except Monday at 3:00 P.M.
Closed Mondays, Thanksgiving, Christmas, New Year's.

ADMISSION: Museum only: Adults $1.50, students $1, under six free.
Combination tickets: Adults $2.50, students $1.50, under six free.

Gainesville

• *Florida State Museum*
Museum and Newell Roads
University of Florida
Gainesville, Florida 32611 *(904) 392-1721*

The buildings in this museum resemble the pyramids and plazas of pre-Columbian civilization in Central America. Inside the museum is a simulated fossil dig with the bones of an extinct, nine-foot ground sloth, a full-sized north Florida cave, and a view of a living forest five hundred years old. Special exhibits highlight the early cultures of Florida and the Caribbean. There is an owl totem pole constructed around A.D. 100 and a re-created Timucuan Indian village. The Bonompak Room is a reconstruction of a Mayan palace. An object gallery has hands-on exhibits, and a collectors' shop sells natural science items. The museum sponsors a decent program to train volunteers to help with the many school projects the museum offers students every year.

DIRECTIONS: The museum is on the campus of the University of Florida, Museum Road and Newell Drive. From I-75, take University or Archer Road exits east to Southwest 13th Street, which takes you to Museum Road (Southwest 8th Street).

HOURS: Monday–Saturday: 9:00 A.M.–4:30 P.M.
Sunday, holidays: 1:00 P.M.–4:30 P.M.
Closed Christmas.

ADMISSION: Free.

Jacksonville

• *Jacksonville Museum of Arts and Sciences*
1025 Gulf Life Drive
Jacksonville, Florida 32207 *(904) 396-7061 or 396-7062*

This wonderful hands-on museum used to be a children's museum and is still a great attraction for young people. A sea tank, Egyptian exhibits, and special exhibits of early Indian life in the Everglades are on display. There is good interpretation of early Florida history, native wildlife and marine life exhibits, and a fine planetarium.

HOURS: Tuesday–Friday: 9:00 A.M.–5:00 P.M.
Saturday: 11:00 A.M.–5:00 P.M.
Sunday: 1:00 P.M.–5:00 P.M.
Closed September, major holidays.
ADMISSION: Museum free. Planetarium $1, under thirteen 75¢.

Miami

• *Historical Museum of Southern Florida*
3280 South Miami Avenue
Miami, Florida 33129 *(305) 854-3289*

The Historical Museum of Southern Florida has displays ranging from early prehistoric times through the Space Age. Special exhibits focus on the Calusa Indians, who lived just south of Tampa Bay, and the Tequesta Indians, who lived north of the Keys on Florida's east coast. There are many other prehistoric and Seminole artifacts on display, along with relics of Caribbean underwater explorations.

In the same building, the Museum of Science and Planetarium have further exhibits on archaeology, astronomy, geology, marine life, and mineralogy. The research library and reference room are open to the public by appointment. Natural science items from South Florida are for sale in the Museum Shop, and picnicking is allowed on the museum grounds.

DIRECTIONS: From I-95, drive 3 miles southwest on U.S. 1.
HOURS (MUSEUM): Monday–Saturday: 9:00 A.M.–5:00 P.M.
Sunday: 12:00 M.–5:00 P.M.
Closed Christmas.
ADMISSION: Free.

Pensacola

Pensacola is a blend of Old South and modern Florida with a dash of colonial Spain. There are no archaeological sites in Pensacola, but the **Temple Mound**

and Park in Fort Walton Beach is only forty-five minutes away, and the city also offers several outstanding museums.

If you are visiting Pensacola, stop in at the **Tourist Information Office** at 802 North Palafox Street (junction of U.S. 29 and U.S. 90) near Seville Square and pick up a free walking tour guide; it will direct you to the many historic sites and museums in the area. Four fine museums in the vicinity have exhibits of prehistoric material.

• *Pensacola Historical Museum*
405 South Adams Street
Pensacola, Florida 32501 *(904) 433-1559*

The museum is housed in the oldest church building still standing in Florida and its exhibits trace the history of Pensacola from prehistoric to modern times.

Local artifacts, pottery, weapons, and tools are on display. The research library is open to the public, and a large collection of artifacts and documents can be examined by appointment. Staff members at this museum are knowledgeable about the aboriginal history of the area and very helpful in identifying local finds.

DIRECTIONS: The museum is at Zaragoza Street in the Old Christ Church.
HOURS: Monday–Saturday: 9:00 A.M.–4:30 P.M.
Closed Sundays, and major holidays.
ADMISSION: Free.

• *West Florida Museum of History*
200 East Zaragoza Street
Pensacola, Florida 32501 *(904) 434-1042*

This museum is just down the street from the Historical Museum and is housed in a converted warehouse. It also has prehistoric exhibits of the Gulf Coast and is the headquarters for the northwest Florida chapter of the **Florida Archaeological Society.**

HOURS: Monday–Saturday: 10:00 A.M.–4:30 P.M.
Sunday: 1:00 P.M.–4:30 P.M.
Closed Thanksgiving, Christmas Eve and Day, New Year's.
ADMISSION: Contributions accepted.

• *T. T. Wentworth, Jr., Museum*
8382 Palafox Highway
Pensacola, Florida 32594

Just twenty minutes away from Seville Square is a wonderful private museum that resembles an overgrown and overloaded country store whose supplies spill onto the front porch and into the yard. In addition to many Indian artifacts, you will find here minerals, stamps, coins, maps, and porcelain related to the history of Pensacola. Some three thousand history books are available for use on the premises.

This is a wonderful place to visit. There is no phone at the museum, and it is open only on the weekends. If you want to check before driving out, anyone at the Pensacola History Museum will be glad to give you the latest information on the hours.

DIRECTIONS: Go 5 miles north on FL 95 to Ensley.
HOURS: Saturday, Sunday, and holidays: 2:00 P.M.–6:00 P.M.
ADMISSION: Free.

• *Gulf Islands Visitors' Center*
Gulf Breeze, Florida 32561

About eight miles across the bay from Pensacola and down Highway 89 is the new Gulf Islands Visitors' Center. Still under construction at press time, this new complex will interpret the several mounds and village sites at the Gulf Islands National Seashore. The center itself is built on a prehistoric village site. Exhibits will trace ancient life along the Gulf shore from the mound period right through European conflict. From Gulf Bay, follow FL 399 and then 399A down to the ruins of old Fort Pickens. Geronimo was imprisoned here and there is a good historical museum on the site.

The Gulf Islands National Seashore has many other sites of historic interest, as well as picnicking, skin and scuba diving, and camping. No pets are allowed on the beach and admission is $1 per car. For more information about the National Seashore, write:

Superintendent
P.O. Box 100
Gulf Breeze, Florida 32561

St. Petersburg

• *St. Petersburg Historical Museum*
335 Second Avenue, NE
St. Petersburg, Florida 33701 *(813) 894-1052*

The major collections are devoted to natural history, science, and Americana, and they focus especially on early Florida history from A.D. 1500. The museum has one of the finest shell collections anywhere in America and some local prehistoric artifacts from Pinellas County. Most of the Indian artifacts, however, date from the 1500s. Other historic exhibits include suits of armor and Civil War hardtack.

HOURS: Monday–Saturday: 11:00 A.M.–5:00 P.M.
Sunday: 1:00 P.M.–5:00 P.M.
Closed Thanksgiving, Christmas, New Year's.
ADMISSION: Adults 75¢, children over four 25¢.

STATE OFFICE

L. Rose Morrell
State Archaeologist
Florida Department of State
Tallahassee, Florida 32304 (904) 487-2333

ORGANIZATIONS TO JOIN

Members of the **Florida Anthropological Society** work diligently to salvage sites and report their findings to the Florida Department of State, which keeps a master site file. As a general rule, the society discourages excavation, except on threatened sites. It has a broad lay-professional membership that includes amateurs from almost every state; there are a dozen local chapters.

The society as a whole strives to locate prehistoric and historic sites and see that they are properly recorded and, whenever possible, preserved. The second major goal is to inform the public of archaeological activities in the state. The society's bulletin *The Florida Anthropologist* comes out four times a year, and a newsletter is published twice a year. Each chapter works independently, but a yearly meeting brings all the local chapters together.

The society has no central headquarters, but its officers can always be reached by writing or calling:

Division of Archives, History and Records Management
Florida Department of State
Tallahassee, Florida 32304 (904) 487-2333

GEORGIA

Three great ruins of the Mississippian culture are open to the public in Georgia: Etowah, Ocmulgee, and Kolomoki. Each was a major ceremonial complex of the Southern Cult, and each has remarkably well-preserved temple mounds and outstanding interpretive centers. A visit to any one of these sites will give you a vivid picture of life in the great farming communities of the Southeast around A.D. 1000.

At Ocmulgee almost every major period of Indian prehistory in the Southeast can be seen. This was one of the first large Indian sites in the South to be scientifically excavated, and it provided many important details in our growing knowledge of prehistoric times.

The settlement in the Etowah Valley reigned as the center of political and religious life to the people who lived here between A.D. 1000 and 1650. In 1817 a group of Cherokee chiefs led the Reverend Elias Cornelius through the underbrush along the Etowah River to stare at these imposing earthen mounds, but the Indians themselves were uncertain about the origin of the great mounds. Only scientific archaeology finally revealed the actual life and culture of the people who lived here.

At Kolomoki both burial mounds and temple mounds built around a ceremonial plaza served a community of more than two thousand people. White settlers seeking treasure dug in the mounds during the early part of the nineteenth century but found only bones. Later, archaeologists sought another kind of treasure and uncovered many fine examples of Mississippian pottery and works of art that now are on display in the on-site museum.

The museum building at Kolomoki is built directly over a burial mound, and visitors can enter the center of the mound and view the ancient skeletons with their burial goods beside them.

Such prehistoric mounds in Georgia are among the most important archaeological sites in the nation. The ancient mound builders had disappeared by the time De Soto and his band of conquistadors came through Georgia in search of gold in 1540. The Spaniards found large Cherokee and Creek Indian villages throughout the region, many concentrated in the northwest corner. Within the next two hundred years, the British arrived, followed by German, Scotch, Swiss, and Irish settlers. By 1775 almost fifty thousand colonists lived in Georgia.

During the early flush of white settlements, the Cherokee willingly adopted the culture of their invaders. Between 1835 and 1838, they set up in New Echota, Georgia, a government modeled on the U.S. Constitution. The Cherokee capital thrived. Stores, farms, orchards, houses, even a print shop, were established. The *Cherokee Phoenix,* the first newspaper printed in the new Cherokee alphabet developed by Sequoyah, was published in Georgia. These brief years of prosperity and cohabitation ended abruptly with one of the saddest chapters in American history, the infamous Trail of Tears.

The Cherokee were forced off their desirable lands and sent with other eastern tribes on a long death march to the Indian Territory of Oklahoma. Their property was confiscated and put up for public lottery, even as Cherokee leaders pleaded for redress. Their villages and crops were raided and burned.

Of the thirteen thousand Indians who began the march of "removal," more than four thousand died before reaching Oklahoma, where descendants of the survivors still live today.

In Georgia the old Cherokee capital of New Echota has been partially restored. The village is three miles northeast of Calhoun (I-75) on SR 225.

Georgia has one other fascinating site called the **Rock Eagle Effigy Mound**—a great eagle (some archaeologists call it a buzzard) made of white quartz rocks. No one knows exactly who created the mound but it is probably about six thousand years old. The mound is in a park near Eatonton and is open to the public.

SITES

Blairsville

- *Track Rock Archaeological Area*
  Chattahoochee National Forest
  Blairsville, Georgia 30512
  (404) 523-4567 (regional Forest Service information number)

If you like pictographs, fifty-two acres of this national forest have been set aside to preserve rock carvings of animals, birds, crosses, circles, and human footprints. The pictographs are protected by iron fencing, but they are right on the main forest road.

DIRECTIONS: From Blairsville (in northern Georgia almost on the Tennessee border), take U.S. 10 and 29 south for 3 miles; turn left (east) on Town Creek Road (95) and follow the signs to the marker (about 5 miles). Service roads often are unmarked, so count your mileage.

Blakely

- *Kolomoki Mounds State Park*
  National Historic Landmark
  Route 1
  Blakely, Georgia 31723 *(912) 723-5296*

I am not partial to skeletons, regardless of their antiquity, but the interpretive museum at Kolomoki offers something that no other museum in the United States has: it is inside a burial mound. When you enter the museum into the core of the mound, a pair of heavy steel and glass doors close like a caught breath behind you, and you see what the archaeologists saw when they first opened the mound. The pottery and other grave goods buried with the bodies have been cleaned, restored, and put back in their place.

The skeletons also lie where they were buried more than seven hundred years ago.

Two groups of people lived at Kolomoki. The first settled there about A.D. 800 and came from the local Swift Creek groups and the Weeden Island people who had lived further south. These people created the Kolomoki culture and began to build burial mounds around A.D. 1000. At its peak Kolomoki was an important population center, a small ceremonial city that served a main compound and many outlying villages.

The site was abandoned about A.D. 1300. Two centuries later the Lamar tribe returned to live in the area and settled along the slopes of Little Kolomoki Creek.

At Kolomoki today seven burial and temple mounds are preserved within the park. Mound A, also known as the Great Mound, is the largest mound east of the Mississippi—nearly 60 feet high, measuring 325 by 200 feet at its base. On its summit are two clearly defined platforms that probably supported temple buildings. There is no definite indication of the usual ramp on the slope; log or clay steps were probably used instead.

Mound E is a burial mound and the first of the mounds in the group to have been scientifically excavated. This is the mound covered by the museum building. Besides the mound's contents, there are many other exhibits inside the museum. Various cultures are portrayed from the Archaic period to the end of the Kolomoki period. Dioramas with life-sized figures show the Kolomoki people at their daily tasks of hunting, fishing, cooking, and planting. Graphics and illustrations show how the Kolomoki built their houses and made their crafts, and one wall of fine exhibits shows a mound being constructed.

Kolomoki is preserved in a well-groomed park, and most of the interesting things to see are inside the museum. But the park is lovely and peaceful. The least crowded time to visit is in the winter months between November and March. All the trails are self-guiding and you can walk or drive. Organizations and school groups should book in advance.

The park is also a recreation area and offers both picnicking and camping facilities, but campsites cannot be reserved in advance. There are also a boat ramp and rental boats, a swimming pool, a children's playground, and a miniature golf course nearby. The park has facilities for group camping that can be reserved. The nearest motels are in Blakely.

DIRECTIONS: From Blakely, in southwest Georgia near the Alabama border, go 6 miles north on U.S. 27 to the park entrance.

HOURS (PARK): 7:00 A.M.–10:00 P.M. daily.

HOURS (MUSEUM): Tuesday–Saturday, holiday Mondays: 9:00 A.M.–5:00 P.M. Sunday: 2:00 P.M.–5:30 P.M.
Closed Mondays, Thanksgiving, Christmas, New Year's.

ADMISSION: Adults 25¢, children under six free.

Cartersville

- *Etowah Indian Mounds*
  National Historic Landmark
  Route 1
  Cartersville, Georgia 30120 *(404) 382-2704*

Etowah is one of the most famous ceremonial centers in the Southeast. The Etowah Mounds site, the largest prehistoric settlement in northern Georgia, was part of the powerful, highly developed Mississippian culture that flourished between A.D. 100 and 1650. It served an enormous agricultural system throughout the Etowah Valley.

Several thousand people may have lived within the compound of this fortified village. The village fronts on the Etowah River and was surrounded on three sides by a wooden stockade and a deep ditch. Within the palisade the people of Etowah built their houses with logs, plastered the walls with clay, and probably thatched the roofs.

The design of a dancer in an eagle costume is embossed on a copper plate recovered from Etowah Mounds, the largest Mississippian settlement in northern Georgia. (Photo courtesy of the Museum of the American Indian, Heye Foundation.)

Several earthen platform mounds rise above the two public squares of the town. The largest, Mound A, is 60 feet high and covers 2.9 acres. Temples and residences for the chiefs and priests stood on its broad top. Mound C was reserved for burial rituals, and several hundred burials have been excavated from its base and beneath the floor of the funeral temple that stood on the summit. The dead had been dressed in elaborate costumes and buried in log tombs.

All of this ranks the Etowah culture with the high Mississippian cultures. The Etowah people were such skilled artisans that they are usually spoken of in the same breath with the master artists of Moundville and Spiro. They participated in the trade network that brought marine shells from Florida, flint from Tennessee, and copper from north Georgia. They used all of these raw materials with great skill, and many outstanding artworks are on display in the interpretive center at the mounds, another outstanding on-site museum that traces life in Georgia from 5000 B.C. One unusual display is a pair of male and female mortuary figures carved from white marble.

Three large mounds are open to visitors, and the site offers a wonderful panoramic view of the Etowah River Valley. You can still see traces of the dry moat that was part of the elaborate defensive system.

Etowah today is slightly off the track in a beautiful rural setting. The town of Cartersville is halfway between Atlanta and Rome and can be approached from several different directions. I drove in from the west along quiet country roads, but that is definitely the long way round.

DIRECTIONS: Cartersville is reached most directly from I-75. Exit west onto Bethany Bridge Road. Take U.S. 41 north and turn west at Cartersville on GA 61. Then turn onto Etowah Mounds Road to the site.

HOURS: Tuesday–Saturday, holiday Mondays: 9:00 A.M.–5:00 P.M.
Sunday: 2:00 P.M.–5:30 P.M.
Closed Mondays, Thanksgiving, Christmas, New Year's.

ADMISSION: Free.

Eatonton

• *Rock Eagle Effigy Mound*
Rock Eagle 4-H Center
Eatonton, Georgia 31024 *(404) 485-2831*

The mound is hardly a mound at all. It is a mosaic made from thousands of white quartz rocks in the shape of a huge bird in flight. The wings stretch 120 feet from tip to tip and spread over a slightly elevated patch of earth in a shady glen. Scientists know very little about this great white bird, but they estimate it was shaped more than six thousand years ago and was probably a religious shrine. The quartz originally may have been eight feet deep but souvenir hunters have greatly diminished its depth. Today, the mound is surrounded by a hurricane fence. You can climb to the top of a medieval-looking stone tower nearby and have a fine view of the whole effigy.

There is no visitors' center or interpretation at the mound. However, it is located in a large 4-H park, and if you would like to swim or picnic, there is a public pavillion. You can also pitch your tent or park your camper in the public campground on a first-come basis. I wouldn't travel across the country to visit the Rock Eagle Effigy, but if you are planning to visit the area, it is a lovely place to stop.

DIRECTIONS: Eatonton is south of I-20 about midway between Atlanta and Augusta. To reach the park, go 7 miles north from Eatonton on U.S. 441 and turn left where a big stone stanchion marks the 4-H center. Follow the signs going off to the right to the Effigy Mound. The public pavillion is straight down the main road to the lake.

HOURS: Open at all times.

ADMISSION: Free.

Macon

• *Ocmulgee National Monument*
1207 Emery Highway
Macon, Georgia 31201 *(912) 742-0447*

The great Mississippian center of Ocmulgee was a bustling, thriving community on the Macon Plateau, and today it retains its sense of vitality because the park that protects it is located near downtown Macon.

People have lived on the Macon Plateau from the days of the Big Game Hunters. They continued to live here after the big game died out, when they settled along the rivers and valleys and depended on shellfish and small game for sustenance. They learned to make pottery and began to cultivate foods. The earliest farmers started their gardens between 1000 and 500 B.C.

In this part of Georgia, people lived in small villages and built simple burial mounds. When the Mississippian culture exploded in the heartland of the Southeast, one group moved into the Macon area and established an outpost of Mississippian culture in the midst of the simpler villages.

The newcomers planted the rich bottom lands with corn, beans, squash, pumpkins, and tobacco. On the bluff above the river bottoms, their fortified town began to grow and one thousand people may have lived within the palisades.

They built many kinds of houses, including temples and round ceremonial rooms, on level ground. The temples were destroyed, covered over, and rebuilt many times. Each time more soil was added until the temples were raised on mound platforms. The people of the Macon Plateau thrived only a short time in the long story of prehistory. Within two hundred years, the town and mounds began to fall into ruin.

The people of the nearby villages did not use the old town site, but about three miles away, they built two new temple mounds in the swamps along the Ocmulgee River. These were the Lamar people, whose descendants, the Creek Indians, held most of Georgia and parts of Alabama in early historic times.

Later cultures and people came to Georgia, but Ocmulgee lay silent until the final chapter of Indian history in Georgia. For a brief time, the Creeks returned and lived among the ghosts of their ancestors. Finally, they came under relentless pressure from the expanding new United States of America, and bit by bit their lands were signed away. The last remaining members of this famous tribe were removed to the Oklahoma Territory, where their descendants live today.

Today the ancient city of Ocmulgee is a big, green leafy park. For a half mile, Temple Mound Drive takes you past the three largest mounds of the Macon Plateau. You can also walk to the mounds by the mile-long Opelofa Nature Trail, where the swamp and forest join along Walnut Creek. Throughout the summer season, artisans demonstrate prehistoric crafts such as flute making and pine needle basket weaving.

The Visitors' Center houses a **major archaeological museum,** with outstanding exhibits gleaned from the Ocmulgee excavations and other Mississippian cultures of the Southeast.

Several times each day, a ranger takes visitors out to a **reconstructed earth lodge.** The circular, heavily framed earthen building rests in the actual site of the original structure ("in" because it seems as if you are walking into a deep hole in the side of a mound; actually, the structure itself is covered and rounded over with earth and you enter through a long tunnel). Opposite the door is a raised clay platform shaped like an eagle. Its design is similar to eagle effigies seen all over the region of the Southern Cult. The eagle has the cult's familiar "forked eye" symbol. There are three seats at the rear of the platform and a low clay bench about six inches high encircles the room and is divided into forty-seven more seats. In the center is a large sunken firepit. This was probably the meeting place for the town's religious and political leaders.

Special group tours of the mounds and museum with a guide can usually be arranged if you call and make arrangements in advance.

A small picnic area for visitors is on the park grounds. The nearest campground is about eight miles west of town at Lake Tobesofkee. (*Note:* The **Museum of Arts and Sciences** in Macon has some small additional prehistoric exhibits. See listing under "Museums.")

DIRECTIONS: Ocmulgee National Monument is on the eastern edge of town on U.S. 80 East. The main access is from I-75 to I-16 East, at the north end of Macon. From I-16, take either the first or second exit and follow the signs 1 mile to the park entrance.
HOURS: 9:00 A.M.–5:00 P.M. daily.
Closed Christmas and New Year's.
ADMISSION: Free.

MUSEUMS

Albany

• *Thronateeska Heritage Foundation, Inc.*
100 Roosevelt Avenue
Albany, Georgia 31701 *(912) 432-6955*

The Thronateeska is a small museum largely devoted to the history of the region since the arrival of Europeans. But it does have a fine selection of local Indian artifacts collected from the banks of the Flint River where the Creek Indians lived. Beautifully chipped stone tools and projectile points reflect the rare colors of the materials quarried in the region. There are also some good specimens of Lower Creek Indian pottery.

The museum also features pre-Columbian urns, tools, and ceremonial objects from South and Central America. Other museum exhibits show an Indian rug collection, rocks and minerals, pioneer tools, seashells, dugout canoes, antique machines, several buggies and wagons, and antique clothing.

DIRECTIONS: The new museum building is at the old railway depot restoration in Heritage Plaza.
HOURS: Monday–Friday: 9:00 A.M.–5:00 P.M.
Saturday: 2:00 P.M.–5:00 P.M.
Closed Sundays and major holidays.
ADMISSION: Free.

Columbus

• *Columbus Museum of Arts and Sciences, Inc.*
1251 Wynnton Road
Columbus, Georgia 31906 *(404) 323-3617*

In this museum several exhibits focus on the role of the archaeologist, and a good selection of artifacts and dioramas traces the story of prehistoric people in Georgia in the Archaic and Mississippian periods.

Other sections of the museum are devoted to permanent and changing art exhibits and extensive gun and doll collections. Outdoors there is a greenhouse and nature trail, and a garden specially prepared and marked for the blind.

HOURS: Monday–Saturday: 10:00 A.M.–5:00 P.M.
Sunday: 2:00 P.M.–5:00 P.M.
Closed major holidays.
ADMISSION: Free.

STATE OFFICE

Louis Larson
State Archaeologist
Office of Planning and Research
Department of Natural Resources
270 Washington Street SW
Atlanta, Georgia 30334 (404) 834-6835

OPPORTUNITIES FOR AMATEURS

If you would like to visit excavations in progress during the summer months, write or call the office of State Archaeologist Louis Larson, and he will tell you which digs are open to visitors.

The **Columbus Museum of Arts and Sciences** sponsors summer field schools to which amateurs can apply. Write or call the museum archaeologist:

Frank Schneel
Columbus Museum of Arts and Sciences, Inc.
1251 Wynnton Road
Columbus, Georgia 31906 (404) 323-3617

Four other institutions in the state have archaeological field schools at varying times throughout the year, and these are good places for amateurs to receive training:

West Georgia College
Department of Anthropology
Carrollton, Georgia 30117

Georgia Southern College
Department of Anthropology
Statesboro, Georgia 30458

Georgia State University
Department of Anthropology
33 Gilmer Street SE
Atlanta, Georgia 30602

University of Georgia
Department of Anthropology
Athens, Georgia 30602

ORGANIZATIONS TO JOIN

The statewide lay-professional organization is the **Society for Georgia Archaeology.** Its members are actively involved with site survey and jointly act as a public watchdog against destruction of archaeological sites. They work with and assist professional groups in various capacities, including environmental review projects and fieldwork. The society is responsible for two prominent publications: *Early Georgia,* a scholarly journal that comes out twice a year, and *Profile,* a quarterly newsletter with up-to-the-minute reports from both professionals and amateurs. A spring and fall meeting bring members together from all over the state. For information, write:

Society for Georgia Archaeology
Department of Anthropology
University of Georgia
Athens, Georgia 30602

LOUISIANA

Much of the history of aboriginal life in Louisiana has been lost in the currents of the marshes, rivers, and inland seas that lace the state. Exposed dry land seems to shift continually and the topography of the state today, with few exceptions, is quite different than it was several thousand years ago. Scientists are not sure when people first began to live in Louisiana, but evidence of their presence in Archaic times around 5000 B.C. is plentiful. However, the great shell heaps that Archaic people left behind, piled up and down the rivers and along the coast, have been bulldozed and used in the roadbeds of Louisiana's modern highways.

The early inhabitants of Louisiana were always somewhat remote from the great cultural traditions that dominated other parts of the Southeast. Here cultural trends such as the Hopewellian and the Mississippian were felt rather than expressed. As these great traditions rose and fell, many of the people in Louisiana continued to practice the Archaic life style and lived by collecting shellfish, gathering plants, and hunting all the way into historic times. For all this, two unusual cultures with a distinctly Louisiana touch were established, and the remains of both of these can be visited at two archaeological sites open to the public. These are the sites at Poverty Point and Marksville.

The Poverty Point culture was a radical departure from the drab hunting and gathering culture of the Archaic period, yet it is still classified as a development of the late Archaic period. It probably reached its height around 700 B.C. but must have had earlier beginnings in northern Louisiana, perhaps around 1500 B.C. The uniqueness of the Poverty Point culture is reflected in some of the earliest earthwork structures seen anywhere: six octagons built one inside the other forming concentric rings. No one knows exactly who the Poverty Point people were or how they lived. There is no direct evidence of farming, yet the village may have supported several thousand people, and that alone indicates that the people must have cultivated some plants.

The early Woodland culture began in Louisiana with the introduction of pottery around 200 B.C., and a transitional culture called Tchefuncte developed. These people made small conical earth mounds to bury their honored dead, and they crafted simple crude pottery as well. As the people of the Tchefuncte culture diffused northward up the Mississippi Valley, they probably met people coming down the river from the Hopewellian centers of the Ohio and Illinois river valleys. This merger created the Marksville culture.

Marksville represents the middle Woodland period in Louisiana. It is basically a continuation of the Poverty Point culture with mounds and earthworks and the addition of rather elaborate burial techniques and distinctive pottery. Marksville today is seen as a distinctly regional variation, a cultural period intervening between the Woodland and Mississippian periods. By A.D. 700 the new Mississippian culture made itself felt.

SITES

Epps

• *Poverty Point State Commemorative Area*
P.O. Box 248
Epps, Louisiana 71237 *(318) 926-5492*

Poverty Point has been one of the most famous sites in the country for many years, but only recently have visitors been allowed to see it. Excavations will continue here for some years, and an on-site museum is under construction to offer interpretation for the public. Eventually, the Poverty Point site will be a major interpretive complex. Now a visitor to Poverty Point has an outstanding opportunity to watch an important site under excavation and have it explained by professionals.

Poverty Point is the site of the earliest aboriginal cultural group yet discovered in the lower Mississippi Valley. Perhaps the most unusual aspect of Poverty Point is that although the community may have supported several thousand people, there is no evidence of farming. These people lived in the late Archaic period and still depended on fishing and hunting for survival. They built the most unusual series of earthworks seen in the Southeast: six octagonal ridges, five to ten feet high, set one inside the other. The outer octagon is three quarters of a mile across.

Today, the concentric octagons are cut in half by the Macon Bayou, which flows past the site and has eroded the original complex. No one knows the purpose of these mound ridges, but they are wide enough to have been foundations for houses. The age, size, and nature of these earthworks place them among the more significant archaeological finds in the country.

In addition to the unusual octagons, there is a gigantic bird-shaped mound rising almost seventy feet at its summit—its wings and tail spreading eight hundred feet. This bird motif is seen all over the East and persists through later cultures even into historic times. At Poverty Point steatite vessels with this same bird carved on their outer surfaces have been found, and small stone beads are also fashioned in this shape.

Poverty Point people had two other distinctive traits that set them apart from other ancient peoples. Before the introduction of pottery, cooking vessels were made of bark or stretched skins. Hot stones were submerged in these vessels to heat liquid. But there are no stones in the lower Mississippi Valley, so the Poverty Point people ingeniously rolled clay balls and hardened them in the sun. These brick-hard balls were heated and tossed into food vessels as a method of cooking. Millions of these clay spheres have been found at Poverty Point. They also made great quantities of small, chipped flint objects, but their use is still a mystery. Poverty Point was a unique culture in Louisiana, and after it was one thousand years old, other parts of Louisiana still followed the old Archaic Tradition of nomadic hunting and fishing.

The early Woodland period did not begin here until about 200 B.C., when pottery was added to the basic Archaic form. This early Woodland culture, called Tchefuncte, was a bridge into the Marksville period.

The museum at the Visitors' Plaza is open daily. There are picnic areas, sightseeing trails, and an observation platform where you can view the overall design of the concentric octagons.

DIRECTIONS: The site is located approximately 40 miles west and north of Vicksburg, on LA 577, north of Epps, Louisiana.
HOURS: 8:00 A.M.–dusk daily.
ADMISSION: Free.

Marksville

• *Marksville State Commemorative Area*
P.O. Box 336
Marksville, Louisiana 71351 *(318) 253-9546*

On a high bluff overlooking Old River, prehistoric walls enclose thirty-five acres of ancient mounds and village sites. Two of the mounds are large, truncated pyramidal mounds and the others are burial mounds. Marksville represents the middle Woodland period in Louisiana, and it is probably a continuation of the Poverty Point culture influenced by the Hopewell culture emanating from the Ohio and Illinois valleys. It is seen as a regional variation of the Hopewell, ending with the rise of the Mississippian Tradition at about A.D. 700.

The Hopewell influence brought very fine pottery and the introduction of fine flint artifacts, as well as the elaborate burial techniques associated with the Hopewellians. The Marksville people made their artifacts with material from as far away as Yellowstone, and marine shells were traded from the Gulf area all the way north into Ohio. The Marksville people made a variety of ornaments in the style of Hopewell: perforated pearl beads, copper ear ornaments, copper beads and bracelets, and platform pipes.

The burial mounds were reserved for nobles or shamans. The charred remains of the dead were scattered across the top of the mound and the whole was covered over with an earth cap. Burials have been found within the mound itself, often accompanied by extra skulls or human jaws that seem to have been used as ornaments.

The Marksville people made ornate pottery for burials and also a more utilitarian plain ware. Vessels commonly were incised with a bird design on the sides, and then a distinguishing band of cross-hatching was incised on the rim.

Old River, as the name suggests, is an ancient channel of the Mississippi that probably flowed through the site when the area was occupied by the early Marksville Indians. The five-foot embankment that surrounds the site ends at the bluff. An aerial view of the area shows several other mound groups along the old flood plain of the river, and much archaeological exploration is still going on in this region.

On the site today, a natural history museum interprets the archaeological background and other natural history aspects of the area. In addition to the museum and field exhibits, there are picnic grounds.

DIRECTIONS: The Marksville State Commemorative Area is located on LA 5, adjacent to the town of Marksville, southeast of Alexandria.
HOURS: Monday–Saturday: 9:00 A.M.–5:00 A.M.
Sunday: 1:00 P.M.–5:00 P.M.
ADMISSION: Adults $1, children 50¢.

MUSEUMS

Baton Rouge

- *Museum of Geoscience*
  Louisiana State University
  Geology Building
  Baton Rouge, Louisiana 70803 *(504) 388-2780*

Prehistoric artifacts from Louisiana and around the world are on display. Especially interesting are the artifacts from the prehistoric Bayou Jasmin site and the exhibits on local folklore and Indian culture.

HOURS: 8:00 A.M.–4:30 P.M. daily.
Closed Christmas.
ADMISSION: Free.

Lafayette

- *Lafayette Natural History Museum and Planetarium*
  637 Girard Park Drive
  Lafayette, Louisiana 70503 *(318) 233-6611 (ext. 546)*

The museum owns many fine prehistoric artifacts, but these are not always on display. The exhibit hall changes three times a year, and only one display is up each time.

If you are in Lafayette it is worthwhile to call and ask about the current exhibit. There is also a planetarium program and nature trail.

HOURS: Monday–Friday: 9:00 A.M.–5:00 P.M.
Tuesday and Thursday till 9:00 P.M.
Saturday and Sunday: 1:00 P.M.–5:00 P.M.
Closed Mardi Gras and holidays.
ADMISSION: Free. Planetarium: Adults $1, children 50¢.

Natchitoches

- *Williamson Museum*
  Northwestern State University of Louisiana
  Natchitoches, Louisiana 71457 *(318) 357-6011*

The Williamson is one of Louisiana's major depositories for archaeological material. Extensive archaeological and ethnographic exhibits from Paleo through historical periods are on display. A one-hundred-foot exhibit hall with wall and floor cases contains artifacts from all over Louisiana and reflects both random surface finds and material recovered from recent excavations conducted by the University of Louisiana in the lower Mississippi and Red river valleys.

It's worth a trip just to visit Natchitoches, a lovely French colonial town that is the oldest settlement in the Louisiana Territory. Many of the old plantation homes along the bank of the Red River are open to tours in the fall.

LOCATION: The museum is in a wing of the Arts and Science Building.
HOURS: Monday–Friday: 8:00 A.M.–5:00 P.M.
Closed weekends and major holidays.
ADMISSION: Free.

Shreveport

• *Louisiana State Exhibit Museum*
3015 Greenwood Road
Shreveport, Louisiana 71109 *(318) 635-2323*

The Louisiana State Exhibit Museum holds some of the rare material excavated from Poverty Point. A diorama portrays the site as it must have been in prehistoric times, and other exhibits show projectile points and pottery from different cultural periods. The exhibit hall also has murals and displays of Louisiana agriculture, industry, and natural resources.

DIRECTIONS: From I-20, take Fairgrounds exit.
HOURS: Monday–Saturday: 9:00 A.M.–5:00 P.M.
Sunday: 1:00 P.M.–5:00 P.M.
Closed Christmas.
ADMISSION: Free.

STATE OFFICE

Kathleen Byrd
State Archaeologist
Department of Culture, Recreation and Tourism
Division of Archaeology and Historic Preservation
P.O. Box 44247
Baton Rouge, Louisiana 70804 (504) 342-6682

ORGANIZATIONS TO JOIN

The **Louisiana Archaeological Society** is open to both amateurs and professionals who believe in conservation and preservation of archaeological sites. Its main goal is public education and members are involved in several programs to encourage interest in the native cultural heritage of Louisiana. A quarterly newsletter contains notes and short descriptive articles, and the annual bulletin features full articles, reports, and commentaries.

The society is statewide and has several local chapters. You can reach them by writing:

Louisiana Archaeological Society
P.O. Box 637
Jonesville, Louisiana 71343

MISSISSIPPI

The story of Mississippi is a story of rivers and the Natchez Trace. There are hundreds of mound sites in the state, many of them lost in marshes and woods. But several sites are located on or near the Natchez Trace, a parkway that runs smoothly from Nashville, Tennessee, all the way to Natchez, Mississippi. A few gaps still interrupt the parkway, but most of its 450 miles are complete.

For thousands of years, the Natchez Trace was a maze of simple trails connecting Indian villages. Prehistoric Indians traded and hunted along it. Many mound and village sites indicate that people lived along the Trace as long ago as eight thousand years. The climate was mild, rainfall abundant, soil fertile, and the forests dense with plants and wild game.

After the mound builders came the Chickasaw, the Choctaw, and the Natchez Indians. French traders, missionaries, and soldiers traveled over the old Indian trade route, and in 1763 France ceded the region to England. British settlers continued to use the Trace. From Natchez to the Choctaw villages near present-day Jackson, the trail was called the "path to the Choctaw Nation." From Nashville, traders traveling south to the Chickasaw villages near Tupelo called it the Chickasaw Trace.

Travel and trade over the trail grew rapidly. Today this forest lane is a modern national parkway. Sections of the Old Trace still can be seen in many places along the beautifully landscaped highway. The parkway crosses and recrosses the historic road in a hundred different places. Nine sections of the Old Trace are interpretive sites with parking areas and roadside exhibits; in some spots visitors can take a walk along the old footpath. The only Visitors' Center, however, is at Tupelo at the north end.

In addition to the sites along the Natchez Trace, four other mound sites are open to the public in Mississippi. Pocahontas and Owl Creek are just off the Trace and are listed with it; Winterville, which has a good interpretive museum, is in the western part of the state; and Nanih Waiya is in the East. Whatever part of Mississippi you are in, there is a wonderful adventure in archaeology nearby.

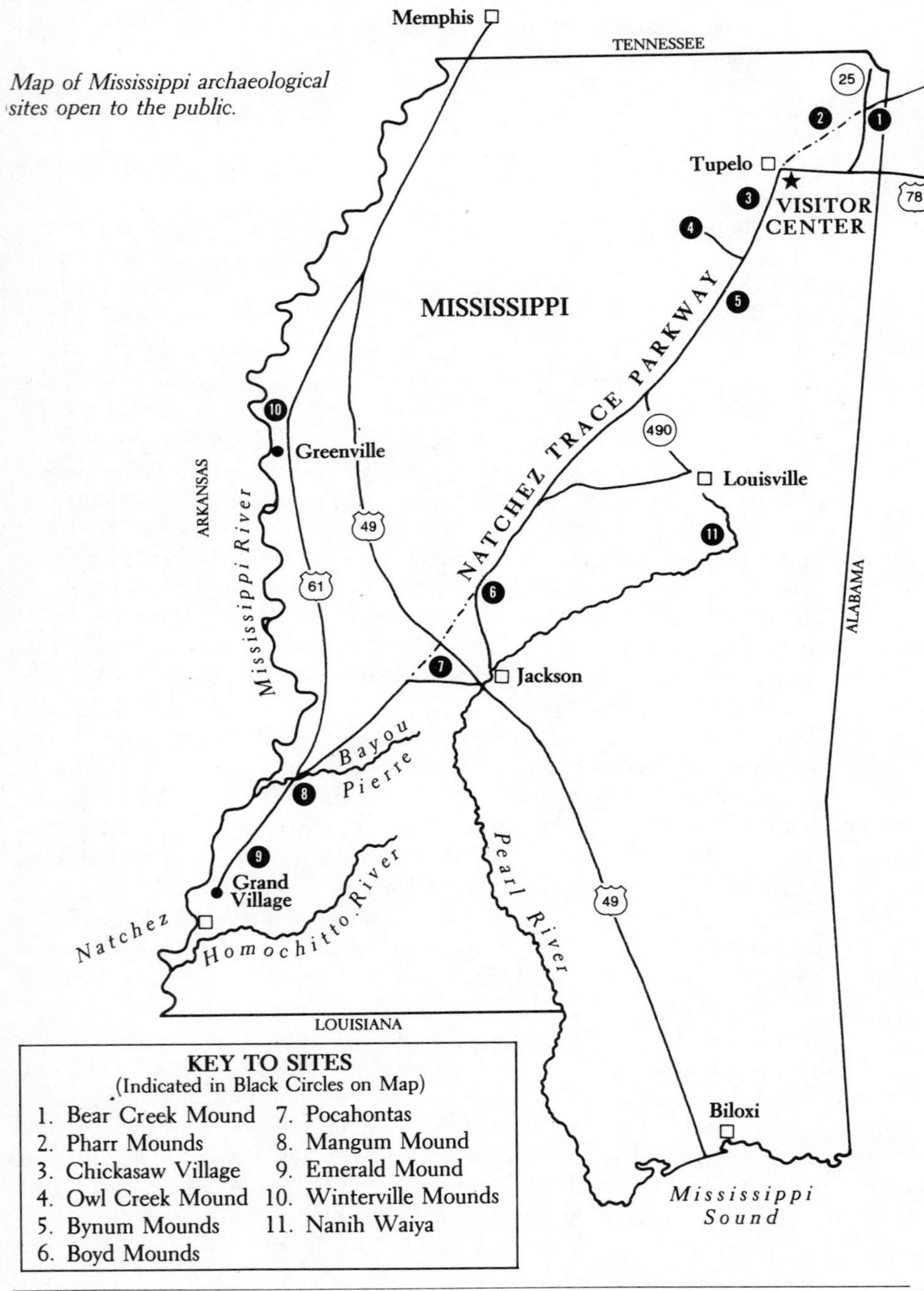

Map of Mississippi archaeological sites open to the public.

SITES

Greenville

- *Winterville Mounds Historic Site*
  Route 3, Box 600
  Greenville, Mississippi 38701 *(601) 334-4684*

Besides the Grand Village at Natchez, Winterville Mounds is the only archaeological site in Mississippi that has a museum and extensive interpretation. It is the largest existing prehistoric mound group in the state. Dominating the site are twelve mounds. The largest of these, the Great Temple Mound, rises some thirty-five feet from its base.

The museum building is constructed from concrete blocks and enclosed in an earthen mound so that its contours blend into the landscape of the garden setting. Skylights light the exhibit rooms, where maps, artifacts, pictures, and murals tell the story of the mound builders. A large glass dome covers an ancient skeleton found about ten miles from the mound. The skeleton's burial goods and jewelry are dated around A.D. 1250.

One portion of the main exhibit hall has a reference library and study room for scholars. Rare books, archaeological publications, field notes, and pottery identification information are available to the public. Special exhibits and programs are frequently presented in the lounge area of the museum.

Within the forty-acre park are picnic shelters, grills, and a concession.

Shelves of pottery are displayed at the Museum at Winterville Mounds Historic Site. (Photo courtesy of the Mississippi Park Commission.)

The nearest campground is at Leroy Percy State Park, six miles west of Hollandale and thirty miles from Winterville Mounds (off MS 12).

DIRECTIONS: The site is 5 miles north of Greenville on MS 1.
HOURS (PARK): Daylight to dusk, daily. Closed Christmas.
HOURS (MUSEUM): Monday–Saturday: 9:00 A.M.–6:00 P.M.
Sunday: 1:00 P.M.–6:00 P.M.
September 15–May 31: 9:00 A.M.–5:00 P.M.
Closed Mondays.
ADMISSION: Adults 50¢, children 35¢.

Louisville

• *Nanih Waiya Historic Site*
Route 3
Louisville, Mississippi 39339 *(601) 827-5436*

Nanih Waiya is considered by many to be the birthplace of the Choctaw Nation. It was occupied from approximately the time of Christ to after European contact. The site is on the Pearl River. Primitive camping, picnicking, and group meeting facilities are available. A stairway takes you up to the top of a tree-covered mound. There is a beautiful nature trail and a swinging bridge across the river.

DIRECTIONS: The site is located 12 miles east of Noxapater off MS 490.

Natchez

• *Grand Village of the Natchez*
400 Jefferson Davis Boulevard
Natchez, Mississippi 39120 *(601) 446-6502*

This Indian village on the banks of St. Catherine Creek in the city of Natchez was the location of the Grand Village of the Natchez Indians. French explorers, priests, and journalists all recorded its thriving presence, and archaeological evidence shows that the Natchez culture reached its zenith here in the mid-1500s. Between 1682 and 1729, the Grand Village was still the center of activity for the Natchez Indians. During this period the French explored and settled the region. Relations between the French and the Natchez were cordial at first but deteriorated in a series of bloody encounters. The Natchez vanished as a nation after their final battle with the French at the Grand Village in 1730.

Three mounds dominate the site: the **Abandoned Mound,** the **Mound of the Great Sun,** and the **Temple Mound.** Early French observers described the Sun's house or temple as a rounded oval raised about eight feet. Upon the death of the "Sun," or chief, his wives and retainers were strangled and interred in the floor of the temple. His house was burned and the mound raised to a new height, upon which the home of his successor was erected. The Tattooed Serpent was the hereditary war chief and brother of the Great Sun. The temple housed the bones of previous Suns and was the scene of funeral rites when a Sun died. A sacred perpetual fire burned in the inner sanctum, symbolic of the Sun from which the royal family descended.

A trail takes you around the mounds and the plaza area. You can take an audio tape tour along with you as a guide. An on-site museum features artifacts recovered in major archaeological excavations. And a fifteen-minute slide/tape program gives a good overall history of the Natchez culture.

Future plans include a reconstruction of the principal houses that once stood in the plaza area: the Great Sun's house, the house of the Tattooed Serpent, and the temple.

DIRECTIONS: This is the southernmost site in Mississippi. The trace joins U.S. 61 above Natchez. Follow U.S. Highway 61 Bypass to U.S. 61 South and exit at Jefferson Davis Boulevard. Directional signs are well posted along the highway.

HOURS: Monday–Saturday: 9:00 A.M.–5:00 P.M.
Sunday: 1:30 P.M.–5:00 P.M.

ADMISSION: Free.

The Natchez Trace

• *Natchez Trace Visitors' Center*
Route 1, Natchez Trace 143
Tupelo, Mississippi 38801 *(601) 842-1572*

Presently, a trip down the Natchez Trace is a road backward through history, into prehistory. Any visit to the many prehistoric sites along the Natchez Trace should begin at the Visitors' Center at Tupelo. Sites are continually being developed as new portions of the parkway are complete and only by checking in at the Visitors' Center can you be sure about which ones are open to visitors. The Visitors' Center also provides free maps and brochures on the dozens of historic and ecological points of interest along the Natchez Trace.

The Visitors' Center shows a fine background film of the history of the trace. Unfortunately, most of the archaeological sites have little interpretation. Except for the extensive exhibits at Emerald Mound and Grand Village near Natchez, you will see mostly mounds. Sometime in the future, the Visitors' Center may display the artifacts recovered from these mound sites.

DIRECTIONS: You reach the Visitors' Center by taking U.S. 78 north about 4 miles from Tupelo. Follow the signs to the Natchez Trace, which will take you around a loop and deposit you in the parking lot of the center. All archaeological sites along the trace are open free during daylight hours.

On The Natchez Trace: Spring and autumn are the best times to travel the Natchez Trace. Summers are hot and humid, winters cold and damp. You can pick up the trace from either end, or from the middle, but the only Visitors' Center is at the north end at Tupelo.

There are no overnight facilities on the trace itself, but motels, hotels, and restaurants are easily accessible in towns just off the parkway. The only service station is at Jeff Busby (Milepost 193.9). Three campgrounds spaced 150 miles apart for the convenience of travelers are limited to stays of 15 days during peak season (no reservations).

DIRECTIONS: The following sites are listed from the entrance to the parkway at Tupelo (Milepost 266). You can make the trip backward approaching from the south, or you can pick it up in the middle. Call or write the Visitors' Center for current information if you are planning to vacation along the trace.

- *Bear Creek Mound*

(Near Milepost 310)
Bear Creek Mound is in the Tennessee River Hills near a narrow fork of Bear and Cedar creeks. The land is rugged with steep hills and deep ravines carved by the creekbeds.

The ten-foot-high mound is square with steep sides and a flat top. Park staffers keep its grassy surface neatly mowed, and a paved road leads directly to the mound and village site. Visitors are not permitted on the mound.

Bear Creek is the oldest archaeological site on the Natchez Trace, and was probably visited by Paleo and Archaic hunters ten thousand years ago. They were followed by the people of the Woodland period who began to cultivate plants and build mounds, although they still relied on the abundant nuts, fruits, game, and fish in the region. Bear Creek is both a temple mound and a burial mound site.

DIRECTIONS: Bear Creek Mound, almost on the Alabama state line, is presently on an unfinished section of the parkway. It can be reached by going around from Tupelo, east on U.S. 78, then north on Highway 25.

- *Pharr Mounds*

(Milepost 286.7)
Pharr Mounds is the most impressive prehistoric site in the northern part of the state, with eight burial mounds scattered over ninety acres. Woodland

Indians used the site to bury their dead around A.D. 200. The ruins of a stockaded village have been located at the edge of the mound area dated around A.D. 1000.

DIRECTIONS: Pharr Mounds is 20 miles north of the Visitors' Center on a part of the trace now under construction. The site should be accessible by 1981. Check with the Visitors' Center before going.

- *Chickasaw Village*

(Milepost 261.8)
This is the site closest to the Visitors' Center. The eighteenth-century Chickasaw settlement was a major meeting place during the historic period. The Chickasaw were closely related to the Choctaw, Creek, and Natchez Indians, and almost two thousand people lived around this village site. But there is nothing to see now at the village site except a patch of grass; at the curb, large interpretive signs relate legendary stories of the Chickasaws.

- *Owl Creek Mound*

(Near Milepost 243.3)
Owl Creek Mound is not part of the National Parkway but it is easily accessible from the trace. This whole area is extremely rich in archaeological sites. Farmers routinely turn up spearheads and points in their plows, and local people speak of stone mounds lying hidden in the forests and under the overgrowth.

Owl Creek Mound is right on a road. A low wooden fence marks its place. The big flat mound is overgrown and covered with shrubs and trees. There is nothing here to attract your eye and you can easily drive right by if you are not accustomed to looking at mounds.

DIRECTIONS: Take the Davis Lake exit off the trace at Milepost 243.3 and follow the signs to Davis Lake. The mound is on your right about 2 miles. It is fenced, but there is no sign. If you reach the Davis Lake camping area, you have passed the mound. Turn around and go back about 1½ miles.

- *Bynum Mounds*

(Milepost 234.4)
The Bynum site is yet another parklike setting with two dome-shaped mounds about ten feet high covered with grass. Prehistoric people occupied the mounds area for about two centuries between A.D. 700 and 900. For some

reason the site was abandoned after this brief interlude and was then later reoccupied in the historic period by the Chickasaw Indians.

Several historic burials were found over the remains of the earlier Bynum people. In the prehistoric period, there were six mounds, a village, and small fields of corn and beans. The original mounds were probably smaller in diameter and higher than the remains today.

A paved road goes from the parkway to a parking lot, and there is a large outdoor exhibit shelter with an audio station. A paved loop walking trail leads from the exhibit shelter through a clearing to the two mounds.

• *Boyd Mounds*

(Milepost 106.9)
Six burial mounds and a small village site were found here against the shore of Ross Barnett Reservoir. One mound and part of the village have been cleared and planted with grass. A sign interprets the site. The cleared mound is low and long, approximately one hundred feet from end to end and only about five feet high. Everything else is covered with a tangle of impenetrable honeysuckle. The other mounds have been plowed repeatedly and are now barely visible beneath the overgrowth. It hasn't been possible to determine when the Boyd village was occupied; the best estimate is somewhere between A.D. 300 and 700.

• *Pocahontas*

This mound is right on the meridian of U.S. Highway 49. At present, U.S. 49 intersects an incomplete section of the parkway. To reach it from the trace, you have to drive around and approach it from Jackson. The mound is about fifteen miles north of Jackson. There is no interpretation, but you can't miss the huge flat-topped mound that sits literally right in the middle of the highway. The mound and borrow pit have been fully excavated. The mound itself is one hundred feet by fifty feet on top and about thirty feet high, and its steep sides are covered with trees. There is a pulloff and rest area from both the northern and southern approaches. There are rest rooms and picnic shelters, and a wooden walkway scales the south side of the mound.

• *Mangum Mound*

(Milepost 45.7)
Mangum is a Southern Cult burial ground that lies on top of an isolated knoll climbing thirty-five feet above level land. Grass and trees grow all over the slope and top of the knoll. The parkway bulges to the south to

create an access road to the site. A paved access road leads to a parking lot at the north end of the mound; then a trail goes from the base to the top of the slope, where a half dozen exhibit markers interpret individual burial sites. The top of the slope overlooks a broad, flat bottom land stretching to the Bayou Pierre, three quarters of a mile away.

- *Emerald Mound*

(Milepost 10.3)
This is the **third largest mound** in the United States. The mound is only thirty-five feet high, but its broad, flat top covers five acres, and it is almost eight acres at its base. Two smaller mounds are built on top of it. Grass blankets the mound, and trees grow on the top and sides. An open grassy plain with scattered trees surrounds the mound for several hundred feet, and a wire fence completely encloses the area. Woods border the fence on three sides.

Emerald Mound, near Natchez, is the third largest mound in the United States. It is nearly eight acres at its base, and rises thirty-five feet to a broad, flat top of more than five acres. Two lesser mounds in the pyramid shape are built on top of the major mound. The broad summit of the mound supported several buildings, and one of the smaller mounds held a special temple. The mound probably served as a ceremonial center for several farm communities, but modern farming has obliterated the village sites. (Photo courtesy of the National Park Service.)

Emerald Mound under excavation, October 1948. (Photo courtesy of the National Park Service.)

A hard surfaced and gravel trail leads from the parking lot to the base of the mound and all the way up to the top. From there steps go up to the top of the secondary mound.

Emerald Mound was built by Mississippian Indians between A.D. 1300 and 1600, and as temple mounds go, it was a late arrival. It probably looked very much then as it does today, although the two secondary mounds may have been slightly higher and more pyramidal in shape, with flat tops. Seemingly dwarfed atop the huge platform, one of these is a large mound in its own right. Several temple buildings stood all over the mound top.

The size of the mound suggests that it was the ceremonial center for several villages, but crop erosion over the last hundred years has obliterated any trace of village features. The builders of Emerald Mound were skillful farmers and artists. They traded with other tribes who brought them shells from the Gulf and copper from Lake Superior. They wove cloth, tanned leather, and enjoyed comforts unknown to the hunters and gatherers who were their ancestors.

More than a dozen other mound groups are located within twenty-five miles of Emerald Mound. These communities were probably still thriving when De Soto's army came through. But when the French arrived in about

1700, only the Natchez Indians lived here and followed the old Mississippian way of life. Nearly all of the villages and ceremonial centers had been abandoned.

Two interpretive panels at the site tell how the Indians constructed this immense earthwork. There is no visitors' center or museum.

The builders of Emerald Mound have been dead for centuries, and wind and rain have softened the contours of its massive bulk. But it still captures and stimulates the imagination.

DIRECTIONS: Drive 12 miles northeast of Natchez on the trace.

MUSEUMS

Starkville

- *Cobb Institute of Archaeology*
  Drawer AR
  Mississippi State University
  Mississippi State, Mississippi 39762 *(601) 325-3826*

The museum has good exhibits from the Mississippian culture. Its major research library is, unfortunately, open only to the faculty of the university.

DIRECTIONS: State College is near Starkville. You can reach it from the Natchez Trace by taking the exit at Highway 82.

HOURS: Monday–Friday: 8:00 A.M.–12:00 M.
Closed school holidays. Always a good idea to call first.

STATE OFFICE

State Archaeologist
Department of Archives and History
State of Mississippi
P.O. Box 571
Jackson, Mississippi 39205

OPPORTUNITIES FOR AMATEURS

No long-term excavations are in progress in Mississippi, but every summer there are several digs throughout the state. Visitors are usually welcome, and volunteers are used at the discretion of the field director. Many times amateurs are welcome and needed, especially in off-season months when students are in school. The state archaeologist recommends that anyone interested in joining a dig get in touch with the following universities:

University of Mississippi
Department of Anthropology
University, Mississippi 38766

Mississippi State University
Department of Anthropology
P.O. Drawer GN
Mississippi State, Mississippi 39762

University of Southern Mississippi
Department of Sociology/Anthropology
Box 445, Southern Station
Hattiesburg, Mississippi 39401

ORGANIZATIONS TO JOIN

The **Mississippi Archaeological Association** is primarily an amateur organization devoted to furthering the knowledge of archaeology in the state. Its primary goal is to let the public know about archaeology and cultivate an educated awareness of the science. Members of three active chapters are involved in several public information programs. Both amateurs and professionals are welcome to join. The present address of the secretary is given below, and the association can always be reached through the state archaeologist at the Department of Archives and History.

Mississippi Archaeological Association
c/o Mary Neumaier
115 Wiltshire Boulevard
Biloxi, Mississippi 39531

NORTH CAROLINA/SOUTH CAROLINA

From the Appalachian Highlands in the west to the Piedmont Plateau all the way to the broad coastal plain, the Carolinas are drenched in the history of early French, Spanish, and British settlers. Because of the dozens of important historical events, much of the archaeological work in these states is devoted to resurrecting the life and times of early white settlers.

But as with other parts of the Southeast, early Americans had lived here thousands of years before the Europeans came. Town Creek Indian Mound in North Carolina is a major Mississippian archaeological site, with reconstructions and good museum interpretation. And the Keowee-Toxaway Park in South Carolina offers a view of early Cherokee life in the region. The Carolinas both sponsor projects in underwater archaeology along the rivers and coastline, and there is more information about this at the end of this section.

NORTH CAROLINA SITES

Mt. Gilead (Albemarle)

• *Town Creek Indian Mound State Historic Site*
Box 306
Mt. Gilead, North Carolina 27306 *(914) 439-6802*

Town Creek is located in a southern wildlife preserve. For over a thousand years, Indians farmed this region in the southern Piedmont. Around A.D. 1450 a group related to the Creek Nation migrated from Alabama and Georgia and moved into the fertile basin of the Pee Dee River Valley, forcing out the Siouan farmers. High on a bluff overlooking the confluence of Town Creek and Little River, the newcomers established a ceremonial mound and plaza that served several farming communities. Their villages thrived along the banks of the river, each village protected by a stockade and watch-towers to protect the compound from the vengeful and determined Siouan tribes. They lived here for a hundred years, until they were driven out again by the Siouan tribes.

The wooden stockades of the Mississippian villages had specially designed gates to prevent surprise attacks. Overlapping wall sections created a narrow twisting corridor, so only one person at a time could enter, and his progress was impaired by the turns in the alleylike entrance. A few bowmen could easily defend such an entrance. At Town Creek a section of the stockade has been reconstructed with this unique gate in place, and to reach the ceremonial plaza you must pass through its narrow corridor.

All political, religious, and social activities took place within the plaza. Important leaders were buried here, and enemies were ceremoniously put to death. But only the priests actually lived within the walls of the compound.

Today several reconstructed buildings stand in the plaza. A temple has been reconstructed on the flat top of a large mound. The paintings and furnishings inside the temple are based on recovered archaeological evidence. Many burials have been located and some have been excavated; one of the thatched-roof burial huts has been rebuilt.

A reconstructed temple tops the crest of the Town Creek Indian Mound in North Carolina. (Photo: JW.)

The paintings and furnishings inside the temple are based on archaeological evidence recovered from the mound. (Photo: JW.)

All of the reconstructions at the center are based on archaeological data and early European journals. Controlled excavations still continue here during the summer months and visitors are invited to observe.

At the Visitors' Center, an introductory slide program sets the scene, and a self-guided tour takes you out to the mound and the various reconstructions. At each area special displays interpret the way of life of the Indians of Town Creek.

Publications can be purchased in the museum building and administrative offices are located within the center. Groups are asked to reserve in advance.

The least crowded months to visit are December through March, and the weather is good year round. Town Creek is well maintained and easily accessible. Nature trails go deep into the wildlife preserve, and you can walk the trails and look at the wonderful birds. (Bring your binoculars.) The site itself can be seen in less than an hour. There is a picnic area at the site, and camping at **Morrow Mountain State Park,** seven miles east of Albemarle (see listing below).

DIRECTIONS: From Asheboro take U.S. 220 south, then head west on NC 731 or NC 73. From Albemarle, take NC 73 east.
HOURS: Tuesday–Saturday: 9:00 A.M.–5:00 P.M.
Sunday: 1:00 P.M.–5:00 P.M.
ADMISSION: Free.

Roanoke

- *Roanoke Indian Village*
P.O. Box 906
Manteo, North Carolina 27954 *(919) 473-2463*

Guided tours take you through exhibits that trace the life of the Roanoke Indians before and after the English attempted to settle on the island. Interpretation is based on old English diaries and records. They tell of the tragedy and destruction of these island people, the other side of the story of the colonial-Indian conflict. The original village site has never been found, but the present reconstruction is somewhere near the alleged prehistoric village. Inside the village exhibits focus on deer tanning, flint napping, and daily living. All tours are guided and last about one to one and a half hours. The village is privately owned; staff members recommend the tour for adults, and children over the age of five.

DIRECTIONS: Historic Roanoke Island is reached by causeway from the east or west. The village is 5 miles from Manteo on Highway 54, about ½ mile past the entrance to Fort Raleigh.

HOURS: Memorial Day–Labor Day:
Monday–Saturday: 9:00 A.M.–5:00 P.M. (Last tour is at 5:00 P.M.)
Open to school tours by appointment the rest of the year.
ADMISSION: Adults $2, children under twelve $1, under six free.

NORTH CAROLINA MUSEUMS

Albemarle

• *Morrow Mountain State Park*
Route 2
Natural History Museum
Albemarle, North Carolina 28001 *(704) 982-4402*

Exhibits in this small natural history museum show artifacts dating back ten thousand years, and small displays represent each of the local prehistoric cultures of the region.

HOURS: May 31–Labor Day
10:00 A.M.–6:00 P.M. daily.
Labor Day–May 30
Weekends only.
ADMISSION: Free.

Note: Morrow Mountain State Park is near Town Creek Indian Mound. The hilly, deeply wooded region is situated on Lake Tillery about seven miles east of Albemarle just off NC 740. It offers a pool and bathhouse, nature trails, picnicking, fishing, boat rentals and a ramp, as well as year-round camping. Summer cabins can be reserved in advance by calling the park.

Chapel Hill

• *Research Laboratories of Anthropology*
Box 561
University of North Carolina
Parson Hall
Chapel Hill, North Carolina 27514 *(919) 933-6574*

This is primarily a research center noted for its large library of archaeology books. Collections include pottery and artifacts from North Carolina.

HOURS: Monday–Friday: 9:00 A.M.–5:00 P.M.
Closed weekends and holidays.
ADMISSION: Free.

Cherokee

- *Oconaluftee Indian Village*
  Cherokee, North Carolina 28719

This is a reconstruction of a historic Cherokee Indian village that was on this site about two hundred years ago. It is also the spot where early prehistoric hunters camped. The village has a seven-sided council house furnished as the Cherokee lived before the white settlers came. All of the cultural and home life of the Cherokee is related here. The rituals handed down from generation to generation come alive as Indian guides take you along to various demonstrations of Cherokee skills, crafts, and arts. There is an authentic Indian herb garden and a wonderful nature trail where thousands of native plants are identified.

Cherokee is the gateway to Great Smoky Mountains National Park. It is the capital of the eastern band of Cherokee who live on the Qualla Reservation at the park's edge. The reservation is the largest east of Wisconsin.

DIRECTIONS: From Cherokee, drive north on U.S. 441, turn at the directional sign, and go ½ mile to the village entrance.
HOURS: Mid-May–October
Complete tours from 9:00 A.M.–5:30 P.M.
ADMISSION: Adults $3, children six to twelve $2.

- *Museum of the Cherokee Indian*
  (U.S. 441)
  P.O. Box 770-A
  Cherokee, North Carolina 28719 *(704) 497-3481*

The Museum of the Cherokee Indian is colorful and modern. Ancient legends are told in a futuristic, molded-plastic style, and the museum is replete with multimedia slide and tape shows that trace Indian life from prehistory to present times. As museums go, it is unique, and many kinds of Cherokee artifacts and crafts merge in the displays. You can also listen on telephones to English texts translated into the Cherokee language.

DIRECTIONS: The museum is on U.S. 441 in Cherokee.
HOURS: Mid-June–August
Monday–Saturday: 9:00 A.M.–8:00 P.M.
Sunday: 9:00 A.M.–5:30 P.M.
September–mid-June
9:00 A.M.–5:30 P.M. daily.
Closed Thanksgiving, Christmas, New Year's.
ADMISSION: Adults $2.10, children six to twelve $1.05; special group rates.

STATE OFFICE

Jacqueline R. Fehon
State Archeologist
North Carolina Department of Cultural Resources
Division of Archives and History
Raleigh, North Carolina 27611

OPPORTUNITIES FOR AMATEURS

The **Archeology Branch,** part of the Division of Archives and History in Raleigh, offers public archaeology programs: informal lectures twice a month and a regularly scheduled volunteer night. Volunteers work in the laboratory on projects such as experimental archaeology, research, cataloging, and cleaning artifacts. There are plans to add an amateur certification program in site survey.

The Archeology Branch also supplies information on field schools offered through the state office or universities on a seasonal basis.

Note: North Carolina is rich in historic sites. If you are interested in more information, write:

Department of Cultural Resources
109 East Jones Street
Raleigh, North Carolina 27611

ORGANIZATIONS TO JOIN

The **North Carolina Archeological Society** is a statewide organization and publishes a fine annual journal, *Southern Indian Studies,* and a newsletter. For current information about the location and address of chapters, write:

Research Laboratories of Anthropology
Box 561
University of North Carolina
Chapel Hill, North Carolina 27514

SOUTH CAROLINA SITES

Santee

- *Santee Indian Mounds*
Santee State Park
Route 1, Box 255-A
Santee, South Carolina 29142 *(803) 854-2408*

This is the only prehistoric site in South Carolina open to the public. It is the largest ceremonial center yet discovered on the coastal plain, representing the hub of late prehistoric activity in the area. The mounds were built between A.D. 1200 and 1400. In shape, they are typical of pyramidal mounds widely distributed throughout the southeastern United States, yet they are a special cultural variety belonging to the South Appalachian Mississippian Tradition.

The mound site is especially interesting because it is one of the places where prehistory blended into history. If it wasn't for the archaeological excavation of an old British fort there may never have been any investigation on this coastal plain, where the most intensive late prehistoric activity in South Carolina took place.

Colonel John T. Watson first discovered the large mound in 1781 and built a fort for the British army on its summit. The fort was captured by American forces during the Revolution. Through archaeology, historians have traced the pattern of military tactics and the everyday life of the soldiers who participated in this eighteenth-century combat. The large mound is eroding from weather and vandalism, but a walkway takes you to the top. There is no museum and little interpretation of the site, but it is an important place in South Carolina's history.

HOURS: Open at all times.
ADMISSION: Free.

SOUTH CAROLINA MUSEUMS

Georgetown

• *Rice Museum*
Front and Screven Streets
Georgetown, South Carolina 29440 *(803) 546-7423*

On the shore of Winyah Bay, Georgetown is a seaport with a long history. It is the site of the first European settlement on the North American mainland. Rice and indigo plantations along the rivers were the main attraction during the early 1700s. Maps, dioramas, and other exhibits are devoted to the history of rice in Georgetown. The museum also has a special section devoted to artifacts recovered from South Carolina's underwater archaeology program. The museum is located inside the 1842 Market Building.

HOURS: Monday–Friday: 9:30 A.M.–4::30 P.M.
Saturday: 10:00 A.M.–4:30 P.M. (April–September)
10:00 A.M.–1:00 P.M. (October–March)
Sunday: 2:00 P.M.–4:30 P.M.
ADMISSION: Adults $1, students and children free.

STATE OFFICE

The University of South Carolina has a central headquarters that is involved in all aspects of archaeology in the state. For information, contact:

Dr. Robert L. Stephenson, Director
Institute of Archeology and Anthropology
University of South Carolina
Columbia, South Carolina 29208 (803) 777-8170

ORGANIZATIONS TO JOIN

The **Archeological Society of South Carolina** is a very active amateur organization that works closely with the Institute of Archeology and Anthropology. Members have regular monthly meetings and an annual conference. The society offers both training programs and fieldwork. Its monthly newsletter and scholarly journal *South Carolina Antiquities,* as well as *The Notebook* of the Institute of Archeology and Anthropology, are available to members. Write:

Archeological Society of South Carolina
Institute of Archeology and Anthropology
University of South Carolina
Columbia, South Carolina 29208

TENNESSEE

Long before De Soto crossed the Mississippi River somewhere near Memphis, Tennessee, this was a civilized region. From Chota in the Great Smoky Mountains, the Cherokees reigned over Tennessee and parts of Georgia and the Carolinas. Before the Cherokee, mound builders thrived here and were part of the great southeastern chain of the Mississippian Tradition.

SITES

Manchester
- *Old Stone Fort*

A long stone wall and natural moats form an almost complete circle on the tip of a high bluff above the fort of the Little Duck and the Duck rivers. Early pioneers were the first white people to notice sections of the wall, and legends of its origin quickly multiplied. Vikings, Welshmen, and Spaniards were the favorite contenders for the title of wall builders. But we know today that the wall was built by prehistoric Indians during the middle Woodland period.

Archaeological excavations show that it took more than four hundred years to build this wall. And yet for all of those centuries of effort, we can find no trace of life except the wall itself. The wall stands four to six feet high, and its various sections total almost a full mile in length. It is made of stone layers with earth sandwiched between them. Some rocks weigh as much as seventy pounds, and each one had to be dragged up the steep slope to the top of the bluff.

A major archaeological excavation of the site revealed little. No one ever lived here, and yet twelve generations of prehistoric people devoted their labor to constructing the wall. Why? It's one of the fascinating mysteries of archaeology. The site may have been a defensive position—but no one knows what the wall might have protected. It may have been a place of worship or a hidden ceremonial center. As one scientist points out, when archaeologists can't identify something, they call it a "ceremonial" center. No one knows the purpose of the stone wall nor the nature of events that occurred within its enclosure.

A visitors' center contains exhibits and artifacts that tell, as much as possible, the story of the "fort" and its legendary builders.

Old Stone Fort is preserved in a six-hundred-acre state park bordered by the two rivers and waterfalls. The park provides a picnic area, campsites, nature trails, fishing, and golf.

DIRECTIONS: From Manchester, drive 2 miles north on U.S. 41.
HOURS: Daylight hours, year round.
ADMISSION: Free.

Memphis

● *Chucalissa Indian Museum and Village Reconstruction*
1987 Indian Village Drive
Memphis, Tennessee 38109 *(901) 785-3160*

Chucalissa (Choctaw for "abandoned houses") was an ancient farming community on a high bluff overlooking the Mississippi River. Between A.D. 1000 and 1500 the village thrived. Farmers, craftsmen, and artists built their houses with steep, shaggy thatched roofs all around the town square. They raised their crops in the river bottoms below the village and made their own tools and pottery. A rectangular flat-topped mound was a platform for public buildings.

Over a thousand people lived here in Mississippian times. But when Father Jacques Marquette, a Jesuit priest accompanying Louis Joliet's expedition down the Mississippi River, passed through in 1673, the town was deserted. No one has ever known who the people of Chucalissa were.

The village site has been excavated extensively and reconstructed, and the outdoor museum has some of the finest archaeological exhibits in the United States. There's a cross-section view of the village midden, and an excavated house floor and burial are left in place. Another exhibit shows how archaeologists reconstruct the appearance of early people from skeletons. Other displays show how pottery and baskets were made and tools fashioned.

Today members of the Choctaw tribe act as guides and demonstrate the skills of Chucalissa artisans. Chucalissa has been under excavation since 1955 and today is part of Memphis State University. In the summer the university continues excavations, and visitors are welcome to watch the work in progress. The reconstruction presently includes nine huts, a chief's house on the main mound, two enclosed excavations, and a village plaza where special events are held during the summer.

The **C. H. Nash Museum Building** is named for the man who guided the development of Chucalissa from its beginning. The museum houses an introductory slide show, case exhibits on the life and archaeology of Chucalissa and the mid-South, and audio-visual programs covering special topics dealing with traditional Indian customs of the region. A library, laboratory, and research collections are all housed in the building.

There is picnicking on the grounds, and you can camp in the state park adjacent to the site.

DIRECTIONS: From U.S. 61 (or I-55) on the southern edge of Memphis, take Mitchell Road 4½ miles west to the museum entrance on Indian Village Drive.

HOURS: Tuesday–Saturday: 9:00 A.M.–5:00 P.M.
Sunday: 1:00 P.M.–5:00 P.M.
(Visitors are not admitted to village area after 4:30 P.M.)
Closed Mondays, Thanksgiving, and Christmas week.

ADMISSION: Adults 50¢, children six to eleven 10¢, under six free.

TOURS: Groups can make an appointment for guided tours if they call or write at least two weeks in advance. Other visitors who would like an escorted tour can inquire at the reception desk; guides are assigned when available.

Shiloh

• *Shiloh Mounds*
Shiloh National Military Park
Shiloh, Tennessee 38376 *(901) 689-5275*

Within this park dedicated to the battle of Shiloh are a group of thirty prehistoric mounds. Six large, flat-topped mounds are similar to the groups of mounds left by the Mississippian people all over the South. There is also a large, oval burial mound and many smaller mounds that were probably used as house foundations.

The Shiloh Mounds probably served as a central plaza for people who lived on this bluff above the Tennessee River around A.D. 1200. And like mound builders everywhere, they had vanished from the region by the time the Europeans arrived in Tennessee.

The cluster of mounds is about a mile from park headquarters. All of the interpretation in the park is devoted to the 1862 battle of Shiloh, a major land engagement in the Civil War. The Visitors' Center one mile from the park entrance has major exhibits and a thirty-minute historical film. You can pick up a self-guided tour folder here and follow the points of interest by automobile. Ask directions to the mounds, which are up on a bluff about a mile from the Visitors' Center.

DIRECTIONS: From Savannah, drive 4 miles west on U.S. 64; then go 6 miles south on TN 22 (near Pittsburg Landing).
HOURS: 8:00 A.M.–6:00 P.M. daily.
Labor Day–Memorial Day: 8:00 A.M.–5:00 P.M.
Closed Christmas.
Guided tours of the park are available in the summer.
ADMISSION: Free.

MUSEUMS

Chattanooga

• *Lookout Mountain Museum*
Point Park
1100 East Brow Road
Chattanooga, Tennessee 37419

During the Civil War, the "Battle Above Clouds" was fought on the slope of this mountain below Point Park. Today the region is part of the Chickamauga and the Chattanooga National Military Park. The museum has Civil War memorabilia, dioramas, and some archaeological displays. Archaic and Mississippian artifacts collected by amateur archaeologists are on display, and there is some Paleo material from a local site. Dioramas and life-sized models show how people of the Archaic Period lived.

It's a fine drive up to Point Park, and the museum offers a good perspective of the story of the region from earliest time through recent history.

DIRECTIONS: From Chattanooga, drive south via Ochs Highway and Scenic Highway. Follow this route to the top of Lookout Mountain, and then to Point Park. The museum is opposite the park entrance.

HOURS: 9:00 A.M.–6:00 P.M. daily.
Closed Christmas.

ADMISSION: Adults 25¢, children six to sixteen 10¢, under six free.

Knoxville

- *McClung Museum*
University of Tennessee
Circle Park Drive
Knoxville, Tennessee 37916 *(615) 974-2144*

Exhibits trace Tennessee's earliest inhabitants from the Archaic through Mississippian periods. The museum houses the collection from the famous Eva site (closed to the public) in Benton County, where Archaic people lived along a tributary of the Tennessee River for seven thousand years and harvested great quantities of clams and mussels. They buried their dead in small round graves, and several dog skeletons were discovered in the burials. This was the first evidence of a domesticated animal in the Eastern Woodlands and perhaps in North America. The most interesting thing about the burials, however, was that many of the Eva people had lived to be sixty or seventy years old, an uncommonly old age in prehistoric times.

The museum also has environmental and scientific displays, art exhibits, and period furnishings.

DIRECTIONS: The campus is on West Cumberland Avenue, U.S. 11 and 70.

HOURS: Monday–Friday: 9:00 A.M.–5:00 P.M.
Closed weekends and major holidays.

ADMISSION: Free.

Nashville

- *Cumberland Museum and Science Center*
800 Ridley Avenue
Nashville, Tennessee 37203 *(615) 242-1858*

The Indian exhibits highlight Tennessee history, and a fine exhibit tells the story of the early mound builders. A display of more than one hundred projectile points traces the hunter's life from Paleo through late Woodland times.

The Cumberland is a general science museum with exhibits designed for young people. It has a live animal room, natural science exhibits, a slide theater, and a planetarium. The natural science research library is open to museum members.

HOURS: Tuesday–Saturday: 10:00 A.M.–5:00 P.M.
Sunday: 1:00 P.M.–5:00 P.M.
Closed Mondays and holidays.
ADMISSION: Adults $1.50, children five to seventeen $1, under five free.

STATE OFFICE

Joseph L. Benthall
State Archaeologist
Tennessee Department of Conservation
Division of Archaeology
5103 Edmondson Pike
Nashville, Tennessee 37211 (615) 741-1588

OPPORTUNITIES FOR AMATEURS

College-level courses in archaeology and museum work are offered at the **Chucalissa site** as part of the state university's program in anthropology. The general public can participate through the Continuing Education division of the university. Call or write to the Chucalissa Museum in Memphis for information on current and planned courses.

The **Tennessee Division of Archaeology** uses amateurs in several of its field programs, including inventorying and excavating sites. For more information, contact the office of the state archaeologist (above).

The departments of anthropology at both **Memphis State University** (Memphis 38111) and the **University of Tennessee** (Knoxville 37916) offer summer field schools in archaeology.

ORGANIZATIONS TO JOIN

There are several archaeological societies in Tennessee. The **Tennessee Archaeological Society** is open to both amateurs and professionals, and can be reached by writing the Tennessee Department of Conservation (above).

The current address for the **Volunteer State Archaeological Society of Tennessee** can also be obtained through the same department.

UNDERWATER ARCHAEOLOGY

Underwater archaeology has become increasingly important, especially in the Southeast where wood, bone, and shell artifacts that seldom survive the surface climate are perfectly preserved in the natural time capsule of rivers and lakes. Artifacts recovered from the water are usually in much better condition than surface finds on dry land, because they have escaped the plow and other damaging human advances. Perfectly intact pottery is common, and the oldest artifact ever found in the state of South Carolina came out of the Santee River.

Marine archaeology involves the same meticulous work as surface excavations. A vacuum is used in place of a hand trowel, but otherwise the scientists follow the same methodical rules of record keeping and preservation for future analysis. Underwater sites are staked out in grids just like surface sites, and everything found in each square is noted, mapped, and collected before it is brought to the surface. This process can become very tricky in deep waters, heavy currents, and sluggish riverbeds where visibility is poor.

A lake bottom in Florida has recently yielded discoveries of a site inhabited by early peoples. The lake bottom slopes gently toward a large sinkhole with a vertical shaft that spreads downward to form a huge water-filled cavity that is at least 240 feet deep. Its mineral-rich, oxygen-poor water has preserved many specimens that would ordinarily have been destroyed long ago.

Toward the end of the Ice Age, the climate in Florida was drier than it is today and the landscape was a semidesert. The sinkhole must have been a source of fresh water to early hunters. It was also a trap for animals that fell over the clifflike walls and could not escape.

Twelve thousand years ago the water level of the lake must have been much lower and people lived on what is now a lake bottom, leaving behind animal bones and artifacts, including a very old hunting boomerang. The boomerang was found on a ledge ninety feet below the lake surface. It is a nonreturning type thought capable of downing game the size of a deer at a range of two hundred feet. Similar boomerangs have been found in Egypt, Australia, and Western Europe, but never before in the Western Hemisphere. Furthermore, its estimated age of twelve thousand years appears to make it older than any boomerang previously found.

At one place at the water's edge, hunters had captured a giant tortoise. They pierced its underbelly with a stake, turned it over, and cooked it. The stake and parts of the turtle's shell and bones have been dated at 10,030 B.C. The giant turtle was at least four feet long and two or three feet tall.

In a swampy bog near the lake, an ancient burial ground containing the skeletons of more than one thousand people has been discovered. It is one of the largest burial sites of Archaic Indians found in North America and dates back to 5000 B.C. The underwater site was excavated by a team of scientists from several institutions led by Carl J. Clausen, former Florida marine archaeologist.

"Underwater" is a specialty of archaeology, and it is studied in conjunction with the rest of the science. It is not a science in itself. The **Institute of Nautical Archaeology** in Texas, under the directorship of George F. Bass, is the center of marine archaeology in the United States. Qualified students of anthropology from Texas A & M and other colleges and universities around the world train here and work in the institute's field schools. Occasionally, the institute accepts volunteers who have special talents, but its supply of volunteers normally far exceeds the demand.

In the Southeast three states have outstanding underwater archaeology programs:

North Carolina: The Underwater Archaeology Branch surveys and inves-

The twisted frame of Brown's Ferry, the oldest known boat in the country, being raised out of the Black River in South Carolina. (Photo courtesy of the Institute of Archeology and Anthropology, University of South Carolina, Gordon Brown, photographer.)

After recovery from the Roanoke River, cannon and empty siege and garrison carriage rest on the deck of an Army Reserves vessel. (Photo courtesy of the Underwater Archaeology Branch, North Carolina Division of Archives and History.)

tigates sites under all the rivers and shores of North Carolina. Groups and students can arrange to visit its laboratory to watch the special drafting and photographic techniques. Actual diving excavations are not open to the general public. Anyone seriously interested in observing an underwater dig can call or write the branch and request permission to visit a site.

Every project uses some students and avocational volunteers. The minimum requirement for actual diving is certification. Other nondiving jobs are available on research vessels. Preliminary training seminars prepare volunteers to join the dig. Field schools are sponsored jointly with other organizations and universities such as the East Carolina University at Greenville. If you would like to volunteer for an underwater excavation, send a résumé of your qualifications to:

Gordon P. Watts, Jr.
Underwater Archaeology Branch
North Carolina Division of Archives and History
P.O. Box 58
Kure Beach, North Carolina 28449

South Carolina: The Institute of Archeology and Anthropology uses a few volunteer divers for its own excavations but only on a local and special-need basis. Divers in South Carolina must be prepared to work in "black" water with almost zero visibility. Currents are harsh and tricky in most places. It's important that all divers be thoroughly familiar with the waters of the region, and only experienced local divers are used.

However, volunteer historical researchers are in demand. Anyone who lives in the area and is willing to devote special research to a particular assignment on a volunteer basis is welcome. One project might be tracing the history of the Santee River from its earliest known habitation through the present day.

Any diver in the state of South Carolina can obtain a special license from the institute to recover artifacts from the river bottoms. Divers are required to file a monthly site report showing where and when the dive took place and what was recovered. The institute checks out the recovered material and has the right to take 25 percent of the diver's recoveries for the state. For information, contact:

Alan B. Albright
Institute of Archeology and Anthropology
University of South Carolina
Columbia, South Carolina 29209

Virginia: Marine archaeology in Virginia is devoted to shipwrecks from the historical period. Divers have been working on shipwrecks lost in the battle of Yorktown, and in 1981—Yorktown's bicentennial year—they will be diving from a barge 350 feet off the public beach and just 100 feet beyond the swimming area. The seagoing archaeologists are happy to have the public observe this dig.

The dive will continue all year, mostly during the early spring through the end of winter. Although the waters are cold in the wintertime, visibility is greatly improved.

A small waterfront museum called the **Yorktown Shipwreck Information Center** is on Water Street. Call (804) 898-7854. The museum describes the underwater projects and also exhibits artifacts recovered from the dig. Visitors can watch preservation treatments being used on an ancient cannon brought up from the river bottom. The cannon is cleaned of corrosion and a kind of reverse electrolysis is used to rejuvenate the iron. The museum also explains different nautical archaeological techniques.

The number of volunteers used on the diving expedition is limited because of the small size of the diving barge. Certified divers and individuals with good skills in record keeping, drawing, or photography are welcome to apply. There are no housing facilities for out-of-town volunteers, but if you plan to spend several weeks of your vacation in the area and have a place to live, the team may very well have a spot for you. Write or call:

John Broadwater
Marine Archaeologist
State of Virginia
Yorktown, Virginia 23690 (804) 887-0970

THE MIDWEST

Illinois

Indiana

Iowa

Kentucky

Michigan

Minnesota

Missouri

Ohio

West Virginia

Wisconsin

THE MIDWEST

From any small rise in the Midwest you can look out across the longest stretch of fertile land anywhere in the world. No ragged peaks or sunken valleys mar the vistas. Before the land was plowed, tall grasses stirred by the wind made an endless heaving sea.

From the earliest times that people were present in North America, the character of this region has been shaped by its climate. The extreme north and south range of this area of the continent makes the Midwest a center of impact for weather fronts coming from every direction. Balmy winds sweep up from the Gulf of Mexico and clash against the hard winds bearing down from Canada. The weather pushes east from the Rockies and crosses the front heading west out of the Appalachians. Below-zero winters and baking summers are the norm.

The climate was responsible for a curious cultural result. The grassy prairie country east of the Missouri River is easily distinguished from the nubby plains to the west. Out on those Great Plains, a sudden reduction in rainfall makes farming risky. Even a slight dry spell marks disaster for crops. Because of this extreme difference in the natural environment, distinctly different prehistoric cultures developed east and west of this river. West of the Missouri, the Archaic lifeways persisted with slight variation, and the people hunted buffalo into the historic period. But east of the river, agricultural communities grew up and a complex network of trade moved along the rivers. Rivers dominate this land: the Mississippi, the Ohio, and the Missouri are fed by the Minnesota and St. Croix and dozens more. The rivers pour into twenty-three thousand lakes in Minnesota, Michigan, and Wisconsin alone.

Paleo-Indians were the first people to live in the Midwest, and their fluted points have been found all over the region. Later, great herds of buffalo made a regular path to the salt licks in Kentucky, and the Archaic hunters followed them wherever they roamed. The Archaic people supplemented their diet with fish and shellfish, and some river banks are still heaped with the clamshells they left behind.

The Woodland period introduced a new art form along with pottery and farming. Around 1000 B.C. the first mounds were constructed. These early structures were small conical or round mounds used for burials. The Adena people were among the earliest mound builders. Other ancient mounds in the Mississippi Valley belong to the Red Ochre culture, dating around 500 B.C. These people placed their dead on a floor and covered them with red ochre.

But the region is probably most famous for the Hopewellian burial mounds; they built monumental earthworks and devised intricate mortuary rituals with rich offerings. The powerful Hopewellian culture overlapped the Adena culture and spread out over an enormous trade network. It spread rapidly out of Illinois and Ohio along a far-flung trading system east to the Atlantic coast, south to the Gulf, north to the Great Lakes. A wide variety of raw materials was required to make the colorful ritual objects for their burials. Through trade, fancy flints were exchanged all over the country, copper came from the Great Lakes, mica from the Appalachians, obsidian from the Rockies, conch shells from the Gulf. Wherever these exotic goods traveled up and down the river highways, the influence of the Hopewellians spread.

When the Hopewell culture suddenly declined, the whole system of trade broke down. The Woodland Tradition continued briefly, and the people who followed the Hopewellians dug graves into the tops and sides of old Hopewell mounds. This was an interim cultural phase, and soon the most powerful tradition ever seen in the prehistoric Eastern Woodlands grew up: The fabulous Mississippian Tradition, which penetrated all the way north to Wisconsin and deep into the Southeast, was based on large-scale farming. The mound builders now built the massive flat-topped temple mounds.

During the Mississippian period great numbers of people lived together in large cities, the largest of which was at Cahokia in southern Illinois. Here the greatest temple mound in North America still stands.

But by the time French explorers Louis Joliet and Father Jacques Marquette paddled their canoes down the Wisconsin River and into the immense Mississippi in the summer of 1673, the great mound cities were deserted. The French saw the huge mounds lining the bluffs along the river banks, but no signs of life were apparent. The scattered groups of Indians they met were friendly and hospitable and shared their prize commodities with the Frenchmen, including the one for which the region is still famous—corn. But the elaborate Mississippian civilizations had disintegrated without leaving behind any record of the cause of their downfall. Their demise remains one of the most stubborn mysteries of archaeology.

The roads of the Midwest today follow the ancient trails of buffalo, early prehistoric hunters, fur traders, and pioneers. The late spring, summer, and fall are the best travel times, although most of the major archaeological sites are open all year. The range of the many sites open to the public in the Midwest is broad; every state offers major archaeological sites that have been interpreted for the public.

ILLINOIS

Cahokia, one of the top archaeological sites in North America, is in East St. Louis, Illinois. Compared to the neatly cut green lawns of the mound groups in the South, Cahokia looks shaggy and unkempt. It is surrounded by a seedy park where baby swings interfere with the serious scientific work at hand. You have to fight your way through a frantic maze of suburban traffic to find the site. Nor does Cahokia have a fancy interpretive center. But the tiny museum's interpretation of a mound-building society and the way archaeologists work is superb.

Cahokia is immense and sprawling. It takes an hour just to climb to the top of the unbelievable Monks Mound, the largest mound north of Mexico and the biggest earth structure anywhere. When you visit Cahokia you are "in the field." There are no neat paths, it's ghastly hot in the summer, and your imagination runs wild as you tramp the roughly laid-out site. It is, in a word, sensational, if you enjoy archaeology in the rough before everything has been smoothed over.

Illinois contains several other important mounds and excavations. Preservation archaeology is critically important in Illinois right now, as the new Interstate 270 prepares to slice through the American Bottom land around St. Louis. The "American Bottom" is a term used to describe the Mississippi River Floodplain. It stretches from Alton, Illinois, in the north to Cheser, Illinois, and from the Mississippi River channel to the east bluff.

All of this region is important to archaeologists. In the Archaic Period wild game and plant foods were plentiful, and later the rich alluvial soils were ideal for farming. The area's strategic location at the confluence of the Mississippi, Missouri, and Illinois rivers led to the development of Cahokia, the highest civilization in prehistoric North America.

The construction of the new highway affects more than fifty archaeological sites. Salvage excavations are being rushed through in an effort to save the stories turned up in the teeth of the bulldozer. Most of the excavations are not open to the public. Only the fieldwork around Kampsville is open to a limited number of visitors during the summer months.

SITES

East St. Louis

- *Cahokia Mounds State Historic Site*
  7850 Collinsville Road
  East St. Louis, Illinois 62201 *(618) 344-5268*

The car edges down a highway glutted with traffic lights and fast-food restaurants. The jazz-modern beat of urban life hammers away as people move along unnoticed and not noticing. Suddenly, Monks Mound looms up like a ragged giant among the nattering Lilliputians. At first sight it seems like a hallucination: the massive almost shapeless hulk could not appear on a city street. But if it isn't Monks Mound, then what *is* it? You have reached Cahokia.

Aerial view of Monks Mound, the largest earthwork in the United States, at East St. Louis, Illinois.

If you are fortunate enough to have come this far, stop at the first building you see, which should be a small yellow museum right there on Collinsville Road. From the museum you can take one of two possible tours of the area. You can rent an audio tour machine and go in your own car or on foot. In the summer you can usually go out with a guide, which is by far the best way. Cahokia is an enormous site with few interpretive signs, and walking around on your own guarantees that you will miss the most interesting parts.

The museum is small in scope but dazzling in value. It is a first-rate, on-site interpretive center. Take the time to look at the finely chosen exhibits and read the excellent interpretive information. The museum also has a sales counter where you can buy pamphlets and books on North American Indians as well as archaeological reports published by the state of Illinois.

After the museum your second stop should be the slide show, which is presented at this time in a trailer annex down the street from the museum. Ask at the museum for directions to the trailer. During the twenty-minute program, you will learn not only about Cahokia but about the mound builders' place in history. Professional archaeologists made this film, and it capsulizes the full range of knowledge about the mound builders and their amazing achievements. (In the near future, both museum and slide show will come together under one roof in a new visitors' center.)

For now, Cahokia is almost shockingly underdeveloped, considering that it is among the most important sites anywhere in the world. Its archaeological secrets have barely been tapped. The great mound and its immediate vicinity are owned by the city, and it has been held in a protected state for decades. However, the team of scientists at the site have a master plan under way for Cahokia that will place it among the leading sites for visitors in the world.

Because of its primitive condition, Cahokia appeals strongly to the imagination. It is not hard to picture the great complex as it might have been nearly a thousand years ago. Even though modern traffic rages up and down its borders, the site is so large that you can easily forget the twentieth century as you ramble along the overgrown paths.

Originally over one hundred mounds dotted the central portion of the city, but many were destroyed by plowing before the turn of the century. Only eighty-seven have been found and twenty of these were almost completely obliterated by modern farming and urban construction. Today about forty mounds are preserved in the historic site, and the remainder are privately owned.

Prehistoric Indians first came to Cahokia around A.D. 700, during the late Woodland period. By A.D. 900 the Mississippian culture had fully emerged, with a well-developed agricultural system. The stable food base, combined with hunting and fishing, supported a complex political and religious community. Cahokia soon became a regional center for the Mississippian culture. There were satellite villages near the modern towns of Mitchell, Dupo, Lebanon, and East St. Louis, Illinois, and St. Louis, Missouri.

Cahokia originally covered about six square miles and had a population of about thirty thousand in the main community. The residential section was extensive and the houses, built along streets or around open plazas, had small gardens. But the main agricultural fields were probably outside the city limits.

The remains of tall log posts staked out in an even circle show these agriculturalists had a sun calendar to predict the changing seasons. Constructed about A.D. 1000 this calendar is an early and impressive exhibit of native American science and engineering.

Around A.D. 1150, the Cahokians enclosed three hundred acres of the central city with a fifteen-foot-high defensive stockade. At least three more walls were erected in the same general location and indicate that the city may have been under siege.

Loading docks, canals, and warehouses were at the heart of the great Cahokian trade system. And above all this activity, the great platform mound reigned. Its base covered fourteen acres, and it rose in four terraces to a height of one hundred feet. On the highest terrace stood a massive building at least 105 feet long and 50 feet high.

Conical and ridge-top mounds were also built around the city. The

Crew member of the summer archaeological team opens up a small excavation site at Cahokia.

Pottery sherds and bone fragments can be seen protruding from the walls of the excavation pit.

Artifacts recovered from the site rest in the bottom of a seive.

exact function of these mounds is not known, but both may have been used for burial purposes. The excavation of one small ridge-top mound revealed nearly three hundred ceremonial and sacrificial burials in mass graves. The main burial appears to be a male ruler about forty-five years old. He was laid on a cape decorated with over twenty thousand marine shell beads and surrounded by attendants who had been sacrificially killed. Among the burial goods were nearly eight hundred arrowheads from various parts of the Midwest. In another part of this mound were the bones of four men with their hands and heads missing. Near them were the skeletons of fifty-three young women between the ages of fifteen and twenty-five.

Aside from this unusual discovery, little else has been excavated at Cahokia. Archaeologists are eager to excavate a matching ridge mound, and there is an enormous amount of important work still to be done at Cahokia. It is one of the great archaeological sites in the country and very much "in a state of becoming." As more of Cahokia is uncovered in controlled archaeological excavations, the site will grow in importance and interest. Any visit to Cahokia over the next several years will bring new discoveries and new adventures in archaeology.

Archaeological excavations continue all summer long, and visitors are welcome to observe. And the Cahokia Mounds Museum Society sponsors an annual field school (see "Opportunities for Amateurs" below).

Presently the site is part of a city park. There are several picnic areas with tables and stoves, playgrounds, drinking water, and restrooms. Family camping is permitted for tents and trailers, with some electricity available. Groups of over twenty-five must have advance permission to enter the site.

Self-guided automobile or walking tours with the audio tape are available year round, and guided walking tours to the top of Monks Mound are regularly scheduled during the summer. Appointments for group tours can be made year round. It would take all day to walk over the entire site, but it is easy to drive around it. A half day is adequate to see Cahokia, unless you want to spend time observing the dig.

DIRECTIONS: Cahokia is in the suburb of Collinsville. Anyone unfamiliar with East St. Louis will never know exactly where he or she is in this heavily built-up area where a dozen suburbs overlap. Make sure you have a map with you and try to follow the directions. If you do stray, call up the museum, tell them where you are, and ask how to reach the site. Advice from gas station attendants or miscellaneous pedestrians will have you wandering all over southern Illinois. From I-55/I-70, take exit 6 and follow Highway 111 to U.S. 40, which is Collinsville Road. Turn left. Once on Collinsville Road, you can't miss Monks Mound.

HOURS: 9:00 A.M.–5:00 P.M. daily.
During the winter the museum sometimes closes on Mondays, and a phone call is recommended. Closed Thanksgiving, Christmas, New Year's.

ADMISSION: Free.

Kampsville

- *Kampsville Archeological Center*
Broadway
Kampsville, Illinois 26053 *(618) 653–4614*

The small river town of Kampsville is headquarters for the **Northwestern Archeological Program.** The great blossoming of archaeological activity in Kampsville is due to an important discovery at a nearby farm known as the Koster site. In well-preserved stratigraphy at the foot of a limestone bluff, scientists found evidence of continuous human habitation going back eight thousand years. For the last ten years, this important excavation on private property has been open to the public through the generosity of Theodore and Mary Koster.

Pairs of Kampsville workers take to the Illinois River to use their washtub flotation system. Soil already sifted for large artifacts at the nearby archaeological dig is introduced into the water to float out fragments of organic material. The tub bottoms are made of fine mesh screen. As one partner gyrates the tub, the heavier material such as potsherds and pieces of stone settle to the bottom. The lighter material, which contains tiny pieces of animal bones, charred seeds and nuts, and even fish scales rises to the top. The second partner skims this organic evidence from the surface with an extremely fine brass screen mesh. (Photo courtesy of the Foundation for Illinois Archeology.)

Riders on the small ferryboat that drifts across the Illinois River at Kampsville grew used to the sight of the Koster workers standing waist deep in the river, gyrating their self-styled floatation system for separating artifacts out of the soil. This system, hailed as a technological breakthrough, was an inspired invention that involved nothing more sophisticated than a washtub with a meshed bottom.

The Koster site owes its fame to the efforts of Dr. Stuart Struever who, by making his work available to the public, has helped the work of archaeologists everywhere and almost single-handedly stirred up public interest in all archaeological sites.

Unfortunately, the operation at Koster was shut down in 1979. In heavy spring flooding, the Illinois River overran its banks and all but destroyed the site. The dig has been backfilled and will not be reopened. But most of the work has been accomplished. The research facility and museum remain open at Kampsville, and archaeologists continue to work at different digs all over the region every summer. Visitors are still welcome and tours can be arranged by calling the Visitors' Center.

The Museum Visitors' Center offers continuing displays of artifacts recovered from Koster and other excavations in the area. Museum staffers are on hand to talk with visitors.

The ongoing programs at Kampsville are partially supported by members of the Northwestern Archeological Program. People from all over the United States have joined and their membership dues directly provide for important research. Members receive the excellent *Early Man* journal that supplies up-to-date information on the projects at Kampsville as well as other archaeological research around the world. For membership information, write:

Northwestern Archeology Program
Box 1499
Evanston, Illinois 60201

There are hotels and motels in the Kampsville area and many reasonably priced local restaurants. The staff at the museum will be glad to give you further information.

DIRECTIONS: Kampsville lies about 70 miles north of St. Louis on U.S. 100 (on the west bank of the river). There is no bridge at this spot, but a free ferry across the Illinois River lets you approach from any direction.

HOURS: The Museum Visitors' Center is open 9:00 A.M.–5:00 P.M. daily, usually beginning around the end of May through Labor Day.

TOURS: Advanced tours of groups can be booked through the director of special programs at (312) 492–5300.

Lewistown

- *Dickson Mounds Museum*
Lewistown, Illinois 61542 *(309) 547–3721*

Dickson Mounds is essentially an indoor site. This region was first used by Archaic people as a campsite seven thousand years ago. People continued to use it throughout the Woodland period and built several burial mounds, some surrounded by a pentagonal earth wall. The people of the Mississippian period lived here around A.D. 900 and started a crescent-shaped burial mound. More than a thousand well-preserved skeletons have been found here. The museum is built directly over this prehistoric mound.

The main exhibit area is on the second floor, where colorful exhibits depict prehistoric life in the region from Paleo through Mississippian times. The museum adds something more with an audio-visual presentation, showing the history of other parts of the world during the same periods.

The actual excavation is the final part of the tour. In one wing of the museum more than two hundred skeletons can be seen in the place they were buried more than seven hundred years ago. On the wall above the skeletons, a slide show describes how these people lived.

Uncovered burials are not everyone's idea of fun, and the museum has plenty to offer besides the skeletons. Outside, at the foot of a hill, is Eveland Village, a prehistoric Indian site. And there is an Indian garden where vegetables grown by these early people are planted. You can buy seeds from the garden in the Museum Shop. There is also a picnic area with a large shelter and a nature trail.

DIRECTIONS: Dickson Mounds Museum is southwest of Peoria. The museum is located 2 miles off Route 78–97 between Lewistown and Havanna.

HOURS: 8:30 A.M.–5:00 P.M. daily. Advance reservations are suggested for group tours.
Closed Easter, Thanksgiving, Christmas, New Year's.

ADMISSION: Free.

PARKS

Three state parks in Illinois are rich in Indian heritage, although none has specific site interpretation. All of the parks have full recreational facilities and are open year round. During freezing and thawing periods, roads may be closed and the only access is by foot.

Grafton

- *Pere Marquette State Park*
R.R. 1, Box 203
Grafton, Illinois 62037 *(618) 786–3785*

In the park commemorating the work of Father Jacques Marquette, there are nature trails, campsites, stables, an excursion boat, and a lodge. Several prehistoric archaeological sites within the park date from around A.D. 1, and there are seven mounds. These sites are not generally open to the public. Ask the park ranger for information.

DIRECTIONS: From Alton, drive 19 miles northwest on the Great River Road to Grafton, then 5 miles west on Illinois 100 to the park entrance.
HOURS: A visitors' center is open from 8:00 A.M.–4:00 P.M. daily. The park closes at 9:00 P.M.

Savanna

• *Mississippi Palisades State Park*
4577 Route 84 North
Savanna, Illinois 61074 *(815) 273–2731*

The name "palisades" was given to these steep limestone bluffs along the Mississippi River because they resembled a similar geological formation on the Hudson River. There are twelve small conical mounds in the park, most of them located high on the bluffs. The mounds are believed to date from the early Woodland period. One small effigy mound appears to be in the shape of a goose. The mounds are unmarked, and there are no trails. If you wish to hike to the mounds, ask the park naturalist for directions.

The park has nearly two thousand acres of bluffs, prairies, and woods and offers a full range of recreational opportunities, including picnicking, camping, boating and boat rentals, and fishing. Groups are asked to reserve in advance. It is open all year and a ranger is on duty. A visitors' center accessible by self-guided trail offers a slide show and educational displays related to the park. It is located next to the park office. Weekend programs during the summer include guest speakers, field trips, and hikes.

DIRECTIONS: The park is located near the confluence of the Apple and Mississippi rivers in northwestern Illinois. It is 4 miles north of Savanna on Route 84.
HOURS: The park is open year round.
ADMISSION: Moderate fees for camping, boat rentals, and fishing licenses.

MUSEUMS

Carbondale

• *Southern Illinois University Museum*
Faner Building
Carbondale, Illinois 62901 *(618) 453–5388*

The museum holds extensive archaeological collections from all of the Midwest, but exhibits are not always up. Call ahead to check the current displays. Guest speakers frequently appear at archaeological seminars to which the public is invited.

HOURS: Monday–Friday: 10:00 A.M.–4:00 P.M.
Sunday: 1:30 P.M.–4:30 P.M.
Closed Saturdays and holidays.
ADMISSION: Free.

Chicago

• *Field Museum of Natural History*
Roosevelt Road at Lake Shore Drive
Chicago, Illinois 60605 *(312) 922–9410*

The Field Museum is one of the largest natural history museums in the world. Established in 1893 it has over ten acres of exhibits that survey the earth's history, including a world-famous collection of primitive art. Major exhibits cover American Indian, Chinese, and Tibetan cultures. Botanical displays, bird and animal dioramas, and a Hall of Gems are only a few of the special exhibits.

The story of prehistoric people in America is fully explored with an emphasis on the North Central region. A special exhibit of prehistoric life around the Chicago area is featured. Other displays describe early life on the Great Plains, in the Great Basin, California, and the Southwest, and on the Northwest Coast. Prehistoric Mexico and Central America are also explored. An especially interesting exhibit traces the relationship between the Stone Age people in the Old World and in North America.

In its collection the Field holds material from the original Hopewell site. Many of the exhibits show material that cannot be seen anywhere else in the world.

The museum also has a large library of natural history books available to the public. There is a restaurant and museum shop in the building. Lectures, films, educational programs for children, and courses open to students from Illinois' major universities are offered.

HOURS: 9:00 A.M.–4:00 P.M. in winter; until 5:00 P.M. in spring and fall.
Till 6:00 P.M. in summer (till 9:00 P.M. Fridays).
Closed Christmas and New Year's.
ADMISSION: Adults $1.50, children and students 50¢, senior citizens 35¢, families $3.50. Fridays free.

Edwardsville

- *Madison County Historical Museum*
  715 North Main Street
  Edwardsville, Illinois 62025 *(618) 656–7562*

Indian and pioneer artifacts are housed in this restored 1836 home. The American Indian collection includes nearly three thousand artifacts, some of which date back over four thousand years. Most artifacts come from local excavations, although some prehistoric material is from the Southwest. Little interpretation accompanies the exhibits.

HOURS: Wednesday–Friday: 9:00 A.M.–5:00 P.M.
Sunday: 2:00 P.M.–5:00 P.M.
Closed national and local holidays.
ADMISSION: Free.

Peoria

- *Lakeview Museum of Arts and Sciences*
  1125 West Lake Avenue
  Peoria, Illinois 61614 *(309) 686–7000*

Beginning in the fall of 1979, the Lakeview will feature an extensive exhibit of material recovered from the famous Koster site. This major archaeological display will be up for at least two years. One section of the museum is devoted exclusively to prehistoric findings from Illinois.

This arts and science center has changing exhibits and features concerts, lectures, and movies in its auditorium. Sky shows in the planetarium change monthly. There is a museum shop and book bazaar in the building.

HOURS: Tuesday–Saturday: 9:00 A.M.–5:00 P.M.
Sunday: 1:00 P.M.–5:00 P.M.
Also open Wednesday from 7:00 P.M.–9:00 P.M. except in the summer.
Closed major holidays.
Planetarium shows are presented on Wednesday, Saturday, and Sunday. Call for current schedule.
ADMISSION: General museum: free. Planetarium: Adults $1.50, children and students 75¢.

Springfield

- *Illinois State Museum*
  Spring and Edward Streets
  Springfield, Illinois 62706 *(217) 782–7386*

This excellent general museum contains natural history and fine and decorative arts exhibits. The major emphasis is on the wildlife and early inhabitants of Illinois. Exhibits of prehistoric people range from Paleo times to the historic period. Material recovered by the museum scientists from the Modoc Rock Shelter is on display, along with several excellent artifacts from various Hopewell sites.

Every summer the museum offers various science field trips. One-day field trips often include visits to archaeological sites and laboratories to trace the relationship among discovery, excavation, and analysis of artifacts. Write or call the museum for information about each summer's schedule.

Scientific reference books and reports on the museum collections are available for use on the premises. The museum also has regularly scheduled lectures and talks on science, education programs for children and adults, and college-level courses.

HOURS: Monday–Saturday: 8:30 A.M.–5:00 P.M.
Sunday: 1:30 P.M.–5:00 P.M.
Closed Easter, Thanksgiving, Christmas, New Year's.
ADMISSION: Free.

Urbana

• *University of Illinois Museum of Natural History*
Natural History Building
Matthew and Green Streets
Urbana, Illinois 61801 *(217) 333–2517*

American Indian and Eskimo cultures are the main focus in this university museum. Several cases of material trace the life of early Illinois people from around 8000 B.C. Tools, pottery, and stone artifacts are on display from every major cultural period. Other exhibits relate to natural history; the museum has more than three hundred thousand cataloged specimens in botany, geology, and zoology.

HOURS: Monday–Saturday: 8:00 A.M.–5:00 P.M.
Closed national holidays.
ADMISSION: Free.

STATE OFFICE

Charles J. Bareis
Secretary-Treasurer
Illinois Archaeological Survey
109 Davenport Hall
University of Illinois
Urbana, Illinois 61801

OPPORTUNITIES FOR AMATEURS

Every summer **Northwestern University** sponsors adult archaeological field schools at several endangered sites. The season is divided into regular and advanced sessions. No prior experience is required to join the regular field school. The advanced field school is reserved for amateurs who have already participated in at least one session of the regular program or have equivalent experience.

Participants may enroll in one- or two-week-long sessions. This gives even first-time applicants the chance to join both the regular and advanced session. For information, write or call:

Director of Special Programs
Northwestern Archaeological Program
P.O. Box 1499
Evanston, Illinois 60204 (312) 492-5300

The **Cahokia Mounds Museum Society** also sponsors an archaeological field school for amateur archaeologists. Members of the team work at different sites within Cahokia; the summer is divided into six sessions of two weeks each. Students work and learn under the supervision of experienced archaeologists and members of the Cahokia Mounds Museum staff. Tuition is minimal and everyone pays his or her own expenses. Primitive camping facilities are usually available.

Field school students must be at least eighteen years old and in good physical condition. Younger students are sometimes accepted with the signed consent of their parents.

Members of the Cahokia Mounds Museum Society receive newsletters that keep them fully informed of the progress at the site as well as opportunities to participate in digs and laboratory work. For information write or call:

Cahokia Mounds Museum Society
7850 Collinsville Road
East St. Louis, Illinois 62201 (618) 344-5268

ORGANIZATIONS TO JOIN

Illinois is a long state and is generally divided into regions. Different archaeological societies work in different parts of the state.

The major amateur organization in the state is the **Illinois Association for Advancement of Archaeology.** Both amateurs and professionals belong to the association, and the organization works closely with the Illinois Archaeological Survey. The main goal of the association is to encourage interest and participation in archaeology. Members of several local chapters join field schools and contribute their services wherever they are needed on digs throughout the state. The organization also publishes archaeological reports from the entire state.

The current president of the association is Naidyne Bridwell. She suggests that people interested in joining the association get in touch with William Iseminger, editor of the IAAA *Bulletin*. Mr. Iseminger is the site interpreter at Cahokia Mounds Museum. You may contact him at:

7850 Collinsville Road
East St. Louis, Illinois 62201 (618) 344-5268

In southern Illinois, the **Center for Archaeological Investigation** does limited work with amateurs. But if you have any questions about archaeology in this region or if you have made a discovery, report your find to this organization and someone will help you. The center plans to develop an amateur program, and seminars and lectures are frequently given at the university museum. For information, write or call:

Center for Archaeological Investigation
Department of Anthropology
Southern Illinois University
Carbondale, Illinois 62901 (618) 536-5529

The **Illinois Archaeological Society** is a private organization for professionals only. However, members hold a workshop for amateurs once a year during the annual meeting. This day-long presentation is widely attended, and it is an excellent opportunity for amateurs and the general public to learn about the latest activities of professional scientists in the state. Each year the meeting is held in a different region of the state, usually in the second week of November. To register, call or write:

Secretary-Treasurer
Illinois Archaeological Survey
108 Davenport Hall
University of Illinois
Urbana, Illinois 61801 (217) 333-1708

INDIANA

Prehistoric life in Indiana followed the pattern of most of the Eastern Woodlands. The first major game animal was the mastodon, and the fluted points of Paleo-Indian hunters have been found all over the plowed surface of Indiana farmlands. In the Archaic Period, the Wabash and Ohio river banks were heaped with shell mounds. And just before the early Woodland period began, the people of Indiana began to construct burial mounds. The Adena and Hopewell cultures were both expressed in this region. Angel Mounds, the largest site open to visitors in Indiana, was a prehistoric town that flourished during the late Mississippian period.

Indiana archaeology owes its outstanding reputation to two remarkable amateurs—Glenn A. Black and Eli Lilly, who together were responsible for developing archaeology in this state. Black began a professional career in archaeology and became the archaeologist for the Indiana Historic Society. Today, the dedication of these two men is reflected in the many museums and sites throughout the state.

SITES

Anderson

• *Mounds State Park*
4306 Mounds Road
Anderson, Indiana 46013 *(317) 642-6627*

This small park has several nature trails that lead through ravines and woods, over streams, and encircle nine prehistoric mounds built by the Adena and Hopewell people. In the spring the trails along the White River are lush with wildflowers. Most of the trails are easy, but two are moderately rough.

In 1968 the central mound was excavated and yielded several artifacts and six human burials. There is no interpretation or visitors' center at the site. You can camp, canoe, and fish in the park. There are also picnic areas and bridle paths.

DIRECTIONS: Drive east of Anderson just off I-69, via SR 109 and 32.
HOURS: Open year round, 8:00 A.M.–11:00 P.M.
ADMISSION: $1.25 per car; no charge in the winter.

Evansville

• *Angel Mounds State Memorial*
8215 Pollack Avenue
Evansville, Indiana 62242 *(812) 853-3956*

Along the banks of the Ohio River is Indiana's largest group of prehistoric mounds. From the Visitors' Center, self-guided trails take you across a small wooden bridge and out to reconstructed dwelling houses, a temple, and a palisade. A dozen mounds rise up across the wide grassy fields. The central mound is one of the largest in the country, measuring over forty-four feet high and four acres at its base.

A large prehistoric village flourished along the river from about A.D. 1300 to 1500. Eli Lilly purchased the site for the Indiana Historical Society in 1938, and noted archaeologist Glenn A. Black directed the excavations from that time until his death in 1964.

A modern interpretive center has a film about the site and also houses a simulated archaeological excavation along with several outstanding exhibits that explain the culture of the town's prehistoric occupants. These exhibits contain almost all of the artifacts recovered from the large site and the variety and interpretation of the displays are impressive.

A museum counter has books on archaeology and North American Indians for sale. No camping or picnicking is permitted in the state memorial.

DIRECTIONS: For some reason directional signs are few, and Angel Mounds is difficult to find. The best approach is from Evansville. Follow U.S. 41 south. Turn left at a marker onto Lincoln Avenue, which runs into Newburgh Road. Newburgh is a busy road overgrown with trees along its shoulders. It is difficult to read the street signs. Approximately 5 miles after the turn, look carefully for another marker at Fuquay Road. Turn right on Fuquay (the only way you can turn) and that road will take you to Pollack Avenue. Turn east on Pollack and that will take you directly to the park entrance.

HOURS: March–October 31
9:00 A.M.–5:00 P.M. daily.
Rest of year
Monday–Saturday: 9:00 A.M.–5:00 P.M.
Sunday: 1:00 P.M.–5:00 P.M.

ADMISSION: Adults 50¢, under twelve free.

MUSEUMS

Bloomington

- *Hoosier Heritage Complex*
University of Indiana — *Lab: (812) 337-9544*
Bloomington, Indiana 47401 — *Museum: (812) 337-7244*

Two important museums are opening in the new Hoosier Heritage Complex. The Glenn A. Black Laboratory of Archaeology (9th and Fess streets) has many interesting archaeological exhibits. A block away is the Mathers Museum, which is strong on the anthropology and folklore of Indiana. The museum holds Eskimo, South American, Southwestern, and Ohio Valley collections, which are intermittently displayed. The Mathers Museum is a new building that should be fully operational by 1981. Stop first at the Glenn A. Black Laboratory for information about the various archaeological exhibits in the complex.

HOURS (LABORATORY): Monday–Friday: 8:00 A.M.–12:00 M. and 1:00 P.M.–5:00 P.M.; appointment on weekends.
HOURS (MUSEUM): Monday–Saturday: 8:00 A.M.–12:00 M. and 1:00 P.M.–5:00 P.M.
Sunday: 1:00 P.M.–5:00 P.M.
ADMISSION: Free.

Indianapolis

• *Children's Museum of Indianapolis*
3000 North Meridian Street
Indianapolis, Indiana 46208 *(317) 924–5431*

This museum has as extensive a collection as most general museums and is a lot more fun. It is one of the finest cultural centers for young people in the nation. Exhibits emphasize natural history, science, and world cultures, and they focus especially on American Indians and early pioneers. Dioramas show children how prehistoric tools, weapons, and utensils were made and used.

The museum is loaded with other items that fascinate both children and adults. Craft classes, nature hikes, story hours, games, and other programs are offered free on the weekends (daily in the summer).

HOURS: Tuesday–Saturday: 10:00 A.M.–5:00 P.M.
Sunday and holidays: 1:00 P.M.–5:00 P.M.
Closed Thanksgiving, Christmas, New Year's.
ADMISSION: Free.

• *Indiana Historical Society*
315 West Ohio Street
Room 350
Indianapolis, Indiana 46202 *(317) 633-5277*

The society is primarily a library known for its outstanding collection of rare historical books, maps, and pictures relating to Indiana and the Old Northeast. The collection is available for use on the premises by any responsible person.

The society is a professional organization. Once a year, usually during the first week of November, members sponsor an annual program in archaeology to which the public is invited. Both professional and amateur archaeologists present reports, and all phases of archaeology in the state are discussed.

Anyone interested in Indiana archaeology should definitely plan to attend. For information and reservations, call the society.

HOURS: Monday–Friday: 8:15 A.M.–4:45 P.M.
Saturday: 8:30 A.M.–12:00 M.
Closed Sundays and holidays.
ADMISSION: Free.

- *Museum of Indian Heritage*
6040 DeLong Road
Indianapolis, Indiana 46254 *(317) 293-4488*

This museum is best known for its extensive collections of American Indian art. Prehistoric and historic Indian exhibits show material from the Eastern Woodlands, Northwest Coast, Southwest, and Plains Indian cultures. The Museum Shop has authentic American Indian arts and crafts for sale. The library's collection of books and films on Indian cultures is available for research.

HOURS: Tuesday–Friday: 1:00 P.M.–5:00 P.M.
Saturday and Sunday: 10:00 A.M.–5:00 P.M.
Other times by appointment.
Closed Christmas and the month of January.
ADMISSION: Adults $1.25, children four to twelve 60¢.

Peru

- *Puterbaugh Museum*
11 North Huntington Street
Peru, Indiana 46970 *(317) 472-3075*

Over 40,000 historical items and circus relics are housed in the Puterbaugh Museum and the neighboring **Miami County Historical Museum.** Generally a historical museum, the Puterbaugh has four large cases of prehistoric artifacts from Paleo, Woodland, and Mississippian times. Several displays and photographs describe the typical Woodland life of Indiana and Ohio.

HOURS: Monday–Saturday: 9:00 A.M.–12:00 M. and 1:00 P.M.–4:00 P.M.
Closed Sundays and holidays.
ADMISSION: Free.

STATE OFFICE

Dr. James H. Kellar, Director
Glenn A. Black Laboratory of Archaeology
Indiana University
9th and Fess Streets
Bloomington, Indiana 47401 (812) 337-9544

OPPORTUNITIES FOR AMATEURS

Indiana University has two summer programs that welcome amateurs. The **Archaeology Field School** is given for credit but anyone can apply. Contact the Glenn A. Black Laboratory (above) for a registration application. The field schools last about six weeks, and the registration fee usually covers all costs.

The **School of Continuing Education** sponsors a summer program for amateurs that is given in a one-week session. This is usually an extension of the Archaeology Field School and team members work together. Participants pay for their own expenses, which are minimal. Contact:

School of Continuing Education
Indiana University
Bloomington, Indiana 47401 (812) 337-4911

Indiana State University in Terre Haute sponsors an **Honors Field Program** for high school students. For information call (812) 232-6311.

ORGANIZATIONS TO JOIN

Amateur groups in the state are very active and associated with universities. The three leading societies work independently but come together for a spring workshop. Members are involved in all phases of archaeological activity including fieldwork and public education. The society addresses change with the election of new officers, and the best way to reach them is through their affiliated universities:

Wabash Valley Archaeological Society
c/o Anthropology Department
Indiana State University
Terre Haute, Indiana 47809 (812) 232-6311

Indianapolis Amateur Archaeological Association, Inc.
Glenn A. Black Laboratory of Archaeology
Indiana University
Bloomington, Indiana 47401 (812) 337-9544

Northwest Indiana Archaeological Association
c/o Anthropology Department
University of Notre Dame
South Bend, Indiana 46600 (219) 283-3873

IOWA

Two archaeological sites are in the northeast corner of Iowa, scattered along the high bluffs by the Mississippi River. In this far corner of Iowa, the Ice Age glaciers failed to level the land. Clear streams rush through ravines, and the rocky gorges are fringed with trees. Fish Farms Mounds and the famous Effigy Mounds National Monument are all in the area. Toolesboro Mounds are also near the river but at the southern end of the state.

SITES

McGregor

● *Effigy Mounds National Monument*
McGregor, Iowa 52157 *(319) 873-2356*

McGregor and Marquette are old Mississippi River towns with all the color that phrase implies. The three-mile road from McGregor to the monument travels along overgrown banks, looking more like the Deep South than northern Iowa. Campsites, canoes, and houseboats line the shore.

Effigy Mounds National Monument protects the famous Hopewell bear-shaped mounds. The Woodland people first lived here around 500 B.C. and built very simple, low mounds. About the time of Christ, the Hopewell people occupied the bluffs and began to construct effigy mounds in the shape of animals. Most of these, for some unknown reason, are shaped like bears. Copper axes, earrings, and bracelets, small pearl and silver-coated beads, and ornate breastplates typical of the Hopewellians have been found in excavations. Large villages grew up on the bluffs during the Mississippian period and the Oneota or Oneida culture appeared about A.D. 1300. Their ancestors, called the Ioway, were still farming here when Louis Joliet and Jacques Marquette explored the river, and it is for them that the state is named.

The bear-shaped mounds are almost completely obscured by woods. The best way to see the mounds is to join a guided walk along a beautiful trail accompanied by a park ranger. These walks last about an hour and are given on a regularly scheduled basis from Memorial Day to Labor Day. The ranger points out the mound groups and describes the life of the region's earliest people. A one-hour walk on a self-guided trail with trailside exhibits and markers leads to the major features within the monument, including the Little Bear Mound, Hopewell mounds, and scenic viewpoints from the

Dozens of prehistoric mounds are protected within Effigy Mounds National Monument. This famous line of Marching Bears is found in the south unit of the Monument. The outline is artificial. (Photo courtesy of the National Park Service.)

three-hundred-foot-high bluff tops. You can take a longer walk by following the Hanging Rock Trail.

Groups should make advance arrangements with the superintendent for guided walks. Stop first at the Visitors' Center, where museum exhibits and a slide presentation explain the background of the region. No camping or picnicking facilities are available here.

DIRECTIONS: From Marquette, drive 3 miles north on Iowa 76.
HOURS: 8:00 A.M.–5:00 P.M. daily (till 7:00 P.M. in summer). Closed Christmas.
ADMISSION: Free.

New Albin

• *Fish Farms Mounds*

This mound group from the Woodland period is all the way up in the far northeastern corner of the state. There is no interpretation here, but a small picnic area is perched on top of a high bluff overlooking the river. It is a beautiful place reached by a drive through the Yellow River State Forest. This is primitive country, full of wildlife, old pioneer farm buildings, and unusual plant life. Trout streams are plentiful in the Paint Creek area of the forest.

DIRECTIONS: From McGregor the most scenic road is north on Iowa 76 and 364 to Harpers Ferry; continue north on the county road to Lansing; take 26 north. Fish Farms Mounds is on Iowa 26, just 3 miles south of New Albin.

Wapello

• *Toolesboro National Historic Landmark*
Wapello, Iowa 52653

Toolesboro is all the way down in the southeastern part of the state, near the confluence of the Iowa and Mississippi rivers. Originally, there were nine Hopewell mounds at this site, but three have been completely destroyed by farming. During the late nineteenth century, the Davenport Academy of Natural Science excavated the three principal mounds and recovered skeletons, pottery, platform pipes, copper axes, mica ornaments, and pearl beads associated with the Hopewell people. Some of the pipes were plain with vase-shaped bowls. But the most spectacular ones were in the shape of frogs, ducks, rabbits, and birds.

This is a small site right on the road, and it's possible to drive by it. The Visitors' Center is open only in the afternoon during the summer, but you can walk through the park at any time. The Visitors' Center has displays and photographs of the Hopewell culture and samples of native grasses and flowers. Outside, there are interpretive signs for those who come by when the center is closed.

DIRECTIONS: The site is on Iowa 99, 8 miles east of Wapello.
HOURS: Memorial Day–Labor Day
1:00 P.M.–4:00 P.M., or by appointment.
Closed Tuesdays and Wednesdays.
ADMISSION: Free.

MUSEUMS

Davenport

• *Putnam Museum*
1717 West 12th Street
Davenport, Iowa 52804 *(319) 324-1933*

This art, history, and science museum is successor to the Davenport Academy of Natural Science, which was instrumental in many important excavations early in the twentieth century. The museum has displays of Mississippian pottery from Tennessee and Arkansas and some important Hopewell artifacts from Iowa and Illinois. A large library of history, natural history, and fine art books is available by special request. The museum has an aquarium, and a museum shop sells books, publications, and other items related to the collections.

HOURS: Tuesday–Saturday: 9:00 A.M.–5:00 P.M.
Sunday: 1:00 P.M.–5:00 P.M.
Closed Mondays and national holidays.
ADMISSION: Adults $1, children five to twelve 25¢, to eighteen 50¢. Free on Saturday between 9:00 A.M. and 12:00 M.

Iowa City

• *Museum of Natural History*
University of Iowa
MacBride Hall
Iowa City, Iowa 52240 *(319) 353-5893*

Mounted mammals, fish, reptiles, and birds are among the displays in this natural science museum. Permanent archaeological exhibits show special material from the Southwest and the Far North. The museum holds large collections of prehistoric artifacts and changes exhibits freqently.

HOURS: Monday–Saturday: 8:00 A.M.–5:00 P.M.
Sunday: 1:00 P.M.–4:30 P.M.
Closed national holidays.
ADMISSION: Free.

Sioux City

• *Sioux City Public Museum*
2901 Jackson Street (at 29th Street)
Sioux City, Iowa 51104 *(712) 279-6174*

Special emphasis is placed on the Plains and Woodland people of this region. Other displays include outstanding exhibits in history, the life sciences, and earth science. In addition to many geological, archaeological, and Indian exhibits, there are displays that portray life in pioneer days.

A museum shop offers seashells, books, Indian art prints, and other items of interest for sale. Classes for children and adults are offered in various fields of science.

HOURS: Tuesday–Saturday: 9:00 A.M.–5:00 P.M.
Sunday: 2:00 P.M.–5:00 P.M.
Closed major holidays.
ADMISSION: Free.

STATE OFFICE

Duane C. Anderson
State Archaeologist
University of Iowa
Iowa City, Iowa 52242 (319) 353-5175

OPPORTUNITIES FOR AMATEURS

Iowa offers a certification program for amateur archaeologists. The program is designed to promote a strong working relationship between professionals and the lay public. Amateurs may train in site survey, fieldwork, and laboratory analysis, and they can receive certification in any one of these programs. For information, write or call the state archaeologist (see above).

The office of the state archaeologist also publishes an educational series describing the various cultures in Iowa's prehistoric past. There are seven pamphlets in the series and you may request them from the above office. Films and filmstrips on North American archaeology are available for preview, rental, or purchase. The films are geared for elementary grades through college-level courses.

The **University of Iowa** also offers correspondence courses in archaeology. Courses are given in the history of Iowa archaeology, Iowa prehistory, and midwestern prehistory.

ORGANIZATIONS TO JOIN

The leading amateur-professional organization in the state is the **Iowa Archaeological Society.** Members are actively involved in preserving and studying Iowa's prehistoric and early historic heritage. They gather, record, publish, and interpret archaeological information and work closely with professional scientists in the state. Members receive the *Journal of the Iowa Archaeological Society*, published once a year, and the quarterly newsletter.

The statewide organization has several local chapters. Call or write the state archaeologist for details.

KENTUCKY

Prehistoric life in Kentucky evolved much the same as the rest of the Eastern Woodlands. Scattered evidence left by Big Game Hunters has been found across the entire state. When the large herds of mastodon and mammoth disappeared, the life style of the prehistoric hunters gave way to gathering wild fruits, nuts, and berries and hunting small game.

In the lower valley of the Green River, Archaic people fished with bone hooks and spears, and they dug mussels out of the river shoals. Their shell mounds litter the length of the river. The hunters moved with the seasons, returning to the same campsites over and over again. For thousands of years, they lived out their lives around these shell mounds and even buried their dead in them. In some seasons they lived higher up in the valley and found shelter in entrances to large caves. It is during this period that Mammoth Cave was occupied for the first time.

SITES

Mammoth Cave

• *Mammoth Cave National Park*
Mammoth Cave, Kentucky 42259 *(502) 758-2328*

The Woodland Tradition reached the region of Mammoth Cave around 1000 B.C. and within five hundred years was in full bloom. Pottery was used and wild plants were cultivated. Mammoth Cave was used intensively during the Woodland period between 1000 B.C. and A.D. 400. Now whole families lived in the entrance to the cave, and people ventured for miles into the deeper recesses to mine gypsum. No one knows why gypsum was so valuable to these prehistoric people—it may have been a salt substitute, a paint base, or a medicinal aid, but there is no direct evidence. One interesting suggestion is that the gypsum served as fertilizer and became more and more valuable as people began to cultivate wild plants. Whatever the reason for its value, the miners traveled as much as two miles into the cave as they exhausted the gypsum supply nearer to the entrance.

The period of early agriculture in Kentucky reached its climax in the Bluegrass region of the state. The Adena culture from the Ohio Valley made its imprint here. The people cultivated a great variety of plants and evolved the complex social system that typified Adena, including elaborate burials for honored dead. As the Adena culture reached its height, people moved away from Mammoth Cave and settled in the Bluegrass region or around the great rivers in the west. By A.D. 400 the cave region was virtually abandoned.

For centuries then, Mammoth Cave was forgotten. It may have been rediscovered sometime after A.D. 1300 by hunting groups paddling up the Green River. Evidence suggests that they found the opening and crawled or walked through many of the passages.

Around 1799 new Americans discovered the cavern. During the War of 1812, saltpeter was mined for gunpowder. It was during this mining operation that the first signs of the ancient people were discovered. A miner discovered a chamber three feet square behind a flat rock. Inside, covered with a blanket, was the mummified body of a young woman. Fabric sandals, deerskins, and a woven knapsack were by her side. The knapsack contained feather headdresses, a deer-hoof necklace, bone needles, two cane whistles, an eagle claw pendant, and two rattlesnake skins.

By 1816 Mammoth Cave was being exploited by promoters. Guides carried smoking torches as large parties of tourists picked their way through the passageways. Sightseers and guides carried off priceless objects made by prehistoric Indians.

More than a hundred years later a guide crawling through a passageway discovered another mummy—the perfectly preserved body of an ancient miner who had been killed by a falling boulder. He had lain on a ledge in the cave for twenty-four centuries.

Today Mammoth Cave and its rolling landscape have been preserved in a national park. A dozen different tours are conducted through intertwining passages totaling more than 190 miles. Tours vary in length from a half mile to five miles and take from one to six hours. Trails are solid, but all trips involve extensive walking and some are strenuous.

Two tours specialize in the history and archaeology of the cave. The **Lantern Tour** starts at the natural entrance of the cave and shows the War of 1812 mining operation. At Mummy Ledge the body of the ancient miner is preserved in a sealed glass case. Worn-out sandals and remnants of ancient torches have been left in place. At one time in recent history, the cave was the scene of an experiment aimed at curing tuberculosis, and the cure "huts" can be seen. The tour also visits the largest cave rooms, and there is a torch-throwing demonstration. The tour is conducted by lantern light. It is three miles long and takes approximately three hours. It is strenuous and involves steep grades, numerous steps, and stooping.

The **Historic Tour** includes part of the Lantern Tour route and features Fat Man's Misery and Mammoth Dome. Indian artifacts are seen, and the tour includes the torch-throwing demonstration. The Historic Tour is two hours and covers two miles.

All cave tours are conducted by experienced park naturalists. Come prepared; wear sturdy walking shoes and a sweater or jacket. (The average temperature inside the cave is 54° F.) The steps are often damp and slippery and lack of proper footwear will keep you off the tour.

There is a special tour for visitors confined to wheelchairs. The distance is about a half mile and takes about one and a half hours.

Above ground, the park covers fifty-two thousand acres of well-forested, rugged terrain bordered for twenty-four miles by the scenic Green River. Nature trails and longer hiking trails lead through forests to springs that emerge from the cave system. Seven miles of wooded trails along the river bluffs offer beautiful vistas. Ranger-guided walks are available. You can also take a one-hour boat trip on the Green River. Fishing is permitted in both the Green River and the Nolin River.

The Visitors' Center has information about all trips and activities in the park. A slide show tells the history of the cave, and a few artifacts recovered from the cavern are on display.

A hotel and heated cottages are open all year; unheated cabins are available from May to September. If you plan to stay in the park in the summer, write or call ahead to the Park Concessions for reservations. Accommodations are also available in nearby towns.

A dining room and coffeeshop are open all year; the service center next to the campground has a post office, service station, laundry, showers, groceries, and supplies.

DIRECTIONS: Drive 10 miles west of Cave City off I-65.
HOURS (VISITORS' CENTER): June–August: 7:30 A.M.–7:00 P.M. daily.
September–May: 8:00 A.M.–5:00 P.M. daily.
Closed Christmas Day.
ADMISSION: Prices vary with the tour.

Wickliffe

• *Ancient Buried City*
Wickliffe, Kentucky 42087 *(502) 335-3681*

Wickliffe is on high ground near the confluence of the Ohio and Mississippi rivers. Here, remnants of a Mississippian village are partially excavated and protected by shelters. Several temple mounds and one burial mound are on the site. This is a privately owned enterprise, and the exploration is not conducted by professional archaeologists. Material recovered from the mounds is on display.

DIRECTIONS: Wickliffe is 5 miles north of Cairo on U.S. 51 and 60. The site is in the northwest section of the city.
HOURS: Monday–Saturday: 9:00 A.M.–5:00 P.M.
Sunday: 12:00 M.–5:00 P.M.
Closed first two weeks in November.
ADMISSION: Adults $2, children $1.

MUSEUMS

Blue Lick Springs

• *Blue Licks Museum*
Blue Licks Battlefield State Park
Mount Olivet, Kentucky 41064 *(606) 289-7479*

For thousands of years animals have worn paths to Kentucky's salt licks. First came the giant mastodons and mammoths; then bison and other animals visited this spring in the northeastern part of the state. Hunters pursued the game and camped near the spring. People who followed the Fort Ancient lifeway (about A.D. 1400) built a permanent village here, now known as the Fox Field site. (Part of the vast Mississippian Tradition, the Fort Ancient people lived along prominent rivers in southern Ohio and in areas of Indiana, West Virginia, and Kentucky.)

The Fox Field site has been excavated, and artifacts recovered from the dig are on exhibit in the museum, which is located in a one-hundred-acre state park. Other exhibits contain projectile points, fishhooks, and stone tools. There is also a display of extinct animal skeletons. The museum also offers fine glassware collections as well as antique guns.

DIRECTIONS: From Lexington, drive 40 miles northeast on U.S. 68 to Blue Lick Springs; then follow directional markers.
HOURS: April 1–October 30: 9:00 A.M.–5:00 P.M. daily.
ADMISSION: Adults 75¢, children six to twelve 50¢.

Bowling Green

• *Kentucky Museum*
Kentucky Building
Western Kentucky University
Bowling Green, Kentucky 42101 *(502) 745-2592*

The university museum is currently undergoing renovation, but there are plans to reopen it in the summer of 1980. The museum houses large collections of prehistoric artifacts from Kentucky. These are always available to scholars by appointment. Exhibits are constantly changing, so it's a good idea to telephone ahead to find out what is on view. Other major displays concentrate on art, decorative arts, and historical items.

HOURS: Tuesday–Saturday: 10:00 A.M.–4:00 P.M.
Closed major holidays.
ADMISSION: Free.

Lexington

• *Museum of Anthropology*
Lafferty Hall
University of Kentucky
Lexington, Kentucky 40506 *(606) 258-4219*

University personnel have put together a history of Kentucky covering the evolution of human life in North America, with emphasis on the prehistoric Indians of Kentucky.

HOURS: Monday–Friday: 8:00 A.M.–5:00 P.M.
Closed holidays.
ADMISSION: Free.

Mount Olivet
(See Blue Lick Spring)

STATE OFFICE

State Archaeologist
Department of Anthropology
University of Kentucky
Lexington, Kentucky 40506

ORGANIZATIONS TO JOIN

All amateur and professional activities in the state are coordinated through the **University of Kentucky.** For information on current organizations and opportunities for amateurs, write the above address.

MICHIGAN

While ice still covered northern Michigan, Paleo-Indian hunters camped together on the shores of the glacial Great Lakes. As the glaciers retreated, everything about their lives changed. The climate grew softer, and the open tundra filled up with forests and dense tracts of conifers. Now the hunters traveled alone in the pursuit of moose, deer, bear, and a host of smaller animals. For the next seven thousand years, Michigan people stalked and trapped game and fish and gathered wild plant foods. This Archaic period in Michigan ends around 500 B.C., and the following interval up to European contact is called the Woodland period. During early Woodland times, men hunted and fished, and women learned to make a thick crude pottery impressed with a cord design. People also began to cultivate wild plants.

Around 100 B.C. the influence of the rapidly expanding Adena and Hopewell cultures reached the region. Isle Royale in Lake Superior joined the far-reaching Hopewell trade network, and burial mounds proliferated along the St. Joseph, Grand, and Muskegon rivers in the west and in the Saginaw Valley in the east. The greatest of these Michigan sites still standing is the Norton Mound group near Grand Rapids.

The agricultural revolution reached Michigan sometime between A.D.

700 and 1100. The late Woodland people of Michigan supplied furs and copper to major trade centers such as Cahokia in Illinois, but they never participated as fully in the great Mississippian Tradition as they had in the Hopewellian culture.

Farming was not practical in many parts of Michigan. Three distinct cultures evolved at this time that persisted into historic times. In the north families gathered together in the summers at large fishing camps. In the winter they scattered, and smaller groups hunted on their own. The pattern is similar to that of the early historic Chippewa.

In the south agricultural groups built large stockaded villages near their fields, similar to those of the historic Miami and Potawatomi. Between these two economic patterns, a third culture evolved in which farming was secondary to trapping and trading furs. These people, related to the historic Ottawa tribes, lived in large village sites and moved frequently.

Only in the nineteenth century did these distinctive patterns of Indian life fade. To some extent they exist even today, especially in northern Michigan where hunting and fishing are still a way of life.

SITES

Detroit

● *Historic Fort Wayne*
6325 West Jefferson Avenue — *(313) 849-0299*
Detroit, Michigan 48209 — *(313) 833-1805*

Fort Wayne is Detroit's most famous landmark. It was built in the 1840s at a strategic bend in the Detroit River. The dry moat, casements, brick tunnels, oak doors, and earthworks are preserved in and around a stone barracks building that is open to the public. American military uniforms and weapons are on display in the museum building.

Originally a group of mounds built twelve hundred years ago stood at this site on the river. All but one were destroyed when the fort was built. The mound was preserved and protected by the fort's commander. In 1944 the Aboriginal Research Club and the University of Michigan excavated the mound and the material recovered is on display in the museum.

HOURS: May–November
Wednesday–Saturday: 9:30 A.M.–5:00 P.M.
Sunday: 11:30 A.M.–7:00 P.M.
Closed Mondays and Tuesdays and all holidays.
The museum is also closed from the end of November until May 1. Visitors should call to check hours before going.

ADMISSION: Adults $1, juniors and senior citizens 50¢, under twelve 25¢.

Grand Rapids

• *Norton Mounds*

These burial mounds were made by the Hopewell Indians, whose culture flourished from about 300 B.C. to A.D. 400. The Norton Mounds are among the best preserved burial mounds in the Great Lakes region. Eleven clearly visible mounds remain from the forty that once stood on this site. Artifacts recovered from the mounds can be seen at the **Grand Rapids Public Museum.** The mound site itself is not interpreted but you can drive by it at any time and take a footpath to the mounds.

DIRECTIONS: From Campan Square in Grand Rapids, drive 4 miles south on Market Street, which becomes Indian Mound Drive.

Greenleaf Township–Sanilac County

• *Sanilac Petroglyphs*

Worn pictures of men, birds, and animals are carved into a ledge of sandstone near a fork in the Cass River. Some are so faded that they can only be seen at dawn or dusk when the angle of the sun's rays lights the surface of the stone. The petroglyphs are preserved in a shelter.

DIRECTIONS: From State 53, take the Bay City–Forestville Road about 4 miles east toward Minden City. Turn south on Germania Road and go 1/2 mile. The petroglyphs are posted, and there is a parking area.

Isle Royale

• *Isle Royale National Park*
87 North Ripley Street
Houghton, Michigan 49931 *(906) 482-3310*

Isle Royale in Lake Superior is an exceptionally primitive national park and one of the country's few remaining wilderness areas. The island is reached only by boat or seaplane, and only foot trails cross its forty-five-mile length. No automobiles or other vehicles are permitted.

Old lava flows on the island yielded various minerals, including the famous Isle Royale copper. Thousands of years ago, prehistoric Indians first dug pits to expose the rich deposits of native copper. One chunk found on the island weighed 5720 pounds. It may have weighed even more at one time. When white miners discovered the mass, it already bore clear traces where ancient tools had chiseled off pieces of copper.

The copper from Isle Royale was shipped up and down the rivers all along prehistoric trade networks for more than four thousand years. Copper from this site has been found in almost every part of the Midwest and Southeast.

Today Isle Royale is a wilderness paradise. Along the over 150 miles of foot trails are the remains of old abandoned copper mines. The island is completely primitive, and there is no development or interpretation of these sites.

There are many inland lakes and pools within the rugged boundaries of the park and the fishing is excellent. Swimming, however, is not recommended. During warm weather leeches are common in the lakes, and you are advised to keep your feet dry and carry salt with you.

The island's dense virgin forests are home to the world's largest herd of moose. More than two hundred smaller islands accessible by boat surround the main island, and there are many bays, inlets, beaches, and streams. Trails reach several small camping sites.

Directions: Isle Royale is in the northern part of Lake Superior and is actually closer to Minnesota than to Michigan. It is reached from Houghton or Copper Harbor in Michigan and from Grand Portage in Minnesota.

From Grand Portage: Only 22 miles separate the mainland from the park. Boats leave regularly. For day trippers a round-trip excursion boat leaves daily with a two-hour lunch or dinner stop at Windigo.

From Houghton: From this locale, 50 miles away, both boats and seaplanes go to the island. Boats also leave from Copper Harbor.

Accommodations: A lodge at Rock Harbor can be reached both from Houghton and Grand Portage; an inn at Washington Harbor is reached from Grand Portage.

For complete travel and lodging information, write the park superintendent at the above address. The park is usually open from May through October, depending on weather conditions.

Midland

• *Chippewa Nature Center*
400 South Badour Road
Route 9
Midland, Michigan 48640 *(517) 631-0830*

Exhibits in the museum start at the very beginning of geologic history and follow through to the present day. The design of all the exhibits fits into the Nature Center's theme of "Man, Through Time, in This Environment." Underwater dioramas represent oceans that were in this area millions of years ago. A series of exhibits follow the life of the prehistoric Indians from fourteen thousand years ago. Tools made by Paleo-Indians in Midland County are on display. Archaic tools and ceremonial objects found on the center's grounds and nearby sites are shown in a separate module. And the life of the Woodland Indians is portrayed in dioramas that display tools and a model of a typical birch-bark canoe. Other stories and legends tell of the coming of the European explorers, missionaries, and trappers.

The Museum Shop features nature books and field guides, Indian crafts, and binoculars. A library, reference collection, and classrooms are on the premises; interpretive programs are offered year round to members of the center.

Nature trails are open year round and you can pick up a trail guide in the center. Bring your binoculars (and skis in the winter).

Oxbow Archaeological District: Artifacts dating back to 5000 B.C. are being recovered from this nearby site and are on permanent display in the Chippewa Nature Center Museum. The area known as the Oxbow Archaeological District is under excavation each year. A field school is open both for credit and noncredit college students. Write or call the Nature Center for complete information.

HOURS: Monday–Friday: 8:30 A.M.–4:00 P.M.
Saturday: 9:00 A.M.–5:00 P.M.
Sundays and holidays: 1:00 P.M.–5:00 P.M.
Closed Thanksgiving and Christmas.
ADMISSION: Adults 50¢, children 25¢. Free to members.
Additional fees for special events.

MUSEUMS

Alpena

● *Jesse Besser Museum*
491 Johnson Street
Alpena, Michigan 49707 *(517) 356-2202*

Through a large collection of artifacts, the Gallery of Early Man traces the story of human life in the Great Lakes region. There is a special exhibit of prehistoric artifacts worked from native copper. Other permanent exhibits include a general store, a toy shop, a nineteenth-century barbershop, and a Foucault pendulum. A museum shop sells books and handicrafts.

HOURS: Monday–Friday: 9:00 A.M.–5:00 P.M. (also 7:00 P.M.–9:00 P.M. Thursday).
Saturday and Sunday: 1:00 P.M.–5:00 P.M.
Closed national holidays.
ADMISSION: Free. Planetarium: 50¢.

Ann Arbor

- *University of Michigan Exhibit Museum*
1109 Geddes Street (at North University Avenue)
Ann Arbor, Michigan 48109 *(313) 764-0480*

This large general science museum shows artifacts from Michigan's Early Indian sites. There are also examples from the prehistoric Eskimo, Northwest Coast, and Woodland cultures.

The connection between the Old World and New World is brought to life by comparisons of tools found on both sides of the Bering Strait.

Other exhibits include minerals and fossils. There is a planetarium. Books and crafts are for sale in the Museum Shop.

HOURS: Monday–Saturday: 9:00 A.M.–5:00 P.M.
Sunday: 1:00 P.M.–5:00 P.M.
Closed holidays.
ADMISSION: Free. Planetarium, 50¢.

Grand Rapids

- *Grand Rapids Public Museum*
54 Jefferson Avenue SE
Grand Rapids, Michigan 49503 *(616) 456-3977*

Material excavated from the nearby Norton Mounds where Hopewell people lived from A.D. 1 to 200 are on permanent display. Dioramas showing the life at the mounds also feature local finds. Of special interest is a historic-period village with streets paved with cedar blocks and lit by gaslight.

HOURS: Monday–Friday: 10:00 A.M.–5:00 P.M.
Saturday, Sunday, and holidays: 1:00 P.M.–5:00 P.M.
Closed Christmas and New Year's.
ADMISSION: Free. Planetarium: Adults $1, children and students 75¢.

Traverse City

- *Indian Drum Lodge Museum*
Camp Greilick
6419 West Bay Shore Road
Traverse City, Michigan 49684 *(616) 947-6379*

The museum is housed in a log cabin that once belonged to Chippewa Chief Peter Ringnose. Exhibits including ceremonial displays and weapons present a complete picture of how the Woodland Indians lived in Michigan before the coming of Europeans.

Traverse City is a frontier timber town that has become one of the largest cherry marketing cities in the country. **Interlochen Center for the Arts** and **Interlochen State Park** are located here, and the town has a charming zoo.

DIRECTIONS: The museum is in Camp Greilick (Scenic Trail Council, Boy Scouts of America), approximately 12 miles southeast of Traverse City on Hobbs Highway. Directional signs are on the highway.

HOURS: Museum hours are geared to camping schedules in the summer.
June–August
Monday–Friday: 1:00 P.M.–2:00 P.M. and 6:30 P.M.–8:00 P.M.
Sunday: 2:00 P.M.–5:00 P.M. and 6:30 P.M.–8:00 P.M.
Closed September to May, except by appointment.

ADMISSION: Free.

STATE OFFICE

John R. Halsey
State Archaeologist
Michigan History Division
Michigan Department of State
Lansing, Michigan 48918 (517) 373-0510

OPPORTUNITIES FOR AMATEURS

At **Fort Michilimackinac,** a major historical excavation goes on each summer. Amateurs are sometimes used on excavation crews. For information, write:

Dr. Donald P. Heldman
Staff Archaeologist
Fort Michilimackinac Historic Park
Mackinaw City, Michigan 49701

ORGANIZATIONS TO JOIN

The Michigan Archaeology Society publishes the quarterly *Michigan Archaeologist.* Members are involved in various archaeological activities and sometimes participate in professional projects. Both amateurs and professionals belong to this society, and the address of its current secretary can be gotten from the office of the state archaeologist (see above).

MINNESOTA

A skull found at Brown's Valley reveals that people have lived in Minnesota for at least twelve thousand years. The prehistoric people in this region followed the lifeways that evolved in most parts of the Midwest, but they continued to hunt and fish as a principal way of life into historic times. The great mound-building societies of the late Woodland period definitely reached Minnesota, and at one time more than ten thousand burial mounds rose in the state. All but a few of these have been destroyed.

Minnesota is home to the nationally famous Pipestone National Monument, a stone quarry sacred to both prehistoric and historic Indians. And the Jeffers Petroglyphs site contains one of the world's largest concentrations of rock pictures.

Minnesota is also home to one of the pre-Columbian Viking sites: The controversial Kensington Runestone was turned up by a farmer plowing his field in 1898. Some historians believe it is genuine, while others consider it a hoax. The original runestone can be seen in the Runestone Museum in Alexandria, Minnesota. A twenty-six-ton replica stands in the middle of Highway 52 in Kensington.

Minnesota is one of the great outdoor states, and wherever you go to look at archaeological sites you will travel in magnificent country.

SITES AND MUSEUMS

International Falls

• *Mound Group*
International Falls, Minnesota 56640 *(218) 279-3332*

Up on the Rainy River, prehistoric people built a group of large burial mounds. Until recently, no one knew who these people were or where they came from. Pothunters had ravaged the site for years, carrying away beautiful objects easily dug out of the sides of the mound. The mounds were not scientifically investigated until 1933. Even with only a few remaining artifacts, archaeologists were able to distinguish several traits specific to these mound builders, whom they identified as the Laurel people.

The Laurel were a Woodland people who practiced an unusual system of burial. They first dismembered the corpse, a common practice among other Woodland clans, but then extracted the contents of the skull and long bones before burying the body in a bundle. Smoothly finished Laurel pottery also was easily distinguished from other Woodland ceramics. And two unusual tools were uncovered at the excavation—a toggle-head harpoon point and a beaver-tooth chisel.

The Laurel people occupied a vast area stretching all the way from the northern shore of Lake Huron to the edge of the Great Plains in east central Saskatchewan. They reigned over this large region from approximately 200 B.C. to A.D. 800, surviving mostly by hunting and fishing.

Tools, pottery, and weapons of the Laurel culture are displayed in the interpretive center at the Mound Group. Early white explorers and settlers gouged many of the mounds in Minnesota for treasure, and most were lost eventually under the farmers' plows. The mounds at this site are among the few remaining in the state. The Grand Mound is about forty feet high and one hundred feet at its base.

International Falls is right on the Canadian border and a long trip from almost anywhere. It is impressive in its isolation, and a drive to the Mound Group up on the Rainy River is a beautiful trip.

DIRECTIONS: The site is 17 miles west of International Falls on State 11.
HOURS: May 1–October 31
10:00 A.M.–5:00 P.M. daily. Rest of year by appointment.
ADMISSION: Free.

Jeffers

- *Jeffers Petroglyphs*
  Jeffers, Minnesota 56145

This is one of the most famous petroglyph sites in the United States and certainly one of the largest. Trails across the flowering prairie of the Little Cottonwood Valley take you to more than two thousand pictures at eighteen different sites. At one site the pictures are carved on pale pink quartzite rippled by waves that rolled over the land a billion years ago. At another place on the trail, ancient people carved a picture of a spear thrower, one of the few petroglyphs where the atlatl is depicted. At other sites stickmen with horned headdresses, bird tracks, and bison are carved.

The pictures are estimated to date from two major prehistoric periods: late Archaic–early Woodland (3000 B.C.–A.D. 500) and late Woodland (A.D. 900–1750). The site is administered by the Minnesota Historical Society in Fort Snelling, St. Paul. Tours for groups can be arranged by calling (507) 877-3647 or (612) 726-1171.

DIRECTIONS: Jeffers is in the southwest corner of Minnesota, off U.S. 71 and MN 30.
HOURS: Open daily during the summer.

Onamia (Mille Lacs)

- *Mille Lacs Indian Museum and Trading Post*
  Onamia, Minnesota 56359 *(612) 532-3632*

This museum has outstanding exhibits that draw on impressive Indian collections. Exhibits describe Sioux and Chippewa tribal life. The customs and activities of the Chippewa—including building canoes, weaving, and tanning hides—are explained. In Onamia the Indians hold their Rice Dance every September before harvesting the season's crop of wild rice. Mille Lacs Lake is one of the state's best for fishing.

DIRECTIONS: The museum is 10 miles northwest of Onamia on U.S. 169.
HOURS: May–September: 9:00 A.M.–5:00 P.M. daily.
Closed October–April.
ADMISSION: Adults $1, under sixteen with an adult, senior citizens free.

Pipestone

• *Pipestone National Monument*
Box 727
Pipestone, Minnesota 56164 *(507) 825-5463*

From earliest times carved pipes and tobacco were used in Indian ritual ceremonials. Four hundred years ago people associated with the Oneota culture began to come to this region to quarry a soft reddish stone they used to fashion ceremonial pipes. The quarriers traveled as much as a thousand miles on foot to obtain the stone. Because the pipes frequently were used to seal treaties, they became known as peace pipes. The quarry was a sacred place known to many tribes over the entire northern region.

Early in historic times, the Sioux controlled the region and retained the quarry until 1893, long after whites had wrested away the rest of Minnesota. Among the early visitors to the site was the painter George Catlin. Catlin observed the quarrying and in the early nineteenth century wrote about the stone and the Indians who used it to make pipes. Eventually the beautiful stone took on his name and became known as catlinite. The monument was established in 1937, and the right to quarry the sacred pipestone was granted exclusively to Indians of all tribes.

The thin soft layer of catlinite is embedded between layers of much harder stone called Sioux quartzite. Catlinite is easily carved when it is first quarried, but hardens after it is exposed to the air. The bed of pipestone is on a slope. As the Indians continued to dig the stone, they had to dig deeper and deeper to reach it. In some areas nearly twelve feet of quartzite have been removed. Heavy equipment and explosives are not allowed in the quarry operations since it would shatter the soft, brittle pipestone.

Nature trails through the park take you through fascinating geological formations and a wide variety of bird and animal life abounds. A small section of virgin prairie is preserved at the monument site.

The **Indian Culture Center,** located within the monument, is a marketplace for Indian art. The Indian people demonstrate how they make many of their traditional crafts, and naturally one of the crafts demonstrated is pipe making.

Begin your visit at the Visitors' Center and Culture Center. Museum exhibits and an audio-visual program give you the history of the site, and rangers are on hand to answer questions. The three-quarter-mile self-guided trail takes you past the quarries and many other scenic and historic points of interest. A trail guide is available at the Visitors' Center.

Lodging is available in nearby Pipestone and other surrounding communities. Camping is allowed at Split Rock Creek State Park (MN 23 south of Pipestone) and Blue Mounds State Park (U.S. 75 south of Pipestone). Rangers can give you the location of private campgrounds and other overnight facilities. A state information center is located at Beaver Creek, directly off I-90.

DIRECTIONS: The monument is just north of the city of Pipestone and can be reached by U.S. 75 and MN 23 and 30.
HOURS: Memorial Day–Labor Day: 8:00 A.M.–9:00 P.M. daily.
Rest of year: 8:00 A.M.–5:00 P.M. daily.
Closed Christmas and New Year's.
ADMISSION: Free.

STATE OFFICE

Christie A. H. Caine
State Archaeologist
Council for Minnesota Archaeology
Hamline University
St. Paul, Minnesota 55104 (612) 641-2253

OPPORTUNITIES FOR AMATEURS

Anyone interested in visiting an excavation-in-progress or volunteering his or her services should write to the **Council for Minnesota Archaeology** (see above).

ORGANIZATIONS TO JOIN

A joint lay-professional effort of the **Council for Minnesota Archaeology** and the **Minnesota Archaeological Society** offers a paraprofessional certification program for amateurs. Once certified, members can work on professional excavations all over the state. The society publishes the *Minnesota Archaeologist.* The address and telephone for this statewide organization are:

Minnesota Archaeological Society
Building 27
Fort Snelling
St. Paul, Minnesota 55111 (612) 726-1630

MISSOURI

From the earliest times of human life in the New World, the region now known as Missouri has been home to many different peoples. Many kinds of pottery, spear points, tools, and ornaments of stone and shell testify to a wide range of cultures dating from Paleo times all the way into the historic period.

Ancient tunnels have been found in parts of the state where prehistoric miners crawled through narrow passages more than twenty feet deep to obtain red and yellow iron oxides to make paint. Flint was used to fashion small objects such as projectile points; granite and other igneous rocks were used for the larger, coarser implements. Knives, scrapers, hoes, and axes have been found everywhere. Metates and grinding stones testify to a time in prehistory when corn was widely grown in the valleys along the Missouri and Mississippi rivers.

All of these remains come together at a few sites, particularly at Graham Cave, where evidence of human occupation is clearly seen in stratification beginning ten thousand years ago and continuing almost into historic times. The cave, which is still being investigated, lies within a state park in the east central portion of the state.

Lifeways in Missouri apparently followed the same pattern of development as the rest of the Eastern Woodlands. Toward the end of the Ice Age, Big Game Hunters lived in bluff shelters; some of these, like Graham Cave, were more or less continuously occupied for thousands of years. Baskets, mats, fine garments of feathers, decorated bones—all have been found in Missouri caves. After the big game died out, Archaic people lived in the region, surviving on seeds, berries, and small game. Cultivation of wild plants introduced the Woodland Tradition and the Hopewellian sphere of influence. Hopewell mounds and artifacts have been found all along the river valleys, particularly in the southeastern corner of the state. Conical, square, oblong, and animal-shaped mounds have been discovered all over this region.

Large pyramidal mounds identified with the later Mississippian culture dominated a swath of land six to ten miles wide, extending from Missouri's Cape Girardeau to northeastern Arkansas. Most of these mounds have been obliterated by weather, farming, or industrial expansion. Stone carvings of animals, human heads, copper objects embossed with eagles, double eagles, and man-eagles have been found in various mound sites. Obsidian, copper, and conch shells all testify that high cultures were present in Missouri. These remains indicate occupation by an agricultural people over a considerable length of time, probably from the early Hopewell through the late Mississippian cultures.

SITES

DeSoto

- *Washington State Park*
  DeSoto, Missouri 63020 *(314) 586-2995*

Hundreds of ancient **petroglyphs** have been discovered within this fifteen-hundred-acre park. The rock carvings are the remains of a once extensive ceremonial ground that probably belonged to people who followed the high Mississippian Tradition (A.D. 1000–1600). Archaeologists believe the carvings were signs to help celebrants enact long, complex religious cermonies.

Many of the petroglyphs have disintegrated due to the highly acidic soil that has washed or blown over them. But many designs of birds, crosses, arrows, footprints, claws, human figures, and snakes can still be made out.

Two major petroglyph concentrations are located in the southern portion of the park along Highway 21 and near the **Nature Museum** in the park. The museum has some archaeological exhibits, and you can pick up a trail folder at the desk that gives directions to the sites.

A dining lodge, general store, and cabins are located within the park. For cabin reservations, call (314) 586-6696. In addition, there are ninety-six campsites in the park, eighteen with electrical hookups. All campsites are available on a first-come basis for a maximum continuous stay of fifteen days.

Washington State Park offers a unique "Learn to Camp" service for beginning campers. During summer weekdays the Division of Parks and Recreation will outfit a family with basic camping equipment needed for a three-day campout. An experienced camp programer stays with the family, teaching each member basic camping skills and suggesting recreational activities. The total cost of the program is $9, including registration and basic camping fees for two nights. For reservations contact:

Division of Parks and Recreation
P.O. Box 176
Jefferson City, Missouri 65102

Swimming, fishing, and canoeing are permitted within the park. Boats can be rented from the concessionaire.

DIRECTIONS: From Bonne Terre drive 15 miles northeast via MO 47 and 21.

East Prairie

- *Towosahgy State Archaeological Site*
  East Prairie, Missouri 63845

Towosahgy, an Osage Indian word meaning "old town," was once a fortified prehistoric village of the thriving Mississippian culture. All of the complex religious and ceremonial aspects usually associated with the Mississippian Tradition may one day be uncovered here. At present the only visible remains are the earthen mounds built within the village area.

Modern agriculture has erased most of the surface evidence of the village, but aerial photographs have helped archaeologists plot the village and outlying fortification. The photographs revealed an outline of trenches. Post holes and charred fragments of three log stockade walls were found beneath the outline. A bastion that may have been used as a watchtower or blockhouse was discovered protruding out from the stockade. Bastions may have been set at intervals along the fortification.

Although the archaeological investigation is still in its early stages, Towosahgy is believed to have been occupied between A.D. 1000 and 1400. The work continues here under the supervision of the University of Missouri, Columbia, in cooperation with the Missouri State Park Board.

Eventually, Towosahgy may be developed as a permanent state park. For the present the site is open to visitors only during summer excavations during June, July, and August. There are no park facilities, and no special programs have been prepared for visitors. For current information about Towosahgy, write:

Division of Parks and Recreation
Missouri Department of Natural Resources
P.O. Box 176
Jefferson City, Missouri 65102

DIRECTIONS: From East Prairie drive east on Highway 80; turn south on County AA for 2 miles and then go south on County FF for 3 miles. After that, go east 1 mile on gravel and then south 1 mile on gravel.

Kirksville

- *Thousand Hills State Park*
  Kirksville, Missouri 63501 *(816) 665-6995*

The unique aspect of this large state park is its petroglyphs site. Although badly eroded over the years by wind and water, many carvings of squares, ovals, circles, bird tracks, footprints, and animals are still clearly visible. Archaeologists think they may have been carved during the Woodland period, sometime between A.D. 400 and 900. During the summer a park naturalist conducts guided nature hikes and evening nature programs.

The park surrounds Forest Lake, a local recreation area for swimming, boating, and fishing. Four campgrounds in the park provide eighty-four campsites, thirty-nine with electrical hookups. Dump stations, restrooms, hot showers, and a laundromat are available in the camping areas. Campsites are available year round on a first-come basis. Five duplex cabins are available for rent by reservation. Call (816) 665-7719.

A dining lodge and a lakefront stand where food and fishing bait are sold are within the park. Boats can be rented from the concessionaire.

DIRECTIONS: From Kirksville in the northern part of Missouri, drive 4 miles west on MO 6, then 2 miles south to the park.

Miami

• *Van Meter State Park*
Miami, Missouri 65344 *(816) 886-7537*

Archaeological evidence uncovered in this park shows that prehistoric people inhabited the hills and valleys of the region as early as 10,000 B.C. After the Big Game Hunters, Archaic people continued to live here. Their long, slender, finely worked spear points have been found all over the area.

Then came the early Hopewell people, who erected earthen monuments to honor their sacred dead. Burial grounds and prehistoric weapons have been located in the nearby "mounds field" and on the bluffs of the Missouri River north of the park. These burial mounds were probably built by the late Woodland people, descendants of the Hopewellians.

The last prehistoric people to inhabit the area were the Missouri Indians, who built a large village here during the seventeenth century. Beneath the meadow and forests of the park lies one of the most extensive and concentrated assemblages of Indian remains in North America. Great storage and trash pits filled with artifacts, skeletons of humans and animals, house foundations, and workshops have been discovered.

Atop a high hill in the park, the people built a large earthwork called the Old Fort. A ditch and embankment parallel one another around the hilltop. The enclosure is more than a thousand feet long and averages about three hundred feet in width. A palisade of logs probably was erected in the inner trench to protect the village area. Even before the new frontier advanced to Missouri, this great village had been abandoned.

The **Lyman Archaeological Research Center,** located on the east side of the park, is engaged in a major excavation of this site (see listing below). During the summer visitors to the park are welcome to observe the dig. Visitors are not permitted to dig or remove archaeological artifacts from the park.

Many hiking trails go through the park, which is one of the most beautiful forested regions of Missouri; picnicking, fishing, and camping are allowed within the park. Camping at the twenty-five campsites is on a first-come basis. There are hot showers, restrooms, and fire grills in the camping area.

DIRECTIONS: From Marshall drive 8 miles north on MO 41 to MO 122; then go 4 miles west to the park.

• *Lyman Archaeological Research Center*
and Hamilton Field School
R.F.D. 1
Miami, Missouri 65344

This 150-acre site is one of the largest archaeological excavations in the country. The principal excavation is the **Utz site,** an Oneota farming and hunting community that began around A.D. 1550 and lasted into historic times (approximately 1712). The dig will continue here for several years and the public is welcome to observe during the summer months. The **Research Center** located on the site is part of the University of Missouri.

The summer excavations usually last from the first week in June until the first week in August. An on-site museum, open during the excavating season, displays the artifacts recovered from all the digs in the area.

University teams are sometimes here in the winter months. If you would like to visit the site off-season, drop a note to the director, Mr. Robert Bray, at the above address.

DIRECTIONS: Lyman is in the west central part of the state. From Marshall drive 8 miles north on MO 41 to MO 122; then go 4 miles west to Van Meter State Park. The center is on the northeastern edge of the park.

HOURS: June 1–September 1: Tuesday–Sunday: 8:00 A.M.–5:00 P.M. Other times by written appointment.

Montgomery City

• *Graham Cave State Park*
Montgomery City, Missouri 63361 *(314) 564-3476*

This 120-foot **natural rock shelter** is one of the most important archaeological sites in the Midwest. At Graham Cave archaeologists first learned that people had inhabited this region during Paleo times.

Prehistoric people did not live continuously in the shelter but hunted and camped in the surrounding region, probably returning to the cave during cold weather. Sometimes the cave was abandoned for years or decades at a time; then dust storms from the north blew in and covered the layers of refuse scattered on the cave floor. During the 1950s archaeologists uncovered layer after layer of well-preserved strata, digging more than six feet into the floor of the cave. The bottom layer contained remains dating back ten thousand years.

The earliest people to live in the cave hunted big game with spears tipped with a lanceolate point called Graham Cave fluted. As the big game died out, the people began to follow the Archaic lifeways, gathering seeds and berries and hunting small game to exploit the changing environment. Pieces of hardened clay carrying a fabric imprint show that weaving was known, although no pieces of actual material have been preserved over these long millennia. Small-eyed bone needles indicate that clothing was sewn and fitted. Pestles and flat rocks, ideal for grinding seeds and berries into flour, also were found.

Graham Cave is named after the first settler to own the cave property, Dr. Robert Graham, who bought the site in 1816. Today, the cave proper is not open to the public because it has not yet been fully excavated. But visitors to the park can approach and peer into the cave, and signs point out interesting discoveries.

There are fifty-three campsites in the park, with a dump station, restrooms, and hot showers. Camping is available year round for a maximum continuous stay of fifteen days; there are picnicking facilities and hiking trails.

DIRECTIONS: From Hermann drive 13 miles north on MO 19 to I-70 West. Take the Danville–Montgomery City exit off I-70, and follow the directional signs to the park.

MUSEUMS

Branson

• *Ralph Foster Museum*
School of the Ozarks
Point Lookout, Missouri 65726 *(417) 334–6411*

This museum has an extensive collection of Indian artifacts found in the Ozark region. On display are artifacts of the Ozark Bluff Dwellers along with material from later Indian cultures. There is also an impressive display of hundreds of samples of Mississippian pottery.

Students from this four-year liberal arts college join museum staff members in local archaeological digs. The museum also has large collections of gems and minerals, mounted animals, arms, apothecary antiques, and art.

DIRECTIONS: From Springfield drive 40 miles south on U.S. 65. The school is 3 miles south of Branson on U.S. 65 at Point Lookout (near Hollister).
HOURS: May 31–November 15
Monday–Saturday: 8:00 A.M.–5:00 P.M.
Sunday: 1:00 P.M.–5:00 P.M.
November 16–May 30
Tuesday–Saturday: 9:00 A.M.–5:00 P.M.
Sunday: 1:00 P.M.–5:00 P.M.
Closed Thanksgiving, Christmas, New Year's.
ADMISSION: Free.

Columbia

- *Museum of Anthropology*
University of Missouri
100 Swallow Hall
Columbia, Missouri 65201 *(314) 882–3764*

This museum houses a particularly fine display from the Mississippian period (A.D. 1100–1500), including a full-sized reconstruction of a Mississippian village house. The exhibits also show examples of Indian cultures from the Paleo to historic times. There are dioramas of a big-game hunt, a Woodland burial mound, and a Mississippian temple mound.

HOURS: Monday–Friday: 9:30 A.M.–12:00 M. and 1:00 P.M.–4:30 P.M.
Saturday: 11:00 A.M.–3:00 P.M.
Closed Sundays and holidays.
ADMISSION: Free.

Jefferson City

- *Missouri State Museum*
State Capitol Building
High Street and Broadway
Jefferson City, Missouri 65101 *(314) 751–2854*

The state museum has among its exhibits a restored Indian burial rescued from a local site that is now flooded by a reservoir. Dioramas show Archaic Indian life, pottery making, and an Indian paint mine. Other exhibits show how some of the artifacts on display were actually made. The museum also houses an excellent collection of firearms and several Civil War relics. It has everything from a zither collection to a display of moon rocks.

HOURS: 8:00 A.M.–5:00 P.M. daily.
Closed Easter, Thanksgiving, Christmas, New Year's.
ADMISSION: Free.

Kansas City

- *Kansas City Museum of History and Science*
3218 Gladstone Boulevard
Kansas City, Missouri 64123 *(816) 483–8300*

The museum, housed in the old R. A. Long mansion, features the cultural and natural history of the Kansas City area. The natural history hall displays North American Indian artifacts from both historic and prehistoric times. In the prehistoric displays there is an extensive collection of Archaic and early Woodland artifacts.

A burial removed from a closed excavation of a Hopewell site in the area is shown here as it was found by archaeologists. Other material from this site is also on display.

The museum also has period costume exhibits, a gift shop, and a planetarium. The historical archives are available for research on the premises.

HOURS: Tuesday–Saturday: 9:30 A.M.–4:30 P.M.
Sunday: 12:30 P.M.–4:30 P.M.
Closed Mondays, Thanksgiving, Christmas, New Year's.
ADMISSION: Free. Planetarium: Adults $1, children 50¢.

- *William Rockhill Nelson Gallery and*
Atkins Museum of Fine Arts
4525 Oak Street
Kansas City, Missouri 64111 *(816) 561-4000*

This impressive museum is famous for its Indian art collections, which are considered among the country's best. Indian pottery and jewelry are displayed in the prehistoric exhibits. Exhibits from Sumerian art of 3000 B.C. to period rooms and contemporary paintings and sculpture are on permanent display. The museum is equally well known for its collection of Chinese art, English pottery, and miniatures.

HOURS: Tuesday–Saturday: 10:00 A.M.–5:00 P.M.
Sunday: 2:00 P.M.–6:00 P.M.
Closed Mondays and major holidays.
ADMISSION: Adults $1, children six to twelve 50¢, under six free.

St. Joseph

- *St. Joseph Museum*
  301 South 11th Street (at Charles Street)
  St. Joseph, Missouri 64501 *(816) 232-8471*

Here is a major collection dedicated to the full spectrum of American Indian life in both prehistoric and historic times. Material from all major cultures and periods is on display. There also are fine natural history and western history exhibits in the museum.

HOURS: May–September
Monday–Saturday: 9:00 A.M.–5:00 P.M.
Sunday and holidays: 2:00 P.M.–5:00 P.M.
October–April
Tuesday–Saturday: 1:00 P.M.–5:00 P.M.
Sunday and holidays: 2:00 P.M.–5:00 P.M.
Closed Thanksgiving, Christmas Eve and Day, New Year's Eve and Day, and winter Mondays.
ADMISSION: Adults 50¢, children under twelve 25¢, senior citizens free.

St. Louis

- *Missouri Historical Society*
  Lindell Boulevard and De Baliviere Avenue
  St. Louis, Missouri 63112 *(314) 361-1424*

Exhibits of prehistoric artifacts here represent all of the major cultural periods from Paleo through Mississippian times. Most of the material displayed was recovered from archaeological excavations in the middle Mississippi River Valley and other parts of Missouri. The museum has an exceptional collection of prehistoric pottery. Other sections of the museum are devoted to period costumes, firearms, decorative arts, and western history exhibits.

HOURS: 9:30 A.M.–4:45 P.M. daily.
Closed July 4, Thanksgiving, Christmas, New Year's.
ADMISSION: Free.

- *Museum of Science and Natural History*
  Oak Knoll Park
  Clayton and Big Bend Roads
  St. Louis, Missouri 63105 *(314) 726-2888*

A hall devoted to the American Indian contains displays of prehistoric material dating from 8000 B.C. to A.D. 1500. Most of the artifacts date from the Mississippian period and were recovered from digs in Missouri and Illinois.

Besides a mineral hall and a hall of physics, the museum features a life-size dinosaur exhibit, a transparent model of a woman, and a simulated earthquake.

HOURS: 9:00 A.M.–5:00 P.M. daily.
Closed on Mondays from November to March.
Closed July 4, Labor Day, Thanksgiving, Christmas, New Year's.
ADMISSION: Free.

STATE OFFICE

Archaeological Survey of Missouri
University of Missouri
15 Switzler Hall
Columbia, Missouri 65211 (314) 882-2121

OPPORTUNITIES FOR AMATEURS AND ORGANIZATIONS TO JOIN

The **Missouri Archaeological Society** is a lay-professional organization that works closely with the Archaeological Survey. Members are kept up to date on opportunities to participate in professional excavations and laboratory work. The society distributes several excellent publications to members, including the annual journal *Missouri Archaeologist*, a monthly newsletter, and at least three other publications each year. Two annual meetings bring members together from various parts of the state. Apply for membership by writing or calling:

Missouri Archaeological Society
15 Switzler Hall
University of Missouri
Columbia, Missouri 65211 (314) 882-2121

OHIO

Burial mounds, effigy mounds, tremendous geometrical earthworks, and great defensive walls—Ohio contains more remains of the mound builders' art than any other state. The Ohio Valley was the home of both the Adena and Hopewell people, and their great earthworks are among the most spectacular prehistoric ruins in North America.

Large-scale geometric enclosures show that the early Hopewell people were capable of highly precise surveying and construction. A connection between the Ohio mounds and earthworks and those of Teotihuacán, an ancient city of pyramids near Mexico City, has always been theorized, but never proved. One recent discovery suggests that the Ohio earthworks were built according to the same standard unit of measure (187 feet) used by the builders of Teotihuacán, but no actual sites have been found to show that people from Teotihuacán ever traveled as far north as Ohio.

The Hopewell were preceded by the famous Adena people, the first mound builders. The Adena were the first to erect earth mounds over their honored dead. It is interesting that these burials were always of men and the mounds apparently were reserved for priests and community leaders. To accompany the burials, the Adena made magnificent bracelets, knives, ornaments from copper, and ornate pipes, but pottery was their major achievement. Thousands of examples of beautiful ceramics have been recovered from Adena burial mounds.

The Adena accomplished all of this without benefit of a stable food supply. They maintained large settlements simply by hunting, fishing, and gathering plant foods. Some archaeologists believe that the Adena disappeared from Ohio soon after the beginning of the Christian era, pushed out by the more powerful Hopewell people. But there is some evidence that they continued to live in the Ohio Valley through 500 B.C., apparently living side by side with the Hopewell.

No one knows exactly who the Hopewell people were or when they came to Ohio. Their earthworks were much larger and more complex than the Adena. Of all the prehistoric societies that lived in the Ohio Valley, the Hopewell were the most skilled and accomplished. Some earthen walls are fifteen feet high and fifty feet wide at the base, and surround as much as fifty acres.

For a thousand years, the Hopewell dominated the Ohio Valley and extended their influence over large areas of the eastern United States. Like the Adena the Hopewell people had no large cities or towns, no vast tracts of farmland. The people lived in scattered villages and survived by hunting and fishing. Yet great numbers of people worked together to construct the large earthen monuments. This kind of organization indicates that an elite group of religious or political leaders headed a system powerful enough to demand homage.

Around A.D. 700 the Hopewell culture suddenly declined. Plague and drought are suggested causes. Or perhaps there was a break in the trade network that supplied the raw material to create their fabulous works of art. Whatever the cause, the whole fantastic culture disappeared.

Many different groups seem to have participated in the Adena and Hopewell cultures, and they are often seen as religious cults rather than full cultures. The idea of making elaborate burial mounds and artworks to honor the high-ranking dead was fostered by cults generally called the Cult

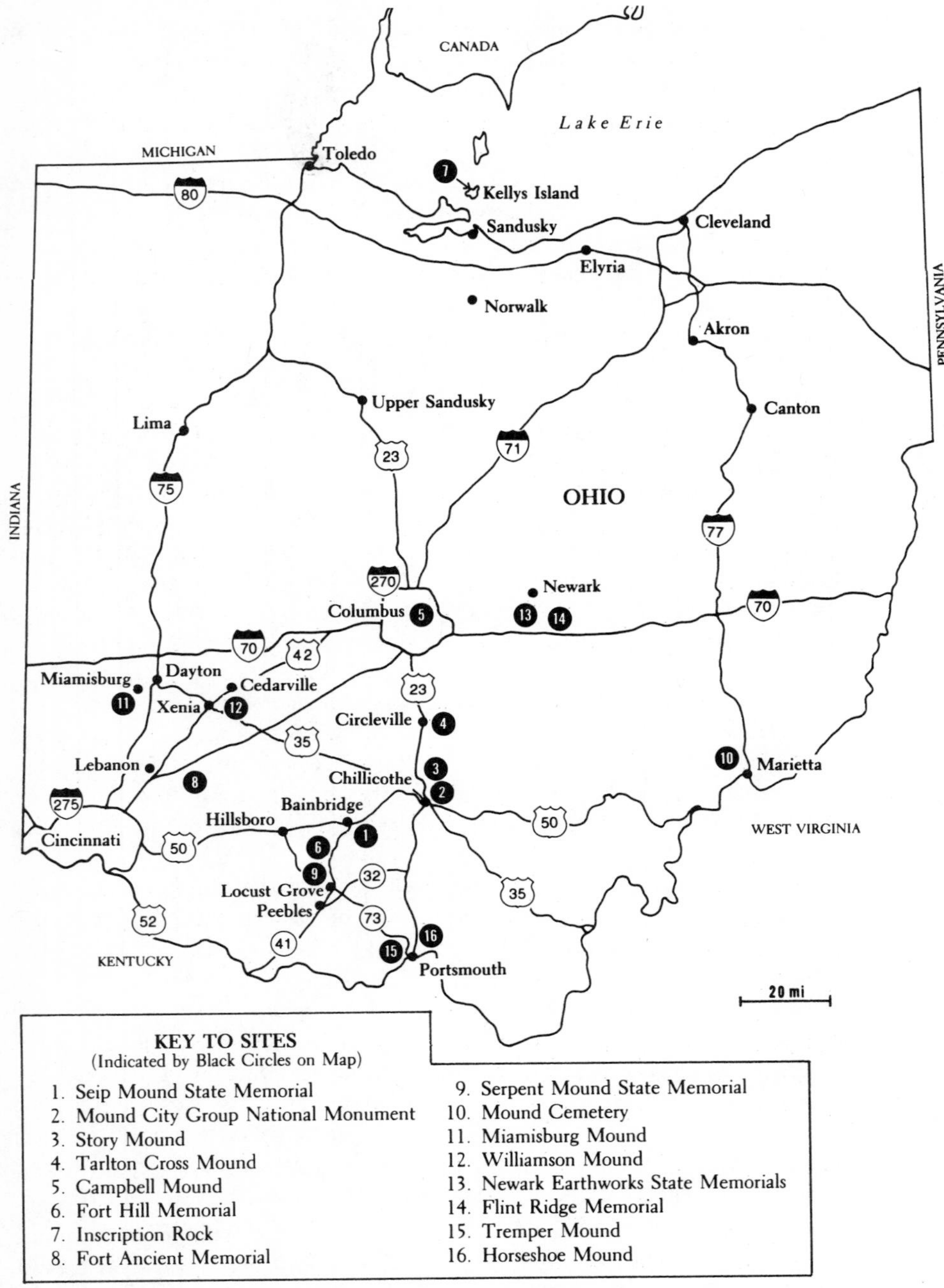

Key map of Ohio showing archaeological sites open to the public.

of the Dead. The concept spread among many small diverse communities and unified them on a religious level.

Ohio today is incredibly rich in archaeological sites open to the public. Because there are so many sites in the state, a map is given to show their locations.

SITES

Bainbridge

• *Seip Mound State Memorial*
Bainbridge, Ohio 45612

Seip is a giant Hopewell mound 250 feet long and 30 feet high. It was the central mound of one of the largest earthworks in Ohio. When Seip was excavated in the 1930s, it yielded the richest assortment of artifacts ever discovered in any mound: ornaments made of copper, mica, and silver, and thousands of pearls. Exposed excavations showed outlines of Hopewell workshops, where artists created these fabulous crafts. Seip Mound was restored after excavations, and its many treasures are on display at the **Ohio Historical Center** in Columbus (see the listing below).

There is an exhibit pavilion and a picnic area at the site.

DIRECTIONS: From Chillicothe, follow U.S. 50 west toward Bainbridge. Three miles before you reach Bainbridge, you will see the marker for Seip.

HOURS: Open daily 8:00 A.M.–6:00 P.M.

Note: Continue on U.S. 50 into Bainbridge and just west of town near the highway you will see **Kilvert Mound,** a picturesque burial mound that has never been excavated.

Chillicothe and Vicinity

• *Mound City Group National Monument*
Route 1, Box 1
Chillicothe, Ohio 45601 *(614) 774-1125*

Here is one of the best examples of Hopewell earthworks in the Scioto Valley. The mound group is often called a "necropolis" because no one ever lived here. The 130-acre enclosed plot was reserved for the honored dead. The mounds may have been monuments to leading artisans or successful traders.

Twenty-four burial mounds are enclosed by a three-foot embankment.

An observation platform on top of the museum building offers a full vista of the monument, and you can also walk the footpaths that cross the park grounds.

From a mound known as Mica Grave, a section has been removed to show an elaborate multiple burial. Exquisite works of art were recovered from these mounds during excavations; many are on display in the fine on-site museum. A special film tells the whole story of the Hopewell people and the archaeological excavations at the site. You can also buy good reproductions of effigy pipes at the museum sales counter.

The mounds were destroyed during excavation and later restored by the Ohio Historical Society. The monument is now administered by the National Park Service.

DIRECTIONS: Take exit 104 off U.S. 35 and drive 3 miles north of Chillicothe.
HOURS: 8:00 A.M.–5:00 P.M. daily (till 7:00 P.M. in the summer). Closed Christmas and New Year's.
ADMISSION: Free.

Note: **Story Mound,** a conical mound built by the Adena people, is in Chillicothe. Although an obscure site, it is interesting because it is similar to the original Adena mound that was destroyed by excavation. Story Mound is undeveloped but can be seen easily from the street. It is on Delano Avenue, one block south of Allen Avenue in Chillicothe.

Another small prehistoric site is southeast of Chillicothe. This is the **Leo Petroglyph** site, a rock carving made by Fort Ancient Indians around A.D. 1200. The site is reached by taking U.S. 35 south from Chillicothe; turn east onto County Road 28 and follow that road to the marker. There are nature trails and picnicking is permitted at the site, which is open during daylight hours.

Circleville Vicinity

- *Tarlton Cross Mound*
  Tarlton, Ohio 43156

This effigy mound in the shape of a Greek cross is believed to have been a Hopewell shrine. The cross is ninety feet wide and three feet high. A foot trail leads to the mound, and there is a picnic area.

DIRECTIONS: From Circleville drive south on OH 56 to OH 159, then north on 159 to Tarlton and continue 1 mile on 159 to the marker.
HOURS: Open during daylight hours.
ADMISSION: Free.

Columbus

- *Campbell Mound*
  Columbus, Ohio

This prehistoric burial mound is an almost perfect specimen of the Adena symmetrical mound. It stands in the center of a neatly mowed acre of grass, enclosed by a stone fence. (See the museum listing below for the nearby Ohio Historical Center.)

DIRECTIONS: Campbell Mound is on the west side of the Scioto River on McKinley Avenue, 5 miles northwest of Columbus.
HOURS: Open during daylight hours.
ADMISSION: Free.

Hillsboro

- *Fort Hill Memorial*
  Fort Hill Road
  Hillsboro, Ohio 45133 *(513) 588-2360*

Fort Hill is one of the most beautiful and best preserved hilltop enclosures in Ohio. Defensive earth walls fifteen feet high enclose some forty acres of the flat hilltop, and a moat runs along the inside of the fort. The enclosure may have been used for rituals or ceremonies, but the great height of the walls suggests it was a defensive point. Test excavations at this site failed to recover any cultural remains, but implements found in the vicinity suggest that the Hopewell were the builders.

Sixteen miles of nature trails cross the area. A two-thousand-foot trail leads up a steep slope to the ancient fortification at the top of the hill, where there is a picnic area and shelter house. A new museum with extensive exhibits depicting the story of Fort Hill and its natural history is on the site.

DIRECTIONS: Fort Hill is 18 miles southeast of Hillsboro near Routes 41 and 124.
HOURS (PARK): The park trails are open every day during daylight hours.
HOURS (MUSEUM): April–October
Tuesday–Saturday: 9:30 A.M.–4:45 P.M.
Sunday and holidays: 11:00 A.M.–6:00 P.M.
Closed Mondays.
ADMISSION: Adults 75¢, children 35¢, under twelve free with an adult.

Kelleys Island

- *Inscription Rock*
  Kelleys Island, Ohio 43438

Kelleys Island is a busy vacation spot in Lake Erie. Inscription Rock State Memorial, a large rock engraved with animals and birds, is just east of the dock on the south shore. The carvings probably were made between A.D. 1000 and 1650.

Auto and passenger service is available to the island from Sandusky and Marblehead. You can camp, fish, and swim on Kelleys Island, and there is a public boat launch. For boat schedules to the island, call:
Neuman Boat Line (419) 626–5557

Lebanon

- *Fort Ancient Memorial*
  SR 350
  Lebanon, Ohio 45036 *(513) 932-4421*

Fort Ancient fringes a bluff rising above the Little Miami River and is isolated by a deep ravine. The fort was built by the Hopewell Indians nearly fifteen hundred years ago. It is the largest and most impressive prehistoric earthwork of its kind in North America. Massive earthen walls often more than twenty feet high enclose an area of one hundred acres, within which are burial mounds.

The fort was abandoned when the Hopewell culture declined. About A.D. 1000 another group of Indians moved into the fort and planted corn in the valleys below the bluff. These people, known as the Fort Ancient Indians, were actually part of the Mississippian culture. They eventually abandoned the hilltop and the fort was empty when the first Europeans entered the region.

Today, nature trails wander over the site and offer splendid views of the Miami River Valley. Artifacts recovered from the fort and nearby prehistoric village sites are displayed in the **Fort Ancient Museum.** The park also has a playground and picnic facilities.

DIRECTIONS: From I-71 north of Cincinnati, exit at SR 350 and follow it southeast to the memorial.
HOURS (SITE): Open daily during daylight hours.
HOURS (MUSEUM): April–October
Tuesday–Saturday: 9:30 A.M.–4:45 P.M.
Sunday and holidays: 11:00 A.M.–6:00 P.M.
Closed Mondays.
ADMISSION: Adults 50¢, children 25¢, under twelve free with an adult.

Note: The **Warren County Historical Society Museum** in Lebanon also holds some material recovered from the Fort Ancient site (see listing below).

Locust Grove

- *Serpent Mound State Memorial*
  Peebles, Ohio 45660 *(513) 587-2796*

America's most famous ceremonial earthwork, the Great Serpent Mound curls nearly a quarter of mile over the grassy countryside. You can climb to the top of an observation tower for a grand view of this extraordinary Adena effigy mound. Serpent effigies are found all over the world, but the Ohio mound is among the largest and most mysterious ever discovered. Within the open jaws of the serpent is an egg-shaped mound thirty feet by eighty-six feet. The effigy is made of small stones packed with yellow clay. Nothing is buried in the mound.

A small on-site museum uses dioramas and graphics to interpret the site. Nature trails criss-cross the sixty-one-acre park, and there is also a picnic area.

DIRECTIONS: From Bainbridge drive south on 41 to Route 73 west. The park is 4 miles northwest of Locust Grove on Route 73.
HOURS (PARK): Open year round during daylight hours.
HOURS (MUSEUM): April–October
8:00 A.M.–5:00 P.M., daily.
ADMISSION: Free.

Marietta

- *Mound Cemetery*

The beautiful river town of Marietta is considered Ohio's earliest city. The town cemetery was named for the thirty-foot-high, perfectly shaped mound on its grounds, which is surrounded by a wide moat four feet deep. The mound has never been excavated but it is believed to be the burial place of a high priest or chieftain. Twenty-four officers of the American Revolution are also buried in this cemetery.

DIRECTIONS: The cemetery is on 5th Street at Scammel.

Miamisburg

- *Miamisburg Mound*
  Miamisburg, Ohio 45342

Miamisburg Mound is the largest conical burial mound in Ohio. Probably built by the Adena people, the mound stands nearly sixty-eight feet high and contains more than a million cubic feet of earth. If you feel energetic, 120 steps will take you to the top of the mound.

DIRECTIONS: Miamisburg is just south of Dayton. From I-75, exit at Miamisburg. The mound is on U.S. 25, 1 mile southeast of town.

Note: Also in the Dayton-Cincinnati area is **Williamson Mound,** a small undeveloped mound site in Cedarville (on U.S. 42, northeast of Xenia).

Newark and Vicinity

• *Newark Earthworks State Memorials* *(614) 344-1920*

The Newark group of prehistoric earthworks originally covered several square miles, but as the modern city of Newark grew, a considerable portion of the earthworks was erased. It is still one of the most extensive works of its kind. The walls and mounds that remain are split up by city streets.

Begin your tour of the Newark Earthworks at the **Mound Builders State Memorial.** In the memorial is the **Great Circle Earthworks,** a grassy embankment twelve hundred feet across with earthen walls as high as fourteen feet. In the center of the Great Circle is an effigy mound shaped like an eagle.

The nation's first museum devoted exclusively to prehistoric American Indian art opened at this site in 1971. Exhibits in the **Ohio Prehistoric Indian Art Museum** represent the artistic achievements of all the known prehistoric cultures in Ohio from 10,000 B.C. to A.D. 1600.

DIRECTIONS: From the junction of I-70 and SR 79, drive 14 miles north on SR 79. The memorial is on the southwest edge of Newark on the left side of SR 79.

HOURS (MEMORIAL): The memorial is open free, year round. A picnic area is on the grounds.

HOURS (MUSEUM): April–October
Tuesday–Saturday: 9:30 A.M.–4:45 P.M.
Sunday and holidays: 11:00 A.M.–6:00 P.M.

ADMISSION: Adults 50¢, children 25¢, under twelve free with an adult.

The Octagon Earthworks: The giant octagon encloses fifty acres and is joined by an avenue to a circular embankment surrounding another twenty acres. Several small mounds are within the octagon.

DIRECTIONS: To reach Octagon Earthworks, travel to Newark on SR 79, and in Newark go to Church Street. Turn left on Church to 30th Street. Then turn left on 30th to Parkview, and right to the park on North 33rd Street.

Aerial view of the Newark Earthworks. (Photo: Ohio Historical Society.)

Wright Earthworks: This is a small section of parallel walls that was once part of a much larger square.

DIRECTIONS: From West Main Street, drive south on South Williams Street and east on Waldo. Wright is at the intersection of James and Waldo.

• *Flint Ridge Memorial*
Box 55, Route 1
Glenford, Ohio 43739 *(614) 787-2476*

This quarry was visited by prehistoric Indians for hundreds of years. They chiseled delicate translucent flint of many colors out of the rock and made weapons and tools. A museum is built over one of the flint pits, and a series of exhibits explains how flint is formed, mined, and made into tools. Several nature trails cross the quarries, and there is a special trail for blind and handicapped visitors.

DIRECTIONS: Flint Ridge is just southeast of Newark. From I-70, take the Brownsville exit; drive north 2 miles on County 668 to the memorial.

HOURS (PARK): The nature trails are open year round, weather permitting. There is a picnic area.

HOURS (MUSEUM): April–October
Tuesday–Saturday: 9:30 A.M.–4:45 P.M.
Sunday and holidays: 11:00 A.M.–6:00 P.M.

ADMISSION: Adults 50¢, children 25¢, under twelve free with an adult.

Portsmouth

• *Tremper Mound*

This large earthwork resembles a large animal. The mound is famous for an enormous cache of pipes that were found during excavation. There is no interpretation at the site and very little to see.

DIRECTIONS: Drive south toward Portsmouth on SR 73; just before you reach Portsmouth turn south on SR 371 to Tremper Mound.

• *Horseshoe Mound*
Mound Public Park
Portsmouth, Ohio 45662

In Mound Park is a horseshoe-shaped mound, one of the many signal-fire mounds used by the prehistoric Indians. Valuable artifacts have been recovered from these kinds of mounds, and the **Portsmouth Public Library** has one of the most valuable relic collections in the region.

DIRECTIONS: The park is in Portsmouth at Hutchins Avenue between Grand and Seventeenth Avenue. The library is at 1220 Gallia Street and may be reached by calling (614) 354-5688.

MUSEUMS

Cincinnati

• *Cincinnati Museum of Natural History*
1720 Gilbert Avenue
Cincinnati, Ohio 45202 *(513) 621-3889*

The museum's walk-through exhibit of Indian cultures contains archaeological material collected in the Ohio Valley. Displays represent the Adena, Hopewell, and Fort Ancient cultures, and a few exhibits highlight material from the Southwest and the Northwest Coast. Of special interest is a small engraved stone tablet recovered from an Adena burial mound near the museum.

This museum also exhibits shells, minerals, fossils, and dinosaur bones. Mounted specimens of extinct and endangered birds can be seen in the gallery of birds. There is also a planetarium and a gift shop. The museum is on a fifteen-hundred-acre nature preserve; a wilderness trail leads to a cavern with a waterfall.

HOURS: Tuesday–Saturday: 9:00 A.M.–4:30 P.M.
Sunday: 12:30 M.–5:00 P.M.
Closed national holidays.
ADMISSION: Adults $1, children under twelve 25¢.

Cleveland

- *Cleveland Museum of Natural History*
Wade Oval
University Circle
Cleveland, Ohio 44106 *(216) 231-4600*

This museum interprets sites inhabited by early peoples and the natural history of the Ohio region. There are exhibits and dioramas of prehistoric Indian cultures of Ohio and other parts of North America. The museum is engaged in fieldwork, and exhibits change as work progresses and new sites are excavated.

Other exhibits include gems, armored fossil fish of the Devonian Period found in Ohio shales, mammals, and birds. The museum has a seventy-foot haplocanthosaurus dinosaur on display. There are live animal programs on weekends. A nature center, aquarium, botanical garden, zoological park, and planetarium are on the grounds. A large research library of natural history books can be used on request.

HOURS: Monday–Saturday: 10:00 A.M.–5:00 P.M.
Sunday: 1:00 P.M.–5:30 P.M.
Closed major holidays.
ADMISSION: Adults $2.00; children six to eighteen, students, and senior citizens 50¢. Free on Tuesday afternoon.

Columbus

- *Ohio Historical Center*
Interstate 71 and Seventeenth Avenue
Columbus, Ohio 43211 *(614) 466-1500*

This is the place to see many of the major discoveries from Ohio's great Adena and Hopewell mounds. Open "pit" displays are arranged along a wide mall. Dioramas interpret historic life at Fort Ancient, Seip Mound, and a prehistoric rock shelter. Each exhibit in the new center has a distinct theme, and together they trace all of Ohio's prehistoric culture from Paleo-Indian times. Also located on the archaeology mall is a reconstructed Adena house, a burial exhibit, and a cremation basin.

The natural history section of the museum has a demonstration laboratory and hundreds of natural science exhibits. The **Ohio Archives and Historical Library** is also housed in the center.

HOURS: Monday–Saturday: 9:00 A.M.–5:00 P.M.
Sunday and holidays: 10:00 A.M.–5:00 P.M.
Closed Thanksgiving, Christmas, New Year's.
ADMISSION: Free.

Dayton

• *Dayton Museum of Natural History*
2629 Ridge Avenue
Dayton, Ohio 45414 *(513) 275-7431*

Although the natural history exhibits here are designed for all ages, the museum is noted for special children's programs. Sometimes the museum conducts archaeological field trips for young people. Prehistoric artifacts range from Paleo times through the Adena and Hopewell cultures and into the later Woodland periods. All the exhibits emphasize the Ohio area.

Small live animals are housed in another part of the museum, and there is also a planetarium and observatory. A natural history research library is open to the public.

HOURS: Monday–Saturday: 9:00 A.M.–6:00 P.M. (Tuesday and Friday till 9:00 P.M.)
Sunday and holidays: 2:00 P.M.–6:00 P.M.
Closed Christmas Eve and New Year's Eve.
ADMISSION: Free Monday through Saturday.
Sunday and holidays: Adults $1, children 50¢ (includes admission to the planetarium).

Elyria

• *Ray Beatson's Indian Ridge Museum*
8714 West Ridge Road
Elyria, Ohio 44035 *(216) 323-2167*

This museum owned by archaeologist Ray Beatson is dedicated to the prehistoric Indian cultures of Ohio. The wide-ranging exhibits include artifacts from the early Woodland (Adena), middle Woodland (Hopewell), and late

Woodland and Mississippian cultures. Most of the artifacts are from the northern Ohio River Valley. Dr. Beatson is usually on hand for conversation and elucidation.

HOURS: Tuesday–Sunday: 1:00 P.M.–5:00 P.M.
ADMISSION: Adults $2, children under twelve $1.

Lebanon

- *Warren County Historical Society Museum*
105 South Broadway
Lebanon, Ohio 45036 *(513) 932-1817*

Both historic and prehistoric exhibits are displayed here in storefronts circling a reconstructed village green. The prehistoric material is from the Hopewell and Fort Ancient cultures. Historic exhibits include household items from a Shaker colony.

Fort Ancient, one of Ohio's most outstanding archaeological sites, is just 7 miles southeast of Lebanon on OH 350.

HOURS: Tuesday–Saturday: 9:00 A.M.–4:00 P.M.
Sunday: 12:00 M.–4:00 P.M.
Closed holidays.
ADMISSION: Adults $1, children five to eighteen 25¢.

Lima

- *Allen County Museum*
620 West Market Street
Lima, Ohio 45801 *(419) 222-9426*

Exhibits at the Allen County Museum include a large collection of artifacts that span the Paleo, Archaic, Adena, Hopewell, Cole Creek, Fort Ancient, and Erie cultures of Ohio. A diorama depicts a Glacial Kame burial along with material recovered from an actual grave site. Glacial Kame was a widespread cultural manifestation of the late Archaic period between 2500 and 1500 B.C. The Glacial Kame people buried their dead in sand and gravel hilltops that had been deposited in the final stages of the Ice Age. These glacial outwashes are called "kames."

In most respects, the Glacial Kame people followed the usual Archaic lifeway, but their burials, found in many Midwestern states, were often elaborate and contained many ornaments and burial goods. Because no Glacial Kame sites are preserved for the public, material recovered from these interesting sites can be seen only in museums. The **Ohio Historical Center** in Columbus has good displays of Glacial Kame material.

In another part of the Allen County Museum, fossil and mineral exhibits are displayed. A special transportation exhibit features steam and electric railroad items, bicycles, and antique autos. There is a completely furnished, detailed model of Mount Vernon.

HOURS: Tuesday–Sunday: 1:30 P.M.–5:00 P.M.
Closed Mondays and holidays.
ADMISSION: Adults $1, children 50¢.

Newark

• *Licking County Historical Society Museum*
6th Street Park (between Church and Main)
Newark, Ohio 43055 *(614) 345-4898*

The museum is housed in a restored historic home built in 1815. Displayed along with the period furniture are some beautiful copper, mica, and pearl ornaments recovered from the nearby **Newark Earthworks.**

HOURS: Tuesday–Sunday: 1:00 P.M.–4:00 P.M.
Closed Mondays and holidays.
ADMISSION: Adults $1, children free.

Norwalk

• *Firelands Museum*
4 Case Avenue (at West Street)
Norwalk, Ohio 44857 *(419) 668-6038*

The people of the Erie Whittlesey Indian culture lived in this area when the Europeans arrived, and exhibits here describe their lifeways. Several cases of prehistoric artifacts represent the Archaic, early Woodland, and Hopewell cultures in Ohio. One case of artifacts contains spearheads and chopping tools dating back more than ten thousand years.

The museum is housed in one of Norwalk's many historic buildings. Historic manuscripts, maps, pioneer relics, firearms, coins, costumes, and natural history exhibits are also on display.

HOURS: May, June, September, October
Tuesday–Sunday: 12:00 M.–6:00 P.M.
July and August
Monday–Saturday: 9:00 A.M.–6:00 P.M.
Sunday: 12:00 M.–6:00 P.M.
April and November
Weekends only: 12:00 M.–6:00 P.M.
Rest of year: By appointment.
ADMISSION: Adults 50¢, children under twelve free.

STATE OFFICE

Martha Potter Otto
Curator of Archaeology
Ohio Historical Center
Columbus, Ohio 43211 (614) 466-1500

OPPORTUNITIES FOR AMATEURS

The **Ohio Historical Society** sponsors several projects each year and sometimes amateurs can arrange to visit the sites or volunteer their services through the curator of archaeology (see above). *Popular Archaeology* magazine also lists ongoing projects in the state that invite amateur participation.

The Ohio Historical Society also offers a year-long calendar of events featuring many programs on archaeology and natural history. For a schedule of lectures and field trips, write or call:

Ohio Historical Society
Interstate 71 and Seventeenth Avenue
Columbus, Ohio 43211 (614) 466-1500

ORGANIZATIONS TO JOIN

The major amateur organization in the state is the **Archaeological Society of Ohio,** publishers of *Ohio Archaeologist.* This is a large, statewide organization with several local chapters. The address of the society changes when new officers are elected, but you can write care of the journal business office:

Mr. Summers Redick
35 West River Glen Drive
Worthington, Ohio 43085

In northern Ohio the **Toledo Aboriginal Research Club** is an extremely active lay-professional organization, which you can contact by writing:

Toledo Aboriginal Research Club
Department of Sociology and Anthropology
University of Toledo
2801 West Bancroft Street
Toledo, Ohio 43600

WEST VIRGINIA

Traces of more than three hundred Adena mounds have been found throughout the Ohio and Kanawha river valleys of West Virginia. Yet prehistoric Indians found the country west of the Alleghenies too rugged to live in year round; instead, they lived on the fringes, entering the region to hunt, fish, and gather salt. However, the Adena people did gain a foothold in the river valleys, where they constructed their classic mounds.

Almost all of these mounds have been obliterated by weather or farming, but one of the most famous in America still stands in West Virginia—the great Grave Creek Mound, also known as Mammoth Mound. And an important ongoing excavation of an Archaic site is being conducted at East Steubenville, just across the river from Steubenville, Ohio. This excavation receives visitors during the summer months. However, there is little interpretation at either Grave Creek or East Steubenville.

SITES

Moundsville

• *Grave Creek Mound*
10th Street and Tomlinson
Moundsville, West Virginia 26041

At one time at least one hundred burial mounds were on the site of what is now the city called Moundsville. One of the few remaining is the famous Grave Creek Mound, one of the most photographed and sketched prehistoric ruins in America. The mound was probably begun in the late Archaic period as a small burial ground for important members of the Adena society. It grew in stages as more and more earth and new chambers were added, until it reached a height of nearly eighty feet.

In historic times the members of one enterprising family realized the possibility of profit and excitedly set themselves to tunneling through the mound.

Near the center of the base, the diggers discovered a burial chamber containing two skeletons and several priceless grave goods and pieces of jewelry and pottery. One skeleton wore an ivory pendant and a necklace of 650 disc-shaped beads. Above this chamber, about midway along the shaft, a second vault contained the skeleton of a woman wearing 1700 ivory beads and 500 shell ornaments around her neck; on her arms were five copper bracelets.

The entrepreneurs turned one vault into a museum. Tourists were guided along the tunnel passage to the dark core of the mound, where they could view skeletons and artifacts lit by smoking candles.

Grave Creek Mound, West Virginia, the largest Adena mound in America. (Photo: JW.)

The macabre museum soon failed, was abandoned, and the tunnel and shaft collapsed. The prehistoric art collection and the skeletons disappeared. There may still remain some unexcavated objects in the mound.

Today, Grave Creek Mound looks very much as it did in the nineteenth century. Trees grow out of its sides, and a path winds around it to the summit. You can see it easily from the street if the inner park is closed. A large, modern museum building stands next to the mound, but no artifacts from the mound are on display.

DIRECTIONS: Grave Creek Mound is accessible off WV 2 at Moundsville.
HOURS: Monday–Friday: 10:00 A.M.–4:30 P.M.
Saturday: 1:00 P.M.–4:00 P.M.
Sunday: 1:00 P.M.–4:00 P.M.
ADMISSION: Adults 50¢, children under twelve with an adult free.

ONGOING EXCAVATIONS

East Steubenville Site

This is the site of an ancient shell midden. The site area, on top of a valley ridge overlooking the Ohio River, was occupied between four thousand

and two thousand years ago. Excavation teams from the College of Steubenville in Ohio will be working here every summer for the next few years, and you can visit the site if you call or write ahead for an appointment. The archaeological field school is usually in progress during the month of June. East Steubenville is just across the Ohio River from Steubenville, Ohio. For permission to visit, write or call:

Mr. Jack Boyde
College of Steubenville
Steubenville, Ohio 43952 (614) 283-3771

STATE OFFICE

Archaeology Section
West Virginia Geological and Economic Survey
P.O. Box 879
Morgantown, West Virginia 26505 (304) 292-6331

OPPORTUNITIES FOR AMATEURS AND ORGANIZATIONS TO JOIN

The **West Virginia Archaeological Society** is a lay–professional organization dedicated to the protection of prehistoric sites. Occasionally members participate in field excavations in cooperation with the Geological Survey. The society may be reached through Wheeling College in Wheeling, West Virginia 26003, or by calling the Geological Survey (see above).

WISCONSIN

Glaciers still gripped the northern part of Wisconsin when Paleo-Indians hunted hairy mammoths along the fringe of the icecap. As the ice retreated, Archaic people pushed further north until they occupied the entire region. In the later Woodland period, tribes from the South migrated up the Mississippi River into Wisconsin, establishing permanent homes and villages. There is evidence that a wide range of cultures migrated in and out of the region. The Hopewell had outposts in the western part of Wisconsin; and the people here were part of the long prehistoric trade system that covered most of the East and continued to expand during the Mississippian period.

Wisconsin was the source of many different kinds of metal, including highly prized native copper. Silver, meteoric iron, flint, pipestone, quartz, and quartzite were quarried all over the state. Lead was not used as a metal until historic times, but these early people ground small cubes of galena into a lustrous mixture of metal dust and probably used it to gild their bodies.

Many different mound-building cultures lived in Wisconsin; enormous panthers, lizards, birds, and even human effigies rise up all across the surface of the state. At least five thousand effigy mounds are concentrated in Wisconsin, almost the sum total of all such mounds known in America. The mounds are anywhere from twenty-five to three hundred feet long and usually between two and three feet high. Their fantastic shapes are unique, and they are in one sense the most mysterious mounds in North America because their builders have never been traced.

While some of the mounds contain burials, almost no artifacts or grave goods have been recovered, making it impossible to identify the skeletal remains. One interesting discovery is that human skeletons are often found buried at a vital place in the effigy body—at the brain or heart or in the joint where a wing or limb joined the body. Archaeologists cannot even tell why or when the effigy mounds were built; they may have been built sometime over the long span of the Archaic period, or they may belong to the late Woodland period.

Most of the effigy mounds in Wisconsin are within state parks, and a few are in municipal parks. With the exception of Aztalan, the most important site in the state, there is little or no interpretation of any of the mounds. Yet the parks are preserving the unique mounds of Wisconsin for future exploration.

If you plan to spend time in the many Wisconsin state parks, you can purchase an annual auto sticker ($5 residents, $8 nonresidents); the daily parking fee is $1.50 for residents, $2.50 for nonresidents, and camping fees are extra. Most of Wisconsin's state parks have special facilities for the handicapped (hard-surfaced roads, modified restrooms, and modified picnic tables). For an excellent state park *Visitors' Guide,* write:

Wisconsin Department of Natural Resources
P.O. Box 7921
Madison, Wisconsin 53707

SITES

Baraboo

- *Devils Lake State Park*
  Baraboo, Wisconsin 53913

On the north end of Devils Lake are two mounds, one bear-shaped, the other shaped like a lynx. At the south end is a bird-shaped mound. The mounds are marked with small signs. In the summer naturalists sometimes conduct guided tours to the mounds. The park is open year round. Camping is available in the park; the nearby town of Baraboo has many resort facilities.

DIRECTIONS: Baraboo is in the south central part of Wisconsin. From Baraboo drive 3 miles south on WI 123 to the park entrance.

• *Man Mound*

In the small town of Baraboo is Man Mound, one of the few effigy mounds shaped like a human figure.

DIRECTIONS: Drive east on Eighth Avenue (WI 33); turn north on County Trunk T and drive to first intersection, then east to the mound.
HOURS: Open daylight hours.
ADMISSION: Free.

Black River Falls

• *Gullickson's Glen Petroglyph Site*
Black River Falls, Wisconsin 54615

Dozens of petroglyphs etched on a high sandstone cliff can be seen from this site. The area has been thoroughly excavated; the recovered artifacts suggest that the artists in stone belonged to the Oneota culture.

DIRECTIONS: Black River Falls is in the east central part of the state on the eastern edge of the Black River State Forest. From town, drive 2 miles south on WI 54, west on Road C for 7 miles, then south 1 mile to the parking lot of the county park.

Lake Mills–Fort Atkinson

• *Aztalan State Park*
Lake Mills, Wisconsin 53551

Aztalan is Wisconsin's most important archaeological discovery. A small group of Cahokians migrated here from Illinois and lived for two hundred years surrounded by the less advanced people of Wisconsin, who still followed the Woodland Tradition. The Cahokian farmers practiced the sophisticated, sometimes brutal, expressions of the great Mississippian Tradition. One of their more unpleasant rituals was cannibalism and probably their most common victims were captive Woodland Indians.

The Cahokians protected their village from attack by surrounding it with a reinforced stockade almost twenty feet high, interspersed by watchtowers. For all of their attempts to defend themselves, they were finally overwhelmed by the Woodland Indians, and the village was burned to the ground.

Today visitors to Aztalan can see some reconstruction of the stockade wall and two restored flat-topped mounds. Exhibit panels tell the story of Aztalan, but the interpretation is minimal. This site probably will be developed extensively in the future.

For now, it is open in the summer only; there is no camping in the park. The nearest campground is at Lake Kegonsa State Park near Stoughton (west) and the southern unit of Kettle Moraine State Forest (to the east). The **Aztalan Historical Society Museum** is at the junction of the County Road and Aztalan Mound Road.

DIRECTIONS: From Lake Mills drive 3 miles east on County Road Trunk B to Aztalan Mound Road, then south to the park entrance.

• *Panther Intaglio*
Fort Atkinson, Wisconsin 53538

The Panther Intaglio is unique because it is scratched *into* the earth. A trench about a foot deep outlines the effigy and it is one of the few intaglios in America. The **Hoard Historical Museum** is also in Fort Atkinson.

DIRECTIONS: From Fort Atkinson, just 13 miles south of Aztalan, drive west on WI 106 to the site.
HOURS: Open daylight hours.
ADMISSION: Free.

Menasha

• *High Cliff State Park*
Menasha, Wisconsin 54952

A large group of effigy mounds is concentrated on a high bluff overlooking Lake Winnebago. The effigies, mostly in the shape of lizards and birds, range from 25 to 285 feet long. A nature trail leads from the parking area up to the mounds. The park is open all year, and there is camping.

DIRECTIONS: The park is in the eastern part of the state. From Menasha drive 10 miles east on WI 114 to the park entrance.

• *Menasha Mounds*
Menasha, Wisconsin 54952

Three panther effigies can be found in Smith Park in the town of Menasha.

Prairie de Chien (Bagley)

• *Wyalusing State Park*
Bagley, Wisconsin 53801

The park is on the banks of the Wisconsin River. Several effigy burial mounds rise all along the top of a ridge, and an easy nature trail has been developed for visitors. The park is open year round and camping is permitted.

From Prairie de Chien you are just across the river from the outstanding **Effigy Mounds National Monument** near Marquette, Iowa.

DIRECTIONS: From Prairie de Chien drive 6 miles southeast on U.S. 18, then 5 miles west on County Trunk C to County Trunk X. Follow that highway to State Park Road, which leads to the park.

Prairie de Chien (Cassville)

• *Nelson Dewey State Park*
Cassville, Wisconsin 53806

Many effigy mounds can be found in this park overlooking the Mississippi River but there is no interpretation of the site.

DIRECTIONS: From Prairie de Chien drive down U.S. 18 and WI 133 south to Cassville. Go 2 miles northwest on County Trunk VV.

Sheboygan

• *Sheboygan Mound Park*
Sheboygan, Wisconsin 53081

More than thirty effigy mounds of all sizes and shapes can be found in this city park. **Sheboygan County Museum** (see listing below) has artifacts from the Old Copper culture.

DIRECTIONS: Drive south on U.S. Business 141, east on County Trunk EE, south on South 12th Street, east on Panther Avenue, and south on South 9th Street to the park.

West Bend

• *Lizard Mound State Park*
West Bend, Wisconsin 53095

Birds, panthers, and lizards are among the thirty-one effigy mounds in this park just north of Milwaukee. A nature trail winds in and around the mound sites. The nearest camping is at the northern unit of Kettle Moraine State Forest near Kewaskum; there are motels in West Bend. The park is open only in the summer.

DIRECTIONS: From West Bend drive 4 miles northeast on WI 144, then 1 mile east on County Trunk A.

MUSEUMS

Beloit

• *Logan Museum of Anthropology*
Beloit College
Beloit, Wisconsin 53511 *(608) 365-3391 (Ext. 305)*

On the Beloit campus are twenty-four prehistoric Indian mounds. One of the effigy mounds on the campus grounds is depicted in a diorama in the museum. All of Wisconsin's prehistoric cultures are portrayed in the museum, which includes limited artifacts from the effigy mound culture and the Oneota culture. One floor of the museum is devoted exclusively to prehistoric cultures of the Southwest. The American Indian and Stone Age displays are constantly changing, but many worldwide archaeological finds are on permanent display.

HOURS: Monday–Friday: 9:00 A.M.–4:30 P.M.
Saturday: 9:30 A.M.–12:00 M.
Sunday: 1:30 P.M.–4:30 P.M.
Closed school holidays. (Call first, since these days change.)
ADMISSION: Free.

Fort Atkinson

• *Hoard Historical Museum*
409 Merchant Avenue
Fort Atkinson, Wisconsin 53538 *(414) 563-4521*

The museum is near the famous **Panther Intaglio.** Displays include thousands of local artifacts from different prehistoric periods, and many tools of Wisconsin's Old Copper culture. The museum also shows the historic **Foster House,** home of the first family to arrive in Fort Atkinson in 1841. The museum staff asks that groups call ahead for an appointment.

HOURS: Tuesday–Saturday: 9:30 A.M.–3:30 P.M.
First Sunday of each month: 1:00 P.M.–5:00 P.M.
Closed holidays.
ADMISSION: Museum: free. Foster House: Adults 50¢, children 25¢.

Green Bay

• *Neville Public Museum*
129 South Jefferson Street
Green Bay, Wisconsin 54301 *(414) 497-3767*

The prehistoric artifacts on display represent several cultures, including the Archaic Old Copper and Red Ochre cultures, the North Bay culture, and the Oneota culture. The rest of the museum is devoted to general history, art, and natural history.

HOURS: Monday–Saturday: 9:00 A.M.–5:00 P.M.
Sunday: 2:00 P.M.–5:00 P.M.
Closed holidays.
ADMISSION: Free.

Madison

• *State Historical Society of Wisconsin*
816 State Street
Madison, Wisconsin 53706 *(608) 262-2704*

Since it is located in the state capital, this museum emphasizes Wisconsin's history from prehistoric times to the present. From the prehistoric period are displays showing how pottery, stone, and copper were used.

There is also a large collection of Old Copper material. A Plains Indian display includes a teepee and a reconstructed pioneer log cabin.

HOURS: September–May
Monday–Thursday: 8:00 A.M.–10:00 P.M. (Friday till 5:00 P.M.).
Saturday: 8:00 A.M.–4:00 P.M.
Sunday: 12:00 M.–4:00 P.M.
Closed holidays.
Summer vacations: 8:00 A.M.–5:00 P.M.; same weekend hours.
ADMISSION: Free.

Milwaukee

• *Milwaukee Public Museum*
800 West Wells Street
Milwaukee, Wisconsin 53233 *(414) 278-2700*

A beautifully colored Haida totem pole from the northwest coast stands at the door of this natural history museum. Inside, displays represent Indian life in both North and South America. Materials excavated at Wisconsin sites are used to show the evolution of Indian cultures. The prehistoric world is brought to life with modern dioramas, films, life-sized models, and audio programs. The whole museum is devoted to American Indians, and even the cafeteria is decorated with Indian crafts.

HOURS: 9:00 A.M.–5:00 P.M. daily.
Closed major holidays.
ADMISSION: Adults $2, children under eighteen 75¢, Milwaukee residents free.

Sheboygan

• *Sheboygan County Museum*
3110 Erie Avenue
Sheboygan, Wisconsin 53081 *(414) 458-1103*

Materials gathered from local finds have been brought together to depict the county's history. Prehistoric artifacts are used to describe the Old Copper, Hopewell, and Mississippian cultures. The museum is housed in a historic home built in 1850. Effigy mounds of many shapes are found in **Sheboygan Mound Park** (see site listings above).

HOURS: April–September
Tuesday–Saturday: 10:00 A.M.–5:00 P.M.
Sunday: 1:00 P.M.–5:00 P.M.
Closed October–March; Easter weekend, July 4.
ADMISSION: Adults 50¢, children five to twelve 25¢, under five free.

Stevens Point

• *Museum of Natural History*
University of Wisconsin
Learning Resources Center
Stevens Point, Wisconsin 54481 *(715) 346-2858*

The University of Wisconsin has brought together here several collections of local artifacts. One display shows a prehistoric burial.

HOURS: Monday–Thursday: 8:00 A.M.–10:00 P.M. (Friday till 5:00 P.M.)
Saturday: 8:00 A.M.– 4:00 P.M.
Sunday: 12:00 M.–4:00 P.M.
Closed holidays.
Summer vacations: 8:00 A.M.–5:00 P.M.; same weekend hours.
ADMISSION: Free.

STATE OFFICE

Joan E. Freeman
State Archaeologist
Wisconsin Historical Society
816 State Street
Madison, Wisconsin 53706 (608) 262-3271

OPPORTUNITIES FOR AMATEURS

Archaeologists in Wisconsin are working on a certification program for lay archaeologists, but as of this writing the program is still in its infancy. If you are interested in this program, stay in touch with the Wisconsin Archaeological Society (see below).

ORGANIZATIONS TO JOIN

The Wisconsin Archaeological Society is a statewide, lay-professional organization. Its publication, *The Wisconsin Archaeologist*, is the oldest continuous state publication in America. The society has several local chapters, and you can reach the central headquarters by writing:

Wisconsin Archaeological Society
P.O. Box 1292
Milwaukee, Wisconsin 53201

THE GREAT PLAINS

Colorado

Kansas

Montana

Nebraska

North Dakota/South Dakota

Oklahoma

Texas

Wyoming

THE GREAT PLAINS

The Great Plains area cuts a wide swath from Canada's southern Alberta all the way south to central Texas. From west to east, the plains spread from the Rocky Mountain barrier through dry desert badlands and scrubby flat prairies, on toward the grassy plains of the Missouri River, which marks the Great Plains' eastern border, separating it from the wetter climes of the Midwest.

In its antiquity the Great Plains was the floor of several oceans. It has been a steaming swamp and even a sheet of ice in the north. It has been forested, although now it is nearly treeless. Giant turtles and crocodiles once existed here; so did camels, huge sloths, rhinoceroses, tiny wild horses, and giant pigs.

Ten thousand years ago, mammoths roamed the Great Plains. The Imperial mammoth was the size of a two-story building, nearly twenty-two feet high at its shoulder. Prehistoric hunters brought it down with their stone-pointed spears. At the end of the Ice Age, the Great Plains went through a hot dry period when the Big Game Hunters all but abandoned the region. Artifacts recovered from sites in Wyoming and Nebraska indicate that a few hunters remained and made the transition to the Archaic Tradition. As the climate improved, bison and later buffalo migrated through an ocean of grass, and the Great Plains once again became a rich hunting ground for prehistoric people.

The Archaic Tradition on the Great Plains represents an intermingling of eastern and western cultures. Woodland farming techniques influenced the people who lived along the Missouri River. They began to cultivate some crops, including corn, and gradually settled into permanent villages. But these people of the plains also continued to hunt and collect wild plant food.

This Archaic-Woodland blend became a Plains Village culture. The Mandan and Hidatsa people living along the river bluffs of the Missouri in North Dakota exemplified this synthesis of traditions. They made pottery, grew corn and squash, and lived a sedentary village life. In the summer and fall, they roamed across the plains in pursuit of buffalo and wild game.

In eastern Oklahoma, Spiro was an outpost of the Southern Cult phenomenon, which arose out of the great eastern Mississippian Tradition. The Spiro people built mounds and made elaborate ornaments and burial offerings.

But in the northwestern badlands of the Great Plains, buffalo hunters continued to follow the Archaic Tradition until white men drove them onto the confines of reservations. In some regions of the plains, hunters began to farm and then abandoned agriculture in favor of buffalo hunting. These were the only prehistoric people known to have given up farming once they had learned it. Thus, on the Great Plains, the Archaic, Plains Woodland, and Plains Village cultures existed simultaneously, often overlapping.

COLORADO

SITES

Prehistoric people probably lived all over Colorado, but they were mainly nomadic hunters. Two early sites on the windy playas of the Colorado plains contribute to the evidence that people may have been in America before 10,000 B.C. At the Dutton and Selby sites, Paleo-Indians brought down mammoths, camels, horses and bison at Ice Age watering holes. Excavations under the direction of Dennis Stanford of the Smithsonian Institution have revealed several layers of cultural material dating from the Clovis period back possibly to twenty thousand years ago. Except for the Clovis points, all the artifacts recovered were made of bone, a finding consistent with other early sites in Alaska.

Another important Colorado excavation is the Lindenmeier site in the far northeastern corner of the state, where bison were slaughtered and butchered more than ten thousand years ago. The ancient campsite of the hunters is nearby. The many artifacts found at the Lindenmeier site all describe the life of people preoccupied with the hunt—dozens of stone and bone knives, choppers and scrapers of all varieties were uncovered. Folsom points were found here along with a thinner, unfluted point known as the Yuma point. The Yuma may prove to be contemporaneous with the Folsom point. Collections of both projectile points can be seen at the Denver Museum of Natural History. This famous museum also houses the original Folsom point discovered in New Mexico.

Little else is known about the early people who inhabited Colorado until the Basketmakers, early ancestors of the Pueblo people, moved into the mesa lands of the southwestern part of the state. The great Anasazi ruins of Mesa Verde and other archaeological sites of southwestern Colorado are described in "Four Corners," in the "Southwest" section of this book.

Although there are no archaeological sites open to the public in the rest of Colorado, it is possible to hike on a section of the ancient **Ute Trail,** which crosses the Continental Divide in Rocky Mountain National Park. Check the map in the Visitors' Center on Trail Ridge Road in the park. (The entrance to Rocky Mountain National Park is two miles west of Estes Park on Colorado 66.) And the **Great Sand Dunes** provide a glimpse into yet another prehistoric life style. As long ago as twenty thousand years, people may have hunted in the San Luis Valley near the Great Sand Dunes.

MUSEUMS

Alamosa

- *Adams State College Museum*
  ES Building
  Alamosa, Colorado 81102 *(303) 589-7011*

This anthropological museum has collections from Paleo times, as well as Pueblo Indian artifacts and pottery. There is a planetarium and observatory.

DIRECTIONS: The museum is on U.S. 160.
HOURS: Monday–Thursday: 1:00 P.M.–4:00 P.M.
Closed holidays and school vacations.
ADMISSION: Free.

- *Grand Sand Dunes National Monument*
  Visitors' Center
  P.O. Box 60
  Alamosa, Colorado 81101 *(303) 378-2312*

Prehistoric people camped just west of the monument about ten thousand years ago. Extinct bison bones have been found together with beautifully fluted Folsom points used to make the kill.

Exhibits in the museum trace the natural and human history of the Great Sand Dunes. Indian artifacts, archaeology, geological exhibits tell the story. In summer the rangers offer nightly programs in the amphitheater and nature walks. Special four-wheel-drive tours through the sand dunes last two and a half hours and leave daily between 8:00 A.M. and 6:00 P.M. Camping is permitted in the park.

DIRECTIONS: The monument is 34 miles northeast of Alamosa on SR 150.
HOURS: 8:00 A.M.–5:00 P.M. daily. Extended hours in summer.
Closed Christmas.
ADMISSION: $1/car/day.

Boulder

- *University of Colorado Museum*
  Henderson Building
  Broadway between 15th and 16th Streets
  Boulder, Colorado 80309 *(303) 492-6165*

The prehistoric panorama of the Great Plains and Southwest is traced in numerous displays and in important collections from ancient kill sites in Colorado and also material recovered by famous archaeologist Earl Morris. The Hall of Man gallery is devoted to the Hohokam, Mogollon, and Anasazi.

One exhibit explains the unique tree-ring dating system that has allowed archaeologists to date archaeological sites accurately in the Southwest. Also, a find collection of Hopi kachina dolls is displayed. Other sections of the museum are devoted to regional geology, zoology, and botany.

HOURS: Monday–Friday: 9:00 A.M.–5:00 P.M.; Saturday to 4:00 P.M.
Sunday and holidays: 10:00 A.M.–4:00 P.M.
Closed major holidays.
ADMISSION: Free.

Colorado Springs

- *Cliff Dwellings Museum*
Manitou Springs
Colorado Springs, Colorado 80829 *(303) 685-5242*

The museum depicts the great Pueblo period between A.D. 1100 and 1300 and describes the lives and architectural achievements of all of the Indians of the Southwest.

DIRECTIONS: West on U.S. 24 Bypass to Manitou Springs.
HOURS: Summers only: May and September
10:00 A.M.–5:00 P.M. daily except Friday.
June–August
9:00 A.M.–6:00 P.M. daily.
ADMISSION: Adults $1.25, children seven to eleven 50¢.

- *Pioneers' Museum*
Old Court House
215 South Tejon Street
Colorado Springs, Colorado 80903 *(303) 471-6650*

Archaeological and historical collections from Colorado and New Mexico are featured. For a full picture of the prehistoric societies of the region, request a guided tour through the museum.

HOURS: Tuesday–Saturday: 10:00 A.M.–5:00 P.M.
Sunday: 2:00 P.M.–5:00 P.M.
Closed major holidays.
ADMISSION: Free.

Denver

- *Colorado State Museum*
Colorado Heritage Center
13th Street and Broadway
Denver, Colorado 80203 *(303) 839-3681*

Mesa Verde is depicted here in dioramas and displays. Other exhibits trace the life of the prehistoric Utes. Western and historical artifacts are also on display.

HOURS: Monday–Friday: 9:00 A.M.–5:00 P.M.
Saturday, Sunday, and holidays: 10:00 A.M.–5:00 P.M.
ADMISSION: Free.

- *Denver Museum of Natural History*
City Park
Montview and Colorado Boulevard
Denver, Colorado 80205 *(303) 575-3872*

In 1926, this world-famous natural history museum sponsored the field trip to Folsom, New Mexico, where a stone point found among the bones of an extinct bison proved for the first time that people had been in North America for at least ten thousand years. That Folsom point is on exhibit, still lodged between the bison's ribs. Archaeological material has been collected from all over the world. Exhibits in two major galleries depict the life of prehistoric people—the Hall of Old World Peoples and Prehistoric People of America.

The Denver Museum is one of the world's finest natural history museums. The first floor displays mineralogy and geology of the Colorado region; the second floor is devoted to mounted animals. Vertebrate and invertebrate fossils, collections of archaeological specimens, and many more exhibits dealing with prehistoric Indian lore and life are found all over the museum.

Natural history items are for sale in the Museum Shop. Stop at the information desk for a floor plan before venturing into the dozens of galleries and halls of this enormous museum.

HOURS: Monday–Saturday: 9:00 A.M.–4:30 P.M.
Sunday and holidays: 12:00 M.–4:30 P.M.
Closed Thanksgiving, Christmas Eve and Day, New Year's Eve and Day.
ADMISSION: Free.

Note: The museum frequently sponsors archaeological field trips for members; the general public is invited if there's room. Check the museum schedule.

STATE OFFICE

Bruce Rippeteau
State Archaeologist
Colorado State Museum
13th Street and Broadway
Denver, Colorado 80203 (303) 839-3681

OPPORTUNITIES FOR AMATEURS AND ORGANIZATIONS TO JOIN

Archaeological societies have been formed in Denver, Fort Collins, and Pueblo, Colorado. For full information about amateur participation, write or call the office of the state archaeologist (see above).

KANSAS

The evolution of cultures in Kansas followed the basic pattern established throughout the Great Plains. The people in the western part of the state pursued the Archaic hunting tradition into historic times. In eastern Kansas Woodland people introduced ceramics and agriculture. A Plains Woodland culture developed here, and several prehistoric villages have been discovered by members of the Kansas Archaeological Society.

The large and powerful Pawnee nation originated in northern Kansas and extended into present-day Nebraska. The Pawnee lived very much as the Mandan Indians of the Dakotas. They were farmers and hunters who built earth lodges along river terraces and farmed the river bottoms. They planted their gardens in the spring, then moved onto the high plains to hunt bison all summer long, returning to their villages for the fall harvest. Some remnants of their way of life can be seen at the Pawnee Indian Village in north central Kansas.

America's first amateur archaeological society originated in Kansas. A full training program is offered to members and yearly fieldwork is carried out at sites around the state.

SITES

Belleville

- *Pawnee Indian Village Museum*
  Route 1
  Republic, Kansas 66964 *(913) 361-2255*

The modern walls of the museum encircle the floor of a Pawnee earth lodge. A walkway rims the inside wall, taking you past recessed display cases that contain artifacts discovered in the Pawnee village. Two enormous dioramas illustrate how the village must have looked when European traders first entered, and the original lodge floor, fifty feet in diameter, is exactly as the Indians left it. Stone, bone, and metal tools have been left as found.

The Pawnee were descendants of ancient peoples whose hunting grounds south of the Platte River included much of Kansas; this village was probably inhabited by about a thousand people in the 1820s and 1830s. Although the Pawnee were a powerful people, the combined pressure from white intruders and attacks by other tribes forced them into smaller and smaller areas. In 1875, they were forced from their remaining lands in Nebraska and northern Kansas and coerced into settling in the Indian Territory of present-day Oklahoma.

The **Kansas Historical Society** has skillfully interpreted this site, making it the best place in the state to learn about early life on the plains.

DIRECTIONS: From Belleville drive 15 miles west on US 36 to KS 266; then drive north 8 miles to the museum.
HOURS: Tuesday–Saturday: 10:00 A.M.–5:00 P.M.
Sunday: 1:00 P.M.–5:00 P.M.
Closed Mondays, Thanksgiving, Christmas, New Year's.
ADMISSION: Free.

Hays

- *Sternberg Memorial Museum*
  Hays, Kansas 67601 *(913) 628-4000*

The Sternberg Memorial Museum has extensive natural history exhibits and excellent archaeological displays. The museum is on the campus of Fort Hays State University at the western edge of town.

HOURS: Monday–Friday: 8:00 A.M.–5:00 P.M.
Closed holidays.
During school vacation: 1:00 P.M.–5:00 P.M.
ADMISSION: Free.

Salina

- *Indian Burial Pits*
  Price Brothers Farm
  Salina, Kansas 67401

Enormous signs all over the highway leading into Salina direct you along a country road to a small farm where a unique archaeological site is "housed." Underneath a tin shed is an open pit, containing the skeletal remains of 146 prehistoric Indians. The flexed skeletons are exactly as they were placed by people of the Smoky Hill culture about eight hundred years ago. The burial ground, certainly the largest uncovered burial other than Dixon Mounds in Illinois, was discovered accidentally in the 1930s and later excavated by an amateur archaeologist.

There is almost no interpretation at the site, but everything has been left in place as it was found, including the few grave goods that lie next to the skeletons. The cemetery was carefully excavated. If you have seen exposed burials at Dixon Mounds or any other lavishly interpreted sites, you'll notice the identical archaeological effect of each skeleton lying on what appears to be a raised dias. No hermetically sealed doors protect the skeletons from the climate, so the bones have been shellacked till they are the color of dark brown molasses. It's been so long a time since anyone's been down into the pit that the old bones, pots, flint knives, and shell necklaces are covered with layers of dust.

Palmer Price, one of the Price brothers, accompanies visitors around the walkway, chatting about the farm. The cemetery complex is much larger than this pit, but there will be no further excavation. Even if you dislike skeletons, this is a special site in Kansas.

DIRECTIONS: From I-70, take the Niles exit and follow the directional signs (over flat dirt road) to the site.
HOURS: 9:00 A.M.–6:00 P.M. daily (or by appointment).
ADMISSION: Adults $1, children under twelve 50¢.

MUSEUMS

Ellsworth

• *Ellsworth County Museum*
Main Street
Ellsworth, Kansas 67439 *(913) 472-3059*

Some prehistoric artifacts are displayed, along with replicas of petroglyphs found in central Kansas.

HOURS: Tuesday–Saturday: 10:00 A.M.–5:00 P.M.
Sunday: 1:00 P.M.–5:00 P.M.
ADMISSION: Free.

Lyons

- *Rice County Historical Museum*
  221 East Avenue South
  Lyons, Kansas 67554 *(316) 257-3941*

This local museum contains a large amount of material recovered from the prehistoric village sites in the vicinity. These sites in Rice County are an important part of the current archaeological work in Kansas, since they are believed to mark Coronado's entrance onto the plains in 1541.

HOURS: Tuesday–Saturday: 10:00 A.M.–5:00 P.M.
Sunday: 1:00 P.M.–5:00 P.M.
ADMISSION: Contributions accepted.

STATE OFFICE

Thomas A. Witty, Jr.
State Archaeologist
Kansas State Historical Society
120 West 10th Street
Topeka, Kansas 66612 (913) 296-3251

OPPORTUNITIES FOR AMATEURS

The **Kansas Archaeological Training Program,** a joint effort of the Kansas Historical Society and the Kansas Anthropological Association, sponsors a two-week dig each summer. The amateurs provide volunteer help, and the society supplies the supervision. A full training program in the theory and techniques of excavation, survey, laboratory analysis, and exhibit techniques offers certification for amateurs.

Visitors are usually welcome to observe summer excavations. If you live in Kansas or plan to be traveling in the state and would like to observe a dig, write the Kansas Historical Society (above address).

ORGANIZATIONS TO JOIN

The **Kansas Anthropological Association** is the leading amateur organization in the state. Its members have statewide and local meetings and yearly field schools. The association works closely with professionals in the state. You can reach the association through the Kansas Historical Society or by writing:

Kansas Anthropological Association
Route 2
Beloit, Kansas 67420

MONTANA

The rugged Bitteroot range divides Montana from Idaho, making it a gateway to the Great Plains. The headwaters of the Missouri River rush out of the mountains and meander across the eastern Badlands, where less than a century ago herds of buffalo grazed.

The Plains Indians of this region gathered wild plants and hunted buffalo. There are several buffalo "jumps" in Montana, places where Indians maneuvered their prey toward steep cliffs and stampeded them over the side. The "jump" technique made these prehistoric hunters extremely efficient even without horses. Most of the jump sites are on private property not open to the public.

Relics found in Montana suggest that it has been inhabited continuously since 3000 B.C. But like other parts of the western plains, no traces of agriculture or pottery have been found here.

Many tipi rings have been found in the state. These circles of stone left by the Indians are found all over the western plains. Their significance is a mystery. They may have been used to hold down tents, for religious rites, as sun calendars, or even for trapping game. Sometimes they are found in clusters, and sometimes only one or two appear on a barren hillside. People often stumble over these circles of stones in parks and wilderness regions on the northern plains. Some circles are small, others quite large.

Few archaeological excavations are conducted in Montana; some museums exhibit material from prehistoric sites.

SITES

Billings

• *Pictograph Cave State Monument*

Three caves at this site are connected to each other by a paved trail. There is evidence that a number of different people used these caves for long periods of time. The walls are covered with paintings of men and animals. Excavation in the caves chronicles two previous occupations including a basket-making culture.

DIRECTIONS: From Billings drive east 7 miles on I-90 toward Harbin; a turnoff will direct you to the site.

HOURS: Open daily at all times.

ADMISSION: Free.

Logan

- *Madison Buffalo Run*

A long cliff at the edge of this prairie was used for centuries to "hunt" buffalo. Herds of bison were cornered and driven over the cliffside. The Madison jump is the only run in Montana open to the public. There is no visitors' center, but interpretive signs explain how the jump was used.

DIRECTIONS: Take I-90 west from Bozeman to Logan. Signs at the exit will direct you 6 miles to the run.
HOURS: Open daily at all times.
ADMISSION: Free.

MUSEUMS

Bozeman

- *Museum of the Rockies*
Montana State University
Bozeman, Montana 59715 *(406) 994-2251*

The small collection of prehistoric artifacts here will be expanded within the next few years. One mammoth skull on display was probably scavenged by prehistoric people.

HOURS: Monday–Friday: 9:00 A.M.–4:30 P.M.
Saturday and Sunday: 1:00 P.M.–4:30 P.M.
Closed major holidays.
ADMISSION: Free.

Browning

- *Museum of the Plains Indian and Crafts Center*
P.O. Box 400
Browning, Montana 59417 *(406) 338-2230*

Although there are few prehistoric museum collections in Montana, many museums are devoted to the historic aspects of the Plains Indians. The most extensive interpretation of Plains Indian life is found at the Museum of the Plains Indian. Many exhibits here show the way in which Indian life was altered by the territorial expansion of the United States. The museum is administered and operated by the Indian Arts and Crafts Board, U.S. Department of the Interior. A craft shop sells items made by the Plains Indians.

DIRECTIONS: The museum is at the junction of U.S. 2 and 89, 1/2 mile west of Browning.
HOURS: June–September: 9:00 A.M.–5:00 P.M. daily.
October–May: Monday–Friday: 10:00 A.M.–4:30 P.M.
Closed Christmas, Thanksgiving, New Year's.
ADMISSION: Free.

STATE OFFICE

There is no state archaeologist in Montana. For information about archaeology in the state, and to report possible sites, write or call:

Museum of the Rockies
Montana State University
Bozeman, Montana 59715 (406) 994-2251

ORGANIZATIONS TO JOIN

The **Montana Archaeological Society** is a lay-professional organization dedicated to the expansion of knowledge about Montana's prehistory. For information, write:

Dr. Les Davis
c/o Sociology Department
Montana State University
Bozeman, Montana 59715

NEBRASKA

Like South Dakota and Kansas, Nebraska opens out under endless skies. The Missouri River forms the eastern border; in the west bone-dry buttes scrape the horizon. The Platte River runs most of its course through Nebraska, at places a mile wide and only a foot deep.

In prehistoric times hundreds of thousands of buffalo migrated through Nebraska. Ten thousand years ago, hunters gathered at watering holes on the slowly drying plains and killed bison, musk oxen, and mammoths, the last survivors of the waning Ice Age. Bison bones, stone tools and Folsom points have been found in many parts of Nebraska.

After the big game disappeared, Archaic hunters concentrated in the more eastern reaches of the state and for thousands of years followed the game animals back and forth across the Platte. Here they probably encountered Woodland Indians entering the region from Iowa and Wisconsin to settle the rich bottom land. Finely crafted bone needles, beads, and tools have been found here. Wooden disc ornaments covered with copper were recovered from one village site along with shell ornaments and conch shells from the Gulf Coast.

SITES

Crawford

- *Fort Robinson State Historic Site*
  Crawford, Nebraska 69339 *(308) 665-2852*

Fort Robinson is in the beautiful Pine Ridge country near the Black Hills, and Plains Indians, soldiers, fur trappers, and pioneers used it as a home base. Nearly fifty of its original buildings still stand. In the post headquarters, a small display describes the life of prehistoric Indians on the plains. Wonderful exhibits of the Plains Indians tell of their buffalo-hunting days before the white man came. The great Sioux chief, Crazy Horse, died in the log guardhouse on the old parade grounds of this fort.

DIRECTIONS: From Crawford drive 3 miles west on U.S. 20.
HOURS: April–November 15
Monday–Saturday: 8:00 A.M.–5:00 P.M.
Sunday: 1:00 P.M.–5:00 P.M.
ADMISSION: Free.

Fort Calhoun

- *Fort Atkinson State Historical Park*
  Fort Calhoun, Nebraska 68023 *(402) 468-5895*

Fort Atkinson is a historical site—the first military post built west of the Missouri River—but it is the only place in Nebraska where a dig-in-progress can be observed. In a major undertaking sponsored by the Nebraska Historical Society, the old fort is being fully excavated and restored. Visitors are welcome in the summer; an on-site museum describes life on the plains during the 1800s.

DIRECTIONS: The park is in Fort Calhoun, just north of Omaha.
HOURS (MUSEUM): Memorial Day–Labor Day: 10:00 A.M.–8:00 P.M. daily.
Groups, by appointment, rest of year.
HOURS (PARK): 8:00 A.M. till sunset, year round.
ADMISSION: Free.

Lewellen

- *Ash Hollow State Park*
Lewellen, Nebraska 69147 *(308) 778-5651*

Ice Age geology, vertebrate fossils, and the story of early peoples come together at Ash Hollow State Park. The bones of extinct mammoths and rhinoceroses have been found here. At a rock shelter toward the north end of the park, early people lived ten thousand years ago. Artifacts are preserved as they were found in the caves.

Paleo-Indians, buffalo hunters, and pioneers trekking westward across the prairie all found shelter, food, and water at Ash Hollow. A visitors' center in the park describes the geology, paleontology, and human occupation of the park. Visitors can enjoy hiking and primitive camping.

DIRECTIONS: The park is on U.S. 26, west of Ogallala, near Lewellen.
HOURS (MUSEUM): May 24–Labor Day: 10:00 A.M.–8:00 P.M.
HOURS (PARK): 8:00 A.M. to sunset, year round. The caves can be visited only in the summer.
ADMISSION: Free.

MUSEUMS

Hastings

- *Hastings Museum*
1330 North Burlington Avenue
Hastings, Nebraska 68901 *(402) 463-7126*

This big, fascinating museum is devoted to the lore and life of the plains. Displays focus primarily on pioneers and historic Indian tribes, but some prehistoric material is mixed in. A resource library is open to the public; special tours for school groups can be arranged.

HOURS: Monday–Saturday: 8:00 A.M.–5:00 P.M.
Sunday and holidays: 1:00 P.M.–5:00 P.M.
ADMISSION: Adults 75¢, children 25¢.

Lincoln

- *Nebraska State Historical Society Museum*
1500 R Street
Lincoln, Nebraska 68508 *(402) 471-3270*

The Nebraska State Historical Society is dedicated to preserving both prehistoric and historic sites in Nebraska. Artifacts from major sites chronicle

Nebraska life from earliest prehistoric times through the pioneer era. Prehistoric material recovered from several excavations along the Missouri River is also on display. The society's library of Nebraskan and western history and the Nebraska State Archives are housed here.

DIRECTIONS: The museum is on the mall, north of the capitol building.
HOURS: Monday–Saturday: 8:00 A.M.–5:00 P.M.
Sunday: 1:30 P.M.–5:00 P.M.
Closed major holidays.
ADMISSION: Free.

- *University of Nebraska State Museum*
212 Morrill Hall
14th and U Streets
Lincoln, Nebraska 68588 *(402) 472-2642*

The best exhibits exploring Nebraska's prehistoric past are in this large museum. Some exhibit materials are drawn from excavations carried out by the museum. A unique projectile point known as the Scottsbluff point, recovered from a bison quarry in southwestern Nebraska, is on display.

Another display from the Lipscomb site in Texas shows Folsom points stuck in the bones of an extinct bison. From Signal Butte in western Nebraska are tools and animal bones left near an Archaic hunters' campsite more than 4500 years ago.

The museum offers special programs for children and students; a major research library is open to the public. The Museum Shop sells books, stamps, rocks, and minerals.

HOURS: Monday–Saturday: 8:00 A.M.–5:00 P.M.
Sunday and holidays: 1:30 P.M.–5:00 P.M.
Closed Thanksgiving, and school Christmas vacation.
ADMISSION: Free.

STATE OFFICE

Nebraska State Historical Society
1500 R Street
Lincoln, Nebraska 68508 (402) 471-3270

OPPORTUNITIES FOR AMATEURS

Unlike most states, Nebraska does not encourage amateurs to participate in archaeology. Most preservation and restoration is devoted to historic sites.

The best way to learn about archaeological developments in the state is to join the **Nebraska State Historical Society Museum** or the **University of Nebraska State Museum.** Both institutions offer memberships.

NORTH AND SOUTH DAKOTA

The prairie spreads flat against a limitless horizon. The Missouri River slices diagonally across the plains then bends down to St. Louis, where it joins the Mississippi. It's hard to believe, but in another geologic era fifteen-foot alligators, crocodiles, and giant turtles thrived here.

At the end of the Ice Age, receding glaciers left broad flat plains of rich soil. The open prairie is studded with the gray mesas and bluffs of the Badlands. The rolling green fields give way westward to scrubby tufts of vegetation.

Stone tools and weapons found in the vicinity of Bismarck, North Dakota, suggest early occupancy, but no one knows just when people first entered the Dakotas. The first traces of human life seem to appear during Archaic times.

Several unusual prehistoric remains have been found in the Dakotas. Unusual mounds and earthworks have been discovered in the eastern regions of the states. Rude cairns that may have been prehistoric road signs occasionally are found piled up on top of hills. More mysterious are the circles of stones found on steeply sloping hillsides. The use of these stone rings, sometimes called "tipi rings," has never been discovered. Turtle effigies outlined in stone also have been found on the open prairie. Turtles may have played some part in the religious ceremonies of the Mandan Indians, but the meaning of these effigies has never been traced.

The Archaic people of the Great Plains were distinct from the tribes further west, as they were cut off by mountain ranges, but the people also followed the Archaic Tradition, surviving by hunting bison and wild game. Then Woodland people from the east penetrated the plains and introduced farming and pottery into the eastern region of the prairie. The two overlapping cultures lived side by side.

On the moist eastern plains near the river basins, the Hidatsa, Arikara, and Mandan people established permanent villages around agricultural centers, creating a Plains Village culture. These people continued to hunt, but farming provided a stable food supply. The origin of these tribes is unknown. The Mandan were probably the first to enter the region. Crowded by other tribes, they may have wandered westward from the Gulf Coast, then moved northward in successive migrations up the Missouri River until they reached the Heart River near Bismarck.

By the thirteenth century, the early Mandan and possibly the Hidatsa were well established in villages between the Knife and Heart rivers. Their rectangular lodges were clustered in small villages on terrace rims above the rivers. From miles away the domed earthen huts of the villages could be seen crowded onto the river bluffs. Each wooden lodge was plastered with mud until it looked like a mound with a long tunnel leading into it. About twenty people lived in each lodge. These earth lodges were built around a central plaza, where the social and religious life of the community took place. The biggest of these villages had more than one hundred lodges.

The Mandan people most clearly represent the special blend of traditions of the plains. They were the most successful gardeners in northwestern North America, growing corn, beans, squash, and sunflowers. In between the spring planting and fall harvest, they hunted buffalo, elk, deer, antelope, and waterfowl.

The Mandan and other culturally related tribes continued their way of life into historic times, trading with the white trappers and settlers who followed Lewis and Clark up the Missouri. Then, like other native Americans, these people were ravaged by diseases introduced by the Europeans. In the smallpox epidemics of 1837 and 1838, the Hidatsa, Mandan, and Arikara may have lost 60 percent of their population. Descendants of the survivors live today on the Fort Berthold Reservation in the northwestern part of North Dakota.

NORTH DAKOTA

SITES

Clustered along the Missouri River near Bismarck are several preserved Mandan village sites that are open to the public. With the exception of the Knife River National Historic Site, these are administered by the North Dakota Historical Society.

Most of the villages were occupied into historic times, but they are strongly reminiscent of those of the prehistoric people. Mandan women built the village lodges, although men assisted them in placing the timbers that supported the thick earth walls. In some sites only pits in the earth can be seen; at others whole earth lodges are intact. All of these sites are open free at all times.

Mandan Village Sites Near Bismarck

Double Ditch Indian Village is the site of an earth-lodge village occupied by the Mandan people sometime between 1675 and 1781.

DIRECTIONS: The village is 7 miles north of Bismarck on Highway 1804.

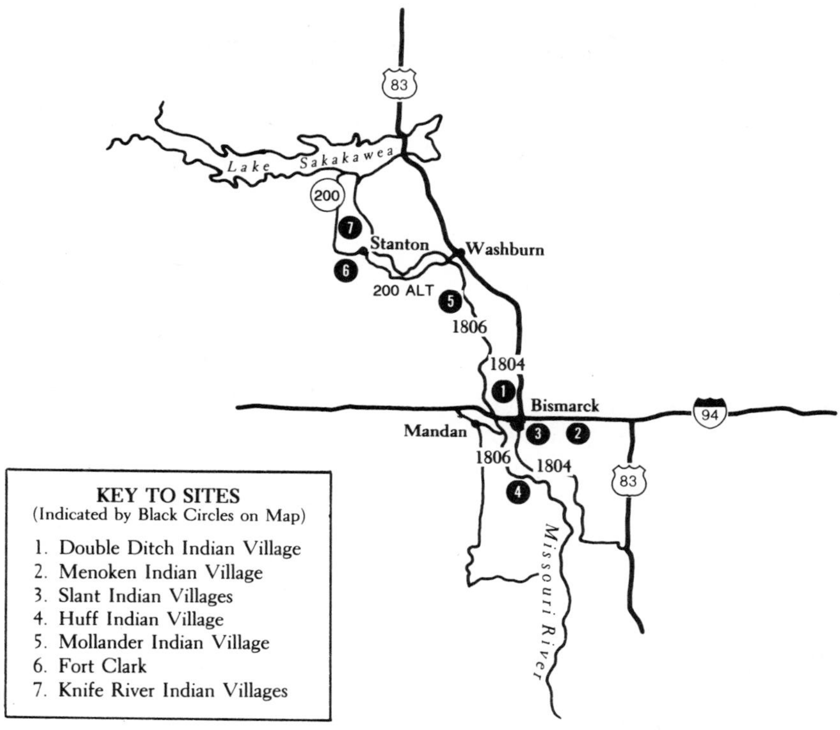

Close-up map of Bismarck area, North Dakota.

Menoken Indian Village Historic Site: The cultural affiliation and dates of occupation of this earth-lodge village are still unknown. It is believed to be the point where Pierre de la Verendrye, the earliest white explorer to enter North Dakota, first visited the Mandan Indians. The site shows the position of bastions and the moat of the old fortification. Saucer-shaped depressions can be seen where earth lodges once stood.

DIRECTIONS: The village is located 13 miles east of Bismarck on I-94.

Slant Indian Villages are part of Fort Lincoln State Park. Reconstructed earth lodges on the site show how the Mandans lived between 1675 and 1781. The village once contained sixty-eight lodges. Five of these have been reconstructed on their original sites; all the details inside and outside the lodges have been very faithfully reproduced, based on archaeological evidence.

At this site visitors can see a prehistoric dwelling very much as it must have appeared before white explorers came to North Dakota. Furnishings inside the lodges portray the daily life of the people, including their tools, mortars and giant pestles, hoes, and shovels. One of the lodges is a ceremonial building eighty-four feet in diameter standing in its original position in the center of the village.

DIRECTIONS: The villages are 4 miles south of Mandan on Highway 1804.

Huff Indian Village Historic Site is an early site, occupied by the ancestors of the Mandan between 1485 and 1545. Legend has it that the Mandan once lived underground. They climbed vines to enter this world through an opening in the earth's crust. Once on the surface, their leader, Good Furred Robe, laid out their first village, placing the houses in rows like corn. The original village of the legend may have been Huff, where the heavily sodded lodge rings suggest great age.

DIRECTIONS: Huff is 15 miles south of Mandan on Highway 1806, on the west bank of the Missouri River. The site is 1 mile south of the town of Huff.

Mollander Indian Village Historic Site was occupied around 1807.

DIRECTIONS: The site is 20 miles north of Mandan on Highway 1806 and River Road.

Fort Clark Historic Site: This interesting site is the scene of an early Mandan village that was later occupied by the Arikara Indians from 1838 to about 1861. The remains of Fort Clark, a fur post built by the American Fur Company in 1831, can still be seen.

DIRECTIONS: The site is located 14 miles west of Washburn on Highway 200 Alt.

Knife River Indian Villages National Historic Site contains the remnants of five villages occupied by the Hidatsa and the Mandan Indians. Over the years the small villages grew to fortified towns. The villages lie on the southern bank of the Knife River, named by the Indians who quarried flint for their knives along the river banks.

Toussaint Charbonneau and his wife Sacajawea were living in one of these villages when Lewis and Clark came through in 1802. Charbonneau was engaged as an interpreter, and Sacajawea joined him on the hazardous expedition. A full portrayal of their story can be seen at the **State Historical Society of North Dakota** in Bismarck.

Archaeologists from the University of North Dakota have been working at the village site for the past several years. During the summer staff members take visitors on a guided tour of the current excavation, explaining the history and archaeological investigation of the village site. The tours take about one and a half to two hours and are free.

The Knife River villages comprise the largest and best-preserved site in North Dakota. The site is located near Stanton at the confluence of the Knife and Missouri rivers, northwest of Mandan. For more information about current excavations, write: Box 175, Stanton, North Dakota 58571.

Fortuna

- *Writing Rock Historic Site*

Writing Rock, a ten-ton granite boulder, stands in a slight hollow at the crest of a hill commanding a view of the wide country below. The top and sides of the rock are covered with lines, dots, circles, and, near the top, a bird with wings outstretched. The petroglyphs apparently were pecked into the stone by many different prehistoric people over the centuries. The rock was regarded as sacred to generations of Indians who made pilgrimages here from Montana and other distant points all the way into historic times. Several graves have been found in the area; excavations yielded hammers, axes, shells, and beads of many shapes and colors. A second, smaller rock also is carved with inscriptions.

DIRECTIONS: Writing Rock Historic Site is in the far northwestern corner of North Dakota. From Fortuna at the junction of U.S. 85 and ND 5, drive south on a small county road to the site.

MUSEUMS

Bismarck

- *State Historical Society of North Dakota*
  Liberty Memorial Building
  Bismarck, North Dakota 58505 *(701) 224-2666*

A new museum building scheduled to open in 1981 will offer extensive exhibits drawing from the society's excavations in the field.

HOURS: Monday–Friday: 8:00 A.M.–5:00 P.M.
Saturday: 9:00 A.M.–4:00 P.M.
Sunday (summer only): 1:00 P.M.–5:00 P.M.

Grand Forks

• *Department of Anthropology*
University of North Dakota
Grand Forks, North Dakota 58202 *(701) 777-3309*

The students change the anthropology exhibits every year; the new exhibits always include some prehistoric material. Visitors are welcome.

HOURS: 9:00 A.M. to 5:00 P.M. weekdays when university is in session.
ADMISSION: Free.

New Town

• *Three Tribes Museum*
Fort Berthold Indian Reservation
New Town, North Dakota 58763 *(701) 627-4477*

Displays trace the history of the Mandan, Hidatsa, and Arikara Indians. Although the artifacts in the museum are not scientifically interpreted, some are prehistoric. The museum is open all year. After Labor Day, the hours vary and it's a good idea to call before going.

DIRECTIONS: From New Town drive 5½ miles west on SR 23 in Four Bears Memorial Park.
HOURS: 9:00 A.M.–5:00 P.M. daily.
ADMISSION: Adults $1.50, students 50¢, under six free.

STATE OFFICE

North Dakota does not have a state archaeologist. Address all inquiries regarding archaeology in the state to:

State Historical Society of North Dakota
Liberty Memorial Building
Bismarck, North Dakota 58505 (701) 224-2666

OPPORTUNITIES FOR AMATEURS

The **University of North Dakota** offers a summer field school open to the general public as well as students. Visitors are usually welcome at these excavations, but the sites are often on private property with restricted access. If you would like to visit or join a summer dig in North Dakota, write:

Department of Anthropology and Archaeology
Box 8242, University Station
University of North Dakota
Grand Forks, North Dakota 58201

ORGANIZATIONS TO JOIN

The **State Historical Society** is encouraging amateur archaeologists in the state to form an association. For current information, write or call the society (see above).

SOUTH DAKOTA

SITES

Mitchell

● *Mitchell Prehistoric Indian Village*
P.O. Box 621
Mitchell, South Dakota 57301 *(605) 996-5473*

On a few acres of land caught between a golf course and a small lake, archaeologists are working to preserve a prehistoric village. At the Mitchell site everyone interested in archaeology is welcome to observe or participate in the dig.

The ancient village was probably occupied for about thirty years somewhere around A.D. 1000. Scientists believe that ancestors of the Mandan people came here to cut timber and left again when the region was stripped of wood. Scientists are not sure who these people were or where they came from.

A fortification trench surrounds the outer limits of the village; a smaller inner moat encircles the central portion. More than forty depressions in the grassy field show where the lodges once stood. As yet, archaeologists cannot tell exactly what these dwellings looked like.

The excavation teams, under the directorship of archaeologist Darrell W. Fulmer, will be working here for several years. There are plans for an on-site interpretation center that will describe the village site and its relationship to other regional cultures, as new information is gleaned from the fieldwork. The work here is urgent, since every day valuable material washes

Field director Darrel Fulmer with crew members in the excavation trench at Mitchell Prehistoric Indian Village, South Dakota.

out into the lake. From the lakeshore you can see the waves lapping against the village site, carrying away shell, bone, and stone artifacts.

A twelve-week **archaeological field school,** given in cooperation with the University of South Dakota, is offered every summer; the site is open to the public during those weeks (usually from June through August). Volunteers can join the dig for a day or a season. A small fee covers the supervisory time spent with novice participants. Long-term volunteers (six or more weeks) can have a free tent in a modern campground and a small food allowance.

Everyone is welcome to apply, including young people. The work at Mitchell offers an excellent opportunity for amateurs to learn fieldwork on a small enough scale so each person can fully participate in all parts of the dig.

The site is open to visitors only during the field school, but if you are in Mitchell at any time during the year, call Darrell Fulmer and he will arrange for you to see the Mitchell Prehistoric Indian Village.

Pottery sherds recovered from the dig are pieced together. Looking on is Theresa Villa, a crew member from the University of South Dakota. (Photo: JW.)

DIRECTIONS: From Mitchell take Highway 37 north to Cemetery Road; turn west on Cemetery Road and watch for a small directional marker to the village.

HOURS: June–August: 8:00 A.M.–8:00 P.M. daily.

MUSEUMS

Interior

- *Badlands National Park*
  Visitors' Center
  P.O. Box 6
  Interior, South Dakota 57750 *(605) 433-5361*

Wasted spires encroach on a stark landscape. This strange backdrop is the richest Oligocene fossil bed in the world. Camels and saber-toothed tigers once luxuriated here when it was a marshy plain. Tiny horses the size of fox terriers, giant pigs the size of cows, and the fantastic-looking protoceras with its long, narrow head and five pairs of horns sticking out of its face at different angles—the fossilized bones of all can be seen in the Badlands.

Campsites of prehistoric Indians have been found all over the Badlands. The earliest radiocarbon dating from these hearths is A.D. 900.

In the Visitors' Center, a major exhibit tells the tragic story of Wounded Knee, the massacre of 250 unarmed Sioux men, women, and children by U.S. soldiers. A second major exhibit traces Indian life in North Dakota from A.D. 500 to the Plains Village period (A.D. 1500), and into the later Siouan times of the historic period. The Visitors' Center has a hands-on exhibit room with wide doors and ramps for handicapped visitors.

In the summer park naturalists give campfire talks and accompany visitors on nature walks. Camping is permitted at Cedar Pass, and there's lodging in the park. For information about facilities, write the park superintendent.

DIRECTIONS: The Visitors' Center is at Cedar Pass.
HOURS: Memorial Day–Labor Day: 7:00 A.M.–9:00 P.M. daily.
Rest of year: 8:00 A.M.–4:30 P.M.
ADMISSION: Free; $1/car/day in summer only.

Vermillion

• *Over Dakota Museum*
University of South Dakota
Clark and Yale Streets
Vermillion, South Dakota 57069 *(605) 677-5228*

Extensive collections of prehistoric material are on display here, along with historical and geological exhibits. The Hall of Man details life in the region from Paleo times. The major focus is on the middle Missouri period when the Plains Indians adopted the burial mound idea and did some limited farming. Natural history exhibits include specimens of birds, mammals, and reptiles of South Dakota.

HOURS: Monday–Friday: 8:00 A.M.–4:30 P.M.
Saturday: 10:00 A.M.–4:30 P.M.
Sunday: 2:00 P.M.–4:30 P.M.
ADMISSION: Free.

STATE OFFICE

Robert Alex
State Archaeologist
Archaeological Research Center
Box 152
Ft. Meade, South Dakota 57741 (605) 347-3652

OPPORTUNITIES FOR AMATEURS

Amateurs and volunteers of all ages are welcome at the **Mitchell Prehistoric Indian Village** site (see listing under "Sites").

ORGANIZATIONS TO JOIN

South Dakota Archaeological Commission
State University Museum
Vermillion, South Dakota 57069 *(605) 347-3652*

OKLAHOMA

Oklahoma has the largest Indian population of any state, most of these immigrants from other parts of the country as a result of the infamous Trail of Tears "removal" that ended in 1839. It is home to more than sixty-five modern tribes who strive to preserve their ancient heritage in a new homeland.

The rich Indian history of Oklahoma after the Trail of Tears is unrelated to its distant past. Long before the removal to Oklahoma, the Cimarron River Valley may have been the cradle of a North American farming civilization. There is evidence that people lived in the valley for eleven thousand years before the Spanish claimed the land.

At the Domebo site near present-day Lawton, Paleo-Indians tracked and killed elephants. Caves in the western part of the state revealed an early Archaic basketmaking culture. And Spiro and Parris mounds were the product of a later farming society that was part of the advanced Southern Cult.

For years Spiro has been famous in the annals of American archaeology, but only recently has the site been opened to the public. It is the westernmost outpost of the Mississippian culture; with Etowah in Georgia and Moundville in Alabama, Spiro completes a Southern Cult triumvirate. Excavations continue at the site, and it is not to be missed by anyone interested in tracing and comparing the societies of the Southern Cult phenomenon.

Many Indian tribes in Oklahoma have their own museums. Even though these focus on more recent events in Indian culture, the exhibits often illuminate the tribe's early ancestry. Several large and beautiful museums in the state are devoted to the art and history of the native American. A visit to any one of these adds another dimension to the picture of Oklahoma.

SITES

Spiro

- *Spiro Mounds*
  Spiro, Oklahoma 74959 *(918) 962-2062*

Spiro is in one region of Oklahoma that lends itself to farming. The Cimarron, Arkansas, Illinois, Canadian, and Red rivers spill into the eastern part of the state, creating a rich, fertile bottom land.

The excavations at Spiro have helped piece together the story of early people's transition from nomadic hunting to a settled village life that surpassed mere survival. Unfortunately, much of the valuable information Spiro might have yielded has been lost to profiteers who "excavated" the site.

The prehistoric people who lived in eastern Oklahoma were probably ancestors of the modern Caddoan tribe. Between 2500 and 1500 years ago, a dramatic change occurred in their life style when maize, beans, and other seeds were introduced from New Mexico. Gradually, they developed a full-scale agricultural society. Permanent villages were established and, due to the abundance of food, the people were free to pursue high forms of art and religion. Through a trade network, Spiro became part of the Southern Cult.

The eight mounds at Spiro were used for both religious ceremonies and burials. Skeletons, tools, weapons, and rich grave goods of prehistoric men and women were found inside the mounds. Engraved conch shells and copper plates, freshwater pearls, and raw materials from the Gulf of Mexico, Florida, Illinois, and Michigan link Spiro to the Mississippian people from all over northern and southeastern America. Spiro may have been a manufacturing center for religious goods traded all across the South.

The elaborate, almost grotesque, sculptures and engravings found here originally led some archaeologist to speculate that the Southern Cult had a premonition of the impending destruction of their culture by Europeans. But recent radiocarbon testing shows that the mounds were built between A.D. 800 and 1100 and were abandoned long before Europeans reached America's shores. The sudden demise of the Southern Cult is as much a mystery as its origins.

Spiro will never reveal all of its secrets. The original excavator was the Pocola Mining Company, which blasted into the mounds in 1933, discarding bones and selling relics around the world. The artifacts were never documented; archaeologists will never know exactly where they were found or what they were used for. In 1935 professional archaeologists began to excavate the site. Two dedicated amateurs, Mr. and Mrs. Henry W. Hamilton, worked tirelessly for sixteen years to locate and reclaim the missing material that was spread across several continents. Spiro Mound contained the largest body of figural and decorated shell art ever discovered in North America.

Spiro is one of the few major sites where visitors are welcome to observe the ongoing excavations. Only one mound has been completely excavated and restored; others are in various stages of excavation.

Interpretation of the mounds and the work of the archaeologists is described in the on-site museum. Most of the artifacts on display are first-rate replicas. The original material can be seen at the **Stovall and Philbrook Museums** and the **Oklahoma Historical Society.**

DIRECTIONS: Drive 5 miles east of Spiro on Route 9. Directional markers point to a side road that goes out to the site. Personnel at the Visitors' Center can advise you about lodging and camping in various towns in the area.

HOURS: May–September: 8:00 A.M.–7:00 P.M.
Rest of year: 8:00 A.M.–5:00 P.M.

ADMISSION: Free.

Warrior effigy pipe recovered from Spiro Mound, Oklahoma. (Photo courtesy of the Museum of the American Indian, Heye Foundation.)

Heavener

- *Heavener Runestone*
  Heavener, Oklahoma 74937 *(918) 653-2241*

A twelve-foot high stone slab with mysterious writing on it has been a sore point among scientists since it was first discovered in 1912. Some are convinced the letters are from the runic alphabet of Vikings, indicating that white men reached the middle-America region long before Columbus touched the shores. The theory is that the Norsemen sailed into the Gulf of Mexico and ventured up the Mississippi and Arkansas rivers.

DIRECTIONS: The Heavener Runestone is in Clem Hamilton State Park, 2 miles east of Heavener in southeastern Oklahoma.

MUSEUMS

Anadarko

- *Indian City U.S.A.*
  Box 695
  Anadarko, Oklahoma 73005 *(405) 247-5661*

Indian City is a large outdoor museum where models of Indian villages are set up. This is very much a tourist-visitor spot, but the displays are well done and convey a sense of sixteenth-century Indian life in America. Buffalo roam across nearby fields; an Indian guide accompanies you on the forty-five-minute tour. Young amateur archaeologists will love it.

DIRECTIONS: Indian City is 2 miles south of Anadarko on OK 8.
HOURS: Summer: 9:00 A.M.–6:00 P.M. (last tour at 5:00 P.M.)
Winter: 9:00 A.M.–5:00 P.M. (last tour at 4:15 P.M.)
ADMISSION: Adults $3.00, children $1.50.

Bartlesville

- *Woolaroc Museum*
  Route 3
  Bartlesville, Oklahoma 74003 *(918) 336-6747*

Getting to this museum is at least half the fun, provided you're not driving an open convertible. The museum is on the old ranch belonging to Frank Phillips, founder of Phillips Petroleum. As you drive through 3500 timbered acres, you may see buffalo and other wild animals, not necessarily friendly.

Among its archaeological collections, the museum displays artifacts from Spiro Mounds. It also features materials dating back to 1000 B.C. from the Plains Indian cultures.

DIRECTIONS: The museum is 14 miles southwest of OK 123; directional signs are clearly posted.
HOURS: 10:00 A.M.–5:00 P.M. daily except Monday, Nov.–March. Closed Thanksgiving and Christmas.
ADMISSION: Free.

Goodwell

• *No Man's Land Historical Museum*
Panhandle State College
Sewel Street
Goodwell, Oklahoma 73939 *(405) 349-2670*

If you find yourself in this desertlike no man's land, visit the museum on the Panhandle State College campus. Artifacts shown go all the way back to Paleo times; other exhibits trace the Archaic Indians, who lived here until European contact. This is the region where an early basketmaking culture lived, and some baskets from archaeological sites are on exhibit.

HOURS: Tuesday–Friday: 9:00 A.M.–5:00 P.M.
Weekends: 1:00 P.M.–5:00 P.M. Closed major holidays.
ADMISSION: Free.

Idabel

• *Museum of the Red River*
Herron Research Foundation, Inc.
812 Southeast Lincoln
Idabel, Oklahoma 74745 *(405) 286-3616*

The museum conducts excavations and research projects in the Red River Valley. Each year, changing displays reflect the work at recent excavations and relevant artifacts are put on exhibit. Amateurs are welcome to join the small field schools (see "Opportunities for Amateurs" below).

HOURS: Tuesday–Saturday: 9:00 A.M.–5:00 P.M.
Sunday: 1:00 P.M.–5:00 P.M.
Closed Monday.
ADMISSION: Free.

Norman

- *Stovall Museum*
  University of Oklahoma
  1335 Asp Avenue
  Norman, Oklahoma 73019 *(405) 325-4711*

The largest collection of archaeological artifacts in Oklahoma is exhibited at the Stovall. Exhibits show how sites were excavated and how the recovered artifacts fit into the overall cultural patterns of prehistoric people. The Stovall also houses the most extensive collection from Spiro Mounds.

HOURS: Monday–Friday: 9:00 A.M.–5:00 P.M.; summer to 4:30 P.M.
Weekends: 1:00 P.M.–5:00 P.M. Closed major holidays.
ADMISSION: Free.

Oklahoma City

- *Oklahoma Historical Society*
  Historical Building, Capitol Complex
  2100 North Lincoln Boulevard
  Oklahoma City, Oklahoma 73105 *(405) 521-2491*

Extensive historic and prehistoric exhibits are presented at this large museum. Particularly interesting are the collections from Spiro Mounds.

HOURS: Monday–Friday: 9:00 A.M.–5:00 P.M.
Library and archives only: Saturday 9:00 A.M.–5:00 P.M.
Closed Sundays.
ADMISSION: Free.

Tulsa

- *Philbrook Arts Center*
  2727 South Rockford Road
  Tulsa, Oklahoma 74152 *(918) 749-7941*

The museum shows a wealth of art and ornaments from the Spiro Mounds. The crafts of prehistoric cultures from all parts of the state are gathered in large art displays.

HOURS: Tuesday–Saturday: 10:00 A.M.–5:00 P.M.
Sunday: 1:00 P.M.–5:00 P.M.
ADMISSION: Adults $2, senior citizens $1, children free.

- *Thomas Gilcrease Institute of American History and Art*
  1400 North 25 West Avenue
  Tulsa, Oklahoma 74127 *(918) 581-5311*

The Gilcrease is the most important art museum in Oklahoma. It also holds several major archaeological collections that illuminate life in Central and North America from prehistoric times to the introduction of European culture. Artifacts twelve thousand years old are shown in some exhibits. The Gilcrease also exhibits what many consider the finest collection of western paintings in the world.

HOURS: Monday–Saturday: 9:00 A.M.–5:00 P.M.
Sunday and holidays: 1:00 P.M.–5:00 P.M.
Closed Christmas.
ADMISSION: Free.

STATE OFFICE

State Archaeologist
Oklahoma Archaeological Survey
University of Oklahoma
1335 South Asp Avenue
Norman, Oklahoma 73019 (405) 325-1028

OPPORTUNITIES FOR AMATEURS

The **Museum of the Red River** sponsors a field school every year in the spring and summer. Everyone is welcome to apply. The school is free to residents of Oklahoma; out-of-state participants are asked to donate $50 for the season. Sometimes even this small fee is waived.

The museum is eager to find a place for all volunteers. All are expected to supply their own food and lodging. A camping area for tents and RVs is provided at the museum. There are plenty of motels nearby.

The museum is a free public museum owned by the city of Idabel and sponsored by the Herron Research Foundation. All materials recovered from excavations belong to the museum. The excavation team works as the weather permits, and the field school is deliberately kept small. Work begins in the middle of April and continues until July. Most volunteers can select the weeks they wish to work. For information, write or call:

Museum of the Red River
812 Southeast Lincoln
Idabel, Oklahoma 73019 (405) 286-3616

ORGANIZATIONS TO JOIN

The **Oklahoma Anthropological Society** works closely with the office of the state archaeologist. Together they sponsor at least one annual dig. Excavations, often on sites that are threatened by vandalism, are supervised by the Archaeological Survey. For information, write:

Oklahoma Anthropological Society
University of Oklahoma
1335 South Asp Avenue
Norman, Oklahoma 73069

TEXAS

Bones from many different kinds of Ice Age animals have been found in **Freisenhahn Cave** on the Texas Coastal Plain. The large variety of now-extinct species suggests that they were in the flush of their time on earth, not bordering on extinction. Under the skeleton of one large tiger lay a crude manmade scraper. Several other crudely flaked stones also were found in the cave. Controversy surrounds this discovery, but it's possible the tools were made before the final advance of the Ice Age—more than sixty thousand years ago.

Near **Lewisville,** Texas, the remains of elephants, extinct bison, and camels have been found at nineteen ancient hearths. At the largest campsite, a fluted Clovis projectile point was found with a piece of charred wood. Scientists expected the wood to yield a radiocarbon date between twelve thousand and fifteen thousand years old. Instead, the charcoal was beyond the range of the lab technique—indicating that it was more than thirty-seven thousand years old. The oldest date ever assigned to any Clovis point is somewhat less than eighteen thousand years.

These two finds in Texas, the sites of which are not open to the public, have stirred up speculation and controversy. They may show that North America was inhabited long before 10,000 B.C., a theory widely held but not definitely proved.

Certainly there is no argument that Paleo-Indians hunted big game in Texas. The distinctive Clovis and Folsom fluted points have been found at a number of kill sites, specific areas where prehistoric hunters slaughtered and butchered big game.

Two well-stratified sites recently discovered in southwestern Texas have revealed a great deal about the life and times of the Paleo-Indians. **Bakers Cave** near Devil's River is a deeply stratified cave first occupied nine thousand years ago. The second site is at **St. Mary's Hall,** a Paleo-Indian site that lies on the grounds of a private girls' school within the city limits of San Antonio. Here the stratigraphy traces the transitional period between Paleo and Archaic times. These in-between periods are extremely important to scientists because they describe how people adapted to change and frequently turned adversity into advantage. Both of these excavations were joint projects of scientists from the **University of Texas at San Antonio,** students, and amateurs.

When the Ice Age animals disappeared from the Texas plains, a new Desert Archaic culture evolved, based on human adaptation to the suddenly arid climate. Earlier, a single mammoth provided food for a large group of people. Now, small families traveled alone, hunting the smallest game, gathering wild plants and berries. People followed this nomadic life for thousands of years.

About A.D. 1000, a new culture penetrated some parts of west Texas. Agriculture, probably introduced by the Mogollon people from New Mexico, was added to the basic hunting and gathering life. The Plains Village Indians also farmed on the Texas Panhandle for a brief time between A.D. 1200 and 1450, building houses similar in style to the pueblos of the Southwest.

In Texas today a flurry of archaeological activity takes place every summer: ongoing excavations, summer digs, and museum expeditions. Amateurs are involved in almost every phase of the science in this state. Two new historical sites are being prepared for the public under the administration of the Texas Parks and Wildlife Department. There are no massive ruined cities or cliff dwellings inTexas, but several unique archaeological sites, such as the Alibates flint quarries and Hueco Tanks, are open to the public.

SITES

Alto

- *Caddoan Mounds State Historic Site*
  Route 2
  Box 85C
  Alto, Texas 75925 *(713) 858-3218*

The University of Texas has conducted excavations at this site for several years, and visitors are welcome to observe the dig in progress. The crew is in the field during June and July. A new visitors' center and interpretive display, scheduled to open to the public in 1980, will be a permanent year-round facility.

DIRECTIONS: The site is on State Highway 21, 6 miles southwest of Alto.

Comstock

- *Seminole Canyon State Historical Site*
  P.O. Box 806
  Comstock, Texas 78837 *(915) 292-4464*

Archaeologists have uncovered more than three hundred archaeological sites on this tract of land and water now confined within the Amistad Recreation Area. The only sites accessible to the public are pictographs. Remarkably well-preserved rock paintings are found all through this region. Ranger-guided tours will take visitors to Fate Bell Shelter, a major pictograph site containing a dry archaeological deposit. The park is scheduled to open in June 1980. The park permits primitive camping in the Amistad Recreation Area.

DIRECTIONS: The site is off U.S. 90, about 40 miles northwest of Del Rio.

El Paso

- *Hueco Tanks State Historical Park*
  Box 26502
  Ranchland Station
  El Paso, Texas 79926 *(915) 859-4100*

This archaeological park contains some of the best-preserved painted rock art in the United States. For ten thousand years desert travelers visited this arid region where rain is caught in potlike depressions in the rock. *Hueco* is the Spanish word for "hollow." Geologists do not agree on the origin of these natural basins in the hard syenite rock, but the catch basins have created a rocky oasis for many kinds of desert life.

Camping, hiking, and picnicking are allowed in the 860-acre park.

DIRECTIONS: The park is off U.S. 180, 32 miles northeast of El Paso; take gravel road exit 2775.

Fritch

- *Alibates Flint Quarries National Monument*
  Lake Meredith Recreation Area
  P.O. Box 1438
  Fritch, Texas 79036 *(806) 857-3151*

For thousands of years, prehistoric Indians of the Great Plains traveled to Alibates to quarry what is perhaps the most beautiful flint in the world. Flint is normally a solid color, but Alibates flint is striped like desert agate in a blend of colors from the deepest green all the way to a pale buff. Prehistoric people chipped and flaked the hard rock into every kind of implement: knives, hammers, chisels, drills, fishhooks, scrapes, and projectile points. Tools made from Alibates flint have been found all over the Great Plains and in the Southwest. The earliest date of occupation for the quarry may have been as far back as 10,000 B.C., and it was probably used until the 1870s.

The quarries are within the Lake Meredith Recreation Area. In the summer you can hike back into the hills accompanied by a ranger to where the ancient quarries still pit the surface of ridges. The pits are wide and shallow, the deep layer of flint lying just beneath the surface of the hillside. Two hikes go out every day, one at 10:00 A.M. and the other at 2:00 P.M. It's a steep climb to the ridge top, and the weather is miserably hot in midsummer. But it's a fascinating expedition. The hike is less than a mile round trip, but allow two hours for the whole tour.

Afterward, the ranger usually gives a flint-chipping demonstration, which will give you a rough idea of the skill required to fashion prehistoric implements.

Camping, boating, and swimming are permitted all over the Lake Meredith Recreation Area, but visitors are permitted on the Alibates Monument site only with a guide. Tours are given in the summer only. If you visit the monument out of season, you will be unable to locate the quarry site. The trail is unmarked and no signs are posted. Special off-season tours can be arranged by writing to the superintendent (at the above address). It's possible that the regular tour schedule will be expanded in the future; call ahead to check the current schedule.

DIRECTIONS: Take SR 136 32 miles north of Amarillo, or 6 miles south of Fritch. Watch for a turnoff on Alibates Road (Cal Johnson Road). Follow the dirt road 6 miles west to contact point where two small trailers are parked. The ranger's office is in the first trailer.

Lubbock

• *Lubbock Lake Site*
Texas Tech University
Box 4499
Lubbock, Texas 79409 *(806) 742-2481*

For several years intensive excavations have been under way at this site in the southern high plains of Texas. At this single locality are human, animal, and geological sequences recorded over a twelve-thousand-year time span. Situated in an ancient meander of Yellow House Draw, the Lubbock Lake site was first discovered during a WPA dredging operation in the 1930s. More than forty years later, scientists from Texas Tech University are only beginning to unravel the intricate pattern of environmental and cultural change buried in the earth.

An on-site museum and permanent exhibits are planned for the future. In the meantime excavations sponsored by The Museum of Texas Tech University continue here every summer. Visitors are invited to observe the dig on Saturday mornings during June and July.

A new interpretive center will be open from mid-May through mid-August (hours: Monday–Friday, 8:30 A.M.–4:30 P.M.; Saturday and Sunday, 1:00 P.M.–4:30 P.M.).

For full information about visiting, call the office of the Lubbock Lake site at the university (see also "Museums" below).

DIRECTIONS: The site is in Yellow House Canyon. Loop 289 and Clovis Highway (U.S. 84) intersect at Indiana Avenue. Follow Indiana Avenue north across the railroad tracks and underneath the overpass to the fenced-in area.

MUSEUMS

Alpine

- *Museum of the Big Bend*
  Sul Ross University
  Alpine, Texas 79830 *(915) 837-8144*

Most prehistoric Indian artifacts here are from Texas and Oklahoma, but some materials are from Mexico and the Apache and Commanche tribes.

HOURS: Tuesday–Saturday: 9:00 A.M.–5:00 P.M.
Sunday: 1:00 P.M.–5:00 P.M.
Inquire for schedule during school holidays.
ADMISSION: Free.

Austin

- *Texas Memorial Museum*
  Trinity and 24th Streets
  Austin, Texas 78705 *(512) 471-1604*

The collections span a breadth of subjects related to the science and natural history of Texas. The archaeological exhibits are diverse and wide-ranging, covering every prehistoric culture group of North America. Special Texas exhibits are drawn from material that can be seen nowhere else. A major science and historical library can be used on the premises.

HOURS: Monday–Friday: 9:00 A.M.–5:00 P.M.
Saturday and Sunday: 1:00 P.M.–5:00 P.M.
Closed major holidays.
ADMISSION: Adults $1, children 50¢.

Canyon

• *Panhandle-Plains Historical Museum*
2401 Fourth Avenue
Canyon, Texas 79015 *(806) 655-7194*

In this wonderful, old-fashioned museum, an entire turn-of-the-century Texas town is re-created. And its Hall of the Southern Plains Indians exhibits one of the best collections of Plains Indians artifacts in the Southwest. The Indian gallery explores the cultures of the Comanche, Kiowa, Arapaho, Apache, and Cheyenne tribes. Some of the science exhibits are short on interpretation, but the museum as a whole is fun, interesting, and definitely worth a stop in the small west Texas town of Canyon.

Each summer, museum crews excavate selected sites on the Panhandle. These include historic, prehistoric, and fossil locales. Some amateurs are accepted as volunteers on the field crew (see "Opportunities for Amateurs").

HOURS: 9:00 A.M.–5:00 P.M. (June–August till 6:00 P.M.).
Sunday: 2:00 P.M.–6:00 P.M.
Closed major holidays.
ADMISSION: Free.

Fort Worth

• *Fort Worth Museum of Science and History*
1501 Montgomery Street
Fort Worth, Texas 76107 *(817) 732-1631*

A collection of prehistoric stone tools and pottery as well as archaeological materials are on display in the Hall of Man. Other interesting science exhibits are in the Hall of Medicine, Hall of Natural History, and Hall of Texas History. There is a large planetarium in the museum; and a library covering the collections is open to the public.

HOURS: Monday–Saturday: 9:00 A.M.–5:00 P.M.
Sunday: 2:00 P.M.–5:00 P.M.
Closed major holidays.
ADMISSION: Free for county residents; all others 50¢.

Longview

• *Caddo Indian Museum*
701 Hardy Street
Longview, Texas 75604 *(214) 759-5739*

The exhibits center on the Caddo Indians—their pottery, tools, and arrow and spear points. Some of these materials are more than two thousand years old. There is also a small library of catalogs and art reference books.

HOURS: 9:00 A.M.–5:00 P.M. daily.
Closed Christmas Eve and day.
ADMISSION: Free.

Lubbock

• *The Museum of Texas Tech University*
Indiana Avenue and 4th Street
Lubbock, Texas 79409 *(806) 742-2442*

The museum exhibits material from the Lubbock Lake site in which fossils of extinct animals and Paleo spear points have been found together (see listing for Lubbock Lake under "Sites"). Historical and cultural exhibits of the Southwest are also featured.

HOURS: Monday–Friday: 8:30 A.M.–4:30 P.M.
Saturday and Sunday: 1:00 P.M.–4:30 P.M.
Closed holidays.
ADMISSION: Free. Planetarium: Adults $1, students 50¢.

Waco

• *Strecker Museum*
Baylor University
Dutton and South 5th Street
Sid Richardson Science Building
Waco, Texas 76703 *(817) 755-1110*

In addition to artifacts from central Texas, there are materials here from a rock shelter dating from around A.D. 1000. Other exhibits feature mounted animals and birds, minerals, and fossils. A fully reconstructed 1835 log cabin is on permanent display.

HOURS: Monday–Friday: 9:00 A.M.–4:00 P.M.
Saturday: 10:00 A.M.–1:00 P.M.
Sunday: 2:00 P.M.–5:00 P.M.
Closed major holidays.
ADMISSION: Free.

STATE OFFICE

Texas Historical Commission
P.O. Box 12276
Austin, Texas 78711

OPPORTUNITIES FOR AMATEURS

Amateurs are involved in many phases of archaeology in Texas. The **Chihuahuan Desert Research Institute** in Alpine offers geological, botanical, ecological, and archaeological expeditions in the field. The institute plans a permanent visitors' center. For information, write:

Chihuahuan Desert Research Institute
P.O. Box 1334
Alpine, Texas 79830

The **Panhandle-Plains Historical Museum** also offers limited opportunities for amateurs to participate in its field trips. For information and the schedule of field trips, write:

Panhandle-Plains Historical Museum
Box 967 W.T. Station
Canyon, Texas 79016

ORGANIZATIONS TO JOIN

Texas has nearly two dozen amateur archaeological societies actively involved in ongoing excavations. For a full list of local organizations, write:

Texas Historical Commission
Box 12276
Austin, Texas 78711

The leading lay-professional association in the state is the **Texas Archaeological Society.** People come from all over the state—and the country—to join the society's yearly field school. In the field professional archaeologists direct the work and training of amateur crew members. A companion program is offered for children. Activities are geared to different age levels so everyone can join in. This is a unique field school for the whole family. The field school is always held in June; camping is usually available at the site. For information, write:

Texas Archaeological Society
Southern Methodist University
Box 161
Dallas, Texas 75275

WYOMING

Ancient campsites, caves containing buried layers of stone and bone tools, burial cairns, and ancient mining shafts indicate that Wyoming was home to the early people of America. Folsom and other projectile points from Paleo and Archaic times have been found throughout the state, along with mysterious rock paintings along old trails.

Little is known of the early inhabitants of Wyoming's vast grassy plains and deep mountain valleys. When white settlers first entered the region, they encountered many great Indian tribes; in the following centuries, their numbers dwindled drastically and today only the Shoshone and Arapaho live in Wyoming.

Great wilderness areas have been preserved in the national parks and forests of Wyoming, and outdoor life is the state's biggest attraction. There is not much in the way of archaeological sites for travelers to see, but this is an exciting state to join in fieldwork.

Rock quarries and traces of extinct animals all point toward early occupation of the region. There are pictographs and petroglyphs all over the state, and several caves have revealed rare red-painted pictographs on their walls. In the Wind River district of central Wyoming, huge pestles five feet long have been discovered. The ball of the pestles are eight or nine inches in diameter with a stem tapering to about four inches. The giant tools were probably used for grinding seeds and berries, and perhaps grain, yet they have not been linked to a particular culture or people.

The archaeological work under way in Wyoming is fascinating. Every year, summer excavations turn up new archaeological evidence, and most of this work takes place in remote, outlying regions. This is archaeology in the rough, and the only way to observe is to participate. The Wyoming Archaeological Society is an active organization that offers amateurs the best opportunity to get involved in the science.

SITES

Lovell

• *The Medicine Wheel*
Big Horn Canyon Recreation Area
Visitors' Center
Lovell, Wyoming 82431 *(307) 548-2251*

On top of Medicine Mountain, about halfway between Sheridan and Lovell, Wyoming, lies a prehistoric shrine beyond reach of history. Indians of Wyoming believe it was built "before the light came" by people who "had no iron."

Here twenty-eight spokes made of small stones radiate out from a central cairn. A circle of small stones marks the outside rim of the wheel. The wheel has a circumference of 245 feet; the rocks laid in a circular pattern have never been removed or disturbed. No one knows who constructed the wheel or when. Five more cairns lie along this outside edge, and a sixth rests at the end of a slightly extended spoke that points to the southwest. The center cairn, about three feet high, probably represents the sun. The twenty-eight rock spokes supposedly correspond to twenty-eight lunar days—one lunar month or "moon."

The study of prehistoric astronomical constructions is called archaeoastronomy. Scientists have learned that prehistoric people of the New World were careful observers of celestial bodies. Many pre-Columbian people of Mexico and South America had sophisticated calendars. The Inca developed a twelve-month calendar, and the Maya were obsessed with time and numbers.

Prehistoric people north of Mexico never seem to have achieved such sophisticated calculations, but they charted the stars and were very much aware of the changing panorama of the heavens. The circular **Casa Rinconada** ruin in Chaco Canyon and the square towers of **Hovenweep** point to celestial knowledge. **Casa Grande** in Arizona may have been a prehistoric sky lab. And some pictographs in the Southwest seem to be sky maps. At **Cahokia** in Illinois, shadows falling across a ring of tall posts broadcast the changing seasons.

The medicine wheels scattered from northern Colorado to the Canadian border are probably astronomical monuments. The Indians use the word *medicine* to indicate magical or supernatural power. At least forty wheels have been discovered on the plains of Alberta and Saskatchewan, but only a half dozen have been found south of the Canadian border.

The Big Horn Medicine Wheel is the best example of these prehistoric monuments. Scientists from the High Altitude Observatory in Boulder, Colorado, found that by sighting across the central cairn from the cairn on the tip of the southwestern spoke, it was possible to watch the sunrise on the summer solstice. From the southeast the center cairn marks the sunset on the same day. Other, even more sophisticated astronomical calculations can be charted from this medicine wheel, making it clearly an important discovery for scientists.

Big Horn Canyon, where the Medicine Wheel is located, is a geologist's dream. A national forest encompasses more than a million acres in these mountains of north central Wyoming. The Big Horn River slices through miles of steep-walled, brilliantly colored canyons. There are resorts and campsites within the forest, and fishing and hunting are permitted under Wyoming state regulations. For information, write:

Forest Supervisor
Columbus Building
Box 2046
Sheridan, Wyoming 82801

The Big Horn Canyon National Recreation Area, which is partially in Montana, is within the National Forest. Camping, fishing, picnicking, and boating are encouraged within the area.

The Visitors' Center for the recreation area is at Lovell, near the junction of U.S. 310 and 14A. It is open daily from 8:00 A.M. to 7:00 P.M. in summer, and from 8:00 A.M. to 5:00 P.M. the rest of the year. The Visitors' Center has full information on visiting the region.

Directions to The Medicine Wheel: U.S. 14A branches off at Burgess on the eastern face of the Big Horn Mountains and scales the summit of the range in long curving sweeps. It passes near The Medicine Wheel and then drops into Big Horn Basin at Lovell. About 23½ miles along this road, there is a junction with a gravel road. Turn north and follow it about 3 miles to the parking area.

The Medicine Wheel is protected by a wire fence, and visitors may not walk on the site or remove anything from the area.

The site is open only during the summer. Portions of U.S. 14A are closed in the winter months, and the gravel road to The Medicine Wheel is usually impassable.

Yellowstone National Park

- *Obsidian Cliff*
  Yellowstone National Park, Wyoming 82190

One place in Wyoming that was visited time and again, perhaps for thousands of years, is Obsidian Cliff, in Yellowstone National Park. The cliff is made of the black volcanic glass with which prehistoric people chipped distinctive points. These points have been found all over the plains and as far east as Ohio. They were highly prized by many different peoples in North America for their sharpness and beauty. A well-worn foot trail marks the route traveled to reach the cliff.

Today you can drive to the glass mountain. But moss and lichen obscure its glittering surface and you would never guess it was the source of the exquisite black points. At the Mammoth Hot Springs Visitors' Center, graphic displays describe how the Indians chipped the volcanic rock and fashioned it into weapon points. No artifacts are displayed.

Mammoth Hot Springs is at the northern entrance to Yellowstone, reached from Livingston and Gardiner, Montana, via I-90, U.S. 10 and U.S. 89. The Visitors' Center is on the Grand Loop just outside the park. For full information about visiting Yellowstone, write:

Yellowstone Park Company
Yellowstone National Park, Wyoming 82190

MUSEUMS

Laramie

• *University of Wyoming Anthropological Museum*
Arts and Sciences Building
Laramie, Wyoming 82071 *(307) 766-5136*

This museum has the largest and most important collection of prehistoric artifacts in Wyoming. The museum, now undergoing renovation, will reopen in 1980 with extensive permanent exhibits.

A major collection of Paleo-Indian artifacts is housed here. Only part of the collection is displayed, but all the museum's holdings are available for study by appointment. Much of the prehistoric material comes from various kill sites, and the museum also will display a large collection of extinct animal bones.

HOURS: Winter
Monday–Friday: 8:00 A.M.–5:00 P.M.
Summer
Monday–Friday: 7:30 A.M.–4:30 P.M.
Closed school vacations and holidays.
ADMISSION: Free.

STATE OFFICE

George Frison
State Archaeologist
Department of Anthropology
University of Wyoming
University Station Box 3431
Laramie, Wyoming 82071

ORGANIZATIONS TO JOIN

The **Wyoming Archaeological Society** is a statewide, lay-professional organization. Members participate in various phases of archaeological activity and receive the quarterly journal, *Wyoming Archaeologist.* For information, write:

Wyoming Archaeological Society
University of Wyoming
Department of Anthropology
Laramie, Wyoming 82071

THE SOUTHWEST

Arizona

New Mexico

The Four Corners Region

THE SOUTHWEST

Thousands of years ago, people lived in caves in the Southwest. Sandia Cave in New Mexico may have been occupied twenty-five thousand years ago. It was in the bottom layer of this cave floor that a large projectile point with a peculiar bulge on one side was found (the Sandia point), together with bones of prehistoric horses and camels. More finely made fluted points discovered near Clovis and Folsom, New Mexico, showed that people had lived and hunted in that region at least twelve thousand years ago.

A western Archaic culture sometimes called Cochise began as the big game animals died off more than ten thousand years ago. It lasted with little variation until around 500 B.C., when farming, introduced from Mexico, revolutionized life in the desert. Until then, the Cochise people had been almost exclusively dependent on wild foods for survival. Their grinding stones for seeds and nuts have been found everywhere in the Southwest. There was almost no game for the hunters. When the Cochise learned how to cultivate plants, a vibrant new life awakened in the desert. With the introduction of corn, ten thousand years of Archaic living faded into prehistory.

Out of the Cochise Desert Tradition four cultures evolved: the Mogollon, the Hohokam, the Anasazi, and the Patayan. They were similar to each other in some respects, but each was marked by distinct characteristics that have charmed and fascinated several generations of American archaeologists and travelers.

After the nomadic desert people settled into permanent villages, they built the most beautiful buildings anywhere in prehistoric America. Not only was the masonry finely finished, but the desert backdrop of the villages lent them a heart-wrenching beauty. Nestled into cliffs that glow like gold in the sun, clustered atop soaring mesas, or quietly settled on the floor of deeply shaded canyons, the Mogollon, the Hohokam, and the Anasazi all built magnificent dwellings. Only the Patayan, a culture that grew up along the Colorado River, failed to build in the classic stone masonry style. Their huts and villages have been buried under silt pouring out of the Colorado River, and little has been discovered about their culture.

In the highland mountains that lie across southern Arizona and New Mexico, the Mogollon culture evolved. This culture is not clearly defined; it may have been a variation of the stronger Anasazi culture further north or a blend of the Hohokam and Anasazi, two cultures that were largely contemporaneous. The Mogollon people, who lived along the Mimbres River, developed a unique pottery that has become famous throughout the world:

black abstract designs of animals, fish, and birds decorate their white ceramic bowls and vessels.

The Mogollon originally dug circular pit houses into the earth; a strong upright post in the center supported a roof of woven saplings. The partially subterranean pit house was warm in winter and cool in the summer. If you climb down into an underground kiva on a blistering August day, you'll be surprised by the sudden drop in temperature. The Gila cliff dwellings in the southwestern corner of New Mexico were built by the Mogollon. Sometime during the twelfth and thirteenth centuries, the Mogollon people disappeared. They may have moved south into Mexico, or they may have been absorbed by the Anasazi.

In southern Arizona, along the Salt and Gila rivers, a culture called Hohokam evolved out of the Desert Archaic. Strong ties with Mexico are reflected in the Hohokam pottery. Pedestal bases, elaborate handles and knobs—all reflect the influence of Mexico. The Hohokam also constructed courtyards that are similar to the ceremonial ball courts of Mexico; they made ornaments of shell, mosaic plaques, and mirrors of pyrite crystals. They also cremated their dead.

All of these characteristics set the Hohokam apart as a distinct culture. But they are best known for the complex and lengthy system of irrigation canals that they built to divert river water into fields far out in the desert. Some of these networks were sixty miles long. The Hohokam had a natural advantage over today's desert dwellers, because there was more rainfall in southern Arizona at this time in prehistory. In addition to the staples of corn, beans, and squash, the Hohokam also grew cotton and were excellent weavers.

Further north, where the plateaus are cut by deep dark canyons and rimmed with gold sandstone bluffs, the most remarkable and best-known culture of the Southwest—the Anasazi—developed.

The early Anasazi farmers had lived in caves, but then learned to build pit houses. By A.D. 700 the Anasazi had become large-scale farmers, and they lived together in large groups. They began to build their houses of stone. The various building stages of the Anasazi culture are divided into different *Pueblo* phases (from the Spanish word for "village").

During the Great or Classic Pueblo Period, from A.D. 1100 to 1300, the Anasazi culture reached its zenith. In the Four Corners region, they built dwellings that soared as high as five stories and housed hundreds of people. They built first on the open mesa tops and then inside large natural caves in the faces of cliffs.

The villages were set like jewels, sandstone dwellings against deep gold walls. In the spring, as snow melted down the mountains, water trickled through the cave walls and into the deep canyons yawning below, making a running, singing sound. On an especially quiet day, you can still hear that musical sound. This supply of running water may have been one reason the Anasazi moved into the caves. There was no water on the mesa tops, where the people practiced dry farming, dependent on the whims of nature for rainstorms.

As the culture expanded, all of the Anasazi skills advanced. Pottery was remarkably fine and beautifully decorated with elaborated designs. Most of the people dry-farmed their fields, relying on available water. Others, like the people of Chaco, built a flooding system by which they trapped water from storms and later released it into the fields.

Three major Anasazi centers evolved, each with its own style of architecture and art that distinguished it from the others. These three centers are still preserved today and are open to the public: Navajo National Monument in northern Arizona, Chaco Canyon in northern New Mexico, and Mesa Verde in southern Colorado. Each of these great centers developed several outlying posts that were tied to them through trade: Salmon and Aztec, Hovenweep, Escalante, Canyon de Chelly, and many others were all part of the Anasazi culture.

The most striking aspect of these Anasazi civilizations is reflected in their building. From the houses they left behind, archaeologists have been able to describe their society. There is no evidence of a hierarchy or ruling class. The dwellings are single rooms—all of a size—built one next to the other. In the cliff dwellings, hundreds of people lived together in a confined space, often almost impossible to reach.

Their story tells of people strongly committed to one another, working together in a spirit of communalism that benefited everyone. No personal glorification of individuals is seen anywhere in the culture. All effort was directed toward the society as a whole. Religion was closely intertwined with everyday life; the gods were the gods of nature, woven into the whole fabric of the society. There is no evidence of internal strife or warfare. As the culture expanded, other groups sometimes merged with the Anasazi or lived side by side with them without conflict.

Then suddenly, all that had been so peacefully and naturally achieved began to break down. The reasons for the decline of the great culture have never been fully discovered. There was a severe, long-lasting drought in the latter part of the thirteenth century. There is evidence at Chaco Canyon that the farmers may have depleted the soil and stripped the region of its natural resources, including timber. There may have been a breakdown in trade networks.

Any and all of these may have contributed to the demise of the culture, and there may have been other factors that left no trace. As the Anasazi weakened, they were easy prey for desert marauders, who lived by raiding farming communities. The Anasazi withdrew into smaller and smaller regions in the South and Southeast.

Over the next two hundred years, generally called the Regressive Renaissance Period, the Anasazi culture was marked by instability, migration, and the shifting of population centers. But the Anasazi preserved remnants of their culture, and their descendants began to gather once more into permanent pueblos in such places as the beautiful Frijoles Canyon in New Mexico.

But the renaissance was cut off by the unexpected arrival of the Spaniards. Archaeologists still speculate on what these remarkable people might have achieved if they had been left to shape their own destiny.

Pueblo life after European occupation is best seen in New Mexico, where the descendants of the Pueblo Indians still live today. The great ruins of the Hohokam are found in Arizona and of the Mogollon in New Mexico. The Anasazi cliff dwellings are concentrated in the Four Corners region.

TRAVELING IN THE SOUTHWEST

It is impossible to say which of the southwestern archaeological sites is the most interesting or the most beautiful. Each is extraordinary, and I cannot think of one ruined village in the Southwest that is not almost overwhelming in its beauty.

Some ruins such as Mesa Verde are so well known that they attract thousands of visitors. Others are relatively obscure, and still others require hours of strenuous hiking to reach. Generally speaking, the more remote settings offer the best opportunity to sit quietly and contemplate the spirit and beauty that inhabit the ruins. For unquestionably, these places are haunted, and many of them are held in reverence by modern Indians.

There are so many sites in the Southwest that there is something for everyone of every age. Some remarkable sites are reached by easily accessible trails that will accommodate wheelchairs. Children love to visit the ancient ruins, and most of them are safe for youngsters. Others require strenuous hiking up steep trails and along sheer cliff tops. Still others require either a horse or several days in the field on foot.

Backpackers can hike into the Gila Wilderness Area and see hundreds of small ruins nudging the canyon walls. A little known valley where the Anasazi lived in northern Arizona can be entered only with a guide. Along the Trail of the Ancients in Utah, you can learn about special places not marked on the map. Several of the famous monuments, such as Navajo and Canyon de Chelly, allow only a few visitors to hike into the canyons with a guide. All of these journeys are away from crowds and modern life. Each requires planning, especially during the summer. But if you take the time to book your arrangements ahead, you will have an experience that few people in America have enjoyed.

It's no good trying to visit every single ruin in the Southwest. Seeing a hundred sites does not compare with taking the time to linger in a single beautiful place. You might choose to spend your time in just one small section. My own choice for an initial visit is the southeastern corner of

Utah, from which Hovenweep, the Trail of the Ancients, Mystery Valley, Navajo National Monument, and Canyon de Chelly are all accessible.

But there are many other places. Every region in the Southwest has prehistoric ruins. In central Arizona there is Walnut Canyon, almost unbelievable in its deep forests, and the sprawling Tuzigoot, and Montezuma Well (much more interesting than the famous Montezuma Castle). The Gila Cliff Dwellings are in the high, remote corner of Southwestern New Mexico. At places like Gran Quivira and Abó, you can see the prehistoric Indian life almost blend with Spanish culture.

The interpretation of these sites is astonishing in its scope. The museums and visitors' centers are unrivaled anywhere in the United States. Here in the Southwest archaeology truly comes alive. It is in the air; it lives in the faces and lives of the Indians who still call this region home.

Many of the archaeological sites in the Southwest are reached by dirt or gravel roads. But almost any car can make the journey. Coming around twisting dirt roads no wider than a deer track, I have met Texas-style Cadillacs and Winnebagos the size of large yachts.

The only serious problem on these roads arises during the sudden rainstorms that lash out at any time of year, most often in spring and summer. Then the red earth and contrasting blue sky suddenly turn all one color—watery brown. In minutes, you are up to your hubcaps in thick mud and are easily trapped on the road, unable to move either forward or backward. Cars not sucked into the mud slip from side to side across the treacherous surface that offers no traction. Even four-wheel drive vehicles are easily caught in these devilish mud traps. The best thing to do is try to reach high ground before you are swamped. In heavy rain, flash floods sweep without warning down dried-up arroyos. It is usually a matter of degree. If the road is made of gravel and is well maintained, it will hold up in light rain. But if it is merely hard-packed dirt, the road soon becomes slick and dangerous. Before setting out across desert roads, ask people in the area about road and weather conditions. If the weather is threatening, put off your trip for another day.

If the site is on paved roads, a rainy day can be a fine time to visit, since it will be quiet and the wet gray clouds throw an entirely different light on the place. One early morning when I was at Hovenweep, it started to rain lightly. But two determined visitors from the east opened a yellow umbrella and picked their way down an invisible trail into the canyon. From the rim, I watched their descent all the way to the bottom, umbrella still unfurled like a badge against the dark canyon walls. So, by all means, don't let the rain stop you. Put on your slicker and boots and go.

Traveling in the Southwest is an adventure from any point of view. But visiting archaeological sites in the Southwest is something else again. The ruined cities offer unmatched opportunities to experience the great cultures of prehistoric America in what many people consider the world's most magnificent natural setting.

ARIZONA

One of the most important sites ever found in the Southwest is Ventana Cave in southern Arizona. This large rock shelter showed deep stratified deposits, proving that prehistoric people used the cave continuously for at least ten thousand years. A few other sites suggest that people may have lived in Arizona twenty thousand years ago or even longer. But Arizona is known chiefly for its remarkable archaeological sites of later times, ranging from the Basketmaker culture and the Great Pueblo Period of the Anasazi in the Four Corners, to the Sinagua culture of the San Francisco Mountains area and the Hohokam culture further south.

Hohokam farmers dug the first known irrigation canals in the New World to carry water from the Gila and Salt rivers across the desert to their fields of cotton, maize, squash, and beans. Traces of these prehistoric canals are found near similar modern irrigation systems that water farm projects in the desert today.

Closely knit Hohokam villages spread across the valleys, each community a miniature republic. The Hohokam had strong ties with people further south in what is now Mexico. We don't know their language or what they called themselves or where they came from. *Hohokam* is the Pima word for "those who have gone."

The Hohokam traded with people as far away as the Gulf of California for ocean shells to make jewelry. They used fermented cactus juice to etch designs on ornaments made of shells; large shells were used to make trumpets.

The great Hohokam centers were around Phoenix. The Hohokam influenced the people around them and were influenced by them. In Arizona many cultures and peoples blended together in the great flowering of the various Pueblo civilizations between A.D. 1100 and 1400. The Sinagua, who came to Arizona from the north through the volcanic San Francisco range, learned their craft and art of building pueblos from the Anasazi and they learned farming techniques from the Hohokam. Long before the Europeans began to stir about in their American melting pot, the original Americans had learned the virtues of merging cultures.

After the great prehistoric cultures had disappeared, Spanish missionaries tried to convert the Indians to Catholicism. In the north the Hopi and other northern tribes remained immune to these efforts. In the south Jesuit Father Eusebio Kino founded two dozen missions in northern Mexico and southern Arizona. Ruins of the great missions still stand in Arizona—places such as Tumacacori, whose spare ruins are now part of a national monument north of Nogales.

Arizona's present is still firmly rooted in its prehistoric past. In the northeastern corner of the Four Corners, the Hopi—probable descendants of the Anasazi—still live in the pueblo villages of Walpi and Old Oraibi atop sweeping mesas that remain much as they were seven hundred years ago. The Hopi practice as part of their religious ceremonials ancient dances like the Snake, Bean, Kachina, and Flute. In southern Arizona the Pima and Papagado are thought to be descendants of the Hohokam. They continue to weave baskets in the way of their ancestors.

Many of the current Indian crafts—pottery, basketry, jewelry, and the ritual kachina dolls—are still made in traditional ways. And on the deep floor of a canyon near the Grand Canyon, the few remaining descendants of one prehistoric Indian tribe continue to live according to the traditions of their ancestors.

Beautiful ruined cities are found all over Arizona, from Walnut Canyon to Tuzigoot to Montezuma Well to Casa Grande, to Tonto—each a different, silent testimony to the advanced culture of the prehistoric people here.

Arizona also has several museums that are showplaces of Indian cultures: The Museum of Northern Arizona in Flagstaff, the Heard Museum in Phoenix, and the Arizona State Museum on the campus of the University of Arizona in Tucson. Arizona also offers full certification for amateur archaeologists and almost unlimited opportunity for amateurs to work with professionals on important projects throughout the state.

SITES AND MUSEUMS

Dragoon (Tucson)

- *Amerind Foundation*
  Dragoon, Arizona 85609 *(602) 586-3003*

Fine collections of artifacts from the Southwest and Mexico are on display in addition to other material from the Great Plains, California, and the Arctic. The facilities include a fifteen-thousand-volume library of research and technical reports as well as a reading room and laboratory. Lectures, guided tours, and films are presented by knowledgeable staff members.

HOURS: Daily, by appointment only.

Flagstaff and Vicinity

- *Montezuma Castle National Monument*
  P.O. Box 68 *Castle: (602) 567-3322*
  Clarkdale, Arizona 86324 *Well: (602) 567-4521*

Within this single monument are two of the most unusual pueblo ruins in the Southwest. High up on the face of a cliff are the remains of a five-story pueblo where fifty people lived some six hundred years ago.

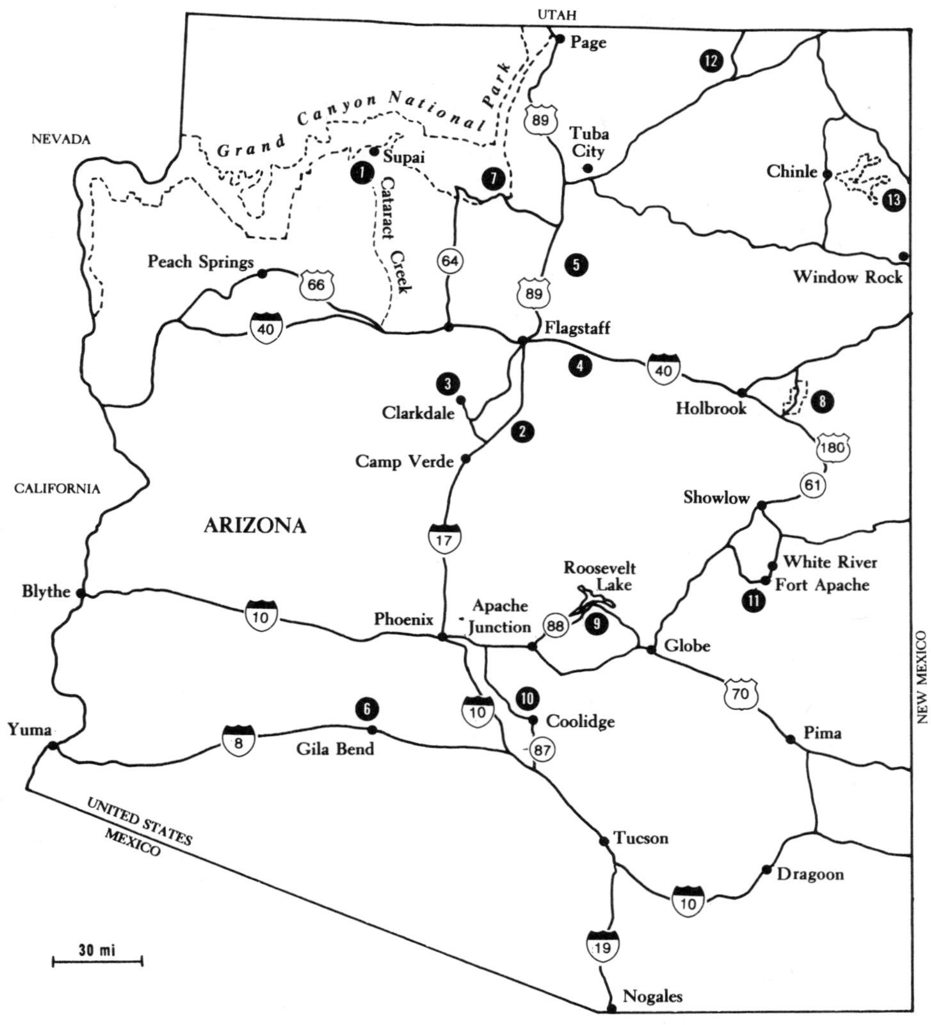

KEY TO SITES
(Indicated by Black Circles on Map)

1. Havasu Canyon
2. Montezuma Castle National Monument
3. Tuzigoot National Monument
4. Walnut Canyon National Monument
5. Wupatki National Monument
6. Painted Rocks
7. Grand Canyon
8. Petrified Forest National Park
9. Tonto National Monument
10. Casa Grande National Monument
11. Kinishba Ruins
12. Navajo National Monument
13. Canyon de Chelly National Monument

Map of Arizona showing location of sites.

The sheer limestone walls of Montezuma Castle curve into the face of the cliff. This national monument in Arizona is one of the best preserved dwellings in the Southwest. (Photo: Neil Felshman.)

Montezuma Castle is one of the best-preserved cliff dwellings in the Southwest. The twenty rooms in the dwelling are built in steplike fashion inside a high cave and shielded by the overhanging rim of the mesa. The sheer exterior walls of the dwellings are made from the limestone blocks laid in mud mortar. They are twelve inches thick and curve to conform to the shape of the cave where the castle is built.

This region was first inhabited around A.D. 700 by the Hohokam, who lived in huts along the streams and creeks in the valley. About four hundred years later, the Sinagua from the north migrated into the area and began to build the stone pueblos of which Montezuma Castle and the ruins at Montezuma Well are examples. The ruins were named when pioneer settlers mistakenly assumed that the Aztecs had built the spectacular structures they found.

Seven miles northeast of the castle is **Montezuma Well.** Here, low-lying cliffs circle a pool of water so tranquil that the sky is mirrored with hardly a ripple in the deep green surface. The pool is a limestone sink fed by an underground stream that moves water through at a rate of one and a half million gallons a day. Prehistoric farmers diverted much of this water into irrigation ditches that emptied into the farmland below. Small ruined dwellings are hidden in the cliffs that enclose the pool, and a trail leads down to the stream outlet where water was channeled into the irrigation canals.

The two ruins within the monument are entirely different from each other in feeling. Montezuma Castle is much better known, and visitors flock to take a look at it. The trail is paved and easily traversed, but you can only stand on the path and look up at the beautiful castle. Montezuma Well, on the other hand, is more remote, less famous, and yet seems more accessible because you can get closer to it. The trail leads all around the pool, past ruined dwellings, flowering cactus, and families of big gray owls roosting in the bushes.

The deep pool of Montezuma Well is fed by an underground spring that supplied water for prehistoric farmlands. (Photo: Neil Felshman.)

DIRECTIONS: The monument is easily reached off I-17, 43 miles south of Flagstaff. There are visitors' centers at both Montezuma Castle and Montezuma Well.

If you are approaching from the north, go to Montezuma Well first; from the south, Montezuma Castle is first. The sites are connected by I-17, but each has its own exit road.

If you want to approach from Tuzigoot, take SR 279 to I-17 north and follow the signs.

ADMISSION: A single entrance fee of $1 per car covers both sites.

• *Tuzigoot National Monument*
P.O. Box 68
Clarkdale, Arizona 86324 *(602) 634-5564*

Crumbling on a hilltop like a medieval castle, Tuzigoot commands a bucolic valley and stream from its limestone ridge 120 feet above the Verde Valley in Arizona. People lived and farmed in this valley in the early tenth century. They raised not only corn but also beans and cotton and pumpkins.

The people who farmed and lived here in the valley were joined by Indians from the north called *Sinagua* (a Spanish word that means "without water") in about A.D. 1125. These new residents began building on the hill, constructing the first cluster of fifteen or twenty rooms where approximately fifty people lived.

The population of *Tuzigoot* (Apache for "crooked water") remained relatively stable for more than a century. Then, people began to drift south from the Four Corners area, where the long drought had made farming difficult. These Pueblo people from the north joined those who had begun the hillside settlement, and by the end of the century, there were ninety-two rooms at Tuzigoot. Within sight of the hillside village at this time were six more pueblos, either newly constructed or expanded by the influx of refugees.

For another hundred years, the Indians lived here in prosperity. Then, sometime during the 1400s, they deserted their pueblos; no one is sure why. When Spanish soldiers reached Verde Valley in 1583, the pueblos were abandoned and in ruins, and the Yavapai Indians of the area were living in thatched huts.

In 1933 the University of Arizona excavated the site, and in 1939 Tuzigoot was established as a national monument. A beautiful old-fashioned museum with screen doors opening onto a wide verandah has been prepared for visitors. Turquoise and shell jewelry and perfect black obsidian projectile points are on display.

The walk through the ruins of Tuzigoot is on a sharply graded, paved footpath. A leisurely tour of the ruins takes about a half hour. From the

The ruined city of Tuzigoot towers above the Verde Valley near Cottonwood, Arizona. (Photo: JW.)

An ancient mano and metate lie abandoned near the crumbling walls of Tuzigoot. (Photo: JW.)

crest of the hill, the ruined city spills down toward the valley where modern farmers plow the fields in geometric patterns.

DIRECTIONS: The monument is near Clarkdale, Arizona, and is easily reached by main roads. From Flagstaff drive 49 miles southwest on U.S. 89A to Cottonwood, then 3 miles northwest to the ruins. There is a campground in Cottonwood.

HOURS: June–August: 7:00 A.M.–7:00 P.M. daily.
September–May: 8:00 A.M.–5:00 P.M. daily

ADMISSION: $1 per car or 50¢ for each adult arriving by bus; children under sixteen accompanied by an adult, free.

• *Walnut Canyon National Monument*
Route 1, Box 25
Flagstaff, Arizona 86001 *(602) 526-3367*

As the Sinagua moved from their volcanic ash-covered farmlands in the Wupatki area during the 1200s, they came into Walnut Canyon, where there was fertile soil and a dependable supply of water. Caves high in the canyon walls also offered protection from the elements and an opportunity for the Sinagua to use some of their newly acquired skills in construction. They built more than 300 rooms in the limestone cliffs, but about 150 years later they abandoned the canyon.

The cliff dwellings in Walnut Canyon stood peaceful and unmolested for six hundred years, until they were spotted in 1883. By the early 1900s they were visited freely—and freely looted. Until the dwellings were taken over by the National Park Service in 1933, pothunters took away almost all of the artifacts left by the Sinagua and vandals defaced and damaged the dwellings. Knowledge of the way ancient people lived here has largely come from investigation at other sites.

The elevation at the rim of the canyon is seven thousand feet. Today a paved foot trail descends for three quarters of a mile into the bottom of the canyon. Stairs have been cut into the rock, but it is a steep climb. The combination of climbing and extreme altitude makes the trek difficult for anyone who is not in good physical condition.

The hike takes at least one hour. Park rangers advise visitors to take it easy on the trail and stop occasionally to rest. The trail passes through twenty-five of the cliff-dwelling rooms, and you can see one hundred other ruins from vantage points. The ruins here are unusual because whole front walls are intact, something seldom seen at any archaeological site.

From the Visitors' Center, another, shorter trail follows one rim of the canyon, where you can see the dwellings across the canyon. This trail offers a wonderful view of the whole canyon. Bring your binoculars.

The first tourists enter Walnut Canyon, Arizona, in 1904. This rare photo was supplied by the National Park Service.

DIRECTIONS: Walnut Canyon is easily reached over a three-mile paved highway that connects with I-40, 7½ miles east of Flagstaff.
HOURS: Memorial Day–Labor Day: 7:00 A.M.–7:00 P.M. daily.
Rest of year: 8:00 A.M.–5:00 P.M.
Closed Christmas, New Year's.
ADMISSION: $1 per car or 50¢ per person arriving by bus or on foot.

• *Wupatki National Monument*
Tuba Star Route
Flagstaff, Arizona 86001 *(602) 774-7000*

In A.D. 1065, the Sinagua farmers who lived among the volcanic peaks of the San Francisco range were warned to abandon their pit houses and huts by rumblings and earthquakes that continued over a period of months. Then, the rumblings exploded as Sunset Crater violently erupted, covering hundreds of square miles with black volcanic ash.

The Indians soon realized that the forbidding-looking soil was more fertile than any they had yet known and that it existed for hundreds of miles around. People returned to the area to plant their crops in the black earth.

The layer of volcanic ash acted as a moisture-retaining mulch, which held water in the soil and permitted farming where it had been impossible before. The Sinagua were not the only ones to return; some of the Anasazi from the north, the Hohokam from the south, and the Mogollon from the southeast also came into the area.

In the 1100s settlements began to spring up throughout the area. The renaissance lasted only about a hundred years, as the volcanic ash cover gradually was blown away. During those years, however, upwards of five thousand people lived and farmed the area of the Wupatki National Monument and hundreds of pueblo ruins are left. Among the major accessible ruins in the monument area are **Wukoki,** a three-story pueblo built on sandstone; **Lomaki; Citadel Ruins,** which had fifty rooms, and has not yet been excavated; and the **Wupatki Ruin.**

Wupatki Ruin is the largest in the area and during the 1100s housed as many as three hundred people. The influence of other cultures on the Sinagua is seen in some of the features of this ruin. The circular amphitheater or "dance plaza" is similar to the Anasazi kivas, but ceremonial trappings are missing and the purpose of the structure can only be approximated. There is also an oval ball court similar to those found in Mexico and Central America, which is closely identified with the Hohokam. The ball court at Wupatki is unique since it is made of masonry while others are usually constructed of adobe.

There is camping available at the U.S. Forest Service campground from May to September, and overnight facilities and restaurants are plentiful in the area.

DIRECTIONS: The Wupatki National Monument is on a looped road connected with Sunset Crater National Monument; it is easily reached off U.S. 89, 32 miles north of Flagstaff.

HOURS: The Visitors' Centers at both monuments are open from 8:00 A.M. to 7:00 P.M. (May to September); and 8:00 A.M. to 5:00 P.M. the rest of the year.
Closed Christmas, New Year's.

ADMISSION: Free.

- *Museum of Northern Arizona*
  Fort Valley Road
  Flagstaff, Arizona 86001 *(602) 774-5211*

The art, archaeology, geology, and natural history of the Colorado Plateau are explored in many extensive displays. Murals and reconstructions cover a wide range of northern Arizona Indian cultures from the Basketmakers through the Pueblo culture. There is a fully staffed research library and museum shop. Two contemporary craft shows are presented each summer: the Hopi in early July and the Navajo in late July and early August.

HOURS: Monday–Saturday: 9:00 A.M.–5:00 P.M.
Sunday: 1:30 P.M.–5:00 P.M.
ADMISSION: Free.

Gila Bend

• *Painted Rocks State Historic Park*

Ancient Indian pictures are preserved in this state park. Well-marked trails go through the park and take you to the most interesting petroglyphs. There are picnicking and primitive camping in the park, but no water.

DIRECTIONS: From Gila Bend drive 15 miles west on I-8, then 12 miles north on Painted Rocks Road.

Globe

• *Clara T. Woody Museum of Gila County*
Mine Rescue Building
Globe, Arizona 85501 *(602) 425-7385*

The Salado people lived in a large village called *Besh-Ba-Gowah* ("Place of Metal") from about A.D. 1225 to 1400. The village is gone, but the material recovered from excavations and preserved in this museum presents a comprehensive view of life in the ancient village.

HOURS: Tuesday–Friday: 10:00 A.M.–4:00 P.M.
ADMISSION: Free.

Grand Canyon

• *Grand Canyon National Park*
Grand Canyon, Arizona 86023

Thousands of years ago western Archaic people lived in caves in the Grand Canyon. But the small ruins that remain in the park today are from the Anasazi people who lived here briefly between A.D. 1185 and 1250 and attempted to farm the canyon bottom along the Colorado River.

Three archaeological sites in the Grand Canyon are open to the public. In a museum adjacent to the ruins on the East Rim Drive, displays illustrate the life of the prehistoric people of the canyon.

On the south rim, the most accessible part of the canyon, is a ruined village called **Tusayan.** The south rim, open year round, is reached from Williams, 59 miles north on AZ 64.

On the north rim is **Cape Royal Ruin** and a site on the Colorado River designated as **G.C. 624.** This latter site is reached by hiking or mule packing down the eight-mile Bright Angel Trail to the canyon bottom. The north rim of the canyon is blocked by snow in the winter. In the summer, it is reached by driving 30 miles south from Jacob Lake on AZ 67.

For information about visiting archaeological sites in the Grand Canyon, write the park superintendent at the address above.

● *Havasu Canyon*
Supai, Arizona 86435

There is so much to take in at Grand Canyon that few people make the special journey to an isolated Indian reservation at the bottom of nearby Havasu Canyon, where a sparkling green waterfall spills into a deep pool, and red canyon walls soar above the stream like ruined temples. The Havasupai people have been living in this secluded spot for thirteen centuries.

More than thirteen hundred years ago, ancestors of the Havasupai lived on the Colorado Plateau. They grew corn, built granaries for their harvests, and fashioned a well-designed pottery. By A.D. 1000 wandering tribes of raiders had driven them off the plateau and onto a canyon floor created by a small branch of the Colorado River called Cataract Creek.

Here, the people continued to thrive and the population expanded across the bottom of the canyon. They built cliff dwellings in the face of the cliffs until every ledge became a home, some of the structures several stories high. To supplement the crops, hunting parties gathered on top of the plateau each winter; these forays into the wider world became a fixed part of Havasupai life: summers in the canyon, winters searching the plateau for game.

But the plateau changed over the centuries. Rainfall diminished. The soil grew drier, and the vegetation more sparse. More and more, the people were confined to the walled canyon.

Although Grand Canyon was discovered by the Spanish in 1540, no European entered Havasu until a Franciscan priest in search of converts penetrated the steep-walled canyon with a guide in 1776. Francisco Thomás Garcés' mile-deep descent took him down a forbidding trail, past dry canyon walls, and suddenly into a lush green oasis where a waterfall the color of turquoise fell into a deep sinking pool in the canyon bottom. Flowers and luxuriant grasses grew along the streams. And here Father Garcés met the *Havasupai*—"people of the blue-green water."

The priest later reported his discovery, but the Spanish settlers themselves never went to the canyon. They continued to search for richer fields across the vast expanses of New Mexico. The Havasupai remained well hidden and safe from the plundering hands of the conquistadors.

They retained their early culture—pottery, clay pipes, stone kivas, bone tools. Through the Hopi and the Navajo, the Havasupai were influenced by the new European lifeways, trading for metal pans, guns, and cloth. When Father Garcés first saw them they already had horses, cattle, and some Old World plants.

The Havasupai have remained peaceful and isolated in their canyon. In the 1850s they accepted a small reservation of only about five hundred acres in the bottom of the canyon, and here they still live in seclusion. These gentle people keep abreast of the outside world through the Hopi and other Indian neighbors. A small group of families live in the village of Supai, and each year a few visitors are invited to descend into the almost untouched gardens of Havasu Canyon.

Early prehistoric remains of villages in the canyon bottom have been lost to spring floods that rush out of Cataract Creek. But dozens of small ruins can be spotted tucked up into the cliffs. These ruins cannot be entered.

Visiting Havasu Canyon: With permission from the tourist manager, you can hike down an eight-mile trail to the canyon, or you can go in by horseback. The round trip is too strenuous for a single day, and you should plan to spend at least one or two nights in the canyon.

Accommodations are available in the tribal lodge, and camping is permitted in three designated campgrounds.

Groceries are available in Supai Village, and a village café serves breakfast and lunch. Tribal crafts are for sale. The mail goes out on pack train from the Supai post office—the only pack train in America. The Havasupai people do not allow liquor, drugs, firearms or other weapons on their reservation.

The journey begins at Hualapai Hilltop, reached by turning north off U.S. 66 about 7 miles east of Peach Spring, Arizona, and driving for 60 miles on a partially paved, all-weather road. No gasoline, water, or other supplies are available after leaving Highway 66, so fill your gas tank and water bottles before turning off.

At Hualapai Hilltop you must leave your car and descend by foot or horseback down the winding eight-mile trail through rugged dry canyons until you reach the lush green canyon bottom.

Reservations. An entry fee of $5 per person is charged. When you arrive at Supai Village at the bottom of Havasu Canyon, you are asked to register at the Tourist Office.

Saddle horses can be reserved through the manager. These reservations should be made well in advance and *confirmed* one day before traveling.

The manager suggests that all visitors wanting space on either the campground or in the lodge in Havasu Canyon give their *arrival* and *departure* date.

Very few people are allowed to visit Havasu Canyon, so make your travel arrangements well in advance. Write or call:

Tourist Manager
Havasupai Tourist Enterprises
Supai, Arizona 86435 (602) 448-2121

Holbrook

• *Petrified Forest National Park*
I-40
Holbrook, Arizona 86025 *(602) 524-6228*

Nearly 100,000 acres of the most beautiful fossilized wood in the world is found in the Petrified Forest. Arizona petrified wood is a rich, deep red streaked with gold and blue. The trees grew 180 million years ago in the high country to the west and southwest and were later washed down by streams and buried in volcanic ash. Millions of years later, the whole region was uplifted and erosion exposed logs of solid stone.

Brilliantly polished cross-sections of petrified logs, some pieces three feet in diameter, are on display in the park's two visitors' centers. Giant stone logs lie in pieces scattered throughout the park. It is strictly forbidden to remove even the smallest fragment of petrified wood from the park. Curio shops around the area sell wood that has been purchased from ranchers who have petrified wood "mines" on their land.

Prehistoric Indians lived all over this region and there are three hundred known Anasazi sites in the park. Two are open to visitors. Near the northern entrance to the park is **Puerco Ruins,** a partially excavated pueblo that originally had about 150 rooms. Just 1 mile south of Puerco is the famous petroglyph site, **Inscription Rock.** Puerco Ruin is 11 miles from the northern entrance. This entrance is also near the rim of the **Painted Desert.**

Agate House, a prehistoric dwelling built from petrified wood, is within walking distance from the Visitors' Center at the southern entrance. The Rainbow Forest Visitors' Center at the southern entrance to the park has exhibits of projectile points and other prehistoric artifacts made of petrified wood. The Visitors' Center also shows a film about the region that describes how the wood was petrified.

Visitors' centers at both entrances to the park have exhibits of fossil plants and bones, fabulous slices of petrified wood, and excellent graphic displays that describe the geology and flora and fauna of the region since the beginning of time.

There is no camping in the park, but you can picnic near the Rainbow Forest entrance and at Chinde Point on the rim of the Painted Desert.

DIRECTIONS: You can drive through the park in a loop. Traveling from east to west, use the northern

(Painted Desert) entrance on U.S. 66/I-40. You can travel through the park and come out on U.S. 180 and continue west to Holbrook. Traveling west to east, reverse the trip and enter at the southern (Rainbow Forest) entrance on U.S. 180 and come out on U.S. 66/I-40, going toward Gallup, New Mexico.

HOURS (PARK): The park is open daily year round during the daylight hours. Sunset and sunrise are the best times to drive into the northern entrance, where you can sit along the rim of the Painted Desert and watch the sun wash the sandstone cliffs in ribbons of color.

HOURS (VISITORS' CENTERS): May 15–September 15: 5:30 A.M.–7:30 P.M.
Rest of year: 8:00 A.M.–5:00 P.M.

ADMISSION: $2 per car.

Phoenix-Globe Vicinity

- *Tonto National Monument*
Box 707
Roosevelt, Arizona 85545 *(602) 467-2241*

The best thing about visiting Tonto National Monument may be getting there. Tonto is about eighty miles from Phoenix and the drive takes two and a half hours. From Apache Junction east of Phoenix, the old Apache Trail parallels the ancient Indian route through the canyons of the Salt River. Indian lore has it that the mountain peaks are images of people turned to stone. The road twists out of Apache Junction into the legendary Superstition Mountains, where many men have died seeking the Lost Dutchman gold mine. It continues to wind through Fish Canyon and just past Roosevelt Lake to the monument.

For one long twenty-five-mile stretch between Tortilla Flat and Roosevelt the paved road turns to gravel and narrowly clings to the sheer mountainside. Luckily, if you are approaching from west to east as the directions above lead you, you are on the inside of the road nudging the canyon walls. The oncoming side drops away sharply into deep gorges.

Leaving the monument, you can drive out on the paved road (Highway 88) to Globe, which is about 28 miles to the east. So the best way to make this trip is to approach from Phoenix and go through to Globe. A reverse journey is ill advised, since the unpaved section of the Apache Trail is precarious going from east to west (although the rangers tell me that people do it all the time).

The road is generally safe but can be treacherous in rainy weather.

All kinds of vehicles come over the Apache Trail, including recreational vehicles and buses. It is a splendid journey if you take your time and enjoy the remote wilderness scenery.

In prehistoric times Tonto was home to farming people who moved into the canyons around A.D. 900 and built villages along the Salt River. The people are called *Salado,* the Spanish word for "salty." Their first homes were pit houses along the river banks. Around 1200 they moved to the easily defended ridge tops and later built stone and mud houses inside natural caves.

The Hohokam people may have already been living in the canyon when the Salado first migrated into the region. Together they exploited the land to its fullest. They hunted, farmed, and gathered wild plants and seeds. From three hundred different desert plants, the Salado Indians made medicines and wove plant fibers into baskets, sandals, and clothing.

They built irrigation canals and grew corn, squash, beans, pumpkins, and cotton in the canyon bottoms. As cotton growers they were unmatched anywhere in the New World, and their woven fabrics are the most beautiful and intricate material recovered from prehistoric America. They created lacy, open-worked fabrics dyed many different colors. Blankets, headbands, sheer gauzy shirts, carrying bags, and breechclouts were all woven from cotton.

The Salado also made ornaments from shell, stone, and turquoise. Their pottery bowls were plain red, painted on the inside with black and white geometric designs. Many of these bowls have been found on other archaeological sites, indicating that they were traded over long distances.

Three Salado villages remain protected in natural caves above the Salt River. Two Lower Ruins are accessible by a self-guided trail, and the Upper Ruins can be reached only on a ranger-guided hike, which leaves the Visitors' Center once each day.

Lower Ruins: A steep half-mile paved trail leads to the Lower Ruins. Many species of native plants used by the Salado people still grow along the trail—barrel cactus, giant saguaro, jojoba, yucca, and many others. The round trip takes about one hour. The trail is open every day from 8:00 A.M. until 4:00 P.M..

Upper Ruins: You can visit the Upper Ruins only when accompanied by a ranger. The one and a half mile trail is steep and rugged. In the spring the hillside is literally carpeted with big yellow poppies. The hike to the Upper Ruins starts promptly at 9:00 A.M., and it takes about three hours to go up and back. You must book your visit at least five days ahead of time. If you like to plan ahead, you can also make a reservation several months in advance.

It takes all day to explore Tonto fully. You can start with the ranger-guided hike in the morning, stop for a picnic lunch, and then walk the self-guided trail to the Lower Ruins in the afternoon. This means that if you are coming in from Phoenix, you will have to start out at dawn, but it's worth it to watch the sun rolling across the canyon walls early in the morning. This is an outstanding day's trip.

Tonto National Monument is open all year, and the best time to visit is between October and June. The Visitors' Center is open every day from 8:00 A.M. to 5:00 P.M. The trail to the Lower Ruins closes at 4:00 P.M.

Tonto National Forest: Three million acres of land surround the monument; approximately one quarter is remote desert and mountain wilderness, where foot and horseback are the only means of travel. You can fish, hunt, and camp along the Salt and Verde rivers.

There are some primitive campgrounds along the Apache Trail and at Roosevelt Lake on the way to the monument. Improved campgrounds are in other parts of the forest. For full information about camping in Tonto National Forest, write:

Forest Supervisor
Tonto National Forest
102 South 28th Street
Phoenix, Arizona 85034

There are motel accommodations in Globe, Apache Junction, and Phoenix.

Phoenix-Tucson Vicinity

• *Casa Grande National Monument*
Coolidge, Arizona 85228 *(602) 723-3172*

Take Arizona Highway 87 south from Phoenix and you travel through the Gila River Reservation to Casa Grande National Monument. Jack rabbits and prairie dogs scamper back and forth across the road, and occasional wisps of dry mesquite drift through the air like brown clouds. Yet on all sides of this dried-up desert, above-ground irrigation sprinklers water lush green crops. The early Hohokam Indians who farmed the Gila Valley two thousand years ago used an irrigation system of canals that carried water for miles into the desert. The Hohokam grew cotton, corn, beans, and squash on vast tracks of arid land. And the adobe walls of one of their villages surround the most perplexing and mysterious ruin in Arizona—Casa Grande.

When you are still miles away, the ancient clay structure protected by a modern steel shelter rises up out of the desert like a mirage. You watch the "Big House" change shape in the hazy distance as the road curves in a wide arc and finally turns into the park entrance.

The four-story building still dominates the Hohokam village. It is closer in style to structures found in Mexico than anything seen in the Southwest.

Remnants of a timbered ceiling give a probable building date of A.D. 1350. The solid adobe walls are from three to five feet thick and still stand twenty to twenty-five feet high, although the central tower is at least thirty feet high.

Was Casa Grande a sentry station or a lookout tower? Certainly its great height would offer a clear view for miles across the flat desert. Was it a fortress or a temple? Its solid high walls and unique shape indicate it might have been either. Or was it an ancient desert observatory? Seven round holes in the upper chamber open to the sky. At night, glittering patches of sky can be seen through these small openings. The actual use may never be discovered, but it is clear that Casa Grande was a building with a special purpose.

By 1450 the Hohokam had disappeared from their village in the Gila Valley. Casa Grande was roofless and abandoned when Jesuit Father Kino first saw it in 1694 and doubtless had been in that condition for centuries. The great structure rising out of the empty desert became a landmark for white men—miners, cowboys, pony soldiers—and hundreds of desert travelers who passed by wrote their names on the crumbling walls.

This very fragile site is usually quiet and uncrowded except on winter weekends. The weather is best between October and May, but the monument is open all year.

In the museum excellent displays clearly show the relationship between the Hohokam and the Indians of Mexico. Unique pottery vessels, copper bells, the design of ball courts—all are similar to those found in the high cultures of Mexico. Some of the finest Hohokam pottery and jewelry in the Southwest is on display in this Visitors' Center.

A well-marked trail leads out of the museum, through an exquisite cactus garden, and along to the ruin. The trail is flat, wide, and easily accessible. A park ranger at the Casa Grande gives an informal talk about the monument and describes the village life of the Hohokam. You are free to walk trails on your own but are asked not to touch the walls of either the ruined houses or the Casa Grande.

The Visitors' Center is ringed with great saguaro cactus. There is a shaded picnic area with tables and water, but no camping is allowed at the monument. The nearest lodging is at Coolidge.

DIRECTIONS: The national monument is *not* in the city of Casa Grande. The monument is reached from either Phoenix or Tucson. From Phoenix drive south on AZ 87 or I-10 about 40 miles. The monument is 1 mile north of Coolidge on AZ 87.

HOURS: 7:00 A.M.–6:00 P.M. daily.

ADMISSION: $1 per car or 50¢ each adult on a tour bus; children under sixteen free when accompanied by an adult.

• *Heard Museum of Anthropology and Primitive Art*
22 East Monte Vista Road
Phoenix, Arizona 85004 *(602) 252-8848*

The Heard has one of the finest Indian art collections in the world. Pottery, jewelry, rugs, and blankets have been collected from almost all of the Indian nations of the Americas. In addition to the changing exhibits, an Indian fair is held in April; the Heard Indian Arts and Crafts Exhibit is held each fall. A library and museum shop are in the building.

HOURS: Monday–Saturday: 10:00 A.M.–5:00 P.M.
Sunday: 1:00 P.M.–5:00 P.M.
ADMISSION: Adults $1.50, children and students 50¢.

• *Pueblo Grande City Park Museum*
4619 East Washington Street
Phoenix, Arizona 85034 *(602) 275-3452*

This museum is built next to a large archaeological site of an ancient Hohokam farming village. Remnants can be seen of irrigation canals, small buildings, and the only completely excavated Hohokam ball court in the Southwest. Trails wind around the site, with signs guiding the way. Inside the museum building, materials that have been collected from the excavation are displayed.

HOURS: Monday–Saturday: 9:00 A.M.–4:45 P.M.
Sunday: 1:00 P.M.–4:45 P.M.
Closed major holidays.
ADMISSION: Free.

Pima

• *Eastern Arizona Museum and Historical Society*
Main and Center Streets
Pima, Arizona 85543 *(602) 485-2761*

Both the Salado and the Hohokam tribes lived in this area. Artifacts from the region and northern Arizona are on display here, along with relics of pioneer days.

HOURS: Monday–Friday: 9:00 A.M.–12:00 M. and 1:00 P.M.–5:00 P.M.
ADMISSION: Free.

Tucson

- *Arizona State Museum*
  University of Arizona
  Tucson, Arizona 85721 *(602) 626-1604*

Exhibits from every major culture in the Southwest are offered in this large museum, including tools, mammoth bones, and artifacts retrieved from Ventana Cave and other Early Man sites in Arizona. Dioramas contrast ancient village life with the life of more modern Indian cultures. A large library of books on anthropology and history is available for use by the public, and there is a reading room on the premises.

HOURS: Monday–Saturday: 9:00 A.M.–5:00 P.M.
Sunday: 2:00 P.M.–5:00 P.M.
Closed major holidays.
ADMISSION: Free.

Whiteriver–Fort Apache Vicinity

- *Kinishba Ruins*

East central Arizona is a beautiful, seldom explored section of the state. At its center is Fort Apache Reservation, which runs along the Salt and Black rivers. Five miles south of Whiteriver, the old Fort Apache now houses the Theodore Roosevelt Indian School and the **Apache Cultural Center Museum.** West of town, over a rough dirt road, are the Kinishba Ruins.

Kinishba is one of the largest and most important ruins in the Southwest. More than a thousand people lived in this village between A.D. 1050 and 1300. The ruins are under the protection of the reservation and are extremely fragile. Until the site is fully stabilized, visitors are only permitted to view Kinishba through a wire fence. There is no interpretation at the site at this time. If you make this trip, stop in at Fort Apache on the way.

DIRECTIONS: From Whiteriver follow AZ 73 south to Fort Apache. A directional marker will take you to old Fort Apache. The Apache Cultural Center Museum is open 8:00 A.M. to 5:00 P.M. weekdays. Call (602) 338-4625.

To reach Kinishba, continue southwest on AZ 73 past the Canyon Day junction (about 7 miles). Turn right at the directional marker, and follow a rough dirt road for 2 miles to the ruin.

STATE OFFICE

Arizona State Museum
University of Arizona
Tucson, Arizona 85721 (602) 884-2585

OPPORTUNITIES FOR AMATEURS AND ORGANIZATIONS TO JOIN

Arizona's full certification program for amateurs includes training in field excavation, survey, rock art recording, laboratory analysis, and report writing. People who join the program participate in both classroom lectures and fieldwork. Once the work has been completed, they are certified to work with professionals.

There is tremendous opportunity in Arizona for trained amateurs to join fully in archaeological activities. Ultimately, those who hold certification may work in paying positions, although that is not the intent of the program. Anyone interested in the program can sign up through a local archaeological society. For information about local chapters, write:

Arizona Archaeological Society
P.O. Box 9665
Phoenix, Arizona 85020

NEW MEXICO

The area that is now New Mexico was an early melting pot of the ancient peoples. In the southwestern section, particularly along the Mimbres River near the Arizona border, the Mogollon culture grew up and flowered. The Mogollon people settled in the area, built their pit houses and, later, aboveground dwellings. They farmed the land, gathered nuts and seeds, and hunted and trapped small game. The remains of one of their most beautiful communities can be seen at the Gila Cliff Dwellings in the southwestern corner of New Mexico.

Some archaeologists do not consider the Mogollon a pure culture. Their lifeway was probably a fusion of different cultures, particularly the Anasazi and the Hohokam, which evolved at the same time in different parts of the Southwest.

Minor shifts in climate caused the Mogollon to move from the New Mexico–Arizona border further north and east, a little at a time, into more central places along trade routes. In such places as Gran Quivira in central New Mexico, they were influenced by the Anasazi, who were moving south from the Four Corners region. The Mogollon may have merged with the Anasazi, or they may have drifted south into Mexico. The culture had disappeared completely before 1400.

The Anasazi culture reached its height between A.D. 1100 and 1200. Hundreds of Anasazi communities thrived in the Four Corners region, some small and others housing hundreds, even thousands, of people. Their fields blossomed in canyon bottoms and on mesa tops. But long droughts in the last half of the thirteenth century forced the Anasazi farmers to move. The great communities began to break apart as family after family drifted away. Some went southwest, other southeast. Over the next two centuries, the culture almost died out completely.

The Anasazi had a democratic society. They were religious, communal, and peace-loving. Wherever they moved, they carried their culture with them and influenced the people with whom they came in contact. They lived side by side with many different peoples.

By the early 1500s, a renaissance began. This was the period when the great dwellings in Frijoles Canyon, now preserved by Bandelier National Monument, were built. Stable communities began to appear throughout the Pajarito Plateau in northern New Mexico. The Anasazi's descendants seemed destined for a new age of greatness when the Spaniards moved north into New Mexico in 1540.

Francisco Vásquez de Coronado had heard the rumors of the fabulous Seven Cities of Cibola, where the walls of the buildings themselves were crafted of pure gold. In 1540 he led an expedition north from Mexico to find the cities and reap the treasure for himself and Spain. The journey was long and difficult. When Coronado finally reached a Zuñi pueblo, he found a community of simple farmers but no gold. Coronado and his men rode from pueblo to pueblo seeking mythical treasures, destroying crops and villages, and killing Indians. When he finally returned to Mexico, he left devastation in his wake.

The Pueblo Indians, basically peaceful people, were no match for the Spaniards who had weapons and horses. After 1580 new Spanish expeditions moved into New Mexico, this time claiming land for the Spanish dominion.

The cornfields were requisitioned to feed the invaders. Indians were flogged, hanged, and sold as slaves. Missionaries followed the soldiers and converted entire populations to a Catholicism that was the product of the infamous Spanish Inquisition. The Indians had no immunity to simple European diseases, and thousands died of foreign illnesses.

The farming pueblos had always been prey for nomadic Indians—the Utes, Comanches, Apaches, and Navajo. Now, the desert marauders stole Spanish horses and even more easily stripped the peaceful pueblos. After years of oppression, the Indians staged the successful Pueblo Revolt in 1680, and the Spanish were driven from the Southwest. For a short time, the pueblo people, led by Po-pe, an old medicine man of the pueblo of San Juan, ruled their own domain. But in 1692 the Spanish returned and reclaimed the land in a bloodless campaign under the leadership of Don Diego de Vargas.

Some Pueblo Indians who refused to accept Spanish rule fled to the rugged Governador country of northern New Mexico. Here they lived for fifty years among their traditional enemies, the Navajo. The many Pueblo traits that appear in the modern Navajo culture may stem from this period.

Other recalcitrant Pueblo Indians joined the Hopis, who were never reconquered by the Spanish.

The Pueblo Indians have clung tenaciously to remnants of their ancient culture. There is usually a chapel in each pueblo, but there is also a kiva where the old religion is practiced. Each pueblo is independent of the others, but there is a strong group unity.

In New Mexico today's Pueblo Indians are direct descendants of the ancient people who first inhabited this part of the world. Many of the places where their ancestors lived are now national monuments. Places such as Bandelier and Gila, Gran Quivira, Puyé, and Pecos allow us to trace the finest aspects of the first Americans' lives.

A good bit of archaeological work in New Mexico is devoted to locating endangered sites. Amateur societies closely cooperate with professional archaeologists. One of their main activities is surveying rock art. Petroglyphs and pictographs are now considered important archaeological records and require extensive study. New Mexico is particularly rich in petroglyphs and pictographs, and several preserved sites are open to visitors.

THE PUEBLOS

The Pueblo Indians of New Mexico trace their ancestry back in time to the earliest known inhabitants of North America. Their immediate ancestors are the people of the classic pueblo cliff dwellings. Many pueblos still existing today were first occupied in prehistoric times.

Acoma may be the oldest continuously occupied town in the United States, excepting perhaps Old Oraibi, the Hopi village in northern Arizona. In the tenth century, Acoma was built on top of a sheer butte. It was a thriving town when Coronado first saw it in 1540. Alongside the butte the legendary Enchanted Mesa rises seventy-three feet above Acoma.

The pueblos have survived the Spanish occupation and the territorial expansion of the United States. Today, the Pueblo Indians cherish and preserve their ancient heritage in nineteen pueblos concentrated in the northern part of New Mexico. They all have similar societies, but the Indians speak six different languages. The **Hall of the Modern Indian,** across the interior patio of the Palace of Governors in Sante Fe, describes Pueblo life of the last hundred years. In Albuquerque, the **Indian Pueblo Cultural Center**—jointly owned by the nineteen pueblos—features art and exhibits of the Pueblo Indians.

In the pueblos today, Catholicism and native religion are blended. Every village has a church and at least one kiva. Many of the churches date from the earliest Spanish occupation. The church at Acoma was built between 1629 and 1641.

Most pueblos welcome visitors. Ceremonial dances and movable feasts, to which the public is sometimes invited, are celebrated at various times throughout the year. Other sacred rituals and dances are closed to non-Indians. In early December the Zuñi "Shalako" celebrates the annual return of the Zuñi Council of the Gods to the Pueblo. Dancers wear colorful bird masks ten feet high. The daylong festival draws thousands of spectators. Visitors are welcome, but—no cameras, sketch pads, or tape recorders.

For those interested in early Indian life, the most interesting and beautiful pueblos are Acoma, Zuñi, Laguna, Taos, Picuris, San Juan, Santa Clara, and Zia. Near Santa Clara and Picuris, ancient ruins within the pueblo are open to visitors.

Pueblos are small, private villages, not geared for tourist traffic and automobiles. Walking or driving through the narrow streets of an ancient pueblo makes one somewhat an intruder, although the Indians are hospitable and friendly. Each pueblo usually charges an admission fee. Cameras and tape recorders are routinely banned, but you can sometimes take pictures if you request permission and pay a small fee. The best times to visit are during those festivals and dances when the public is invited. Ceremonial dances seldom can be photographed.

When you visit a pueblo, always stop at the Tribal Office and request permission to enter. In some villages art and crafts are sold in the trading post or from private homes.

A booklet published by the Tourist Division describes each pueblo, and lists the scheduled festivals and ceremonial dances open to the public. For the booklet *Indians of Mexico,* write

Tourist Division
Department of Development
113 Washington Avenue
Santa Fe, New Mexico 87503

SITES

Albuquerque and Vicinity

- *Coronado State Park and Monument*
  Bernalillo, New Mexico 87004

In 1540 Coronado camped near this prehistoric Anasazi village called **Kuaua.** Several kivas or ceremonial chambers have been excavated at this site. In one kiva archaeologists uncovered seventeen layers of painted murals on the walls. The murals were removed layer by layer in a unique process fully explained in the Visitors' Center. The inside walls of a reconstructed kiva at the site are painted with detailed copies of the original murals.

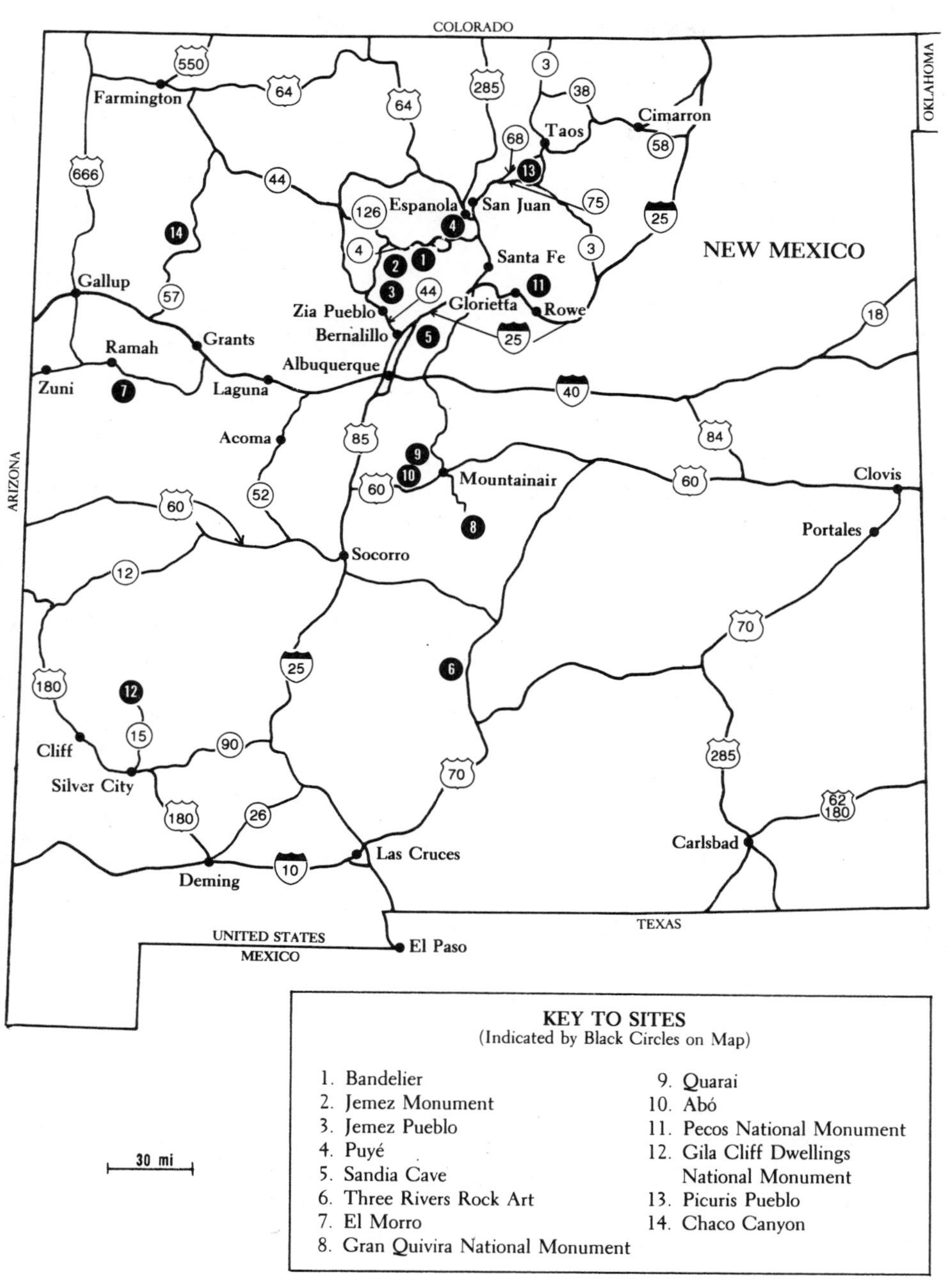

Map of New Mexico showing location of sites.

DIRECTIONS: From Albuquerque drive 20 miles north on I-25, then 5 miles west on NM 44.
HOURS: Thursday–Monday: 9:00 A.M.–5:00 P.M.
Closed Tuesdays, Wednesdays, and holidays.
ADMISSION: Free.

Note: From the monument you can continue north on NM 44 to **Jemez State Monument**; then east on NM 4 to **Bandelier** and **Puyé** (see listings under Los Alamos). While these ruins are all in the same area, it takes time to appreciate each one's unique aspects. If your time is limited, it's better to visit one or two sites rather than rush through them all.

• *Indian Petroglyph State Park*

This site contains petroglyphs carved on lava formations between A.D. 1100 and 1600 by ancestors of the Pueblo Indians. There is a trail here for the handicapped.

DIRECTIONS: From Albuquerque drive 9 miles west on Atrisco Road.
HOURS: May–October: 9:00 A.M.–7:00 P.M. daily.
November–April: 9:00 A.M.–5:00 P.M. daily.
Closed holidays.

• *Sandia Man Cave*

Most people reach the crest of the Sandia Mountains on the aerial tram. If you drive, the road takes you past the cave where the Sandia projectile point, the unusual point with the distinctive bulge on its shoulder, was first discovered. The Sandia may be contemporary with or older than the Clovis point.

The drive up the mountain, partially on unpaved road, is spectacular. You can go up one way and down another on a loop, each turn in the road offering unmatched views of some 10,000 square miles of valleys and mountain ranges as far away as Colorado.

Take I-40 east out of Albuquerque into Tijeras Canyon and turn left on SR 14; turn left again at the San Antonio junction (SR 44). The landscape is heavily forested and offers several good places to stop for picnicking. At the crest the altitude is 10,678 feet.

An unpaved road leads down the other side of the mountain to the village of Placitas. On the way down, the road passes Sandia Man Cave. A sign and a parking area mark the site, and an easy trail leads to the cave. There is no interpretation—nothing to see except the inside of an extremely dark, deep cavern. But this is the place where some of America's earliest inhabitants lived.

SR 44 continues down the mountain and comes out on I-25. It's easier and shorter to make the trip from I-25 up, turn around, and come down the same way. But if you choose this route, you'll miss the splendid trip to the Sandia crest.

Carrizozo

- *Three Rivers Rock Art*

Hundreds of rock carvings made by the Mogollon people can be seen in this specially preserved area. A mile-long, tree-shaded trail takes you through the site.

DIRECTIONS: From Carrizozo drive 28 miles south on U.S. 54 to Three Rivers; then go 5 miles east on gravel road. Follow the directional marker to the site.

Note: Five miles north of Carrizozo is **Valley of Fires State Park,** a river of lava six miles wide that poured out of Little Black Peak. This is a fascinating side trip, and there is camping in the park.

Grants

- *El Morro National Monument*
Ramah, New Mexico 87321 *(505) 783-5132*

A spring-fed pool at the bottom of a cliff has attracted desert dwellers and travelers for centuries. Soaring some two hundred feet above the valley floor a massive sandstone *morro,* or bluff, is shaped dramatically against the sky. Here, on the sheer face of the mesa wall, Don Juan Oñate scratched his name in 1605. Don Diego de Vargas followed him, and dozens of explorers, soldiers, and cowboys added their names. **Inscription Rock,** as the bluff has come to be called, is a historic register of names.

But long before these adventurers passed by, prehistoric Zuñi Indians left their messages here in hundreds of symbols and designs carved into the buff-colored stone. Two Pueblo villages lie in ruins just behind the mesa. A visitors' center at the site tells the colorful story of El Morro. Ancient hand and footholds are dug into the face of the cliff, but an easier, well-marked trail leads from the Visitors' Center along the base of the cliff and onto the top of the mesa. The trail to the ruins is rough and steep in places. Camping and picnicking are permitted.

DIRECTIONS: From Grants drive 43 miles west vai NM 53. From Gallup drive 53 miles southeast via NM 32 and 53.
HOURS: Memorial Day–Labor Day: 8:00 A.M.–8:00 P.M. daily.
Rest of year: 8:00 A.M.–5:00 P.M. daily.
ADMISSION: $1 per car or 50¢ per person.

Los Alamos and Vicinity

- *Bandelier National Monument*
Los Alamos, New Mexico 87544 *(505) 672-3861*

The achievements of nature and ancient man merge in this fertile place, dazzling in its variety. The steep cliffs, gently rolling wooded hills, mesas, and deep, shaded canyons are composed of tuff—a soft volcanic ash that over centuries has become rock—together with a basaltic lava that many centuries ago showered from the Jemez Volcano.

Here, in the canyon formed by the Rito de los Frijoles (Bean Creek), settlements of the Anasazi people flourished from about A.D. 1100 until the late 1500s. Like the Anasazi throughout the Four Corners region, these people were primarily farmers who raised corn, beans, and squash along the banks of the creek in Frijoles Canyon. They wove garments from cotton and made the distinctive black and white Anasazi pottery.

Although they lived here in the canyon for more than four hundred years, drought, soil erosion, and marauding tribes of nomadic Indians finally drove them into other areas. The people of the nearby pueblos of San Ildefonso, Cochiti, and Santa Clara are direct descendants of the early dwellers of the canyon.

More than four hundred separate ruins dot this small area. Some are only of one room, but there are many dwellings with as many as forty rooms, and several large pueblos, including Tyuonyi, have about four hundred rooms.

Bandelier was established as a national monument in 1916. It was named

The circular ruins of Tyuoni near El Rito de los Frijoles, Bandelier National Monument. (Photo: JW.)

Long House stretches along the base of cliff in the main ruins area of Bandelier National Monument. (Photo: JW.)

for the Swiss-American writer and archaelogist, Adolf Bandelier, who explored and studied the Pueblo cultures in New Mexico in the 1880s.

The experience of exploring different ruins within the monument varies widely. By hiking back over the trails that crisscross Bandelier's nearly fifty square miles, you will find small unexcavated sites where feelings of privacy, peace, and connection with the past are intense.

The most accessible ruin is **Tyuonyi,** which means "meeting place" or "place of treaty" in the Keres language. In places the pueblo was three stories high and contained about four hundred rooms. The pueblo is built in a wide circle around a central plaza to which there is just one entrance. In the center are three kivas that were probably owned and used by different clans or societies.

Visitors must hike over remote wilderness trails to reach the ancient shrine of the Stone Lions which is hidden within Bandelier National Monument. (Photo courtesy of the National Park Service.)

A Tsankawi vessel recovered from Bandelier. (Photo courtesy of the National Park Service.)

A well-marked trail leads from the circular ruins up into the shadow of sheer cliffs, where several dwellings are built into caves.

The **Talus House** here was reconstructed of rock debris (called talus) from the cliffs. It is a good example of the houses as they were more than four hundred years ago. The **Long House** stretches more than a hundred feet along the base of the cliff. Above the remaining walls are many small holes that once were fitted with timber to support the roof beams. On the sheer cliff face above the holes, petroglyphs representing birds, people, and lightning are carved into the rock.

While Tyuonyi is in the main ruins area reached over a one-and-a-half-mile trail, most of the monument is practically undisturbed wild land, with more than sixty miles of trails leading to remote sites. Hiking or backpacking into the wilderness is the only way to reach them.

The ancient shrine of the **Stone Lions** is a twelve-mile round trip on foot over wilderness trails. Also deep in the wooded country are the gorges of **Alamo Canyon, Painted Cave,** and the pueblo ruins of **San Miguel** and **Yapashi.**

An easier trip is the eleven-mile drive from the Visitors' Center to the large **Tsankawi** pueblo. This unexcavated ruin is atop a high mesa with stunning views of the surrounding countryside. From the highway (NM 4), it's a two-mile hike round trip to the ruin.

DIRECTIONS: Bandelier National Monument is 46 miles northwest of Santa Fe. It can be reached by taking U.S. 285 north and then heading west on NM 4, a paved road that leads past the Tsankawi section and then directly to the Visitors' Center at the monument.

ACCOMMODATIONS: There are accommodations and restaurants in the nearby towns of White Rock and Los Alamos and, of course, in Santa Fe. Overnight camping and backpacking are permitted. If you plan to backpack into the canyons, it's a good idea to telephone the rangers ahead of time to check weather and trail conditions.

Two campsites are available for vehicles: the Ponderosa Campground for groups and 93 developed sites for family units at the Juniper Campground. There are no trailer hookups, but there is a dump station. Campsites are $3 per night with a fourteen-day limit; reservations are not accepted.

HOURS (VISITORS' CENTER): September–May: 8:00 A.M.–7:00 P.M.
Rest of year: 8:00 A.M.–5:00 P.M.

ADMISSION: $1 per car or 50¢ per person.

Note: From Bandelier it is a short drive to **Jemez State Monument** or **Puyé Cliff Ruins.**

• *Jemez State Monument*
Jemez Springs, New Mexico 87025 *(505) 829-3520*

The ruins of a massive seventeenth-century Franciscan mission stand beside the fragile remains of a prehistoric pueblo called Guisewa. An interpretive trail winds through the beautiful, crumbling sandstone and adobe ruins. A visitors' center is on the site.

DIRECTIONS: From Los Alamos drive 39 miles west and south on NM 4. The monument is 1 mile east of Jemez Springs.
HOURS: Thursday–Monday: 9:00 A.M.–5:00 P.M.
Closed Tuesdays, Wednesdays, and holidays.
ADMISSION: Free.

Note: To reach Jemez Pueblo, continue south on NM 4. The descendants of the people of Guisewa live at Jemez. This is the pueblo where the seventeen survivors of Pecos took refuge and became part of the community (see listing under Santa Fe). Ceremonial dances are held each August 2 and November 12. The public is invited, but no photographs are permitted.

• *Puyé Cliff Ruins*
Santa Clara Indian Reservation
Box 580
Española, New Mexico 85732 *(505) 753-7326*

The sprawling mesa commands the breathtaking countryside, a vista unchanged in the thousand years since a village flourished here. To the east, the white-capped peaks of the Sangre de Cristo Mountains sparkle in the sun. The green hills of the Jemez Mountains to the west are softer, streaked by rain.

The road to the mesa top is steep, first sloping around the base, and then winding in a tight coil to the summit. The empty face of the cliff is pockmarked with small, regularly spaced holes that once supported roof beams for dwellings, most of which now lie crumbled along the base of the cliff. The holes and caves that backed the dwellings seem to continue for miles along the cliff's face. This now-deserted place was once a teeming and prosperous city, long before Columbus sought a sea route to the spices of India. On top of the mesa alone are the remnants of a village of more than two thousand rooms.

The ruins on the tabletop mesa are of the typical red-brown adobe. Here and there, houses of two and three stories still stand, and a roof of wood and adobe shields the circular interior of a restored kiva. Many of the cliff dwellings are intact, and it's possible to climb down into some, although the craggy boulders at the bottom of the cliff loom ominously some sixty feet below a sheer drop.

The regularly spaced holes along this sheer cliff face once supported beams for hundreds of prehistoric dwellings at Puyé. (Photo: Neil Felshman.)

Remnants of an eleventh-century city still stand on the flat mesa top above the cliff. (Photo: Neil Felshman.)

A rough trail down the cliff face leads to intact dwellings at Puyé. (Photo: Neil Felshman.)

Drought forced the original inhabitants from these dwellings some time in the eleventh century, but in the late 1600s, during the Pueblo Revolt, many of the Pueblo people came here for shelter. The descendants of the original inhabitants are the Santa Clara Indians, who live on their forty-seven-thousand-acre reservation, of which Puyé is a part. There is a small visitors' center with rest rooms.

Puyé is 32 miles from **Bandelier National Monument.** It is owned and run by the Santa Clara Indians.

DIRECTIONS: Puyé can be reached from Española. Drive southwest on SR 30 to the directional marker, then go 9 miles west on SR 5. Or from Los Alamos take NM 4, 30, and 5.

HOURS: Summer: 8:00 A.M.–6:30 P.M.
Rest of year: 8:00 A.M.–5:30 P.M.

ADMISSION: An entrance fee of $1 per person is charged at a gatehouse.

Note: On the last weekend in July annually, the Santa Clara Indians hold a ceremonial, with dances and other rites to commemorate their ancestors at the Puyé Cliff Dwellings. The public is welcome, and pictures may be taken.

There are a number of motels and restaurants in Española and Santa Fe is not too far.

Mountainair

• *Gran Quivira National Monument*
Mountainair, New Mexico 87036 *(505) 847-2770*

The ridge on Chupadero Mesa is a good place to see the surrounding country. The land sloping away from this high place is covered with deep grasses that whisper quietly in the wind. But it is the abandoned city on the crest of the ridge that captures and holds the voices. The pale gray stones, painstakingly fitted, in places still mortared together, record the passage of centuries. The outlines of rooms, one on top of the other, honeycomb the entire ridge. Time has taken its toll; nothing keeps out the sky on the meticulously made dwellings, where once civilization was centered.

We call it Gran Quivira. The people who first came here about twelve hundred years ago called it Cueloze. The area was a crossroads where early cultures met and mingled. The first were probably the Mogollon people. They built a small cluster of pit houses here around A.D. 800. They farmed along the ridge, gathered nuts and berries, and trapped small game. They made the brown and red pottery that is generally identified with the early cultures of southern New Mexico and Arizona.

Inside the walls of the Church of San Buenaventura at Gran Quivira National Monument. (Photo: Neil Felshman.)

Approximately two hundred years later, the influence of the Anasazi from the northeastern section of New Mexico and Arizona began to be felt in the village. By A.D. 1200 the culture was definitely Anasazi. Fine basket weaving and black and white pottery were prevalent. There were structural changes, too. Surface dwellings built from adobe and timber and community houses of limestone masonry replaced the pit houses. But the pit house construction was retained for religious observance in the kiva, which was at the center of a concentric circle of rooms.

Located at the edges of two separate cultures, the pueblo became a variation of the Mogollon and Anasazi cultures. Its location at a crossroads of travel created trade with peoples from both eastern and western coasts.

The pueblo expanded slowly and then, in the mid-sixteenth century, the culture changed once more. There was a spate of building and a new sort of pottery was made. In addition to the traditional methods of burying the dead, now there were also cremations.

No substantiated reason for these changes has been found, but the best guess is that a new and unrelated group of people moved into the village and were accepted by the people who were already in residence. From all appearances neither group dominated the other, but they lived peacefully in the same place. The merging of two cultures once again created a third culture, compatible with those that had gone before it.

By the end of the sixteenth century, the first contact with Europeans occurred. Searching for fabled riches in a land up north called Quivira, Don Juan de Oñate and his party came upon the large village. Since he had visited other villages of the Hamanas Indians on his journey, he called this one the Pueblo de las Hamanas. What Oñate saw was the largest settlement in the area. The people grew corn, squash, and beans; they hunted deer, quail, rabbit, and most important, bison. They raised turkeys and used the feathers for blankets and adornment. And they gathered seeds and whatever fruit grew in the dry climate.

Other Europeans came. The churchmen of Spain came and built settlements throughout the area. In the 1660s they built a large church and mission at the pueblo, and many of the walls still stand, the same gray color as the earlier buildings, but slightly sharper, a little less timeworn.

But there was little opportunity to worship in this edifice. The enormous village and the ridge itself was completely abandoned by both Indians and Spaniards in 1670, probably as the result of a prolonged drought. It has remained uninhabited to this day.

At the small Visitors' Center you can borrow or buy a trail guidebook. If the Visitors' Center is closed, the pamphlets are kept in a small box at the beginning of the trail. The trail is easy, and it takes about a half hour to walk through the ruins.

Gran Quivira is one of three sites within easy reach of each other near the town of Mountainair, New Mexico. Mountainair is a small town with two or three restaurants, one of which is usually open, and the same number of motels, which are neat and reasonably priced, but not elaborate.

DIRECTIONS: To reach Gran Quivira from Mountainair, head south on NM 14, a paved, well-cared-for, slightly undulating road that passes through small farms for 26 miles.
HOURS: 8:00 A.M.–5:00 P.M. daily.
Closed Christmas.
ADMISSION: Free

• *Quarai State Monument*
Mountainair, New Mexico 87036

From Mountainair the road winds back and forth through fields where a few goats and an occasional cow look up to idly mark your passage. Then, as the road abruptly makes a right turn of ninety degrees, across a field of tall grass, are the red-brown towers of Quarai. A pair of horses graze beside the ruin, lifting and tossing their heads as though aware of the picture they make against the majestic, crumbling mission.

C. F. Lummis said that Quarai was "an edifice in ruins . . . but so

Quarai's red sandstone walls rise more than thirty feet. (Photo: Neil Felshman.)

tall, so solemn, so dominant of that strange, lonely landscape. . . . On the Rhine it would be a superlative; in the wilderness of the Manzano it is a miracle."

Although Quarai is close to both Gran Quivira and Abó (see below), the area was not inhabited before the Spaniards came. Rather, it was probably first occupied around 1620 as the result of a resettlement of people in the surrounding area.

The pueblo, priest's dwelling, and large church, which was called La Purísima Concepcion de Cuarac, were all built of the local red sandstone. Many of the walls still stand, even those that soar thirty feet and more.

The church was the New Mexico seat of the Spanish Inquisition in the mid-1600s. Terrible tribute was extracted from the Pueblo people until the raids of the Apaches coupled with the drought and famine of the late 1660s finally forced them to seek new homes. By 1675 Quarai was deserted.

There is a visitors' center at the site. There is full interpretation on signs in both English and Spanish and access is over flat trails that are easily traversed. In a quiet grove of cottonwoods, a picnic area has been set aside; camping is permitted in nearby **Menzano State Park.**

DIRECTIONS: Quarai is a New Mexico State Monument, 8 miles north of Mountainair on SR 14.

HOURS: Thursday–Monday: A New Mexico ranger is present from 8:00 A.M. to 6:00 P.M. in summer and 9:00 A.M. to 5:00 P.M. at other times.
Closed Tuesdays, Wednesdays, and holidays.

• *Abó State Monument*
Mountainair, New Mexico 87036

Behind a chain link fence, the delicately balanced red sandstone walls of the ruined Abó look almost modern. On the rise above a gully where water freely crosses the road, what is left of the Mission Church of San Gregario de Abó is, like the land itself, as one with the surrounding small houses. On a bright spring morning, an old man suns himself on a front porch and watches the quietly grazing sheep.

More than three hundred years ago, this church was the most magnificent in the area, with an organ and choir and a parish of more than fifteen hundred souls.

The people of the pueblo of Abó had been here for more than four hundred years before the Spaniards came. These were the Tompiros, mountain-dwelling relatives of the Piro Indians who lived in pueblos along the Rio Grande in the Socorro region.

Only a short distance from the much larger pueblo of Gran Quivira, the people here were also affected by the long drought in the late 1660s.

The Mission Church of San Gregario de Abó, now a New Mexico State Monument. (Photo: Neil Felshman.)

Abó lay on the principal trade route between the Rio Grande and the Salt Lakes, and local salt lagoons were a source of wealth for the people of the pueblo. But when the mission was attacked and burned by Apaches in 1672, the village was abandoned by both the Spaniards and the Indians.

DIRECTIONS: Abó is a New Mexico State Landmark, easy to reach on a short, well-marked road off U.S. 60, 10 miles west of Mountainair. The site is fenced off and there is little space for parking.

Santa Fe

- *Pecos National Monument*
  Drawer 11
  Pecos, New Mexico 87552 *(505) 757-6414*

The earliest journals of the Spanish missionaries in the 1600s describe a "splendid temple of distinguished workmanship and beauty" rising up at Pecos. But no ancient temple was ever found here—until 1967. Archaeologists digging under the ruins of the massive eighteenth-century church that stands on the site discovered the foundations of another, older church that matched the description of a "magnificent temple adorned with six towers, three on each side." This earlier structure, now believed to be the largest church north of Mexico at that time, was destroyed in the rebellion of 1680.

Pecos was a large, thriving pueblo when the Spanish first arrived in

1540. Two thousand people lived here in more than 650 rooms. The pueblo was a trading center for Indians from the Great Plains, the Rio Grande Valley, and up and down the Pecos River.

The Spanish missionaries attempted to convert the people to Christianity. With the help of the Indians, they built the great church and encouraged the people to give up their kivas and religious practices. The Pecos people joined the other Pueblos in the revolt against the Spanish in 1680, burned the church, and banished the missionaries. Twelve years later the mission was reestablished.

The rapid decline of the pueblo followed. Comanche raiders and European diseases ravaged the Indian population. A final epidemic in 1788 nearly annihilated the people. Only seventeen Pecos Indians survived.

The people of Jemez to the west invited the survivors to take refuge with them, and the two groups have lived together at Jemez Pueblo ever since. Each year on August 2, descendants of the Pecos people observe the feast of Our Lady of the Angels, patron saint of extinct Pecos.

The ruins of the red adobe eighteenth-century church and two pueblos of Pecos can be seen on a self-guiding trail. One kiva has been restored, and visitors are permitted to enter. Unscheduled groups tours are usually available during the summer. A small visitors' center is at the entrance to the monument.

DIRECTIONS: From Santa Fe drive 25 miles southeast on I-25. Use the Glorieta exit, and follow the directional markers to the monument. Coming from the east, exit at Rowe and follow the markers.

HOURS: 9:00 A.M.–5:00 P.M. daily (till 4:00 P.M. in the winter).

ADMISSION: Free.

Pecos Wilderness Area: The village of Pecos is the gateway to the Pecos Wilderness Area. From the monument, State Highway 63 winds north 20 miles along the Pecos River until it ends at Cowles. From the campsites at the end of the road, all foot trails lead into the wilderness high country.

Silver City

- *Gila Cliff Dwellings National Monument*
  Route 11, Box 100
  Silver City, New Mexico 88061 *(505) 388-1986*

New Mexico's Route 15 begins just east of Silver City, and it ends at the Gila Cliff Dwellings. Along the way the road tortuously winds through the mountains of Gila National Forest and some of the most impressive greenery in the Southwest.

At the road's beginning, a sign warns: "Gila Cliff Dwellings—40 miles—2 hours." And it would be hard to average any more than twenty miles per hour over the twisting, steeply graded, blacktop Route 15. In contrast to the long straight drives through the arid landscape of much of the Southwest, the recently completed road to the Gila Cliff Dwellings climbs and drops quickly through forest lands so lush that the trip is made in almost full shade, and views are breathtaking from both low and high vantages. The road follows the path of the Gila River through the mountains and approximates the route traveled by the ancient people to their homes in these woods.

The oldest ruin found here is a pit house that was constructed sometime between A.D. 100 and 400. The circular shelter was built below ground level, with an entrance two feet wide and ten feet long. This sort of dwelling was prevalent in the area until about A.D. 1000, when the people began to build above-ground square houses of masonry, adobe, and woven twigs. At the same time, dwellings within the caves in the surrounding cliffs were constructed, usually, of stone and timber.

The people who lived here are called the Mogollon, a name that archaeologists derived from Don Juan Ignacio Flores Mogollon, governor of New Mexico from 1712 to 1715. The earliest of the Mogollon people hunted, gathered wild plants, and cultivated corn and beans. They crafted nets, baskets, and plain brown pottery.

Later residents of this area farmed on the mesa tops and along the river. They planted corn and beans and also raised squash and tobacco. They were a small, wiry people who, in addition to farming, lived from their hunting and gathering wild berries and nuts. They were skilled weavers and potters. The pottery from later periods is distinctive: well-shaped vessels and bowls, some black-on-white, others brown on the outside with black interiors. People here traded for cotton, projectile points, and ornamental shells.

The cliff dwellings of the Mogollon were built in the 1200s. There are seven natural caves high in the cliff facing southeast above the west fork of the Gila River. Forty rooms were built in five of these caves. The walls are made of flat stones bound with mud carried up from the river bottom. The Indians felled ponderosa and other pines of the region and shaped the timber into beams for the roofs and ladders to enter the houses.

These people ground their corn and baked a bread like the tortilla. The ceilings of the caves are black from the smoke of their ancient cooking fires.

Sometime before 1400 the Mogollon left this area. No one is sure why, but it seems that a slight shift in the climate made their methods of dry farming difficult, and so they sought more promising farmland.

In 1884 the ruins were first discovered by the prominent archaeologist

The Gila Cliff Dwellings near Silver City, New Mexico, are built into natural caves above the Gila River. (Photo: JW.)

Well-matched stones were fitted with mortar made from river mud. (Photo: JW.)

A storage bin built into a cave at Gila Cliff Dwellings. (Photo: JW.)

Adolf Bandelier, who was led to the site by stories told by frontiersmen. According to Bandelier the ruins were in much better condition in 1884 than they are now. The roofs were still intact but were subsequently destroyed by vandals in the early 1900s.

All of the caves have been excavated by archaeologists, and seven burial sites were recorded and removed from the area, which now has been stabilized and prepared for visitors.

From the parking area, you cross the Gila River by a footbridge, then follow a tree-shaded path winding around and over a stream to the dwellings themselves. The path is well marked but quite steep in places. In the surrounding country and on the path itself, it is easy to go back in time. The stream gurgles underfoot, birds call to each other in the trees, and there is no other sound.

HOURS: The main cliff-dwelling area is well tended and marked. There are rangers on duty at the site from 8:00 A.M. to 6:00 P.M. in the summer and from 9:00 A.M. to 4:00 P.M. the rest of the year.

Wilderness Area: A trip through the dwellings takes about an hour, but there are other ruins dotted throughout the area not so accessible. There are many beautiful sites for camping, a horse trail, and the "Trail to the Past." Hiking, horseback riding, and camping are permitted and encouraged in the Gila National Forest, the oldest and most isolated designated wilderness area in the United States. Detailed maps for backpacking are available in the Visitors' Center.

Along Route 15 to the cliff dwellings is the **Gila Hotsprings Vacation Center.** From this center you can arrange for various kinds of trips into the wilderness, including outfitting and guide services. Guides are adept at pointing out small ruins hidden in the cliff sides. For information about packing into the Wilderness Area, write or call:

Becky Campbell
Gila Hotsprings
Route 11
Silver City, New Mexico 88061 (505) 534-9951

Most people enter the Wilderness Area in midsummer, on holiday weekends, and during the fall hunting season. Make your arrangements with the Campbells well in advance.

Silver City: Silver City is 75 miles from I-25 on U.S. 90 over the Black Mountains. Much of this is twisting mountain road. Allow at least two hours to reach Silver City from the Interstate. There are camping sites at **Iron Creek** in Gila National Forest about 35 miles after you make the turn off I-25. Silver City, once a boom town, is a copper and cattle center for the southwestern region of New Mexico.

Several modern motels are in town. Just outside of town, the **Bear Mountain Guest Ranch,** a 1920s lodge with the feeling of an English country home, offers good food, large and airy old-fashioned rooms, and interesting company in a nostalgic setting among piñons and junipers. Myra McCormick, an enthusiastic amateur botanist and ornithologist, takes her guests on tours of the cliff dwellings and nearby ghost towns and accompanies them on nature hikes. Birds find Myra's ranch a civilized place to congregate, and you will see a fine array of feathered visitors every morning through the wall-to-wall windows of the enclosed breakfast porch. For information:

Bear Mountain Guest Ranch
P.O. Box 1163
Silver City, New Mexico 88061 (505) 538-2538

Kwilleylekia Ruins: Kwilleylekia is a large site where the Salado people built blockhouses in the Gila River Valley. The site is on private property and is usually open to the public during summer excavations. However, there is no regular schedule of hours. If you are in Silver City with time to spare, drive 30 miles northwest on U.S. 180 to Cliff. Then go 9/10 of a mile on NM 211; bear left on NM 293, 1.9 miles to entrance. The day I was there the gate was closed; a letter and telephone call elicited no response from the owner. But Kwilleylekia looked fascinating, and I would try again if I were in the area.

Taos (Penasco)

- *Picuris Pueblo*
P.O. Box 228
Penasco, New Mexico 87553 *(505) 587-2519*

Located in the mountains south of Taos, Picuris was established between A.D. 1250 and 1300 by Indians who moved from a larger pueblo now known as Pot Creek ruin.

The Pueblo Indians living at Picuris are friendly and will provide a guide to excavated parts of the pueblo. A community building houses a museum and training center for artisans; arts and crafts are for sale. August 10 is the feast day of San Lorenzo, celebrated with festivities that include a corn dance. Photographs are permitted.

DIRECTIONS: From Taos take NM 68 west and branch south on NM 3. From Española take NM 76 north, and NM 75 east.
HOURS (MUSEUM): 9:30 A.M.–4:00 P.M. daily.
HOURS (PUEBLO): 8:00 A.M.–5:00 P.M.
Closed major holidays.
ADMISSION: A small fee is requested to enter the pueblo.

MUSEUMS

Albuquerque

- *Indian Pueblo Cultural Center*
Menaul Boulevard and 12th Street NW
Albuquerque, New Mexico 87100 *(505) 843-7270*

Contemporary Indian art and exhibits on early life in the Southwest are shown in this museum, which is owned and operated by the Indians of New Mexico's nineteen pueblos. There is a craft shop, and a restaurant serves pueblo foods. Indian dances performed on summer weekends.

DIRECTIONS: From I-40, exit off 12th Street and go north two blocks.
HOURS: 9:00 A.M.–5:00 P.M. daily.
Sunday: 10:00 A.M.–5:00 P.M.
ADMISSION: Contributions accepted.

• *Maxwell Museum of Anthropology*
Roma and University NE
Albuquerque, New Mexico 87131 *(505) 277-4404*

Archaeology in the Southwest is the emphasis at the Maxwell. Extensive permanent exhibits drawn from university collections focus on human life in the Southwest. Fine examples of prehistoric pottery and baskets are displayed. The museum also has stunning collections of minerals and fluorescent stones. There are also guided tours and special programs for children, adults, and students. The museum has a garden and a reading room.

HOURS: Monday–Friday: 9:00 A.M.–4:00 P.M.
Saturday: 10:00 A.M.–4:00 P.M.
Sunday: 1:00 P.M.–5:00 P.M.
ADMISSION: Free.

Cimarron

• *Ernest Thompson Seton Memorial Library and Museum*
Philmont Scout Range and Explorers Base
Cimarron, New Mexico 87114 *(505) 376-2281*

Thousands of Indian artifacts, western drawings and paintings, and a large research library are housed in this **national camping center** for Boy Scouts and Explorers.

The **Kit Carson home and museum** (1849) and old mine cabins are preserved.

DIRECTIONS: Drive 4 miles south of Cimarron on NM 21.
HOURS: June–August
8:00 A.M.–5:00 P.M. daily.
September–May: Library only
Monday–Friday: 8:00 A.M.–5:00 P.M.
The museum is closed during the winter except by appointment.
ADMISSION: Free.

Gallup

• *Gallup Museum of Indian Arts*
Convention Center Area
Red Rock State Park
Gallup, New Mexico 87311 *(505) 722-6196*

This new museum is serious in scope; exhibits of prehistoric material trace chronologically the development of native Americans from early Paleo hunters to modern times. Classes in archaeology, conducted by museum director Dr. Caroline Davis, are open to the public.

DIRECTIONS: From Gallup, 4 miles east on I-40 to turnoff sign.
HOURS: Monday–Friday: 8:00 A.M.–5:00 P.M.
ADMISSION: Free.

Las Cruces

- *New Mexico State University Museum*
University Avenue
Las Cruces, New Mexico 88003 *(505) 646-3739*

There is a history museum on campus with exhibits related to anthropology, archaeology, history, and science. Other exhibits explore the colorful history of Las Cruces. Local collections of prehistoric Indian material and some Mogollon pottery and stone tools dating from A.D. 800 are displayed.

HOURS: 1:00 P.M.–5:00 P.M. daily.
Closed major holidays.
ADMISSION: Free.

Portales

- *Blackwater Draw Museum*
Portales, New Mexico 88130 *(505) 562-2303*

Blackwater Draw is the first site where the fluted Clovis point was found together with the bones of extinct animals. This strip of land between Portales and Clovis, New Mexico, is an ancient lake bed. Since 1932 archaeologists digging at various sites in the area have uncovered primary evidence of the early inhabitants of North America. Stone and bone knives and scrapers, classic Folsom points, and the grooved Clovis points have been found with the bones of extinct bison and mammoths.

Digs continue at Blackwater Site, but none is open to the public. The museum, however, offers a unique opportunity to study the early peoples of America. Exhibits and graphic displays are devoted to human life in America from the initial entry across the Bering Strait to the end of the Archaic period. The museum is affiliated with Eastern New Mexico University; it stands in the middle of the desert, midway between Clovis and Portales. It is a fascinating and informative place to visit.

DIRECTIONS: Take U.S. 70 south from Portales (or north from Clovis); the museum is just off the highway.
HOURS: Fall and spring semesters: Monday–Friday: 10:00 A.M.–5:00 P.M.
Saturday: 9:00 A.M.–12 M.; summer schedule varies.
ADMISSION: Free.

• *Miles Museum*
Eastern New Mexico University
Portales, New Mexico 88130 *(505) 562-2202*

The Miles Museum is part of a large museum complex on the campus of Eastern New Mexico University. Displays illuminate archaeological discoveries from the Southwest. Artifacts, pottery, and bones are exhibited.

HOURS: Monday–Friday: 8:00 A.M.–12 M.; 1:00 P.M.–5:00 P.M.
Saturday: 9:00 A.M.–12 M.; 1:00 P.M.–4:00 P.M.
Sunday: 1:00 P.M.–4:00 P.M.
ADMISSION: Free.

• *Paleo Indian Institute and Museum*
Eastern New Mexico University
Portales, New Mexico 88130 *(505) 562-2303*

Dr. George A. Agodino, director of the Miles Museum and the Blackwater Draw Museum, has unusual exhibits and photographs of Early Man sites throughout the Western Hemisphere, including graphic displays showing how archaeologists discovered and excavated the sites.

HOURS: Same as these for Miles Museum (see above).
ADMISSION: Free.

Santa Fe

• *Palace of the Governors*
P.O. Box 2087
Sante Fe, New Mexico 87503 *(505) 827-2934*

The Palace of the Governors, America's oldest public building (1610), has become a classic museum of the Southwest. Extensive archaeological and historical collections of the Spanish, Mexican, and territorial periods are shown throughout the long, low-roofed adobe building. Across the inner patio, the Hall of the Modern Indian exhibits describe Indian life in the pueblos.

You can easily spend all day walking through the fascinating historical rooms of this museum. The Museum Shop has fine pottery, jewelry, and an outstanding collection of books on history, archaeology, and western art. On the plaza in front of the palace, Indians sell arts and crafts.

DIRECTIONS: The building is on the north side of the plaza on Palace Avenue.
HOURS: 9:00 A.M.–5:00 P.M. daily.
Closed Mondays (October 15–June 15).
Closed Christmas and New Year's.
ADMISSION: Free.

- *Laboratory of Anthropology*
  Camino Lejo
  P.O. Box 2087
  Sante Fe, New Mexico 87503 *(505) 827-3241*

The Laboratory of Anthropology is a research and study center for anthropologists of the Southwest. Volunteers are welcome to apply for staff work. Amateurs who live in the area or can remain for several months at a time can sometimes join excavations sponsored by the laboratory.

Changing exhibits include large and varied collections of Indian pottery and silverwork. The comprehensive reference library is open to the public on weekday mornings; private collections are available for study by appointment.

DIRECTIONS: Follow Camino del Monte Sol south to Camino Lejo.
HOURS: Monday–Friday: 8:00 A.M.–5:00 P.M.
ADMISSION: Free.

Taos

- *Kit Carson Museum*
  Old Kit Carson Road
  Taos, New Mexico 87571 *(505) 758-4741*

The Kit Carson Memorial Foundation preserves and restores both prehistoric and historic sites. The Anasazi, the Spanish, and the early fur traders all lived at Taos. The Kit Carson home has been restored and is open to the public. Many relics of the Spanish colonial period and the early territorial fur trade are on display.

An Indian Culture program is dedicated to locating and surveying archaeological sites in the Taos area. A new Indian museum to be built near one prehistoric pueblo will portray Indian life and culture from 3000 B.C., the oldest recorded date of human habitation of the area.

The new building will house an archaeology laboratory. Depending on the season and the number of projects under way, the foundation sometimes accepts applications for amateur assistance. Write for information.

DIRECTIONS: Exit Kit Carson Road on U.S. 64, half a block east of the plaza.
HOURS: Summer: 7:30 A.M.–7:30 P.M.
Winter: 8:00 A.M.–5:00 P.M.
Closed Thanksgiving, Christmas, New Year's.
ADMISSION: Fees vary at each site.

STATE OFFICE

Stewart L. Peckham
State Archaeologist
Museum of New Mexico
Box 2087
Sante Fe, New Mexico 87503 (505) 827-2934

ORGANIZATIONS TO JOIN

The **Gallup Archaeological Society,** among the oldest amateur groups in the country, and the **Plateau Sciences Society** both offer field schools. For information, write or call: Dr. Caroline Davis, Director, Gallup Museum of Indian Arts, Box 328, Church Rock, New Mexico 87311; (505) 722-6196.

The **Archaeological Society of New Mexico** sponsors a Rock Art Field School, summer excavations, and workshops in field and laboratory techniques. New Mexico has a certification program for amateurs that is offered to members of all archaeological societies in the state. The **Albuquerque Archaeological Society** is another active society involved in digs; the society distributes several high-quality publications about its work.

For information, write the office of the state archaeologist (above) or: Archaeological Society of New Mexico, P.O. Box 3485, Albuquerque, New Mexico 87110.

THE FOUR CORNERS REGION

It is the only place in the United States where four states have a common boundary: Arizona, Colorado, New Mexico, and Utah join together in a desert region of soaring bluffs and deep canyons. But long before there were any state boundaries—or any states—sometime before the birth of Christ, a cultured people inhabited this area and a great society grew up here.

The people are called the Anasazi, and their way of life is called the Pueblo culture. No one yet knows when the first Anasazi came here, but by A.D. 1 they had already developed a stable society.

Archaeologists have divided the Anasazi culture into several different stages. The earliest-known group probably learned farming from people farther south, from Mexico or Central America. While hunting and trapping as well as gathering food were an important part of survival, the Anasazi also established a way of life based on farming.

They lived in caves or other natural shelters and stored their corn and squash in stone-lined bins built into the caves. They used spears and spear throwers called atlatls for hunting and defense. They also used various plants, particularly the yucca, to weave fine baskets and garments. The people of this time are called the Basketmakers, and this period is therefore named the Basketmaker Period.

Almost five hundred years later, the Anasazi acquired the art of making pottery and moved out of the caves into pit houses, which were partially underground and roofed with wooden frames covered with mud. The pit houses were entered through a hole in the roof, which also served as a chimney. Initially during this period, individual families lived apart from each other and the pit houses were lone outposts of civilization. But within a few decades, small villages of pit houses dotted the region. Farming became more firmly entrenched, and hunting with spears and clubs gave way to the bow and arrow. This is called the Modified Basketmaker Period.

By the year A.D. 700, the Anasazi began to build houses completely above ground—the Pueblo Period had begun. The word "pueblo" refers here to the building stages of the Anasazi culture. In the Developmental Pueblo Period, the houses had only three or four rooms, which were built alongside the pit houses. But soon the Anasazi began to build aboveground structures with many large rooms. These larger structures were usually built in a semicircle with a partially enclosed courtyard. The people used adobe as their main building material, with sticks and some stone as support.

Within the next hundred years, the pueblos were built almost entirely of stone. The pit houses were no longer places to live but had become temples of worship, or kivas, and the Anasazi during this time became a highly religious and organized people. They grew cotton and wove fine textiles, and made their most distinctive pottery.

Shortly after A.D. 1100 the Pueblo culture in the Four Corners came into its golden age, called the Great or Classic Pueblo Period. The population increased dramatically, and the great multistoried houses at Mesa Verde, Aztec, Chaco Canyon, and Kayenta were built. These houses, built entirely of stone, were often more than four stories high and had hundreds of rooms. The arts and crafts of the Pueblo people were also refined at this time and were the most sophisticated that the people had yet produced.

This great flowering of the Anasazi culture lasted less than two hundred years. The end of the thirteenth century was marked by twenty years of continual drought. As the water disappeared, the culture went into a decline. By A.D. 1300 the Anasazi had all but deserted the magnificent buildings and the area where they had made their homes for more than a thousand years.

Most of the ruined Anasazi villages are on Navajo land, the largest Indian reservation in America. Yet the Navajo are not descendants of the Anasazi. They are comparative newcomers into this territory that is so closely identified with them. The Navajo originally came from the north and may be related to the Alaskan Indian tribes. Along with the Apache, they are supposed to have entered the Southwest some time between A.D. 1200 and 1400.

The Navajo people today have a somewhat inscrutable attitude toward the people they have named Anasazi—"the ancient ones." It's difficult to know whether their silence is due to a natural reticence toward Anglos, a reverence for the Anasazi, or perhaps indifference toward a people to whom they are not related. Whatever the reason, the Anasazi ruins are seldom discussed, although many Navajo act as guides to the more remote sites.

To trace the great prehistoric archaeological sites in the region of the Four Corners, we will begin in the northwest corner of New Mexico, follow in a circle into southern Colorado, turn across to southeastern Utah, and finish in northern Arizona. This big circle ends almost at its starting point.

NORTHWEST NEW MEXICO

Bloomfield and Vicinity

• *Chaco Canyon National Monument*
Star Route 4
Box 6500
Bloomfield, New Mexico 87413 *(505) 786-5384*

Two mesas, sheer cliffs at times, mark boundaries about half a mile apart in a narrow canyon stretching back twelve miles, formed by some long-forgotten tide. Wandering desert people first came to Chaco more than five thousand years ago. As Europe entered the Christian era, a few families settled here and began to farm the land. They thrived in this sparse desert for over twelve hundred years.

In Chaco Canyon the story of a civilization's rise and fall is recorded in the great number and variety of places where the American Indians lived and developed their way of life, their religion, their architecture, and their art. There are more than four hundred ruins in the canyon, ranging from

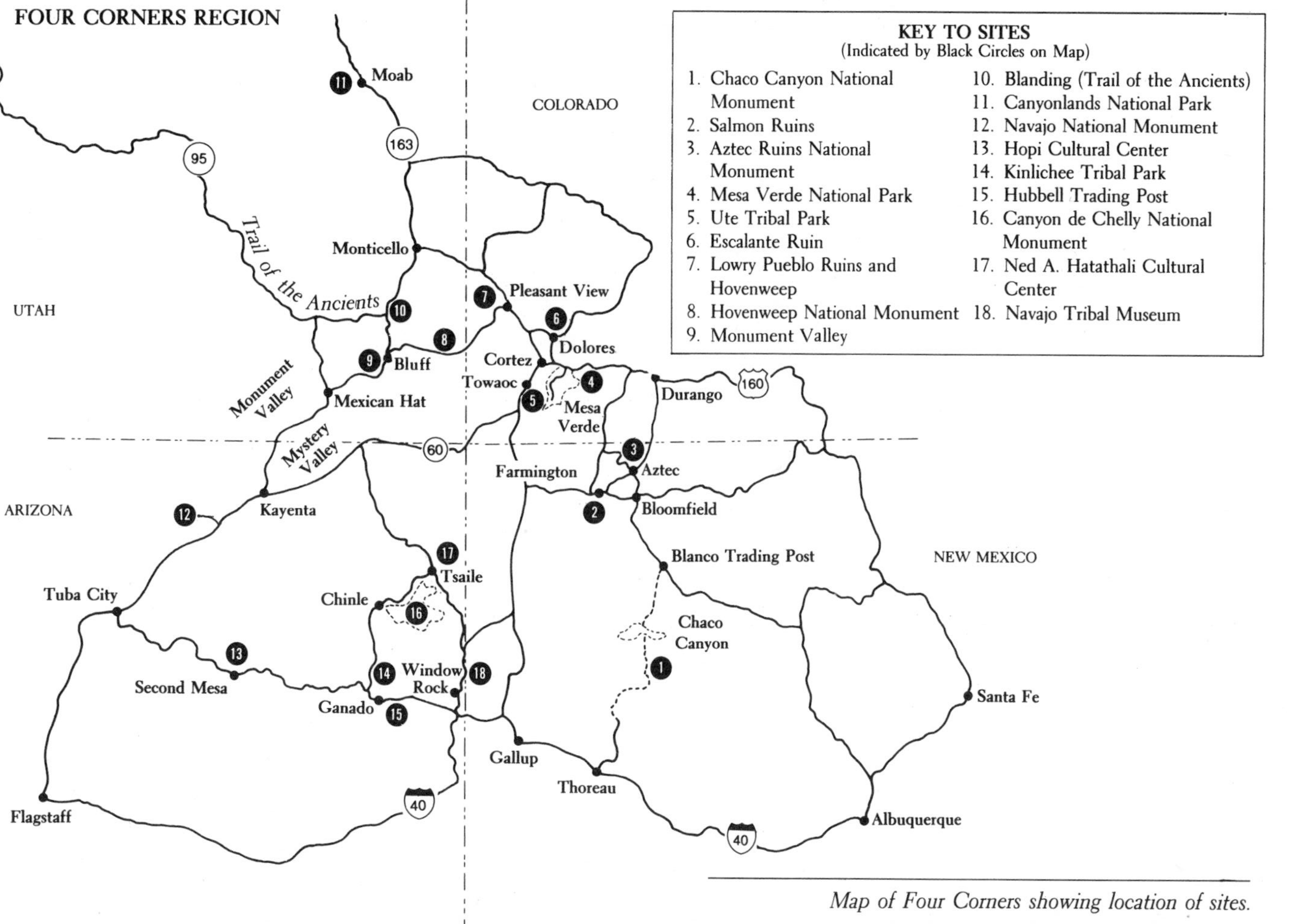

Map of Four Corners showing location of sites.

early single-room structures to the Pueblo Bonito, a town that contained buildings five stories high with eight hundred rooms, thirty-two ceremonial chambers, and large plazas that sprawled over a three-acre tract. Twelve thousand people lived and worked at Pueblo Bonito. At the peak of the civilization, more than seven thousand people inhabited the canyon in many urbanized villages built with incredible care and skill.

The history of the Anasazi in Chaco Canyon follows the same pattern as that of the other ancient peoples throughout the Four Corners area. But in size, Chaco was the largest settlement. The pottery found here differs from the type made farther north in Mesa Verde. Both types are decorated in intense black and white designs. But while the Mesa Verde people painted thick bold lines on their vessels, the Chaco artisans etched fine, geometric motifs. Their architecture, too, differs. The masonry in Chaco Canyon was the finest in the Anasazi world. At the height of the Great Pueblo building period, intricate designs were wrought in the placement of stones and chinking. The Chacoans were masters of the art of building. They were also a deeply religious people. Even the smallest village had its ceremonial kiva. The most impressive Great Kiva in Chaco Canyon is called **Casa Rinconada,** which is sixty-four feet in diameter.

The builders of Chaco also constructed an elaborate network of roads that connected villages within the canyon; other roads lead out of the Chaco area. No one knows the purpose of these roads. There were no horses or beasts of burden in prehistoric America, perhaps one reason why the people never developed the wheel. The roads may have been used for ceremonial processions or to deliver trade goods to other settlements.

The Chacoans participated in an extensive trade network that extended deep into Mexico. Jet and turquoise came from their near neighbors, raw cotton from southern Arizona. From Mexico came parrots, shells, and tiny copper bells, the only metal objects known to the people of Chaco.

Some scientists have suggested that the broad prehistoric highways lacing this area may have been canals. Certainly the control of water and rainfall was a major part of the success of Chacoan farmers. They developed a complex damming system to trap rain and later release it into their fields. This method of flood farming may have played a part in depleting the soil, because, after twelve centuries, the people began to leave Chaco Canyon.

Apparently no single reason caused their exodus, which preceded the extinction of other Anasazi centers by almost one hundred years. Completely stripped of timber for fuel and building material, the landscape had begun to erode. A shift in climate seems to have brought little steady rainfall, but harsh sudden storms washed away topsoil and cut deep arroyos across the farmland. The soil, continuously farmed for centuries, became anemic. There is no direct evidence of drought in Chaco Canyon, but dry spells of two or three years' duration were common in this region. Such a period

Casa Rinconada, the Great Kiva of Chaco Canyon National Monument. (Photo courtesy of the National Park Service.)

would create devastation in a society already crippled by other environmental crises.

Another interesting theory has been suggested. The demise of civilization at Chaco Canyon coincided with the Toltec decline in Mexico. Were the ties between Chaco and Mesoamerica stronger than suspected? A link to the Toltec civilization would explain why the Chacoans developed different art forms than other groups of Anasazi. Was Chaco, in fact, a Toltec colony? Great portions of Chaco still remain unexcavated, but perhaps advanced technology and future archaeological work will answer some of these puzzling questions.

The Chacoans did not leave the canyon all at once. Like other Anasazi later driven from their lands by severe drought, the Chaco people drifted farther south, shifting, moving, without permanency or homes. But the Anasazi were resourceful people. Their vitality and peace-loving nature had always made them good neighbors. These characteristics ensured their future in new territories. Within a few centuries they settled in new areas and began to reestablish their culture. Wherever they went, the Anasazi influenced and joined with other groups. They emerged into history as the Pueblo Indians, although no one knows exactly which modern Indian tribes are their descendants.

When Chaco Canyon was first discovered by white men during a military reconnaissance in 1849, the ruined villages were almost buried in sand. Seven subsequent expeditions by the National Geographic Society cleared away some one hundred thousand tons of dirt from the ruins so they could be more easily admired. Chaco was made a national monument in 1907.

A visit to Chaco Canyon usually takes at least a full day. This is because of both the wealth of things to see and experience and the difficulty in reaching the site. There are hundreds of small ruins in the canyon. Interpreted trails take you through the largest at Pueblo Bonito, Chetro Ketl, and the Casa Rinconada. Each of these trails can be walked through in about an hour.

DIRECTIONS: To reach Chaco from the north, turn off SR 44 to Blanco Trading Post and follow unpaved Route 57 for 23 miles to the Visitors' Center. From the south turn north on Route 57 from I-40 (at Thoreau) over 44 miles of paved road. At the marker turn onto the dirt road for another 20 miles to the monument.

NM 57, the only road to the monument from either direction, is a rough dirt road that is usually passable for cars but may be impassable when it rains.

There is a thirty-six-site campground near the Visitors' Center, and a fee of $2 per night is charged from April 15 to October 15. But there are *no commercial services* of any kind at the monument—neither meals nor groceries and gas. The nearest services are at Nageezi or Blanco Trading Post, 40 and 30 miles from the monument, respectively. There is a picnic shelter at the monument just off the graded road between Casa Rinconada and Chetro Ketl.

When you leave Chaco, you can take SR 57 north to Blanco Trading Post, the continue north on Route 44 to Bloomfield, where the Salmon and Aztec ruins are located (see below).

• *Salmon Ruins*
Route 3, Box 169
Farmington, New Mexico 87401 *(505) 632-2013*

The sense of archaeology at work pervades Salmon Ruins. You walk down a steep, paved, winding path from the sleek new **Archaeological Research Center,** past the small wooden house of George Salmon, who homesteaded these acres in the early 1900s and for whom the ruins are named, across a field littered with digging equipment to a grassy slope where beautifully constructed masonry walls are now being uncovered.

Salmon Ruins under excavation. (Photo courtesy of the Archaeological Research Center, Salmon Ruins.)

Aerial view of Salmon Ruins. (Photo courtesy of the Archaeological Research Center, Salmon Ruins.)

Pottery recovered from Salmon Ruins in northwest corner of New Mexico. (Photo courtesy of the Archaeological Research Center, Salmon Ruins.)

Building began here in A.D. 1088 and was completed by 1095. The architects were the Anasazi from Chaco Canyon, who carried the sandstone from thirty miles away to construct this pueblo. It was built in the shape of a square C, 430 feet long at the back, 150 feet at the sides, and two stories high. The pueblo was a structure of more than 250 rooms with a Great Kiva in a central plaza and an unusual elevated, or "tower," kiva as well. Excavation is going on now, and many walls are shored up with wood buttressing for stability.

Most of the excavation takes place during the summer and guided tours that let you observe the archaeologists in action can be arranged at the research center. There is camping nearby, and restaurants and overnight accommodations are available in the surrounding towns of Farmington, Aztec, and Bloomfield.

DIRECTIONS: From Farmington drive 11 miles east on U.S. 64 to the site. From Bloomfield drive 2 miles west on U.S. 64. The site is only a few miles north of Aztec Ruins National Monument.

HOURS: 9:00 A.M.–5:00 P.M. daily.

ADMISSION: Adults 50¢, children 25¢.

• *Aztec Ruins National Monument*
P.O. Box 4
Aztec, New Mexico 87410 *(505) 334-6174*

Pioneers settling in New Mexico's Animas Valley during the 1870s came upon this meticulously built abandoned city. Tales of the great golden civilization of earlier centuries in Mexico came into their heads, and they called the ruins and the nearby town Aztec. But the architects of this great achievement in the desert were not exotic wanderers from other climes—they were, of course, the Anasazi.

Aztec lies between two major Anasazi settlements, Mesa Verde and Chaco Canyon, and the cultural influence of both these settlements is seen in the architecture and art of Aztec. While pottery and basketmaking at Aztec show the hand of both Mesa Verde and Chaco people, the architecture of the pueblo is strongly characteristic of Chaco Canyon.

The entire city appears to have been planned and laid out before building began. Sandstone blocks were expertly laid and fitted in an E-shape surrounding a plaza. The exterior walls of the city are as high as three stories in places, 360 feet long on the north and south, and about 275 feet on the east and west. In the twelfth and thirteenth centuries, 450 people probably inhabited the city's 500 rooms.

The Great Kiva at Aztec Ruins National Monument, New Mexico. (Photo: JW.)

Interior of the Great Kiva, Aztec Ruins National Monument. (Photo: Superintendent, Aztec Ruins National Monument.)

A large round building dominates the plaza. This is the Great Kiva, which was the center of the community's religious life. This kiva was reconstructed in 1934. To enter its dark coolness in the day's heat is to get a taste of the peace and refuge that the Anasazi experienced in religious life.

The large kiva combines architectural features of both the Chaco Canyon and Mesa Verde kivas. The fire pit and ventilator are similar to the Chaco style, while roof supports fashioned of stone columns are typical of Mesa Verde.

Aztec National Monument is in the town of Aztec, and the actual ruin is right on the road. There is camping nearby; restaurants and overnight lodging are available in town.

Just outside the monument are trading posts which sell film and various souvenirs of the area. Access to the monument is on level paths, some paved. Wheelchair access is possible.

DIRECTIONS: From Farmington drive 14 miles north on U.S. 550 to the directional marker in Aztec, then ½ mile west on Ruins Road to the monument's entrance. From Bloomfield drive 7 miles north on NM 44 to Aztec.

HOURS: Summer: 7:00 A.M.–7:00 P.M. daily.
Winter: 8:00 A.M.–5:00 P.M.

ADMISSION: $1 per car or 50¢ for each adult arriving by bus or on foot; children under sixteen and senior citizens free.

SOUTHERN COLORADO

Cortez and Vicinity

• *Mesa Verde National Park* *(303) 529-4543*
Colorado 81330 *529-4461*

Mesa Verde was one of the three great centers of the Anasazi culture. From A.D. 700 until A.D. 1200, the people lived and farmed on the tops of the mesas. Then, beginning in the thirteenth century, they began to build houses several stories high in the natural caves in the sides of the cliffs. No one is sure why the Anasazi moved from the open mesa tops into the caves. The caves may have provided better shelter or defense, or they may have been a source of water. Probably eight thousand people lived within the canyons of the two main mesas of Mesa Verde.

The Anasazi had disappeared from the region before the Spanish came, and the cliff dwellings remained hidden until they were discovered by a surveying team in the 1870s. The largest dwelling, the two-hundred-room **Cliff Palace,** wasn't discovered until Richard Wetherill and Charles Mason accidentally came across it in 1888.

The 520,000-acre national park was set aside in 1906 and carefully developed for visitors; it is a masterpiece of the National Park Service. The interpretation at Mesa Verde surpasses that of any other archaeological site in the country. The famous park attracts visitors from all over the world, and it is almost unbearably crowded in midsummer.

From the park entrance on U.S. 160, it takes an hour to drive up the steep twisting road to the Visitors' Center. In the summer cars and campers chug bumper to bumper up the mountainside. Yet summer is still the best time to visit Mesa Verde, because it is only then that all the facilities are open and the park is fully staffed. Recent winters have taken a terrible toll on the roads, and sometimes the park is closed because of mud slides. It is always a good idea—no matter what the time of year—to call ahead and check if the roads are open. Last year the roads to Mesa Verde were still closed in the middle of June.

It takes at least two days to see Mesa Verde. The two main mesas, Wetherill and Chapin, jut out across the plateau in opposite directions, and it is difficult to reach both in a single day.

As you start up the mountain from the entrance, **Morfield Campground** is the first stop and no trailers are permitted beyond that point.

Far View Visitor Center, the gateway to **Wetherill Mesa,** is next. You cannot drive onto Wetherill Mesa; a bus trip out to the mesa begins at the Visitor Center and covers twelve miles. It takes about four hours to see the ruins. The tours are not actually guided, but park rangers are on duty to answer questions.

An excellent lodge and restaurant are located at Far View; and a cafeteria serves meals throughout the day. People staying in the Morfield Campground usually come up to the cafeteria to eat dinner.

Chapin Mesa. To reach the other side of the park, continue past Far View on the road to Chapin Mesa, headquarters for the park. The museum here contains the best archaeological collections recovered from Mesa Verde, and also offers many intriguing books on archaeology for sale. Dioramas and exhibits explain the life style of the people who lived here centuries ago.

• From Chapin Mesa, two short hiking trails lead into **Spruce Tree Canyon.** Visitors must register at the ranger's office before using either of these trails. Spruce Tree is the only ruin open in the winter, weather permitting. It is in the canyon behind the museum, and has 114 rooms and eight ceremonial kivas.

By car, two six-mile loops take you out to vantage points on the canyon rim. Vantage points on the road overlook several different ruins.

Balcony House, out on the end of the mesa, is a small, extremely fragile ruin that can be entered only with a ranger. It is the only ruin in the park not visible from a roadside or overlook. Trips to Balcony House leave from the parking area at **Chapin Mesa Museum.** If you arrive at the museum by 8:00 A.M., you have a chance to get on the early morning tour, which is usually not crowded (and not always announced). The trip to Balcony House takes about an hour.

All the other ruins on the mesa can be seen from overlooks on the canyon rim. The enormous and spectacular Cliff Palace, set into the face of a three-hundred-foot cave, is twenty minutes away from the museum.

If your time is limited to one day, the simplest way to see Mesa Verde is first to stop at the Far View Visitor Center. Then continue on to Chapin Mesa and explore the museum. From Chapin you can drive the two six-mile loop roads that take you out onto the rims of the canyon. When you return down the mountainside to Far View, you can take the four-hour bus tour out to Wetherill if you have time.

If you have more time, you can take advantage of the many other opportunities to visit archaeological sites in the park. All summer long rangers conduct guided tours through several of the cliff dwellings. Check at the Chapin Museum or Far View Visitor Center for the current schedule.

Camping: Campsites at the Morfield Campground cannot be reserved. Single and group campsites are available for tents and trailers. There are tables, benches, wood or charcoal grills, but no utility hookups. The campground is open from May 1 through October 31; when closed, camping or overnight parking is not permitted anywhere in the park. Groceries, a gasoline station, showers, and laundry facilities are available.

Lodging: Good accommodations are available at Far View Motor Lodge within the park. Outside the park, Cortez is the nearest town to offer motels and restaurants.

For information about lodging at Far View, call or write:

Mesa Verde Company
P.O. Box 277
Mancos, Colorado 81328

Out of state: (800) 525-5421
Colorado: (800) 332-5759

Hiking: There are several hiking trails in the park. Bicycling is encouraged on the paved roads (except to Wetherill). You can rent bicycles at park headquarters on Chapin Mesa.

DIRECTIONS: It's possible to visit Mesa Verde without a car. Scheduled airline flights and buses go to Cortez and Durango; buses run from Cortez to the park from the middle of May to the middle of October. From the lodge at Far View, a conducted bus tour goes through the park.

The entrance to the park is on U.S. 160, about 40 miles west of Durango and 10 miles east of Cortez. By car, allow at least one hour to reach the Visitor Center from the park entrance.

- *Ute Tribal Park*
Towaoc, Colorado 81334 *(303) 565-8471*

Just west of Mesa Verde, an exciting adventure is available to those interested in remote, seldom-visited, and completely undeveloped archaeological sites. When Mesa Verde was set aside, one canyon was left outside the national park boundaries in lands reserved for the Ute Mountain Indians (a branch of the Ute Indian tribe).

Like the Navajo the Utes entered the Four Corners long after the Anasazi disappeared. But the Anasazi ruins in **Lion Canyon** are now protected by the people of the modern Ute tribe. These were the first ruins ever found in Colorado, and the Ute Mountain Indians have set aside 120,000 acres of their reservation to preserve this land of many ancient dwellings.

The Utes hope to hold this land in its primitive state. Visitors are welcome to the Ute Tribal Park, which encompasses Lion Canyon, but each person must be accompanied by a guide from the Ute Mountain tribe. These canyon lands are completely deserted. Occasionally visitors will run across university archaeologists carrying out excavations in the dozens of sites within the park, and the journey offers a rare opportunity to observe a southwestern dig.

It's possible to reach only a handful of the more than four thousand sites in the canyon. Some are single dwellings, while others are large multistoried buildings. Outlines of ruined villages are seen everywhere, breaking the swells of sand in the canyon bottom. Other ruins are tucked into wide-faced caves. Pictographs are lavishly painted on canyon walls.

For adventure and a sense of discovery, the remote Ute Tribal Park offers splendid, untouched country as well as freedom and isolation. No more than fifteen people are permitted to enter the region on any given day. You travel in your own car, and a member of the Ute tribe accompanies you. The trip covers ninety miles and takes roughly eight hours. Most of the journey is on gravel and dirt roads. You spend a lot of time out of the car, since most ruins are reached by hiking trails. You must bring your own lunch and drinking water. This is a full, exhilarating day in the field.

The trip into Lion Canyon leaves from Towaoc at 9:00 A.M. As yet, there are no accommodations or campsites in this small community. Cortez, only twelve miles north, is the nearest town where food and lodging are available. Allow twenty minutes to reach Towaoc from Cortez. You meet your guide at the pottery factory located at the turnoff to Towaoc on U.S. 666.

Other trips: Energetic souls can hike into the canyon instead of going by car, covering in a single day much of the same area, but going deeper into the canyon and visiting more remote ruins. Overnight campers can use a primitive campground on the banks of the Mancos River, and the park offers a special overnight trip that takes in all the main ruins on the reservation. Backpacking trips can be arranged at a charge of $65 a day (up to four days).

A trained guide accompanies all of these trips, but except for the backpacking journey, there is no formal charge. Donations are suggested ($10 per person), and special groups are welcome.

For full information about entering Lion Canyon, write or call the Ute Tribal Park.

DIRECTIONS: From Cortez drive 12 miles south on U.S. 666 to Towaoc.

● *Escalante Ruin*
Dolores, Colorado 81323

Escalante is another Anasazi village easily reached from Cortez. Two hundred years ago, while on an exploring expedition to the Spanish missions in California, two Franciscan friars recorded the first ruined villages ever found in Colorado. The friars, Fray Francisco Antansio Dominguez and Fray Silvestre Velez de Escalante, saw many mysterious ruins on their journey across the Southwest in 1776; one of these became known as Escalante.

The ruins of the Anasazi village lie at the top of a hill overlooking the Dolores River and the Montezuma Valley. Although the village is near Mesa Verde, it was actually built by the people from Chaco Canyon, 125 miles further south in New Mexico. Escalante apparently was part of the Chaco trade network. The village was occupied for only ten or fifteen years, when Mesa Verde was at its zenith and Chaco was beginning to decline. The outpost at Escalante may have been a last effort of the Chaco people to revive their waning culture.

The site has been fully excavated and stabilized, but the ruins here are fragile. As at all archaeological sites, visitors are asked to step cautiously and protect the remaining walls.

DIRECTIONS: From Cortez take Colorado 145 to Dolores. Escalante is located 3 miles southwest of Dolores on Highway 184.

Pleasant View

• *Lowry Pueblo Ruins and Hovenweep*

Lowry is a ruined Anasazi village that has been closed to the public for several years for stabilization. It is scheduled to reopen in 1980. Lowry was repeatedly occupied and abandoned many times during its 150-year history. People returned to it because its great ceremonial kiva was considered a holy place. The Great Kiva is partially uncovered and can be seen at the site.

DIRECTIONS: Lowry Pueblo Ruins are reached from Pleasant View on U.S. 666, north of Cortez. (From Escalante Ruins, return to U.S. 666 via SR 147 and turn north.)

At Pleasant View turn west onto a partially paved road that points the way to Hovenweep. Lowry is about 9 miles west on this road. If it is open, the directional marker will be up; if it is closed, you will drive by and never know it's there.

This same road, unpaved, continues for miles to Hovenweep. It is a long trip, but if you start from Cortez early in the morning, it's possible to visit Escalante, Lowry, and Hovenweep in a single day. If you prefer to visit only one site, choose Hovenweep.

• *Hovenweep National Monument*

The trails to Hovenweep pass isolated Navajo hogans. The small round cedar lodges squat like overturned bowls on the desert. Occasionally in the distance you spot the bright red shirt of a Navajo boy herding his small crowd of

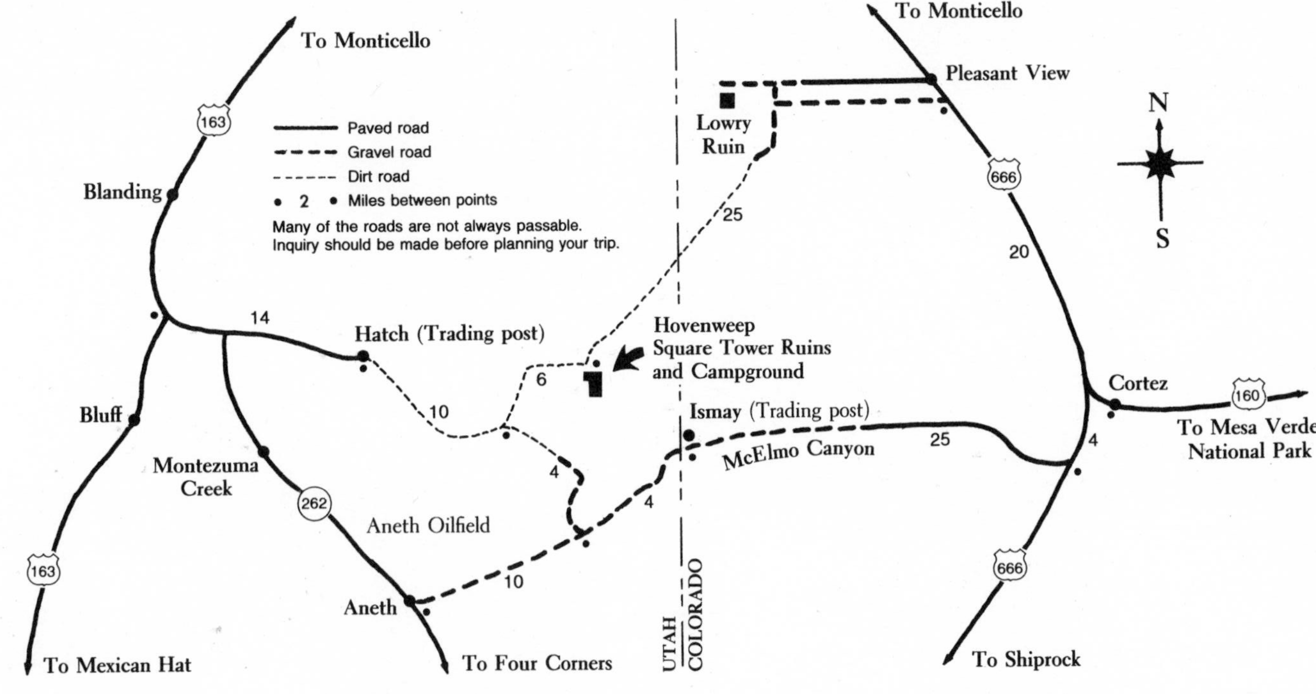

Map of Hovenweep. (Courtesy of the National Park Service.)

The abandoned stone towers of Hovenweep. (Photo: JW.)

sheep. During the summer the Navajo live out here under the sky, following very much the old ways of their ancestors. Winters, when the frosts and snows come, they move into Blanding and other nearby towns. These dirt roads, rutted with ice and mud, are often impassable in winter.

You won't see Hovenweep until you are at the very edge of the canyon. The stone towers command the canyon rims and look out over the desert. They may once have been watchtowers, or storage granaries, or water towers. But today they have an almost religious aura. Sitting beside these silent guardians, one feels the wind coming up coolly from the deep drop below. These ruins, in the quiet headlands of the canyon, have the power to summon their old spirits. The stones are carefully fitted, and although most of the mortar has long since disappeared, some walls still stand more than twenty feet high.

Cajon, Holly, Hackberry, Cutthroat, and **Goodman Point** are the names of some of the ruins clustered within the monument site. The towers are oval, square, circular, and D-shaped. They are isolated and difficult to reach. Only **Square Tower Ruins** are accessible, and even these are reached over dirt roads.

Hovenweep is a lonely, haunted place. The Navajo named it "deserted valley." You will never see many people here, especially in the fall and winter. An interpreted trail leads through the ruins of the Square Tower group, and a faint path goes down into the bottom of the canyon. A ranger is on duty all year.

There is a campground near the ranger station, but no supplies are available at the site. Hatch Trading Post and Ismay Trading Post sell groceries and gasoline. The nearest overnight accommodations are at Blanding and Bluff in Utah, and Cortez in Colorado.

The monument and campground are open all year. The superintendent of Mesa Verde National Park is in charge of Hovenweep Monument. For information, write:

Mesa Verde National Park
Colorado 81330

DIRECTIONS: Hovenweep is approached from the Colorado side via the turnoff at Pleasant View. The paved road soon turns to gravel and then to dirt. To reach Hovenweep, continue to follow the directional markers south and west as the dirt road winds for 25 miles on its way to Hovenweep. The road that appears as a simple straight path on the map is full of turns and you actually follow a zigzag pattern across the desert. Every time you are ready to give up, another tiny marker pops up alongside the road and directs you another 3 or 12 or 6 miles to Hovenweep. These signs bear little resemblance to actual mileage. In due course, if you continue to follow the markers, you will arrive at the site. Allow at least one hour from Pleasant View.

From Hovenweep, you can go back out to the Colorado side, or continue through to the southeastern corner of Utah into Bluff or Blanding.

SOUTHEASTERN UTAH

Bluff

Several places in the southeastern corner of Utah offer opportunities for visitors to explore archaeological and geological sites in remote country. Bluff—an old pioneer town settled by the Mormons—is surrounded by prehistoric ruins, and the town itself has many abandoned houses that the early settlers built with stones from Anasazi ruins. Bluff is a little town full of adventure.

Headquarters for Ken Ross's **Wild River Expeditions** are just down the road. And from **Recapture Lodge,** a lovely, civilized, reasonably priced retreat, geologist Gene Foushee will help you explore Monument Valley, Mystery Valley, and the ancient river terraces of the San Juan River. A day in the field with Gene is no armchair adventure. Most of the time you're out of the jeep, scrambling up cliffs and down ravines. If you want to know what going out to breakfast is all about, get up at 5:00 A.M. and trundle out onto the desert with the Foushees for a sunrise cookout. Gene and Mary Foushee have spent years exploring this region, and whatever kind of trip you would like to make—either on your own or with guides—they can put you on the right path.

A trip down the San Juan River with archaeologist/geologist Ken Ross is worth four years in college. When Ken beaches the raft, you may discover a hidden Anasazi ruin or ancient pictographs. Or he may show you an ocean of fossil shells that line the high bluffs along the river.

The advantage of going into the field accompanied by scientists is that they are explorers rather than tour guides. The farther off the track you want to go, the more interested they are in taking you. And if you are interested in science, they willingly share their knowledge of this incredible terrain.

Other scientific adventures are offered by **Wild & Scenic,** an outfit that gives you your own raft to paddle downriver. Each cluster of rafts is accompanied by a scientist, and the trips focus on different sciences: geology, botany, archaeology, and others.

From Bluff, it's a short drive north to Blanding and the **Trail of the Ancients** (see next listing).

About forty-five miles south on U.S. 163 from Bluff is **Goulding's Lodge** in Monument Valley, one of the classic watering holes of the west. The story of Goulding's is as fascinating as any tale of the Old West, and perhaps that is why it has been the scene of western movies since the late 1930s. Harry Goulding was a sheep herder and trader who brought the attention of Hollywood and the American public to Monument Valley—that unbelievable prehistoric world where monoliths tower two thousand feet above the desert floor, and fossilized animal tracks make the only trails.

Over the years, Goulding's has grown from a small trading post to a comfortable lodge. The Gouldings have donated the lodge to Knox College in Galesburg, Illinois, where profits go to scholarships for Navajo students attending the college.

The rooms at Goulding's are modern and reasonably priced, and there is a small landing strip for chartered planes. The lodge sits in the middle of the valley, and there is absolutely nothing on either side except the mesas that break the horizon. Meals are served family style; and the trading post has Indian crafts, rugs, jewelry, and books for sale. A KOA campground is adjacent to the lodge.

The lodge offers several tours into Monument Valley and other areas, and these are the big tourist attraction of the region. Tours are made in air-conditioned, four-wheel drive vans that carry about ten people, and there are plenty of stops for picture taking but no rough walks or climbs. The vistas in Monument Valley are spectacular; you will see no Anasazi ruins here, only small pictographs on massive cliff walls.

The trip to inquire about is Mystery Valley. Here are hundreds of untouched and unexcavated Anasazi ruins, hidden in cave shelters that look out over the hogans of the Navajo. It's not unusual to have this trip all to yourself, since most people automatically sign up for Monument Valley.

You needn't be a guest at Goulding's to dine in the dining hall or sign up for the various tours. Most of the tours are accompanied by Navajo guides. **Howard Valle's Trading Post** in Mexican Hat also takes tours into Monument and Mystery valleys.

For information about tours and guides for Mystery Valley, Monument Valley, and the San Juan River, write or call:

Gene and Mary Foushee
Recapture Lodge
Box 31
Bluff, Utah 84512 (801) 672-2281

Goulding's Lodge and Tours
Box 1
Monument Valley, Utah 84536 (801) 727-3231

Howard Valle's Trading Post
Box 516
Mexican Hat, Utah 84531 (801) 683-2226

Ken Ross
Wild River Expeditions
Box 110
Bluff, Utah 84512 (801) 672-2244

Patrick and Susan Conley
Wild & Scenic, Inc.
P.O. Box 2123
Marble Canyon, Arizona 86036

Blanding

- *Following the Trail of the Ancients*

The Trail of the Ancients is part of the new Highway 95 that connects Blanding with Hanksville via **Natural Bridges National Monument** and **Lake Powell.** There are dozens of unique archaeological and geological sites along this trail; the map shows only the few outstanding sites located between Blanding and the Natural Bridges National Monument. Some easily accessible sites right on the road are severely stabilized with poured concrete. Don't

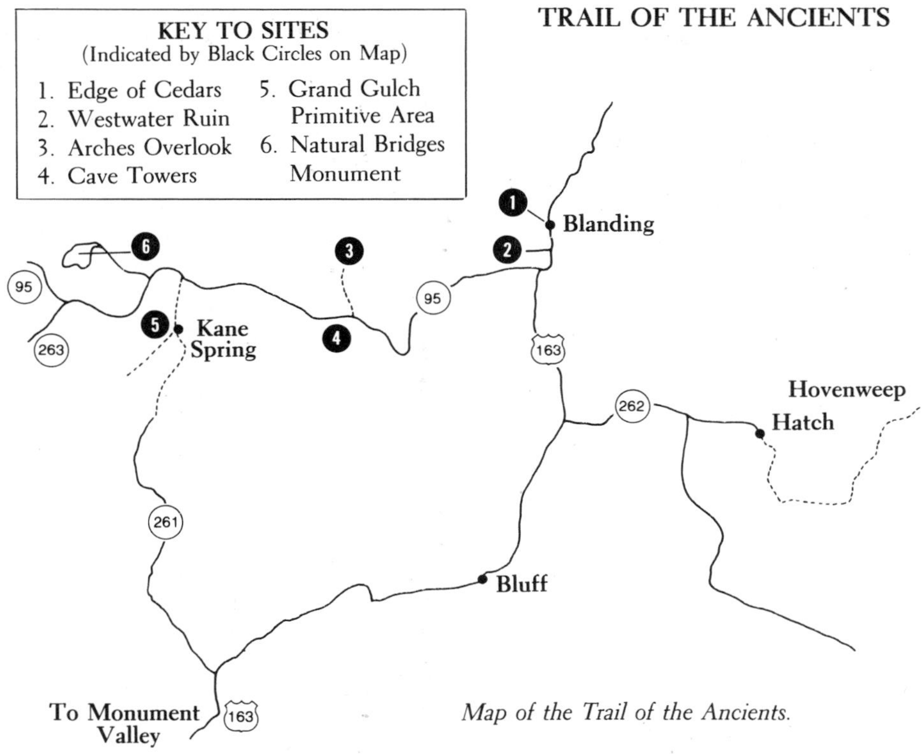

Map of the Trail of the Ancients.

be disillusioned by these trail-side exhibits. Many beautiful and unknown Anasazi ruins are just a short hike off the highway.

Most sites on Highway 95 are marked. They are reached either over rough dirt roads or hiking trails. Many other ruins can be seen from overlooks. The most exciting archaeological adventure in the region is in **Grand Gulch Primitive** area—but it requires an adventurous heart and a lot of stamina.

Some of the sites are very fragile, and the number of visitors entering the ruins is restricted. For this reason the exact location of all sites is not given here. The best thing to do is drive along Highway 95 to the Natural Bridges National Monument and ask the rangers on duty for information. In this way the rangers have some control over the number of people entering the ruins.

Go out of your way to ask about **Cave Tower Ruins**—seven stone towers guarding a canyon rim about half a mile off the highway. These ruins are reached only on foot, and there is not even a trail across the rocky plateau. The turnoff on the road is not marked. Ask the ranger at monument headquarters for directions.

Edge of Cedars State Historic Monument in southeastern Utah lies under a blanket of snow. (Photo courtesy of the Utah Division of Parks and Recreation.)

Area Sites

- *Edge of Cedars State Historical Monument*
P.O. Box 48
Blanding, Utah 84511 *(801) 587-2238*

This small Anasazi village on the edge of Blanding was discovered by Anglo settlers in 1905. The ruin has been fully excavated, and there is a modern interpretive museum next to it. Edge of Cedars is easily accessible, located just northwest of Blanding at 660 West and 400 North.

HOURS: May 16–September 15
8:00 A.M.–7:00 P.M. daily.
September 16–May 15
9:00 A.M.–5:00 P.M. daily.
Closed Thanksgiving, Christmas, New Year's.
ADMISSION: Free.

- *Westwater Ruin*

Westwater is a beautiful Anasazi ruin tucked into a cliff side across a wide canyon. A natural stone bridge and a swinging bridge span the canyon, but it is dangerous to cross over or enter the ruin. There is a spot to leave your car, and it's nice just to sit on the canyon rim and look at the ruin.

DIRECTIONS: Driving south from Blanding on U.S. 163, turn west on an unmarked road just *before* you reach Highway 95. After the turn, continue almost 2 miles to the end of the road. The directional signs on the road have been removed, but the site is well known in the area and easy to find.

• *Arches Overlook*

You reach Arches Overlook by a graded dirt road. Cars can make it, but trailers are advised not to try. Turn off 95 at the sign to Texas Flat. Travel north 2.2 miles until you see a four-wheel drive road going off to your right. You can park here and follow this road, which becomes a hiking trail, for a quarter of a mile. Bring your binoculars. This area has very high cliffs, so take care with children and pets.

The overlook offers a spectacular view of Arch Canyon. Cliff dwellings are clustered in every wall of the canyon. Most of these are believed to be storage granaries built between A.D. 1050 and 1150, when the Anasazi still used the open mesa tops for their homes.

The overlook is a perfect place to picnic.

• *Cave Towers*

These beautiful towers are just west of Arches Overlook, on the opposite side of Highway 95, but the road is unmarked. Continue on to the Visitors' Center at Natural Bridges National Monument and inquire for directions to Cave Towers. It's a fairly long hike out to the ruins, but it is flat and no strenuous climbing is required.

• *Grand Gulch Primitive Area* *(801) 587-2201*

For viewing archaeological sites, backpacking into Grand Gulch may be the most exciting wilderness adventure in the Four Corners. Grand Gulch begins along the Trail of the Ancients at Kane Spring. Guides are not required, and rangers patrolling the area greet visitors and provide interpretation and protection as needed.

There are strict quotas on the number of people entering Grand Gulch, and a reservation system may be established in the future to help backpackers plan ahead.

Small groups of four to six are recommended, although groups of up to fifteen people are allowed to enter the region. All hikers are asked to stop by Kane Spring Ranger Station to obtain a free-use permit. Large parties should call ahead for reservations.

The rangers are knowledgeable about the archaeology and prehistory of the region. They also show an interpretive slide program to orient you before you pack into the wilderness.

There are many sites to discover within the rugged area, but the rangers will not tell you exactly where they are. You are asked to check back in at the ranger station when you come out of the area.

Backpackers should plan to spend at least three days in the enormous canyon; the average stay is five days. However, rangers also can advise you on good one-day hikes.

Guide services for backpacking and horseback trips are available. Horses should be used only with experienced guides, as the canyon trails are dangerous for animals. Groups using horses are required to pack their own horse feed, tie their horses at night, and lead them back and forth to the watering area.

A list of commercial operations that provide guides into the Grand Gulch Primitive Area can be obtained by writing:

Bureau of Land Management, Moab District
San Juan Resource Area
P.O. Box 7
Monticello, Utah 84535

The bureau at Monticello also has information about many other primitive areas in southeastern Utah that can be reached by backpacking, horseback riding, or by river raft.

- *Natural Bridges National Monument*

More than two hundred archaeological sites lie within this monument noted for its three magnificent natural bridges. These bridges are outstanding examples of how water erosion has worn through the red rock landscape. A visitors' center and campground with water are available. Information about the area can be obtained from the ranger on duty.

An eight-mile loop road has several overlooks to view the bridges. Hiking trails go out to each bridge; some of them involve strenuous climbing up and down canyon walls.

Thunderstorms in the summer may cause flash floods. Get out of the canyon bottoms when thunderstorms are threatening upstream. And stay away from the overlooks during lightning storms.

Before venturing onto the many foot trails that enter the monument, check in with the duty ranger, and he or she will help you plan your hike.

You are asked not to enter any prehistoric ruin you might come across in the canyon.

HOURS (VISITORS' CENTER): March 15–November 15: 8:00 A.M.–4:30 P.M. daily.
Rest of year, weather permitting.

Moab

• *Canyonlands National Park*
466 South Main Street
Moab, Utah 84532

Administrative Office:
(801) 259-7166

More than three hundred thousand acres of remote wilderness surround the confluence of the Green and Colorado rivers. Within the rugged canyons are fragile remains of prehistoric Anasazi villages.

The roads in Canyonlands National Park are unpaved, and some sections demand four-wheel drive. Many small ruins and pictographs are found throughout the park. Guided jeep trips are available, and this is probably the best way to locate some of the hidden sites.

DIRECTIONS: The northern section of the park, which includes Grand View Point and Upheaval Domes, is accessible by car over unpaved roads. Drive 12 miles north of Moab, on U.S. 163, then 24 miles southwest on paved or partially paved roads.

The south section, called Needles, is reached by driving 15 miles north of Monticello on U.S. 163, then 38 miles west on SR 211. All other roads in the park are unpaved.

For full information about touring in Canyonlands, write the park superintendent (see above).

NORTHEASTERN ARIZONA

Kayenta Vicinity

• *Navajo National Monument*
Tonalea, Arizona 86044

(602) 672-2366

Three great cliff dwellings at Navajo National Monument mark the culmination of Anasazi culture in the Kayenta region: **Betatakin, Keet Seel,** and **Inscription House.** All three of these magnificent ruins are reached and explored only with difficulty, and only a few visitors each day are admitted. The ruins are extremely fragile. Betatakin requires a three-hour hike, and Keet Seel is reached either by horseback or a day's travel by foot.

All hikes to the ruins are rough and demanding. Trails creep up and down towering red sandstone walls, through groves of trees in the canyon bottom, and across streams and rivers. The Navajo people who occupy this land have their sheep camps in the canyon, and visitors are guests on their land.

The Navajo are newcomers to this region. They came from the north about a hundred years ago. But some descendants of the Anasazi remain in the region—the Hopi Indians, who live on their mesa tops just east of Kayenta, still show Pueblo life as it might have been seven hundred years ago at Betatakin, Keet Seel, and Inscription House.

All Trips: If you plan to make any of the trips into the monument aside from the Sandal Trail tour, it is best to arrive the day before to get an early start in the morning. There are motels in Kayenta, and camping is permitted near monument headquarters.

The ruins are open in the summer only, usually between May 25 and September 15, depending on the weather. The best times to go are at the end of May and after Labor Day. Visiting Navajo is a great outdoor adventure. To fully enjoy the trip, you must plan ahead, since only a few people each day are allowed to hike into the ruins. Arrangements to visit are easily made with a phone call or letter to the monument headquarters.

Visitors' Center: Plan to spend some time in the Visitor Center before starting out on any trip to the ruins. Exhibits and a slide program describe the life of the Anasazi and show examples of their art. In summer, campfire programs are given on archaeology and the natural history of the monument. The Navajo Tribal Guide concession in the Visitor Center sells various crafts made by the Indians.

DIRECTIONS: From Kayenta drive southwest 22 miles on U.S. 160. From Tuba City drive 50 miles northeast on U.S. 160. From this point, a 9-mile paved road runs from the highway to monument headquarters.

HOURS: The Visitor Center is open year round from 8:00 A.M. until 5:00 P.M. (till 6:00 P.M. in the summer). Hiking trails to the ruins usually stay open from about May 25 to the middle of September. The self-guiding Sandal Trail is open all year, weather permitting. Call ahead for reservations information and about guided trips.

ADMISSION: Prices vary depending on the trip you choose.

The Ruins

Betatakin: "Ledge House" was discovered in 1909 by Byron Cummings, a pioneer archaeologist in the Southwest, and John Wetherill, a rancher and trader who, with his brother Richard, discovered many of the major Anasazi cliff dwellings in the San Juan region. The 130-room pueblo is the most accessible of all the ruins at Navajo and contains six tiers and a balcony of apartments.

You can visit Betatakin only if you are accompanied by a park ranger. In the summer two tours leave each day, at 8:30 A.M. and 1:30 P.M. They are limited to twenty people each. The tour is on a first-come basis. The round-trip hike takes about three hours and involves strenuous climbing on the way back. Park officials say it is like climbing down *and up* a seventy-story building. The altitude is seventy-two hundred feet, and the hike is tiring. If you're going to attempt it, you should be physically fit.

Sandal Trail

You can *see* Betatakin from a distance if you walk out to the end of Sandal Trail. Take your binoculars; the round trip takes about one hour. Sandal Trail is open all year except when the snow is heavy. (Snowfall at Navajo has been known to reach thirty inches.)

Keet Seel: This is the largest cliff dwelling in Arizona; it has 160 rooms—living quarters, storage rooms, and five or six kivas. Keet Seel means "broken pottery" in Navajo. The long, sixteen-mile journey to Keet Seel does not take you through Betatakin. The round-trip to Keet Seel, limited to twenty persons per day, can be made either by horseback or on foot.

Horses are rented from a local Navajo family. The Navajo wranglers care for the horses and accompany you to Keet Seel as trail guides. When you arrive, a park ranger guides you through the ruin itself. Rangers suggest that children should be at least twelve years old to make this trip. You bring your own lunch and carry your own water. There is no drinking water in the canyon.

This is an exceptionally remote ruin lying eight miles up canyon from Monument headquarters. The trail follows a dirt road for 1.5 miles, then suddenly drops 1000 feet in the next mile, and follows the canyon floor for the last 5.5 miles.

Make sure you bring the right equipment and clothes. Wear a hat and a long-sleeved shirt for protection against the sun. Your saddle pack will hold a camera, lunch, water (two quarts), and other *small* items.

You must make a reservation and pay an advance fee for this trip, and you can do this by mail or telephone. Phone reservations must be made by 5:00 P.M. the day before you ride, but if you have your heart set on this trip, make your reservations well in advance. The $35 advance deposit (per person) is nonrefundable, which means that people seldom cancel their reservations. Don't count on getting a space at the last minute. The deposit is a down payment on your trip and confirms your reservation.

Stop at the Visitors' Center to pick up your permit (you can do this the day before you ride); then meet your guide at the horse corral between 8:00 and 8:15 A.M. It's a three-hour trail ride to Keet Seel, and you may have to hike the first 1000 feet straight down a rough trail. At the ruin, you have plenty of time to visit Keet Seel, have lunch, and enjoy the country before heading back. Riders usually reach the horse corral between 5:00 and 6:00 P.M.

A Day's Hike. You can also hike into Keet Seel, but plan to start very early in the morning. Hikers obtain a permit at the Visitors' Center, and need to be on the trail by 10:00 A.M. The ranger at the Visitors' Center will show you a map of the canyon and explain the route to Keet Seel. When you arrive at the ruin, another ranger will guide you through. Do not enter the ruin without the ranger. Hikers arriving later than 3·30 will not be allowed to tour the ruin.

Since only five people can enter the ruin at one time, you may have to wait two or three hours if there are people ahead of you. Allow *at least* three hours for the return trip.

With permission, you can spend the night at a primitive campground near Keet Seel. Get your overnight permit before you leave the Visitors' Center and check in with the ranger at the site when you arrive. Camp only in the designated area and away from the canyon walls. The sandstone walls continually change and shift. Overnight backpackers should travel light, but include a lightweight shelter and sleeping bag. Carry enough food for four meals.

Wear a hat and long-sleeved shirt, and comfortable waterproofed hiking shoes. The route continually crosses Keet Seel Creek, which is usually ankle deep. Thunderstorms come up fast in the canyon during the summer and temperatures drop rapidly. Rangers suggest you carry a rain poncho and a wool shirt in the event you get wet. Hikers and backpackers should also check in when they return from this trip, so the park rangers know you are safely out of the canyon.

Inscription House

For the first time in several years, the famous Inscription House—which has seventy-four rooms, granaries, and a kiva—is open to a few visitors. This is an extremely fragile ruin, and only ten people in a day will be taken to the site on a ranger-guided trip. This ruin is at the base of a high-arching sandstone cliff on the northern side of the Nitsin Canyon. The site is reached by dirt road and a two-mile hiking trail.

Second Mesa

- *Hopi Cultural Center*
  P.O. Box 67
  Second Mesa, Arizona 86043 *(602) 734-2401*

The small Hopi nation is completely surrounded by Navajo country. At Second Mesa the clean, modern lines of the new Hopi Cultural Center blend into the austere desert background. A fascinating museum, crafts center, restaurant, and motel are all part of the center. The motel is modern, and the unimposing restaurant serves blue corn pancakes, Indian fry bread with honey, and several other Indian dishes along with the standard steaks and hamburgers.

In the museum Hopi arts and crafts are shown, and in the Silvercraft Guild you can watch artists working in silver overlay, the technique the Hopi use to produce their distinctive black on polished silver designs. The Hopi are magnificent artists; their silver rings, bracelets, and pendants are justifiably renowned. Artists also make the famous Hopi kachinas, dolls carved from wood and clothed in fantastic costumes. The kachinas, spiritual beings who come at regular intervals to help and advise the people, permeate Hopi life and religion. The dolls are replicas of the costumes Hopi men wear during ceremonial dances.

Only fine arts and crafts are sold at the Cultural Center and most of them are expensive. A beautifully crafted kachina doll will cost between $40 and $75; pottery bowls will cost in the hundreds, and jewelry can soar into the thousands.

The ancient Hopi villages that ride the crests of the mesas are like medieval garrisons; many of them have been occupied continuously since prehistoric times. Every day that passes, their very existence is threatened, and there is no way of knowing how long these representatives of ancient cultures can survive. Visits should be undertaken with care.

Old Oraibi, thought to be the oldest continuously inhabited community in America, is closed to visitors. **Walpi,** clinging to the tip of First Mesa, does permit visitors but one must enter on foot. The people are friendly, but there are no shop windows for the tourist to look into. Windows and doors open directly onto narrow streets, and usually visitors find themselves looking unhappily into someone's living room.

Perhaps the best time to visit the villages is during ceremonial events or dances when the public is invited and *everybody* goes. Under these circumstances visitors don't feel out of place and they can relax and enjoy themselves. Another way to visit is to go with a guide from the Hopi Cultural Center; someone takes visitors out every morning and afternoon.

The lodging and restaurant at the Hopi Cultural Center are excellent and reasonably priced. For reservations and full information about visiting the Hopi villages, write or call the Cultural Center. It is open year round.

Ganado

- *Kinlichee Tribal Park*

Just east of Ganado on AZ 264 you will see a sign at the Cross Canyon Trading Post that turns off on a dirt road. Follow the road 2½ miles to the small Anasazi ruin. The ruin is under the protection of the Navajo people; there is a short self-guiding trail.

HOURS: Open daylight.
ADMISSION: Free.

• *Hubbell Trading Post National Historic Site*
Box 150
Ganado, Arizona 86505 *(602) 755-3475*

The Old Hubbell Trading Post hasn't changed much since John Lorenzo Hubbell first opened the doors in 1876, except for the large collection of Navajo art displayed in the trader's home: baskets, blankets, rugs, and silverwork. Hanging on the walls are small paintings executed by E. A. Burbank that show Navajo rug patterns. These stand as an example to modern Navajo artists, who still bring their rugs and crafts to the post to be sold. In the summer weavers demonstrate their craft in the storeroom at the back of the post.

You are free to explore and discover the trading post on your own. Park Service staff are on the grounds to show you around, and a guide takes you through the Hubbell home to see the vast personal collection of art and artifacts of Lorenzo Hubbell.

The tours set off promptly on the hour, and last about forty-five minutes. Each tour is limited to fifteen persons, and a guide fee of 50¢ each is charged. (Those under fifteen and senior citizens may take the tour for free.) Winters are cold, but an off-season visit to Hubbell has its merits. It is less crowded and more fun.

DIRECTIONS: Drive 1 mile west of Ganado, just off Arizona 264 and 63.
HOURS: 9:00 A.M.–4:00 P.M. (till 5:00 P.M. in the summer).

Chinle

• *Canyon de Chelly National Monument*
P.O. Box 588
Chinle, Arizona 86503 *(602) 674-5436*

One of those rare places of awesome physical beauty is the Canyon de Chelly. Along the rims of the mesas above the canyon, views are breathtaking. Sheer gold sandstone walls drop away to the pale, sandy canyon bottom laced with blue streams.

There are nine separate overlooks on the north and south rims that provide the best vantage points to see the ruins and natural landforms.

On the north rim, which oversees the **Canyon del Muerto,** the first

Antelope House ruin tucked beneath the rim of Canyon de Chelly's sandstone walls. (Photo courtesy of the National Park Service.)

overlook is the vantage point over **Massacre Cave.** The people who first lived in this canyon were the Anasazi, the ancient ones who left in the general migration out of the Four Corners area following the droughts of the late 1200s.

In the 1700s the Navajo moved into the canyon, and it became a Navajo stronghold. The Navajo raided surrounding settlements belonging to other Indians and the Spanish, and they then used the canyon as a safe retreat. In 1805 the Spanish sent a war party into the canyon. A large number of Navajos, mostly women and children, hid in a cave a thousand feet from the canyon floor under the mesa's rim. The Spaniards, looking down from above, discovered their location and began firing into the cave. They killed 115 Navajo people and captured 33.

The second overlook provides a view of **Mummy Cave.** There are seven rooms in this ruin, including a three-story tower. The people who built this pueblo around 1284 were from the Mesa Verde area. The cave received its name when an archaeological expedition in the late 1800s found two naturally preserved mummies just below the site.

The third overlook on the north rim provides a vantage of the **Antelope House Ruin.** Its name comes from a fine series of paintings of antelope on the wall to the left of the ruin. The paintings are thought to have been done in the 1830s by a Navajo named Little Sheep (Dibe Yazhi). A pit house under the main structure was found by archaeologists, who put a date of A.D. 693 on its habitation. The main ruin here was abandoned in 1260.

Ledge Ruin is at the fourth overlook on the northern rim. The ruin is in a cave one hundred feet above the floor of the canyon. There was a pueblo here of two stories with about fifty rooms and two kivas. It was occupied between A.D. 1050 and 1275.

On the south rim are five more overlooks: **Tsegi, Junction, White House, Sliding Rock,** and **Spider Rock.** White House, the most famous ruin in the Canyon de Chelly, is named for a long wall in the upper part of the ruin painted with white plaster. White House Ruin is the only one that you can enter without a guide; a footpath leads down to the ruin from the overlook. The round trip to the ruin takes two hours.

Another spectacular sight from the south rim is the Spider Rock overlook, which looks down on an eight-hundred-foot spire of sandstone named Spider Rock from a thousand-foot vantage point where Canyon de Chelly and Monument Canyon meet.

Visiting the Monument: To visit the floor of the canyon, you must have a Navajo guide, which can be arranged with one day's notice through the Visitors' Center. You can enter either on foot or by four-wheel drive vehicle. On a motor tour, you must provide the vehicle. Travel on the canyon floor is restricted to May through October, although the rim drives are open all year, weather permitting.

Justin's Thunderbird Lodge is a concession located just south of the Visitors' Center. The lodge has pleasant, air-conditioned rooms and motel units that are reasonably priced. There is a cafeteria-style restaurant that serves good Mexican and American food. Jeep tours of the floor of the canyon are available at Justin's from April 1 to October 31 for either half a day (leaving at 9:00 A.M. and 2:00 P.M.) or for a full day (from 9:00 A.M. to 5:30 P.M.). The "jeeps" are open vehicles where everyone sits on hard benches in the back. It's a rough ride, but fun. For information you may write or call:

Box 548
Chinle, Arizona 86503 (602) 674-5433

There is another motel in the town of Chinle, and **Cottonwood Campground** at the monument has ninety sites equipped with picnic tables and fireplaces. There are no hookups, and while there is a rest room, there are no showers.

DIRECTIONS: You can approach the monument entrance at Chinle from the north or the south on Route 63. Route 63 intersects U.S. 160 just west of Mexican Water or Arizona 264 at Ganado.
HOURS: The Visitors' Center, rim drives, and campground are open year round from 8:00 A.M. to 7:00 P.M. in summer and 8:00 A.M. to 5:00 P.M. in winter except Dec. 25 and Jan. 1.
ADMISSION: Free.

Tsaile

• *Ned A. Hatathali Cultural Center*
Navajo Community College
Tsaile, Arizona 86515 *(602) 724-3311*

From the northern rim of the Canyon de Chelly, AZ 64 continues northward toward the Chuska Mountains. As you near the mountains, a square butte flares up out of the desert. Beside it, a great, pink, glass, eight-sided building faces the rising sun. This is the new Cultural Center of the Navajo Community College. Founded by Ned Hatathali, the school is the first Indian-owned and operated college on an American reservation. College courses emphasize Navajo history and culture and also include many vocational subjects. Displays in the Cultural Center concentrate on Navajo history, but there are many exhibits from other Indian cultures.

DIRECTIONS: From Tsaile (SAY-lee), Navajo 12 weaves back and forth across the state line to Window Rock, tribal headquarters for the Navajo nation. Allow an hour and a half for the 50-mile journey.
HOURS: Monday–Friday: 8:30 A.M.–4:30 P.M.
Closed weekends and holidays.

Window Rock

- *Navajo Tribal Museum*
  Window Rock, Arizona 86515 *(602) 871-4941*

Headquarters of the Navajo tribal government are in Window Rock. Look for the heavily beamed, sandstone headquarters building set dramatically against a ridge. Just east of the junction of SR 264 and Navajo 12 is the **Navajo Arts and Crafts Guild,** where displays show old and new Navajo art.

The Navajo Tribal Museum emphasizes the culture of the Navajo Indians but also shows many Anasazi artifacts from the Four Corners region.

DIRECTIONS: The museum is 1 mile south of Window Rock on AZ 264 on the Tribal Fairgrounds.
HOURS: Monday–Saturday: 8:00 A.M.–5:00 P.M.
Sunday: 1:00 P.M.–5:00 P.M.
Closed national and tribal holidays.
ADMISSION: Free.

THE GREAT BASIN

California

Nevada

Utah

THE GREAT BASIN

The Great Basin is that desert bowl rimmed by the Sierras on the west and the Rockies on the East. The southern portions of Oregon and Idaho, all of Nevada, a large portion of Utah, and the arid regions of California comprise this area. Once the bottom of a huge inland sea, much of the basin is now crusted with salt.

During the Ice Age, the basin was moist and humid, although even then there was little rainfall. The great depressions filled with water as snow and ice melted into streams and poured off the mountains into the basin sinks. The Great Salt Lake is such a place. Animals and humans congregated all around the shores of these enormous lakes. Although the Rockies were something of a barrier, Paleo hunters found passes across the Continental Divide where they trailed ground sloths, mammoths, and camels from the Great Plains into the Great Basin. Traces of these early hunters have been found in rock shelters at Gypsum, Lovelock, and Danger Caves.

After the glaciers retreated, the basin began to dry out. There was almost no rain. The existing pools of water continued to drain off, and the basin grew increasingly hot and arid. The animals disappeared, and only a few people persisted in the desolate environment. The region may have been almost abandoned for several centuries. Those who remained and newcomers migrating from the east and south developed a method of survival that took advantage of the plant and animal life grudgingly yielded by the desert.

Small groups of people roamed the basin with a desperate purpose. They came to know intimately the hostile eccentricities of the desert. They learned to pluck berries and seeds from desert flora without uprooting or destroying the plant itself. They learned when varieties of plants would come into fruit or seed and would return to harvest the same plants year after year. They learned to hunt and trap the smallest animals, reptiles—even insects.

They wove baskets, sandals, fish nets, and mats, and even made little reed ducks to set out on the marshy lakes as decoys. Many of these woven pieces have been found in seasonal campsites in rock shelters, along with tools, projectile points, and sickles used to cut the marsh grasses. But little is known of their society, religious customs, or art. This way of life waxed and waned with shifts of climate and persisted with little change into historic times. The people of the desert never farmed, never made pottery, and built no permanent villages.

On the southerly and far western fringes of the Great Basin, a few attempts were made to alter this meager existence. The Anasazi from the Great Pueblo cultures of northern Arizona and southeastern Utah tried to farm the region along the Colorado River, but they abandoned their villages within two hundred years. The remains of their farms were buried by damming of the Colorado.

In California the Desert culture blended with the life style of the people further north in the plateau region of Idaho, Washington, and Oregon. What distinguishes these early Californians is their prolific use of the millingstone and mano to grind seeds. Small holes worn into flat rocks have been found by the tens of thousands throughout California.

Those desert dwellers who reached the California coastline became skilled boatmen who hunted seals and fish on the open sea. Life was much easier for these coastal people, as they had a permanent source of food. Some of their villages may have grown quite large, but since their homes were made of wooden poles and woven marsh grasses, little remains to describe their life except the great shell mounds they piled up along inland streams.

There are several famous excavated archaeological sites in the Great Basin; however, most of these are rock shelters and there is little for the visitor to see. The Great Basin is especially rich in rock art. Many amateur groups spend long hours in the desert locating and recording these sites, which are becoming increasingly valuable to scientists. Very little is known about the meaning of prehistoric rock paintings or carvings, and so far little investigation has been devoted to analysis of these sites. This is a wide, promising area of research and one in which amateur assistance is valuable and welcome.

CALIFORNIA

California may have been the first part of North America to be inhabited—or it may have been the last. We know people were living inland, in the region of the Great Basin, during the Ice Age. As the ice melted, the lakes of the basin were filled with water and provided abundant hunting and fishing grounds. But as the water continued to run off, the whole region grew desolate and dry with almost no rainfall. The prehistoric people began to migrate toward the wetter, more hospitable climes of the coast.

Were these the first people to enter California? Or had people already traveled down the coast from the Bering Strait, reaching California soon after the first entry onto the North American continent? Underwater archaeology along California's coastline may eventually solve this problem. And the Calico Mountain site near Barstow points to the possibility that people may have lived in California seventy thousand years ago. If so, this would be the oldest known trace of human life in the hemisphere.

It is certain that people did migrate to California from various desert regions around 5000 B.C. Many different groups evolved different cultures, yet all continued to follow a basically Archaic lifeway. They never learned to farm or make pottery. Little evidence of their lifeways remains; their baskets and thatched houses have long since decayed and disappeared. The only trace they left behind are thousands of millingstones that are found all over the state, even in the desert. Archaic Californians probably began to use millingstones and manos to grind and crack seeds seven thousand years ago.

Along the coastline food was abundant in the almost perfect climate. People built seasonal villages, fished in the streams, and gathered wild plants in the woods. The Costanoans who lived in the San Francisco Bay Area between 1500 B.C. and A.D. 1400 left hundreds of shell mounds all over the region, but only a few of them have been preserved.

Far inland, across the California deserts almost to Arizona, are the strangest prehistoric remains in America—the Blythe desert intaglios, giant figures scratched across the surface of the dry, undulating desert landscape. No one has ever discovered who made the figures, nor why, nor when. They are one of the great mysteries of American archaeology.

SITES

Barstow

- *Calico Mountain Project*

Calico Mountain is located in the heart of the high Mojave Desert. This famous archaeological dig offers an opportunity to join both an excavation in progress and a raging controversy.

Archaeologists have found flakes from tools here that may date back seventy thousand years or more. These rock chippings could be the oldest evidence of human occupation ever found in the Americas; or, as some experts believe, they may be only rubble shaped by years of geologic wear and tear. Findings recovered from the dig can be seen at the **San Bernardino County Museum** in Redlands (see listing below).

Anyone interested in field excavation can join the exploration under the supervision of the professional staff. Amateurs over the age of sixteen are given some preliminary digging instructions and are then allowed to excavate a small section of the enormous tract of land. This is the only early Pleistocene site in the United States that allows amateurs to join the dig. Volunteers must provide their own camping or hotel accommodations.

Visitors are welcome and can go directly to the site without an appointment. Guided tours of the site are given hourly with no charge. The tour takes approximately one hour and includes the main portion of the site, descriptions of the geology of the region, the history of the dig, and the location of the major finds.

The **Barstow Museum** and the **Bureau of Land Management Way Station** also have interesting displays that describe the site.

If you would like to join the dig, make an appointment with the county archaeologist:

Ruth D. Simpson
San Bernardino County Museum
2020 Orange Tree Lane
Redlands, California 92373

Or write the resident curator of the site:

Fred Budinger
P.O. Box 581
Yermo, California 92398

DIRECTIONS: From Barstow drive east on I-15. Just past Yerma, a small county road will take you north to the site.
HOURS: Wednesday–Sunday: 8:00 A.M.–4:30 P.M. year round.

• *Inscription Canyon*

This magnificent petroglyph site is accessible only by primitive roads. Road conditions vary during the year. If you stop at the Bureau of Land Management Way Station in Barstow, you can pick up detailed maps of the region along with information about road conditions.

Blythe

• *Giant Desert Intaglios*

Fifteen miles north of the desert town of Blythe, ancient drawings are sprawled over sloping hills. Animals, serpents, and human figures were scratched on the surface of the desert and laid over with small stones. The origin and meaning of the intaglios are unknown. You cannot really see the intaglios from ground level; at best you see part of a leg or an outstretched arm. The ideal way to view the mysterious etchings would be from an airplane or an observation tower, but neither is forthcoming.

The intaglios have been severely damaged by vandals skimming across the surface on motorcycles or in jeeps. As a result, no off-the-road vehicles are permitted past the main road to the intaglios.

DIRECTIONS: From Blythe drive 15½ miles north on U.S. 95 to the marker. Turn left and follow a rocky dirt road that has a wooden fencing along both sides. When you reach the end of the fencing (about 1 mile), stop your car. No vehicles are allowed past this point. You can walk farther into the site if you wish, but stay on the trail. The intaglios are almost underfoot. They are both difficult to see and easily destroyed. Visibility improves at a distance. Do not attempt to take your car farther since the road is deeply rutted and dangerous.

Fremont

- *Coyote Hills Regional Park*
8000 Patterson Ranch Road
Fremont, California 94536 *(415) 471–4967*

Coyote Hills is a wildlife oasis in the midst of the urban sprawl of the East Bay. For thousands of years prehistoric Indians occupied the area around the salt and freshwater marshes along the bay. Their burials, tools, and other artifacts have been recovered by archaeologists from four shell mounds within the park. One of these mounds, still sliced open from the excavation, may be visited on a tour led by the park naturalist.

The tour leaves every Saturday afternoon at 2:00 P.M. and takes about two hours. The naturalist guide is knowledgeable and the trails are easy, although there isn't much to see at the site. A shell mound in California is not a great pile of white oysters. It is a large earthen mound with tiny specks of shell all through it. But the interpretation offered by the guide is fascinating, and the park itself is beautiful and undisturbed by the highways that roar all around it.

DIRECTIONS: From Newark drive north on Newark Boulevard. Turn left onto Patterson Ranch Road into the park.
HOURS: Summer: 8:00 A.M.–10:00 P.M.
Winter: Open till dusk.
ADMISSION: Free.

Jackson

- *Indian Grinding Rock State Historic Park*
P.O. Box 177
Pine Grove, California 95665

Acorns were part of the diet of half the Indians of North America, but they were a staple for the Miwak Indians of California. A single Miwak family consumed two thousand pounds of acorns every year. Bedrock outcroppings in this state park are pitted with 1158 mortar holes ground down to a depth of five or more inches. The Miwak ground twenty-five different kinds of seeds as well as mansanita berries and acorns in these holes called *chaw ses.*

The Giant Intaglios spread across the California Desert near Blythe.

More than a thousand mortar holes are ground into bedrock outcroppings in Indian Grinding Rock State Historic Park. (Photo: JW.)

The state park is beautifully situated in the California Mother Lode country. The reconstruction of a round ceremonial dwelling with a roof made of whole logs dominates the park, and modern Indian tribes still gather here on the last weekend in September. Picnicking is permitted and camping as well, with permission.

DIRECTIONS: From Placerville take Route 49 south to Jackson, then east 9.1 miles on Route 88 to Pine Grove Road. There is no marker to the park; watch for the sign to Volcano. Turn left on Pine Grove Road, and go 1.4 miles to the park entrance.
HOURS: Open at all times.
ADMISSION: $1 in the summer.

Ridgecrest

• *Renegade Canyon Petroglyphs*
China Lake, California

For thousands of years, prehistoric Indians carved pictures into the rocks of Renegade Canyon; more than twenty thousand sites have been recorded, making this one of the largest collections of petroglyphs in the world.

Renegade Canyon is on the China Lake Naval Weapons Range and can be entered only with special guides. The **Maturango Museum** arranges approximately eight tours each year. Visitors take their own cars (four-wheel drive is recommended but not required), and each group of cars has a military escort who describes the life of the Indians who lived here. At Renegade Canyon you leave your car and hike four miles to reach the concentration of petroglyphs. The trip takes all day, and it is a fascinating excursion into the desert.

You must book your reservation several months in advance for the tours, which go only on weekends in the spring and fall. The fee is $2 per vehicle, surely the least expensive fully guided daylong expedition in America. For reservations, write or call:

Maturango Museum
P.O. Box 1776
Ridgecrest, California 93555 (714) 446–6900

The museum has a small collection of artifacts from the Mohave Desert, including projectile points, knives, and baskets. Other exhibits include fossils and rocks of the region. A booklet that describes the petroglyphs at Renegade Canyon is for sale.

HOURS (MUSEUM): Monday–Saturday: 2:00 P.M.–5:00 P.M.
ADMISSION: Free.

Twentynine Palms

- *Joshua Tree National Monument*
  74485 National Monument Drive
  Twentynine Palms, California 92277 *(714) 367–7511*

In the Mojave and Colorado deserts, the Joshua Tree National Monument preserves the giant yucca and other colorful vegetation that decorate the glowing desert landscape. Several archaeological sites have been excavated at the monument, and there are many petroglyph locations. Rangers will direct you to the rock carvings. Some of these prehistoric pictures have been painted by film crews so they would show up in the movies.

Artifacts and displays in the Visitors' Center show the special adaptation made by the people of the Great Basin to their desert environment. Camping is restricted to eight campgrounds with limited facilities. Bring your own firewood and water.

DIRECTIONS: The monument is between I-10 and CA 62 east of Palm Springs and is reached from several different points.
HOURS (MONUMENT): Open at all times.
HOURS (VISITORS' CENTER): 8:00 A.M.–5:00 P.M. daily.
ADMISSION: Free.

Avalon (Catalina Island)

- *Catalina Island Museum*
  Casino Boulevard
  Avalon, California 90704 *(213) 510–2414*

The museum offers a different perspective on early life in California. The prehistoric people who lived on the Channel Islands were skilled seamen and fishermen. The displays at the museum explore their life and culture and include artifacts recovered from excavations on the islands. Other exhibits describe the history and natural history of Catalina.

Reaching Catalina Island is a California-style adventure. The boat trip from San Pedro or Long Beach takes about two hours each way and costs $15 round trip. As one voyager points out, if you get seasick it seems like years. Take a motion sickness pill and enjoy the ride. Avalon is something of a tourist center, but you can rent a jitney to tour the more isolated parts of the island.

For information about visiting Catalina Island, write or call:

Catalina Chamber of Commerce
Department M
Avalon, California 90704 (213) 831–8822

HOURS (MUSEUM): Easter–November: 1:00 P.M.–4:00 P.M. and 8:00 P.M.–10:00 P.M. daily.
Rest of year: 1:00 P.M.–4:00 P.M. weekends and holidays.
ADMISSION: Free.

Berkeley

• *Robert H. Lowie Museum of Anthropology*
University of California
College Avenue and Bancroft Way (Kroeber Hall)
Berkeley, California 94720 *(415) 642–3681*

Changing exhibits are drawn from a large collection of archaeological material from California and other parts of the Americas. Other ethnological exhibits come from Africa, Asia, Europe, and Oceania.

HOURS: Monday–Friday: 10:00 A.M.–4:00 P.M.
Saturday and Sunday: 12:00 M.–4:00 P.M.
Closed major holidays and university holidays.
ADMISSION: Adults 50¢, children 25¢.

Death Valley

• *Death Valley National Monument Museum*
Death Valley, California 92328 *(714) 786–2331*

Displays in the Visitors' Center trace human life in Death Valley from 7000 B.C. through the present time. A herbarium of living plants indigenous to the region and a library of history books are open to visitors. Maps, slides, and postcards are for sale at the desk.

HOURS: May–October: 8:00 A.M.–5:00 P.M. daily.
November–April: 8:00 A.M.–9:00 P.M. daily.
ADMISSION: Free.

Lompoc

• *Lompoc Museum*
200 South H Street
Lompoc, California 93436 *(805) 736–3888*

Displays include stone tools and ornaments of the Chumash culture and other prehistoric Indian cultures of North America.

HOURS: Tuesday–Friday: 1:00 P.M.–5:00 P.M.
Saturday and Sunday: 1:00 P.M.–4:00 P.M.
Closed major holidays.
ADMISSION: Free.

Los Angeles

- *Natural History Museum of Los Angeles County*
900 West Exposition Boulevard
Exposition Park
Los Angeles, California 90007 *(213) 746–0410*

Some of the artifacts displayed in this large, diverse museum date from 8000 B.C. In addition to displays of archaeological materials from California, other exhibits explore the Hohokam and Anasazi cultures of the Southwest. Models and dioramas illuminate interesting aspects of prehistoric life in California.

Fossil remains of extinct animals and habitat displays of North American and African mammals are shown in the natural history galleries. Ice Age fossils exhumed from Hancock Park (La Brea tar pits) are on display here. A large research library is open to the public for use on the premises. Natural science items, reproductions, and books are for sale in the Museum Shop.

HOURS: Tuesday–Sunday: 10:00 A.M.–5:00 P.M.
Closed Thanksgiving and Christmas.
ADMISSION: Free.

- *Southwest Museum*
234 Museum Drive
Highland Park
Los Angeles, California 90065 *(213) 221–2163*

Wide-ranging exhibits explore Indian cultures from North and South America. The museum's collections of Californian and Southwestern Indian art are among the best in the country. A fine library of comparative anthropology, history, and art books is open to the public by appointment. The Southwest Museum was founded by Charles Lummis, first City Editor of the Los Angeles *Times* and intrepid traveler and reporter on the Southwest.

The museum is situated in the hills east of San Fernando Valley. There is parking on the hillside above the museum, but if you park at the bottom of the hill you can enter through a tunnel where wonderful dioramas of American Indian life are recessed in the walls. From the tunnel, an elevator speeds you up to the museum building.

HOURS: 1:00 P.M.–5:00 P.M. daily.
Closed major holidays.
ADMISSION: Free.

Oakland

- *Oakland Museum*
  History Division
  Civic Center, 10th and Oak Streets
  Oakland, California 94607 *(415) 273–3401*

The galleries and gardens of the Oakland Museum spread across four city blocks. Changing and permanent exhibits explore the history and art of both the prehistoric and historic people of California. Archaeological materials recovered from several sites in the Bay Area are on display. Other exhibits are devoted to natural history, ecology, and science.

HOURS: Tuesday–Saturday: 10:00 A.M.–5:00 P.M.
Sunday: 12:00 M.–7:00 P.M.
Closed major holidays.
ADMISSION: Free.

Redlands

- *San Bernardino County Museum*
  2024 Orange Tree Lane
  Redlands, California 92373 *(714) 792–1334*

Archaeological displays cover all of the Northwest and Southwest cultures with special emphasis on prehistoric Indians of southern California. Special displays are devoted to artifacts and photographs from the **Calico Mountain** site. Anyone especially interested in this site can make an appointment with the curator to see additional material.

The museum also has outstanding history and natural science exhibits. The Museum Shop sells rocks and minerals, slides and pamphlets. A new publication called *Pleistocene Man at Calico* describes the work at Calico Mountain site.

HOURS: Tuesday–Saturday: 9:00 A.M.–5:00 P.M.
Sunday: 1:00 P.M.–5:00 P.M.
Closed Thanksgiving, Christmas, New Year's.
ADMISSION: Free.

Sacramento

- *California State Indian Museum*
  2618 K Street
  Sacramento, California 95816 *(916) 445–4209*

Dugout canoes, prehistoric tools, pottery, and baskets are on permanent exhibit. Changing displays reflect the life of California Indians from prehistoric times to the present.

The museum is located in **Sutter's Fort State Historic Park,** where exhibits include restored carpenter and blacksmith shops of the early 1900s.

HOURS: 10:00 A.M.–5:00 P.M. daily.
Closed Thanksgiving, Christmas, New Year's.
ADMISSION: Adults 50¢, under eighteen free.

San Diego

- *San Diego Museum of Man*
Balboa Park
San Diego, California 92100 *(714) 239–2001*

The museum is famous for its research on early American cultures. A wide variety of archaeological material from southern California and the Southwest is displayed in permanent and changing exhibits. Artifacts from North, Central, and South America are shown in fascinating comparative displays. The skull of **Del Mar Man,** possibly the oldest human bone ever found in America, is on display here.

The museum is housed in the unique California Building, built for the 1915 Panama-California International Exposition. Its Spanish-Renaissance tower and decorated facade make the building a San Diego landmark.

HOURS: 10:00 A.M.–4:30 P.M. daily.
Closed Thanksgiving, Christmas, New Year's.
ADMISSION: Adults $1, children six to sixteen 75¢, under six free.

San Francisco

- *Josephine D. Randall Junior Museum*
199 Museum Way (at Roosevelt)
San Francisco, California 94100 *(415) 863–1399*

Featured here are exhibits about Indians of northern and central California, focusing particularly on the Costanoan culture of the Bay Area. Prehistoric artifacts recovered from shell mounds in the area are on display in the museum, along with explanation of the archaeological techniques for recovery. The Randall Museum is an outstanding educational center and offers special tours for school groups.

HOURS: School year: Tuesday–Saturday: 10:00 A.M.–5:00 P.M.
Summer: Monday–Friday: 10:00 A.M.–5:00 P.M.
Closed holidays.
ADMISSION: Free.

Santa Ana

- *Charles W. Bowers Memorial Museum*
2002 North Main Street
Santa Ana, California 92706 *(714) 547-8304*

A cogged stone is a round studded stone that may have had a religious significance to prehistoric people; its actual purpose is still undetermined. Great numbers of these unusual stones have been found in Orange County and other parts of southern California, and some of them are displayed in this museum. Other prehistoric artifacts recovered from local excavations are also on display, along with some pre-Columbian ceramics.

The history and natural science of the Pacific coast are explored in other exhibits. A library is open for use on the premises.

HOURS: Tuesday–Saturday: 9:00 A.M.–5:00 P.M.
Sunday: 12:00 M.–5:00 P.M.
Closed Mondays and major holidays.
ADMISSION: Free.

Santa Barbara

- *Santa Barbara Museum of Natural History*
2559 Puesta del Sol Road
Santa Barbara, California 93105 *(805) 682-4711*

Interesting exhibits explore the life of prehistoric people living on the Pacific coast. Grinding stones that may have been used ten thousand years ago are on display. Dioramas show the way people lived in caves and out on the desert. Collections in the museum are extensive, and the scope of the exhibits is wide-ranging and comprehensive. Fine collections of gems and minerals, mounted birds and animals are shown. A research library is open to the public.

HOURS: Monday–Saturday: 9:00 A.M.–5:00 P.M.
Sunday and holidays: 1:00 P.M.–5:00 P.M.
Summer: Sunday and holidays: 10:00 A.M.–5:00 P.M.
Closed Thanksgiving and Christmas.
ADMISSION: Free.

STATE OFFICE

State Archaeologist
Department of Parks and Recreation
P.O. Box 2390
Sacramento, California 95811 (916) 322-3454

ORGANIZATIONS TO JOIN

The **Archaeological Survey Association of Southern California** (ASA) is a lay-professional society involved in training programs, excavations, and laboratory analysis. This organization has been active in archaeological work in southern California for thirty years. The ASA Research Center in La Verne houses an artifact lab, a basket lab, an ethno-botany lab, and an osteological lab. The laboratories are open to the public on an annual open-house day or by appointment for tours. The labs offer training for new members, and a certification program is planned that will make it possible for amateurs to receive training acceptable to professionals in excavating, surveying, or laboratory assistance. For information, write:

Archaeological Survey Association of Southern California
P.O. Box 516
La Verne, California 91750

The **Society for California Archaeology** is a statewide lay-professional organization dedicated to encouraging interest in California archaeology. This society is active throughout the state. For information, write:

Society for California Archaeology
Department of Anthropology
California State University
Fullerton, California 92634

NEVADA

Almost all of Nevada lies in the heart of the Great Basin, where the wind wears the landscape away to nothingness. The desert is flecked with sage and little else—in some places, sheets of saline form a crust over the land. Only in the southern corner of the state is there any fertile soil, and even this balance is delicately maintained.

A prehistoric city once stood under what is now Lake Mead. Its inhabitants, who may have been related to the Pueblo Anasazi of the Four Corners region, tried to farm the flood plain along the Colorado. They mined salt for trade and made jewelry from turquoise. But this "Lost City" was finally abandoned because floods and drought made survival almost impossible, and farming upset the desert's water table even more.

The only culture able to weather the hazards of the desert for a long period of time was the Desert Archaic, which began here soon after the end of the Ice Age and continued almost unchanged into historic times. People of the desert exploited the fragile environment to its fullest. They knew every variety of desert plant and when to harvest each one. So skilled were they in their selection that they themselves were part of the natural balance of the desert. Several museums in Nevada trace the life of the Desert Archaic culture. And a few places where prehistoric people lived are open to the public, but there is little or no interpretation at these sites.

SITES

Boulder City Vicinity

- *Lake Mead National Recreation Area*
  601 Nevada Highway
  Boulder City, Nevada 89005 *(702) 293-4041*

People first began to live in this region ten thousand years ago, when various groups arrived from the east and south. Many significant archaeological sites in the Great Basin were inundated by the damming of the Colorado River.

Petroglyphs discovered near Davis Dam in the Lake Mead Recreation Area, Nevada. (Photo courtesy of the National Park Service.)

Hundreds more above water level are yet to be excavated. A few sites within the recreation area are accessible by trails or boat.

Christmas Tree Pass is a small oasis 5 miles east of Lake Mojave on Highway 77. A footpath goes out to **Grapevine Canyon,** where hundreds of ancient petroglyphs carved into the rock are still visible.

Willow Beach, 11 miles south of Hoover Dam, is the site of a prehistoric campground dating back to 250 B.C. Pueblo pottery and Pacific seashells found here indicate that the site was a trading center for people from the West and South. Most of the site is submerged in the clear cold waters of Mojave Lake, but petroglyphs are carved onto the slopes of Black Canyon across the water. Boat tours of the lake pass by these ancient carvings.

The Allan Bible Visitors' Center (Highway 95 just west of Hoover Dam) has full details about visiting the recreation area. The best way to see the park is on a boat trip that goes through both Lake Mead and Lake Mojave. For information, write or call the Visitors' Center (above).

• *Valley of Fire State Park*

Just west of Lake Mead are the dramatic red and white Aztec sandstone canyons of Valley of the Fire. Beautiful examples of rock art are found throughout the park. Early Basketmakers once occupied this area, followed briefly by Anasazi farmers. No single group stayed very long in this region, although various peoples returned to it intermittently over the centuries.

Petroglyph Canyon, reached by trail off Nevada 40, has exceptionally fine rock carvings. **Atlatl Rock** is reached by a gravel road that intersects Route 40 just past the entrance to the park.

Exhibits in the Visitors' Center explore the ecology, geology, and prehistory of this spectacular park. For information write or call:

Nevada State Park System
201 South Fall Street
Carson City, Nevada 89701 (702) 394-4088

DIRECTIONS: From I-15, exit at Route 40 and follow directional signs to the Visitors' Center.
HOURS: Open year round.
ADMISSION: Free.

Las Vegas Vicinity

• *Gypsum Cave*

This famous archaeological site revealed the earliest evidence of the Desert culture in the Great Basin. A diamond-shaped projectile point was discovered, together with the bones of a now-extinct sloth. Radiocarbon dating of material found in the cave averaged about 10,500 years old. The upper strata of the cave floor held artifacts from Basketmakers, Anasazi, and the more recent Paiute Indians. All the material recovered from the site is housed in the **Lost City Museum** in Overton (see listing below).

The site is open at all times. There is no interpretation, and all visitors will see is a large limestone cave, 300 feet long and 120 feet wide.

DIRECTIONS: The cave is 15 miles east of Las Vegas off Route 15.

• *Rocky Gap Site*

This rock shelter contained remnants of a very early primitive people who were probably ancestors of the Paiutes. The site has been fully excavated and the artifacts removed, but three roasting pits still remain, and petroglyphs are carved into canyon walls near the site. There is no interpretation at the site. For information call:

Bureau of Land Management (702) 385-6403

DIRECTIONS: From Las Vegas drive 15 miles west off Route 15 in the Red Rock Recreation Lands. To reach the rock shelter, follow the park road until it ends at Willow Springs. Then follow the directional markers ¼ mile on a trail to the cave. The rock carvings are on the western canyon wall.
HOURS: Open year round.
ADMISSION: Free.

MUSEUMS

Carson City

• *Nevada State Museum*
North Carson Street (Capitol Complex)
Carson City, Nevada 89710 *(702) 885-4810*

Housed in what was once the United States Mint Building, the museum shows dioramas that explore many facets of Paiute Indian life, including a full-scale reproduction of a Paiute camp. Archaeological materials recovered from sites on the Great Plains and in the Southwest are also on display. A research library is open to the public; arts and crafts are for sale in the Museum Shop. An old mine tunnel that runs underneath the building is open to visitors.

HOURS: 8:30 A.M.–4:30 P.M. daily.
Closed Christmas.
ADMISSION: Free.

Las Vegas

• *Museum of Natural History*
University of Nevada
1310 Ascot Drive
Las Vegas, Nevada 89154 *(702) 739-3381*

The excellent exhibits of historic and prehistoric Indian artifacts show how these pieces were used in solving the problem of living in the desert. Early mining equipment, fossils, and living lizards in a terrarium are shown in other sections of the museum.

HOURS: Monday–Friday: 8:00 A.M.–5:00 P.M.
Weekends by request.
Closed major holidays.
ADMISSION: Free.

Overton

• *Lost City Museum of Archeology*
Overton, Nevada 89040 *(702) 397-2193*

Several hundred prehistoric sites were found along the banks of the Muddy River, where the Lost City people raised corn fifteen hundred years ago. Most of these sites were flooded by Hoover Dam, but rescued artifacts are preserved in the museum.

From excavated materials a village typical of the Lost City people has been reconstructed. The prehistoric Paiute culture is also described here; material recovered from the famous **Gypsum Cave** site is also on display.

HOURS: 9:00 A.M.–5:00 P.M. daily.
Closed Thanksgiving, Christmas, New Year's.
ADMISSION: Free.

Reno

• *Nevada State Historical Society*
1650 North Virginia Street
University of Nevada
Reno, Nevada 89504 *(702) 784-6397*

In this fine museum, the emphasis is on prehistoric materials dating from 9000 B.C. On display are artifacts recovered from several important archaeological sites in the region including **Lost City, Lovelock Cave,** and **Fishbone Cave.** None of these sites is open to the public. But there is a large research library where books are available for use on the premises.

HOURS: Monday–Friday: 8:00 A.M.–5:00 P.M.
Saturday and Sunday: 9:00 A.M.–5:00 P.M.
Closed state and major national holidays.
ADMISSION: Free.

STATE OFFICE

Nevada State Museum
Department of Anthropology
Carson City, Nevada 89701

ORGANIZATIONS TO JOIN

Am-Arcs of Nevada
P.O. Box 552
Reno, Nevada 89504

Archeo-Nevada Society
Box 5744
Las Vegas, Nevada 89102

UTAH

There are twenty-five thousand identified archaeological sites in Utah; more than two thousand of these have been excavated, and many are open to the public. The greatest concentration of sites is in the southeastern corner of the state, where Anasazi ruins are hidden away in remote canyons accessible only on foot or horseback. The Anasazi built their apartmentlike dwellings in the canyons and cliffsides and farmed the alluvial banks of the Green and Colorado rivers. A description of some of these sites and ways in which they can be visited are found in the "Four Corners" section.

Most of Utah falls into that region classified as the Great Basin, where wind and water have sculpted surreal formations in the vermillion rock, creating what many people consider the most hauntingly beautiful landscape in the world. Early people roamed into all of these empty canyons. They left few reminders of their presence except for the mysterious rock paintings and carvings found everywhere in Utah. In almost all of the state's national parks and forests, traces of prehistoric people are found, although few major archaeological sites are prepared for the public. Perhaps the most famous rock in Utah is **Newspaper Rock** in Indian Creek Park northwest of Monticello on UT 211.

Many of Utah's parks are remote and difficult to travel through. Check maps carefully and get travel information from park headquarters before venturing into wilderness areas. Many roads are unpaved and are sometimes closed due to various weather and road conditions.

SITES

Boulder

- *Anasazi Indian Village State Historic Park*
  Boulder, Utah 84716 *(801) 335-7308*

This ancient village sits at the southern edge of the Aquarius Plateau, just north of the **Glen Canyon Recreation Area.** A band of Anasazi farmers moved here from the southeastern corner of Utah around A.D. 1050. It is thought to have been the largest Anasazi village west of the Colorado River. For reasons never discovered, the village was burned and abandoned 150 years later.

The village has been excavated, but much of it was later backfilled to protect it from further erosion. One dwelling made of willow poles and stone masonry has been reconstructed on the original site, and more of the village eventually will be uncovered and stabilized. Meanwhile, a diorama and artifacts in the on-site museum portray village life at the peak of its development. A well-marked trail winds through the site.

From the Calf Creek campground about twelve miles west of the village, a hiking trail leads past petroglyphs and granaries tucked high into canyon walls. Another granary can be seen from the point where SR 12 crosses the Escalante River; a marker on the road indicates the spot.

The Anasazi village is located in the farming town of Boulder, 75 miles east of Bryce Canyon. Boulder has two general stores, and one private home provides lodging and home-cooked meals. There is no overnight camping at the site, but picnicking is permitted. A Bureau of Land Management campground is about twelve miles west along Calf Creek.

DIRECTIONS: The park is on Route 12, near the town of Boulder.
HOURS: The museum and site are open 8:00 A.M.–5:00 P.M. daily, all year.
ADMISSION: Free.

Torrey

- *Capitol Reef National Park*
  Visitor Center
  Torrey, Utah 84775 *(801) 425-3871*

Capitol Reef is a sixty-five-mile-long red sandstone cliff striped with bands of blue and green and topped with a ribbon of white sandstone. Its name comes from huge domed formations that resemble the nation's capitol building. The Fremont Basketmakers lived in caves and grew corn along the Fremont River in this region, leaving many petroglyphs that are now protected within the boundaries of the national park.

In the Visitor Center, Fremont artifacts and tools recovered from nearby sites are on display. Remains of a Fremont pit house and granary can be seen from the Hickman Bridge nature trail. A ten-mile scenic drive over an unpaved road begins at the Visitor Center, and many hiking trails and jeep roads crisscross the park. During the summer rangers offer guided walks. The park is open all year and campgrounds are available.

DIRECTIONS: The park is reached from the east or west via UT 24. The Visitor Center is six miles from the west entrance and 12 miles from the east.
HOURS (VISITOR CENTER): May–August: 8:00 A.M.–8:00 P.M. daily.
Rest of year: 8:00 A.M.–5:00 P.M.
Closed Christmas.
ADMISSION: Free.

Wendover

- *Danger Cave*

Between 1949 and 1951, archaeologists excavated fourteen feet of stratified deposits in the floor of Danger Cave. Thousands of flaked tools and grinding stones were discovered, along with nets, mats, and baskets in a steady progression that probably originated ten thousand years ago.

The cave is located at the western edge of the Bonneville Salt Flats and was a stopping place for roving bands of desert dwellers who returned here every summer for thousands of years. It was named "Danger" when the roof collapsed on top of an archaeologist working inside, almost burying him alive. Danger Cave is open to the public, but there is no interpretation of the site and nothing to see except the deep cavern. Some of the artifacts recovered from the cave are on display at the **Utah Museum of Natural History** in Salt Lake City (see listing below).

DIRECTIONS: The cave is near Wendover, on the Nevada-Utah border, on Highway 40.

MUSEUMS

Price

• *College of Eastern Utah Prehistoric Museum*
City Hall
Price, Utah 84501 *(801) 637-5060*

A dinosaur skeleton looms over a collection of local Indian artifacts from the Fremont culture. Fossils, petrified wood, rocks, and minerals are included in the geology exhibits. The museum has directions and field guides to a nearby dinosaur quarry and prehistoric petroglyphs in the area.

HOURS: Winter: 10:00 A.M.–5:00 P.M. Monday–Saturday.
Summer: 10:00 A.M.–6:00 P.M. Monday–Saturday.
ADMISSION: Free.

Salt Lake City

• *Utah Museum of Natural History*
University of Utah
Salt Lake City, Utah 84112 *(801) 581-6927*

Artifacts recovered from **Danger Cave** are on exhibit as well as material from other archaeological sites in the Great Basin. The museum has a historical Hall of Man and galleries devoted to fossils, geology, and the plants and animals of Utah.

HOURS: 9:30 A.M.–5:30 P.M. daily.
Closed Thanksgiving, Christmas, New Year's.
ADMISSION: Adults $1, children 50¢.

Vernal

• *Utah Field House of Natural History*
National History State Park
Main Street
Vernal, Utah 84078 *(801) 789-3799*

Utah Field House is primarily devoted to the geology and paleontology of this fascinating region that encompasses **Dinosaur National Monument.** A skeleton of diplodocus, that famous long-necked giant that once thrived here, stands at the entrance to the museum. Artifacts recovered from the Fremont people who lived in the region of the monument are on display in this museum.

HOURS: June–August: 8:00 A.M.–9:00 P.M. daily.
Rest of year: 8:00 A.M.–5:00 P.M.
Closed Thanksgiving, Christmas, New Year's.
ADMISSION: Free.

STATE OFFICE

David B. Madsen
State Archaeologist
Department of Development Service
Crane Building, Suite 1000
307 West 2nd South
Salt Lake City, Utah 84101 (801) 533-6000

OPPORTUNITIES FOR AMATEURS AND ORGANIZATIONS TO JOIN

Amateurs willing to participate in long-term excavations are welcome to write to the state archaeologist for information about fieldwork.

The state archaeological society can be reached by writing:

Utah Archaeological Society
University of Utah
Museum of Natural History
Salt Lake City, Utah 84112

NORTHWEST COAST AND INTERIOR PLATEAU

Idaho

Oregon

Washington

Alaska

NORTHWEST COAST AND INTERIOR PLATEAU

In the far Northwest, only the merest trace of Big Game Hunters has ever been discovered. But submersion of the continental shelf after the Ice Age may explain the absence of Paleo artifacts. A few projectile points recovered from caves in Idaho and western Washington reveal that hunters brought down camels, giant sloths, and other now extinct animals in a prehistoric time when glaciers still covered most of the northern regions. The Paleo Tradition blended into a unique Northwest Tradition called the Old Cordilleran.

Early Americans in the Northwest followed a hunting and gathering tradition from about 8000 B.C. into historic times, with little change in their habits or life styles. They tipped their hunting spears with a distinctive leaf-shaped projectile point.

The nomadic inland Indians led an unsettled life complicated by a hard struggle for survival. They could not afford to support large villages and eked out an existence gathering seeds and hunting the smallest game on the dry Columbia Plateau.

But along the coast, all the way down from Alaska to northern California, an abundance of fish and marine mammals made life much easier. The prehistoric villages grew large. The affluent people of the Northwest Coast grew to venerate wealth and art, and out of this comparatively luxurious life came a ceremony called the potlatch. A potlatch was a joyous celebration in which people gave away their most valuable possessions. A person's worth and wealth were defined by what he could afford to give away.

Today, Indians of the Northwest Coast still travel by canoe and make many beautiful crafts. The Quinault Indians at Amanda Park in Washington will take you for an exhilarating **canoe ride** thirty-five miles down the Quinault River to the open sea. (Write Olympic National Park, Washington, for information.)

The Ozette site on the northern tip of the Washington coast offers amateurs an outstanding opportunity to watch a major dig in progress. And a very small site in Alaska is an excuse for an adventure in one of the wildest and most remote regions of the world.

IDAHO

Geographically, Idaho is comprised of three regions different in their topography and climate: mountain plateaus, desert basins, and plains. The earliest prehistoric Indians in the three regions had common life styles. Hunters and gatherers, they lived largely on wild plant foods and fish all the way into historic time. They had little pottery and did not farm. Some evidence shows that early inhabitants of Idaho were related to the tribes of southeastern Alaska.

Camels, giant ground sloths, and other extinct game once wandered freely in Idaho. At one early man site in Idaho's Wilson Butte Cave, archaeologist Ruth Gruhn discovered a bifacial stone tool alongside some prehistoric camel bones. The weapon may be over 14,500 years old.

A number of markers along modern highways in Idaho give some information about archaeological excavations, although none of these sites is open to the public. Wilson Butte Cave is on Idaho 25 near Twin Falls. At the Lost Trail Visitors' Center (U.S. 93 at the Montana border) visitors can see artifacts recovered from the Alpha Rockshelter, where people lived from 6000 B.C. to 1000 B.C. Most artifacts recovered from excavated sites have been removed to museums around the country. The best exhibits in the area are at the Washington State University Anthropological Museum in Pullman, Washington, and at the Idaho Museum of Natural History at Idaho State University in Pocatello.

SITES AND MUSEUMS

Pocatello

● *Idaho Museum of Natural History*
Box 8096
Idaho State University
Pocatello, Idaho 83209 *(208) 236-3168*

This museum is one of the top natural history museums in the west and the only museum in Idaho with extensive prehistoric holdings. The museum possesses the world's only collections from the northern Great Basin, and the central and northern Rocky Mountains. New galleries have been expanded recently to show off as much of this material as possible. Special galleries focus on other North American cultures.

Members of the museum staff will provide you with up-to-date information on archaeological resources and excavations around the state. The museum also has one of the country's major vertebrate fossil collections, a herbarium, and a large collection of artifacts from the Shoshonean culture.

HOURS: Monday–Friday: 8:30 A.M.–4:30 P.M.
Closed holidays.
ADMISSION: Free.

Salmon

• *Alpha Rockshelter*

People first inhabited this rock shelter around 6000 B.C. and continued to come here until 1000 B.C.—nearly five thousand years of continuous occupation. From a platform visitors can look into the cave and see the rock paintings on the cave's roof. Unfortunately, there is little else to see since most of the findings have been moved to the **Lost Trail Visitors' Center** (on U.S. 93). Nevertheless, if you are in the area the drive is beautiful.

DIRECTIONS: The Alpha Rockshelter is located near Salmon in the west central part of the state. From Salmon drive 20 miles north on U.S. 93 to North Fork. Take the Forest Service Road past Shoup. Continue across the Salmon River about 4 miles to the marker.

Spalding

• *Nez Percé National Historical Park*
P.O. Box 93
Spalding, Idaho 83551 *(208) 843-2685*

A feeling for the history of the whole region comes with a visit to this park, which is divided into twenty-three sections. Located on the Washington border near Lewiston, Idaho, the park is the home of the Nez Percé Indians, whose celebrated Sacajawea escorted Lewis and Clark across the state. People of the tribe were friendly to white explorers and trappers until they found their lands diminished by the westward-moving settlers. Forts and battle sites within the park commemorate the ensuing struggle.

At a number of sites in the park, archaeologists have found the artifacts of prehistoric hunters. The **Weis Rockshelter,** excavated in the 1960s, is one of the most interesting examples of a cave shelter in the state. Needles, awls, and points indicate that people began using these niches in the mountains around 5500 B.C. and continued to do so into historic times. Another site recently open to the public at **Lenore** was used intermittently as a campsite during the same time span.

Unfortunately, there is little archaeological material left in the park, as most artifacts recovered from these sites have been removed. A new museum at Spalding, scheduled to open in 1980, will feature displays and exhibits describing the various cultures that have lived in the region. Anyone interested in seeing the artifacts collected here should visit the **Washington State University Museum** in Pullman.

For full information about visiting Nez Percé National Park, call or write the Visitors' Center (above).

DIRECTIONS: The park is on U.S. 95, 12 miles east of Lewiston.
HOURS: May–September: 8:00 A.M.–6:00 P.M.
October–April: 8:00 A.M.–4:30 P.M.
ADMISSION: Free.

STATE OFFICE

Thomas J. Green
State Archaeologist
Idaho State Historical Society
610 North Julia Davis Drive
Boise, Idaho 83706 (208) 384-2120

OPPORTUNITIES FOR AMATEURS

Many archaeologists in the state welcome both volunteers and visitors to sites during the summer. For information, get in touch with the office of the state archaeologist (above).

ORGANIZATIONS TO JOIN

The **Idaho Archaeological Society** is an amateur society that works with professionals during the summer months. For information, write:

Idaho Archaeological Society
P.O. Box 7532
Boise, Idaho 83702

OREGON

Divided down the middle by the Cascade Mountains, Oregon is made up of the mountainous Columbia Plateau, the harsh dry Great Basin, and the wet coastline. In its topography, climate, and abundance of fish and other marine life, Oregon resembles Washington, and together the two coastlines comprise the Northwest Coast.

Archaeologists have found traces of human habitation dating back well over nine thousand years in Oregon. At Fort Rock the oldest examples of woven material found anywhere in the world were recovered from a dry cave. The cave is not open to the public, but a marker on Oregon Highway 31 about eighteen miles north of Silver Lake describes the site.

Oregon was the home of many peaceful Indian tribes. The people living east of the Cascades were nomads, surviving on the sparse vegetation and game of the interior region. West of the mountains, early inhabitants lived in long cedar houses and fished for the heavy salmon that literally clogged the rivers and streams. During the winter the people survived easily on plants and game from the forests.

Along the Columbia River, running across the Washington-Oregon border, prehistoric people developed a high culture based on the tremendous runs of migrating salmon. From the town of The Dalles to the mouth of the Snake River, dozens of archaeological sites have yielded large quantities of stone artifacts.

People probably began to live along this stretch of river twelve thousand years ago. Archaeological evidence shows how they adapted to many drastic changes over the millennia. The River culture apparently reached its peak about 1500 A.D. These people of the Columbia River Valley created many fine examples of stone ornaments and carvings from hard granite and gemstones found in the riverbed. Thousands of tools and artifacts have been recovered from the river basin, and many are on display in museums in Oregon and Washington.

Almost all of the prehistoric sites in the Columbia River Valley are on the northern or Washington side of the river. However, three important sites were discovered on the southern side; these were at The Dalles and at the mouth of the Deschutes and John Day rivers. At these sites both carved and chipped artifacts were recovered, including ornaments, beads, bangles, rings, mortars and pestles, pipes, and clubs.

None of the sites is open to the public. The Dalles, the town that marked the end of the Oregon Trail, is an interesting historical place to visit. Here visitors can get an idea of the kind of life led by the Indians thousands of years ago when they camped beside the swiftly running rapids and falls.

Even though artifacts belonging to several different prehistoric cultures have been recovered in Oregon, only a few are presently on exhibit in museums. In the next few years, two new museums are scheduled to open that will fill this gap and be of special interest to amateur archaeologists. In Eugene, the **Oregon State Museum of Natural History** will be part of a large new museum and park complex near the university. The museum will display some of the prehistoric collections belonging to the University of Oregon. And in Bend, the new **Oregon High Desert Museum** is scheduled to open in 1981. This museum will have important displays related to the Great Basin Indians.

MUSEUMS

Klamath Falls

- *Favell Museum of Western Art and Indian Artifacts*
  125 West Main Street
  Klamath Falls, Oregon 97601 *(503) 882-9996*

The museum has a large collection of artifacts from the Columbia River Valley, wood carvings from the Northwest Coast, plus a fine collection of projectile points made from various gemstones of Oregon. Many of these artifacts were recovered by local collectors. Most of the local material has not been documented, and the overall interpretation leans toward the poetic rather than the scientific. Yet this is a large and beautiful museum, and it's a pleasure to browse among the collections.

Other prehistoric collections include pottery from the Southwest and pre-Columbian artifacts from Mexico. In the museum gallery, many regional Indian crafts are combined with western painting and sculpture.

Outdoors, the **Riverside Nature Trail** along the Link River follows an old roadbed where Indians once camped. Pheasants, geese, and small birds shelter in the bushes along the trail.

HOURS: Monday–Saturday: 9:30 A.M.–5:30 P.M.
Sunday: 1:00 P.M.–5:30 P.M.
Closed Mondays from January to April.
ADMISSION: Adults $2, children $1.

- *Klamath County Museum*
  1415 Main Street
  Klamath Falls, Oregon 97601 *(503) 882-2501*

Many local archaeological artifacts are displayed in the museum, but again the interpretation is minimal. One fine display traces the history of the Modoc Indian War that took place between 1872 and 1873. Other exhibits are related to the geology, wildlife, and people of the Klamath Basin.

HOURS: Tuesday–Saturday: 9:00 A.M.–5:00 P.M.
Sunday: 1:00 P.M.–5:00 P.M. (expanded summer hours).
ADMISSION: Free.

The Dalles

For thousands of years, prehistoric people gathered near Celilo Falls to trade and fish for salmon. French fur trappers of Hudson's Bay Company named the site *les dalles* because the basalt cliffs flanking the Columbia River reminded them of the flagstone pavement in their home villages. In pioneer times The Dalles was the end of the Oregon Trail.

Today, The Dalles has many historic sites and buildings. A new **Information Center** is in the planning stage for the town. The building will be on the river bank and will house many of the prehistoric artifacts recovered from the Columbia River Valley.

The **Fort Dalles Museum** is housed in the last remaining building of an old post established during the Yakima Indian wars. The museum is devoted to pioneer memorabilia and history. Covered wagons, stagecoaches, and pioneer relics are on the grounds and inside the museum.

From Seufert Park a free train shuttle takes visitors out to **The Dalles Dam,** where a forty-five-minute tour of the powerhouse, fish ladders, and fish-counting station is available. Here you can visit **Celilo Park,** the old Indian fishing grounds where fishermen speared salmon leaping across the rapids. Celilo Falls is now submerged by waters backed up by the dam, and it's hard to imagine that at one time these falls and rapids were so dangerous that they were almost impassable by boat.

STATE OFFICE

Oregon Archaeological Survey
Oregon State Museum of Anthropology
University of Oregon
Eugene, Oregon 97403

ORGANIZATIONS TO JOIN

The **Oregon Archaeological Society** in Portland is the major amateur organization in the state. The OAS is the largest amateur archaeological society in the Pacific Northwest and one of the largest in the nation with more than 750 members from Alaska to Pennsylvania.

Until recent years the society was known as a collector's organization. Within the last ten years, OAS members have revised their purpose, which is now the preservation and conservation of archaeological sites. Recently, two members successfully lobbied to push two Indian burial protection laws through the Oregon legislature in the face of active opposition from artifact traders.

OAS members participate in professional digs and join in a wide variety of activities that include field trips to excavations all over the Pacific Northwest, monthly meetings with guest speakers, and museum tours; members receive an excellent newsletter called *Screenings.* You can reach the society by writing:

Oregon Archaeological Society
P.O. Box 13293
Portland, Oregon 97213

The **Oregon Archaeological Preservation Committee** is comprised of volunteers dedicated to preserving Oregon's archaeological heritage through public education and legislative action. The OAPC is one of the sponsoring organizations for the **McIver Park Project,** a long-range experimental archaeology program. At McIver Park volunteers and specialists are building a full-size replica of a Chinook plank house, using the same kinds of tools and techniques the Indians did 150 years ago.

During the construction, builders learn and teach authentic Indian crafts and skills, including stone toolmaking, cedar bark processing, and rope making. All of these skills are used to build the house.

When complete, the house will serve as a permanent interpretive center. There will be displays, field trips, and educational programs for children and adults. The McIver State Park is on the Clackamas River, a few miles from Estacada, Oregon. For full information about visiting the project, write:

Oregon Archaeological Preservation Committee
19790 South Old River Drive
West Linn, Oregon 97068

WASHINGTON

Deep rain forests on the Olympic Peninsula, towering, magnificent Mt. Rainier, the Columbia River rolling through rich farmland in the east—all make Washington one of the most splendidly diverse states in the country. The Cascade Mountains, running out of British Columbia all the way to Oregon, are a tough barrier between the dry Columbia Plateau and the damp Pacific coast. The traces of prehistoric Indian life here chronicle a story of hunters and gatherers from earliest Archaic times to the present. People lived from hunting small game and gathering seeds and wild plants. They did no farming and developed no pottery.

Indian tribes living on the plateau east of the Cascades were nomadic hunters, although a few seasonal villages have been discovered. Little changed in their life until contact with Europeans. The oldest human skeletal remains found in the Americas were uncovered at the **Marmes site,** in southeast

Washington. And excavations of the Windust Caves documented the continuous occupation of the area from 7000 B.C. to the present.

Faint migration trails indicate that the coastal Indians of the Pacific Northwest moved westward from the Interior Plateau. Although their life style came to resemble cultures of the Alaska Panhandle, they did not reach this region by traveling down the Alaska coastline. Like their ancestors to the east, the coastal Indians began as hunters and gatherers. Only later did the abundant marine life on the western shore come to define their culture. Over a span of thousands of years, they developed subtle and sophisticated methods of hunting whales, sea lions, and sea otters.

The ongoing excavation at the Ozette site on the Olympic Peninsula has provided a great quantity of new information about the Northwest Coast Indians and has also deciphered some clues to the life of Archaic people in other parts of North America. This is one of North America's most outstanding archaeological sites. A visit to Ozette on the far northern shore of the Olympic Peninsula offers a magnificent day in the field as well as an opportunity to observe one of the most important scientific investigations in the United States.

Washington also offers a wealth of opportunity for the amateur archaeologist; amateurs work with professionals on a great variety of projects including field and laboratory work. The State University Museum in Pullman has major exhibitions from all the important sites in the Northwest.

SITES

Ozette

- *Ozette Village Site*

Two thousand years ago, sudden mud flows seeped through and buried an entire prehistoric village that thrived on Washington's far north coast. In a disaster similar to the eruption of Mount Vesuvius at Pompeii, an entire living society was frozen forever in time. Houses, clothing, and wooden objects that ordinarily would have decayed over the centuries were preserved here intact and in place. The mud-encased village has given archaeologists a rare opportunity to explore a complex and rich prehistoric society.

Life here on the spectacular Olympic Peninsula was relatively opulent, compared to the tough struggle for existence faced by the Indians who lived further inland. Seals and whales migrating to and from the polar region provided the people of Ozette with a plentiful year-round food supply. They specialized in fishing skills and crafts and developed a trading system along the coastline using their long canoes to carry goods and exchange ideas.

In 1966 Dr. Richard Daugherty began to examine the village with his students from Washington State University. Since 1970 a joint excavation undertaken by Dr. Daugherty and the Makah Indians has uncovered whole houses with their furnishings still in place.

The disaster arrested the society in mid-life and preserved it for the future. Findings at Ozette also have provided missing clues to prehistoric life in other parts of the world. Archaeologists are accustomed to finding pieces of stone artifacts and projectile points and can only guess what the original implement looked like. At Ozette the mud has preserved whole weapons, including the wooden shafts. Whole houses are fully preserved—and all manner of new and worn household objects, tools, and implements. Scientists have learned not only how these items were used but how they were made and repaired.

Ozette is an archaeological masterpiece and perhaps the most beautiful remote North American site outside the Southwest. A fine introduction to the site is the multimillion-dollar **Makah Tribal Museum** at Neah Bay, which houses the best material collected from the Ozette site. Neah Bay belongs to the Makah Indians, whose village rests on an ancient shell mound built up by their ancestors. The Makah are famous for their enormous dugout canoes that were used to hunt whales on the open sea.

You have to walk four miles across a gently rolling hillside to reach Ozette, but the walk does not deter sixty thousand people from visiting the site each year.

DIRECTIONS: Follow Washington 112 along the north coast of the Olympic Peninsula toward Neah Bay. Four miles west of Sekiu, turn south on the Hoko Cutoff and follow it 28 miles to Ozette Lake. The road is paved but twisting and rough in spots. There is a small visitors' center at the lake. The 4-mile trek to the ocean is along a wooden walkway.

HOURS: Ozette is open year round, but there is usually little to see in the winter. During the summer tours gather at the Visitors' Center at 9:00 A.M., 11:00 A.M., 2:00 P.M., and 4:00 P.M. A guide takes you through the village and describes the life of the Ozette people. A full excavation crew is usually on hand in the summer months.

The nearest hotels and motels are in Sekiu and Neah Bay; camping sites can be found along Routes 102 and 112.

ADMISSION: Free.

Pasco

• *Sacajawea State Park*
Pasco, Washington 99301 *(509) 545-2361*

At Sacajawea State Park, extensive displays describe the life and times of the Indians who inhabited the Columbia River Basin for ten thousand years and developed one of the highest cultures of the Northwest. Artifacts ranging from crude stone bowls and giant pestles to finely chiseled projectile points made of gemstones are on display.

This state park is one of the many Lewis and Clark campsites. A full range of park services is available, including a boat launch, docking facilities, swimming, and fishing.

DIRECTIONS: From Pasco drive 2 miles southeast off U.S. 12.
HOURS (VISITORS' CENTER): April 15–September 30
10:00 A.M.–6:00 P.M. daily.
ADMISSION: Free.

Vantage

• *Gingko Petrified Forest State Park*
Interpretive Center
Vantage, Washington 98950 *(509) 856-2700*

Amid Washington's farming heartland lies an ancient fossilized forest comprised of two hundred different kinds of trees that lived fifteen million years ago. The state park has rescued a group of petroglyphs that would have been submerged when a new dam raised the water level of Lake Wanapum. Whole slabs of engraved basalt were chiseled out of the cliffside and taken to the museum. Camping year round.

DIRECTIONS: From Moses Lake drive 45 miles west on I-90 to Vantage; follow the directional signs to the park.
HOURS: April 15–September 30: 9:00 A.M.–6:00 P.M. daily.
Rest of year: Weekends only: 8:00 A.M.–5:00 P.M.
ADMISSION: Free.

MUSEUMS

Cashmere

• *Willis Carey Museum*
East Sunset Highway
Cashmere, Washington 98815 *(509) 782-3230*

The museum has large exhibits related to both prehistoric and more recent Indians of the Columbia River Basin, including the Congdon collection of artifacts and human bones.

HOURS: Monday–Friday, holidays: 10:00 A.M.–4:30 P.M.
Saturday and Sunday: 1:00 P.M.–5:00 P.M.
ADMISSION: Free.

Ephrata

- *Wanapum Dam Tour Center*
Box 878
Ephrata, Washington 98823 *(509) 754-3541*

This small, interesting museum displays tools and crafts recovered from the Columbia River Basin. The interpretation describes where the material was found and how archaeologists can trace the life of early people by analyzing excavated artifacts.

HOURS: June–September: 10:00 A.M.–8:00 P.M. daily.
Closed rest of year.
ADMISSION: Free.

Goldendale (Maryhill)

- *Maryhill Museum of Art*
Goldendale, Washington 98620 *(509) 773-4792*

The place where the town of Maryhill now stands was once inhabited by prehistoric people who fished in the river and quarried colored stones near its banks. Large quarry pits where Indians mined a seam of colorful agatized material can still be seen near the basalt bluffs in Maryhill. This stone was used for knives, projectile points, and ornaments. Some artifacts recovered from the river basin are on display in the Maryhill Museum.

The museum is primarily an art museum devoted to sculpture, painting, and ceramics. It has a large collection of Rodin originals and many other fine artworks.

HOURS: March 15–November 15: 9:00 A.M.–5:00 P.M. daily.
Closed rest of year.
ADMISSION: Adults $1.50, senior citizens $1, children six to eighteen 50¢.

Neah Bay

- *Makah Tribal Museum*
Makah Indian Reservation
Neah Bay, Washington 98357 *(206) 645–2711*

This wonderful new museum is located on the Makah Reservation, one of the most picturesque and beautiful regions in the country. Neah Bay at the Northwestern tip of the Olympic Peninsula is known for its spectacular beauty.

In a joint undertaking, archaeologists and members of the Makah tribe have been excavating the nearby **Ozette site.** The museum displays the best material recovered from the dig. Many interpretive exhibits of basket weaving, woodwork, and artifacts detail the art and survival techniques of these prehistoric Indians. Across the museum walls, magnificent murals portray the Ozette village as it must have looked two thousand years ago. As you travel on the Makah Indian Reservation, you are asked to respect the privacy of its citizens.

HOURS: 11:00 A.M.–6:00 P.M. daily in summer.
ADMISSION: Free.

Pullman

• *Museum of Anthropology*
Washington State University
Pullman, Washington 99164 *(509) 335–8556*

This university museum has the most impressive archaeological collection in Washington, including an exhibit of prehistoric basket weaving techniques, displays from the Ozette dig, and the important St. Lawrence Island excavation in the Bering Strait. Other important displays are from the Marmes dig in the Palouse River Valley near Pullman. Before the site was submerged by water from a new dam, skulls, scrapers, and needles more than ten thousand years old were found in the soil.

HOURS: Monday–Friday: 10:00 A.M.–4:00 P.M.
Closed school holidays and vacations.
ADMISSION: Free.

Seattle

• *Thomas Burke Memorial State Museum*
University of Washington
Seventeenth Avenue Northeast and Northeast 45th Street
Seattle, Washington 98195 *(206) 543-5590*

This large museum has some prehistoric artifacts, but the displays are short on interpretation. The major Indian collections from the historic period reflect the life of peoples of the Pacific rim. The life styles, beliefs, crafts, and art of the Northwest Coast Indians are explored in extensive exhibits. The Nootka, Makah, Kwakiutl, Tlingit, Haida, and Tsimshian are some of the Northwest tribes represented. Other exhibits come from Southeast Asia, Australia, and the islands of the South Pacific.

Outdoors, nature walks take visitors to a great variety of native plants and trees. An exhibit guide book is available at the sales counter.

HOURS: Tuesday–Saturday: 10:00 A.M.–4:30 P.M.
Sunday: 1:00 P.M.–4:30 P.M.
Closed university holidays.
ADMISSION: Free.

Spokane

- *Cheney Cowles Memorial Museum*
West 2316 First Avenue
Spokane, Washington 99200 *(509) 456-3931*

Collections and dioramas trace the development of regional Indian cultures from prehistoric times to the modern age, with special emphasis on the arts and artifacts of the Interior Plateau Indians.

HOURS: Tuesday–Saturday: 10:00 A.M.–5:00 P.M.
Sunday: 2:00 P.M.–5:00 P.M.
Closed major holidays.
ADMISSION: Free.

- *Museum of Native American Cultures*
East 200 Cataldo Avenue
Spokane, Washington 99200 *(509) 326-4550*

Spokane, called the "hub of the Inland Empire," is very different in topography and climate from coastal Washington. Survival was harder here than in the more opulent region to the west. The contrasting cultures that evolved within these distinct geographical regions are explored in this museum, which may have the largest collection of Indian artifacts in the Northwest.

HOURS: Monday–Saturday: 9:00 A.M.–5:30 P.M.
Sunday: 12:00 M.–5:30 P.M.
ADMISSION: Free.

Tacoma

- *Washington State Historical Society Museum*
315 North Stadium Way
Tacoma, Washington 98403 *(206) 593-2830*

The museum is devoted to archaeological and historical study of the Pacific Northwest. A small display is given over to prehistoric artifacts.

HOURS: Tuesday–Saturday: 9:00 A.M.–4:00 P.M.
Sunday: 2:00 P.M.–5:00 P.M.
Closed Mondays and holidays.
ADMISSION: Free.

Wenatchee

- *Rocky Reach Dam*
  Wenatchee, Washington 98801 — *(509) 663-8121*

Exhibits in the Information Center of the Rocky Reach Dam trace life along the river for over ten thousand years. There is also a Gallery of Electricity that traces the history of electric power. Visitors to the dam can view fish swimming upstream along a 1350-foot fish ladder.

DIRECTIONS: The dam is 7 miles north of Wenatchee on U.S. 97.
HOURS: 8:00 A.M.–5:00 P.M. daily (till 8:00 P.M. in summer).
ADMISSION: Free.

Yakima

- *Yakima Valley Museum and Historical Association*
  2105 Tieton Drive
  Franklin Park
  Yakima, Washington 98902 — *(509) 248-0747*

The museum houses a small number of prehistoric artifacts and some pictographs rescued from a reservoir. About three miles from Yakima, a group of Indian painted rocks are located on a firing range. You can ask museum personnel for information about visitors' permits.

HOURS: Wednesday–Friday: 10:00 A.M.–5:00 P.M.
Saturday and Sunday: 12:00 M.–5:00 P.M.
ADMISSION: Families $1.50, adults $1, students 50¢.

STATE OFFICE

Sheila A. Stump
State Archaeologist
Office of Archaeology and Historic Preservation
111 West 21st Street
Olympia, Washington 98504 — (206) 753-4405

OPPORTUNITIES FOR AMATEURS AND ORGANIZATIONS TO JOIN

Washington State offers amateurs an opportunity to participate in archaeology at almost every level. The state archaeologist invites, "anyone who wants to get involved in archaeology can call me. We'll find a place for him."

Plans for field schools and workshops are under way, and the state will soon offer a qualifying program that will permit trained people to be hired as paraprofessionals and be paid for their services. Washington is the only state that has a special elite amateur group called "qualified archaeologists." These are people who have completed at least three years of training and who are recommended by two professionals.

Because there is so much opportunity for amateurs to participate in the state, the fines for unauthorized diggings are severe. Each day's violation carries its own $10,000 fine—and the office of archaeology does not hesitate to prosecute.

Amateur Societies: Clearly, there is work for everyone interested in archaeology in this state. The office of archaeology issues excavating permits to members of the state's two amateur societies and works closely with both of these groups. The two societies are: the **Washington Archaeological Society** and the **Mid-Columbia Archaeological Society.** The current address of both organizations can be obtained from the state archaeologist.

Visiting Digs: Almost all of Washington's excavations welcome visitors during the summer. For information about excavations-in-progress, contact the state archaeologist.

ALASKA

Alaska is a major hunting ground for archaeologists. If there is proof to be found that America was inhabited earlier than 10,000 B.C., it is here—at this northern entry point—that scientists expect to find it. This northernmost part of the United States was never covered by ice sheets and may have been inhabited even during the most severe periods of glaciation.

Hundreds of prehistoric sites were turned up during the construction of the eight-hundred-mile Alaskan pipeline. Flint scrapers, small microblades, and projectile points were uncovered by the thousands. The location of the sites indicates that the early inhabitants of Alaska were nomads, depending on caribou herds and fish runs for their livelihood. Ancient whalebone sled runners and white mink bones, along with copper and obsidian, were found hundreds of miles north of their origin, pointing to a mobile way of existence.

It's ironic that Alaska should be the place where the first people entered America, since today it is the most difficult state to reach and explore. It is over twice as large as Texas and has more coastline than the entire "lower 48" as Alaskans call the continental United States. The state has few paved highways, and most roads are gravel or dirt. Travel in Alaska means airplanes. Every conceivable type of air transportation, from commercial airliners to small planes fitted with skis or pontoons, flies Alaska. Up the inland water route from British Columbia, ferryboats ply the waterways carrying freight and tourists.

Perhaps the most interesting and adventurous way to enter Alaska is through the Yukon by way of the Alaska Highway. Between Dawson Creek, British Columbia, and Fairbanks, Alaska, most of the 1520-mile road is gravel and towns are scarce. Jeeps and pickups have the easiest time, but regular automobiles can and do trek along the all-weather road. Yukon windshields are scarred from pebbles coughed up by fast-moving trucks; these are proud (and common) emblems for Al-Can trekkers.

Except for a small igloo within Katmai National Park, no archaeological sites have been prepared for the public in Alaska. But the state offers unique opportunities to visit with descendants of the earliest Americans. One-fifth of Alaska's present population are Native Americans who stem from three main groups: Eskimos (Inuit), Aleuts, and Indians. The Eskimos, who live along the coasts of the Bering Sea and the Arctic and the deltas of the Yukon and Kuskokwim rivers, are by far the most numerous.

Southeastern Alaska and the north central interior are Indian country. The Tlingits, Haidas and Tsimshians once had thriving communities in the southeast. Today, their descendants live in villages near Sitka and Ketchikan. In the interior the Athapascan Indians were isolated nomads who hunted moose and caribou across the Alaskan tundra. Several hundred years ago, some of the Athapascans moved south and became the Navajo and Apache Indians of the Southwest.

The smallest remaining group are the Aleuts, who have lived in villages along the fog-soaked Aleutian Island chain for two thousand years. The Aleuts were ruthlessly persecuted by the Russians, and their numbers were drastically reduced. The few remaining full-blooded Aleuts live in villages on the Priboloff Islands, the Alaskan Peninsula, and the Aleutian Islands.

Native Alaskans are friendly and hospitable, and it's an adventure to reach some of their remote villages in the Alaskan wilderness. Since most small villages have no overnight accommodations, travelers must rely on the generosity of the villagers for sustenance and shelter. Most villages can be reached only by bush plane. There are hundreds of bush pilots in Alaska, all willing and happy to go adventuring. These excursions are unique and exciting, also expensive—but if you are prepared for the cost, few trips could be more enlightening.

Before heading for Alaska, it's a good idea to explore the literature about this rugged state. Travelers must depend on small airplanes and bush pilots to reach outlying areas in this vast region of rain forests, glaciers, open tundra, and icy coastlines. Check all schedules and tour packages ahead of time. Airlines are happy to send you colorful brochures on different regions. For full information about visiting Alaska, write:

Alaska Division of Tourism
Pouch E
Juneau, Alaska 99811

Map of Alaska.

Since Alaska is so large, sites and museums will be listed according to region in the state, moving from south to north, as well as by city or town location. The map shown here should help identify the areas discussed.

SOUTHEASTERN PANHANDLE

Alaska is divided into the southeastern panhandle and the larger "cup." The major towns of the panhandle, including Juneau, are not connected by road; the narrow strip of coastland is separated from Canada and from northern Alaska by impassable ice fields. Boats are the main form of transportation in the southeast.

This is the home of the Tlingit Indians, who have lived in this rainy region since prehistoric times. Today in the southeastern panhandle of Alaska, the Tlingits and their neighbors to the south, the Haidas, nurture their cultural heritage in Sitka, Ketchikan, and in smaller villages nearby where they continue to follow their traditional ways.

The Tlingits and the Haidas migrated to this region thousands of years ago. They slowly established a rich culture based on fishing, hunting, and collecting wild plants. In this lush, productive country, they developed a highly artistic culture. They lived together in villages comprised of family clan houses, each house big enough for fifty or sixty people. In the spring villagers fished and prepared food for the winter. Winter was the time for art, woodcarving, and music making.

Although Sitka was first settled by the Russians in 1799, the fur trappers never conquered the Tlingit country further north. These tribes defended themselves against all intruders, including other Indian tribes. They were fierce warriors and they tenaciously protected their villages and continued their pursuit of the civilized arts.

Tlingit art is unique and easily recognizable. Flowing lines create abstract designs of animals and people, colored in muted shades of yellow, blue, and red. The Tlingits carved oceangoing canoes and totem poles from cedar logs. They erected the poles in villages and sometimes inside their houses. It takes experience and knowledge to read the designs on a totem pole. Mythology, politics, art, and social life are all recorded in the designs that circle the poles all the way to the top—a height sometimes exceeding sixty feet.

The wood and colors of the totem poles deteriorate rapidly in the damp salty air of Alaska. When the population of the Indians decreased, the art of totem-pole making began to decline. As remaining Indians adjusted to the life of their invaders, few totem poles were made to replace those that were disintegrating. By the 1930s most existing poles had been removed to protected totem parks near Ketchikan and Klawock. Some of the best examples can be seen today at **Totem Bight,** a state park near Ketchikan. The art of totem-pole making is being renewed at the **Alaska Indian Arts, Inc.** in Port Chilkoot.

Port Chilkoot is adjacent to Haines, Alaska (see listing below). The Alaska Indian Arts program was created to perpetuate the art and craft of the Tlingits, mainly the Chilkat tribe. Here in old **Fort William Seward,** visitors are welcome to walk around the parade grounds and observe various ongoing projects. Every summer, in the barracks gymnasium, the colorful Chilkat dancers perform. Dancers make their own costumes and instruments. In classrooms visitors can watch crafts—soapstone, ivory and wood carvings, and work in silver and copper—being skillfully reproduced. Totem poles in various stages of sculpturing can be seen on the grounds.

You can pick up a town map and a walking tour pamphlet at the **Halsingland Hotel** or the Chamber of Commerce in Port Chilkoot. There is lodging in the hotel and camping and trailer space behind the Halsingland. The **Glacier Camper Park** just north of Haines has complete camping facili-

This Eskimo ceremonial doll is carved from ivory and has inlaid copper eyes. At one time it was dressed in an elaborate costume and beads which have long since been lost. Circa 1850, Point Barrow, Alaska. (Photo courtesy of the Museum of the American Indian, Heye Foundation.)

ties. To fully grasp the colorful history of these two towns, visit the **Sheldon Museum** housed in its new building near the Haines waterfront.

Haines

- *Alaska Indian Arts, Inc.*
P.O. Box 271
Port Chilkoot
Haines, Alaska 99827 *(907) 766-2160*

Although there are some artifacts from prehistoric periods on display here, the main purpose of this enterprising cultural center is to provide a marketplace for contemporary Indian arts and crafts. Every effort is being made to perpetuate the heritage of the Tlingit Indians. The museum is in an old hospital in Fort William H. Seward. Replicas of a small Indian village and tribal house have been constructed on the parade grounds. Dances, demonstrations, and classroom activities are all open to visitors.

DIRECTIONS: Haines and Port Chilkoot are side by side on the northern end of the panhandle. They are accessible by inland waterway or air. From the Alaska Highway, the Haines Highway splits off 100 miles west of Whitehorse in Yukon Territory.

HOURS: Monday–Friday: 9:00 A.M.–12:00 M. and 1:00 P.M.–5:00 P.M. Closed weekends.

ADMISSION: Free.

Juneau

- *Alaska State Museum*
  Whittier Street (near Egan Drive)
  Juneau, Alaska 99811 *(907) 586-1224*

Politicians, residents, fishermen, and tourists converge on the small capital city of Alaska in cruise ships, ferryboats, and yachts. Small planes equipped with floats land at the city dock, and there's a regular airport for jets. But there are no roads in or out of Juneau. The town is edged by a dense rain forest that climbs the steep slopes of a nine-thousand-foot mountain range. Above the forest rises the vast Juneau ice field, source of massive glaciers and an awesome sight to airborne visitors. Just thirteen miles from downtown Juneau is the Mendenhall glacier, with its two-hundred-foot ice face.

The Alaska State Museum is a storehouse of artifacts dating back as far as two thousand years and represents the rich cultures of the Aleut, Athapascan, and Tlingit Indians. Many other fascinating exhibits trace the city's colorful Russian history. The museum is housed in large new headquarters within walking distance from the main waterfront area.

HOURS: Summer: Monday–Friday: 9:00 A.M.–9:00 P.M.
Winter: Saturday and Sunday: 1:00 P.M.–9:00 P.M.
Museum closes at 5:00 P.M. daily.

ADMISSION: Free.

Sitka

- *Sitka National Historical Park Museum*
  P.O. Box 738
  Sitka, Alaska 99835 *(907) 747-6281*

Sitka was once the center of the Tlingit Indian nation. This museum was built to commemorate the battle between the Tlingit and the Russians in 1804, in which the Tlingit were defeated. The few displays of blanket weaving, totem poles, and other crafts are rich examples of the Indian culture before the Europeans arrived. Remnants of old totem poles can be seen on the park grounds. Footpaths trace the foundation of the last Indian fort in Alaska, and lush ferns, mosses, and shrubs overgrow the trails.

Guides and personnel in the Visitors' Center are knowledgeable about the history of the Tlingit Indians. In one section of the museum, visitors can watch native artists at work.

HOURS: Summer: 8:00 A.M.–8:00 P.M. daily.
Winter: Monday–Saturday: 8:00 A.M.–5:00 P.M.
Closed Thanksgiving, Christmas, New Year's.

ADMISSION: Free.

Note: On Sitka's lively waterfront is **Totem Square** where Tlingit Indians carved a fifty-foot war canoe that stands outside the Centennial Building. There are hotels and motels in Sitka, and campers have their choice of two Forest Service primitive campgrounds: one next to the ferry building and the other about seven miles from town. These campgrounds are part of **Tongass,** the largest national forest in the United States.

THE INTERIOR

The interior is an immense sprawling region enveloped by the Alaska and Brooks ranges. Most of the land is a roadless wilderness. The great Yukon River wanders past small native villages on its way to the Bering Sea. Here in the very center of Alaska, the temperature drops and soars to extremes: −75° F in the winter, and 90 or 100° F in the brief summer.

For thousands of years, the Athapascan Indians have called this territory their own, fishing for salmon in summer and hunting caribou and moose in the winter. They roamed all over the interior, never staying long in any one place. Today, many Athapascans live in native villages along the Yukon and Kuskokwim rivers. At Fort Yukon, just north of the Arctic Circle, a museum housed in a log cabin shows some good examples of Athapascan crafts (see below).

Fairbanks is the hub of the interior. During the 1902 gold strike, fortune hunters flocked to the banks of the Chena River, making Fairbanks the most exciting boom town in the world. In the 1960s the oil strike created another boom. Through the years the town has retained some of its rough edges and frontier informality. But the area has grown rapidly. Fairbanks is crowded, prices are high, and housing is scarce. But for archaeological interest, Fairbanks should not be missed; the University of Alaska Museum (see listing below) houses the finest collection of prehistoric material in the state.

Anchorage

● *Anchorage Historical and Fine Arts Museum*
121 West Seventh Avenue
Anchorage, Alaska 99501 *(907) 264-4326*

Anchorage is the prosperous, rough-hewn melting pot of a city that 175,000 Alaskans call home. Its growth has been unchecked in the past two decades and promises to continue. Shopping centers, skyscrapers, and suburbs are all a part of the metropolis that sits on the fringe of a wilderness.

The Historical and Fine Arts Museum has exhibits illustrating the history and art of all the many cultures of Alaska. There are some prehistoric artifacts, but most exhibits come from more recent periods.

HOURS: Summer
Monday–Saturday: 9:00 A.M.–5:00 P.M.
Tuesday and Thursday: 9:00 A.M.–9:00 P.M.
Sunday: 1:00 P.M.–5:00 P.M.
Winter
Tuesday–Saturday: 9:00 A.M.–5:00 P.M.
Sunday: 1:00 P.M.–5:00 P.M.
Closed national holidays.
ADMISSION: Free.

Fairbanks

- *University of Alaska Museum*
Eilson Memorial Building
University of Alaska
Fairbanks, Alaska 99701 *(907) 479-7505*

The University of Alaska, just northwest of Fairbanks, is a center for Arctic research and the major university in the state. The Institute of Arctic Biology explores the plants of the Alaskan tundra. And at the Geophysical Institute, scientists launch probes into the aurora borealis in an attempt to discover the origin of the northern lights. The university has a total of eighty-five hundred students in nine communities, including Anchorage.

The University of Alaska Museum has the most important archaeological collections in Alaska. The exhibits chronicle the rise of prehistoric cultures from the five major regions of the state, with emphasis on the far northern tribes. During the construction of the Alaska pipeline, 181 new sites were discovered, and the museum has added recent collections from these sites. Also featured are Masterpieces of Prehistoric Eskimo Art.

A collection of early artifacts brought from St. Lawrence, an island in the Bering Strait just forty miles from Siberia, is particularly exciting since archaeologists are striving to trace the movements of the early travelers on the now nonexistent land bridge. Tours of the museum can be arranged at the Information Desk.

DIRECTIONS: The campus is 4 miles northwest of Fairbanks in College.
HOURS: Summer
9:00 A.M.–5:00 P.M. daily.
Winter
1:00 P.M.–5:00 P.M. daily.
Closed Christmas, New Year's.
ADMISSION: Free.

Homer

- *Pratt Museum*
P.O. Box 682
Homer, Alaska 99603 *(907) 235-8635*

It's worth a trip to visit this picturesque town set against mountain glaciers and ringed by deep icy harbors. The Pratt has some anthropological and archaeological exhibits as well as totem poles and other Alaskan Indian crafts. The personnel at the Information Center are knowledgeable about the colorful history of the Kenai Peninsula and helpful to travelers.

Homer is a developing resort area with good motels, hotels, and restaurants. There are tours of Kachemak Bay where whales sound and porpoises frolic. The whole region has a distinctly Russian flavor blended with the native Alaskan heritage.

HOURS: Summer
10:00 A.M.–5:00 P.M. daily.
Sunday: 1:00 P.M.–5:00 P.M.
Winter
Tuesday–Saturday: 10:00 A.M.–5:00 P.M.
Closed December and January.
ADMISSION: Adults $1.

King Salmon

- *Katmai National Monument*
  P.O. Box 7
  King Salmon, Alaska 99613

It takes an adventuresome, not to say hardy, traveler to make this one hour and twenty minute journey by jet and pontooned plane from Anchorage to Katmai. But the rewards are great, for Katmai is one of the nation's wildest and most beautiful parks. The region is a national game preserve where hair seals and sea lions sun themselves on the rocks along the rugged coastline, and caribou and moose run free in the woods. The world's largest carnivore, the Alaska brown bear, is sometimes seen (hopefully from a distance) fishing for salmon along the water's edge. Katmai was the scene of a sudden volcanic eruption in 1912 that drove its population from the peninsula.

Archaeological evidence of two nomadic cultures dating back six thousand years and forty-five hundred years have been found here. Through the millennia the prehistoric people from Bristol Bay gradually merged with the older gulf tribes as trade through the Katmai Pass brought them closer together.

Because there is only one road through the park, the archaeological sites are difficult to reach in the rough back country. However, near Brooks Camp an Eskimo igloo, or barabara, has been found and restored. Interpretive displays illustrate how the igloo was constructed and how it served the prehistoric people who lived here.

DIRECTIONS: The usual way to reach Katmai is by Wien Air Alaska, which operates regular flights to Brooks Camp via King Salmon from

June 1 to September 7. For information about air reservations and lodging in the park, write or call:
Wien Air Alaska
4100 International Airport Road
Anchorage, Alaska 99502 (904) 277-5501

THE YUKON

Canadian Yukon

A valley in the northern Yukon—the **Old Crow Basin**—is the scene of current archaeological excitement. Every year, the old Crow River, swollen by the spring melt, rushes over its course, gouging out the fossilized bones of dozens of species of Ice Age animals from beneath layers of sediment. Many of these old bones show distinct signs of human alteration: some are broken by butchering, others chipped into knives and scrapers. If these tools are as old as scientists believe, the earliest human implements were made of bone, not rock.

The first traces of human habitation of the Old Crow Basin were discovered by Peter Lord in the summer of 1966. Lord, an expert trapper and hunter, joined a field expedition led by Canadian paleontologist C. R. Harington. One day in the field, Lord picked up a finely chiseled caribou bone lying on the surface at the river's bend. The serrated tool appeared to be a "flesher," used to scrape animal hides. The artifact was turned over to Dr. William Irving of the University of Toronto for radiocarbon dating. The result of the test sent a tremor of anticipation through the scientific community. The carved bone gave a reading of twenty-seven thousand years, a finding that may extend the date of human entry onto the continent thousands of years.

Since the initial discovery of the flesher, two major archaeological assaults have been launched on the basin: the Northern Yukon Research Programme, under the direction of Dr. Irving, and the Yukon Refugium Project, led by Dr. Richard E. Morlan of the National Museums of Canada. Both teams are digging out thousands of fossilized animal bones—bones of tigers, horses, and mammoths washing out of the muddy river bank are being inspected for signs of human alteration. Fossilized bone is difficult to date by radiocarbon analysis and the information coming in from the Old Crow site is still indefinite, but scientists believe that some of the material may prove to be twice as old as the flesher.

The important work at the Old Crow site will continue for years, but this Yukon site, like nearby Alaskan sites, is not open to the public.

Fort Yukon

● *Dinjii Zhuu Enjit Museum*
P.O. Box 42
Fort Yukon, Alaska 99740 *(907) 662-2345*

This museum is a natural stopping point for anyone who ventures north of the Arctic Circle, where temperatures are reputed to run from 100° F to −78° F. **Fort Yukon,** hub of the Yukon Flats area, has the largest Indian population in Alaska. Its museum, housed in a log cabin, exhibits artifacts from the early Athapascan Indians who share a common ancestry with the Navajo and Apache who now live in the Southwest.

HOURS: Summer: Monday–Friday: 1:00 P.M.–4:00 P.M.
Winter: By appointment.
ADMISSION: $1.

THE ARCTIC

The Eskimos, Alaska's largest native population, make their home on the state's outer rim, bordering the Arctic Ocean and the Bering and Chukchi seas, all the way to the northernmost tip of the continent. Beginning around the year 1800, outsiders began to explore the Arctic and returned with stories of adventure along with the furs and other wealth they sought.

Since the early 1950s the Arctic has become a place for sightseers, via Wien Air Alaska, and today you can visit the region at any time of year. The Arctic, still unique, is rapidly changing, although the Eskimos cling tenaciously to their traditional ways. They are perhaps the world's most hospitable people.

Whether you leave from Anchorage or Fairbanks, if you want to visit the Eskimos, you must fly. The Arctic's three major cities—Nome, Kotzebue, and Barrow—are reached by regularly scheduled jet flights. From these cities bush pilots fly to Prudhoe Bay, Point Hope, and to many smaller Eskimo villages including Egegik, Ugashik, and Anaktuvuk.

Wherever you go, you will see all the phases of culture and art with which the Eskimos enrich their life in these remote corners of the world: music, games, sledding and hunting, boatmaking, and blanket tossing. Eskimo crafts are meticulously fashioned from ivory, gold, bone, jade, soapstone, and various skins and furs. You can purchase arts and crafts directly from the native people or browse through many small shops and museums.

Scientists at the **Naval Arctic Research Laboratory,** just four miles out of Barrow, sometimes turn up prehistoric artifacts while studying polar bears in the field or exploring for oil. After they are recorded, the artifacts

This Tlingit copper mask represents the Broad Bear, a mythological creature. It is decorated with abalone shell and fringed with bear fur; the teeth are made of mountain-goat horn. Circa 1875, Sitka, Alaska. (Photo courtesy of the Museum of the American Indian, Heye Foundation.)

are shown in a small exhibit room at the laboratory, along with exhibits of Arctic plants and animals and other interesting displays. The laboratory is open to the public during regular office hours between 8:00 A.M. and 5:00 P.M., Monday through Saturday. For information, call (907) 852-7333.

DIRECTIONS: Munz Airlines is one of the best ways to fly the Arctic. If you have any special place you would like to stop, you can check with the airline and ask when it is making a trip. There are regular flights as well as special charters. Munz Northern Airlines flies out of Nome, Kotzebue, and St. Mary's.

STATE OFFICE

Douglas Reger
State Archaeologist
Department of Natural Resources
619 Warehouse Drive, Suite 210
Anchorage, Alaska 99501

OPPORTUNITIES FOR AMATEURS AND ORGANIZATIONS TO JOIN

Anyone interested in participating in archaeological work in Alaska should get in touch with:

Alaska Anthropological Association
University of Alaska
2651 Providence Drive
Anchorage, Alaska 99504

POTHUNTERS, VANDALS, . . . AND AMATEURS

I thought more than twice about closing with a word about pothunters. Amateur archaeologists are not pothunters and are tired of being associated with them. But some of the misunderstandings that continue to exist about pothunters versus amateurs should be cleared up.

In the 1930s professional archaeologists disdained and distrusted amateurs. The so-called amateur was destroying archaeological sites before professionals could get to them. At that time most sites were on public land, and many people figured that since they qualified as "the public," they had a license to dig. They tunneled into mounds and carried away fabulous artifacts. They broke into silent cliff dwellings where no one had trod for centuries and carried away truckloads of exquisite pottery. It is easy to understand why the cold war between professionals and amateurs lasted for so many years.

Scars from this "open season" on public sites are still seen today. Scientists in the Midwest have added a fourth category to the basic mound groups: conical mounds, flat-topped mounds, effigy mounds—and donut mounds, where pothunters have scooped out the crowns and dug through to the center.

Often this destruction of precious sites was perpetrated by overzealous amateurs trying to excavate scientifically. In the process they inadvertently destroyed the sites.

Amateurs and professionals finally have begun to bridge the abyss between them. There is so much important work to do that serious amateurs are now welcome in many different capacities. Amateurs, often called avocational archaeologists, observe, record, and report their findings. They also assist professionals in the field and in the laboratory. Today, amateurs have a vital role in the scientific community, and most scientists appreciate their contribution. Further, amateur archaeologists are aligned with the professionals against pothunters who use valuable sites for their own personal gain.

Granted, some scientists are still amateur-shy. But at hundreds of sites around the country, I learned that most professionals value amateur assistance and are eager to help serious people become productively involved in scientific work.

Dr. W. Fred Kinsey, director of the North Museum at Franklin and Marshall College in Pennsylvania, works regularly with amateurs in the field, the laboratory, and the museum. "Their motivation varies from superficial and gee whiz to deep, sustaining, and thoughtful," says Dr. Kinsey. "Some amateurs are more professional than some professionals." His view is shared by most professionals today.

Unhappily, some people continue to destroy archaeological sites. Perhaps the most unnecessary situation occurs when a well-meaning amateur wants to dig but has no proper training. He finds a likely site but doesn't report it to his local archaeological society or university. Instead, he tackles it himself, and destroys the site because he neither excavates properly nor records his findings.

Amateurs complain that professionals ignore them when they report sites; if they didn't dig (and, in some cases, dive), the sites wouldn't be excavated at all. This is an unfortunate situation. The amateur is frustrated, the professional is irritated, and the science suffers.

Again, because of the great need for the work to get done (plus the amateurs' growing awareness of the need to protect sites), the situation is beginning to improve. There is more help for amateurs today, and they don't have to excavate on their own. As more and more states offer certification programs and more lay-professional societies are formed, the unwitting destruction of sites will become a thing of the past.

The pothunter is a different fish entirely. There are many kinds of pothunters. First, there is the person avid to collect and possess something from the past. This trait is so human that anyone can understand it. You walk across a plowed field and discover a projectile point or arrowhead at your feet. Who wouldn't put it in his pocket and take it home to contemplate? Or a broken fragment of pottery, or even a handful of ancient clam shells washing out of a river bank. This kind of collector is easily converted to serious amateur. The public education programs, sponsored by amateur archaeological societies, have helped collectors recognize the importance of leaving artifacts in place and reporting sites.

Much more dangerous are pothunters who loot known sites for treasures that can be sold to private collectors. With total disregard for everyone else, they steal valuable artifacts and profit from their theft, destroying important sites in the process. The collectors who buy from them are equally guilty. It is said that the finest collections of prehistoric pottery in the Southwest will never be seen in any museum. Instead they reside in private homes.

There is yet a third category of "pothunter"—far more common and even less understandable than the others: vandals. Countless valuable sites have been destroyed by sheer vandalism. The giant desert intaglios along the California-Arizona border are perhaps the most shocking instance. These great figures of animals and people carved out of the desert are as long as 130 feet. Nowhere else on the continent can such drawings be found. No one knows who fashioned them, or when, or why. They are figures of great beauty and mystery and of enormous scientific interest.

The intaglios lie in a remote desert away from main roads. You must go miles out of your way to find them. Yet people with jeeps and motorcycles have raced back and forth across their outlines, deliberately trying to erase the magnificent drawings.

To defend the fragile desert pictures, a team of amateurs set up a "desert watch" in an effort to protect them. I saw the intaglios in 1979. The access road was clearly posted, "No 4-wheel drive," and it is impossible to take a regular car into the rough terrain. Legally, the only way to approach is to leave your automobile at the end of the access road and proceed on foot. Still, there was no one to prevent off-road vehicles from trespassing.

All over the country, site after site has been closed to the public because of vandalism. Going down the San Juan River in the southeastern corner of Utah with Ken Ross—archaeologist, geologist, and old-time river man—we beached the raft and hiked a half mile inland to look at some petroglyphs pecked on a high sheer wall. As we drew close to a beautiful etching of three people standing side by side with their arms across one another's shoulders, like three youngsters walking down Main Street, I saw writing scrawled across the body of the picture.

"It's my fault," Ken said, peering over my shoulder. "I brought some people out here on an expedition, and this lady reached up and scratched her name over the picture. I couldn't believe it. And you know, she was a *schoolteacher.*" There was a trace of disillusionment in his voice.

These days, Ken keeps some of his secret places to himself. Even students and scientists are sometimes held back until the river man is sure of their intent. For example, he no longer takes geology students (who never go anywhere without picks and rock busters) to ancient coral fossil beds that line the cliff tops. "They're too fast for me," says Ken, who was the interpretive archaeologist when Mesa Verde opened in the 1930s and today must be well into his sixties. "I turn my head for a minute, and they're up there hacking away at the coral with their picks. It's just instinct with them . . . they want a specimen to take home and put under a microscope."

In this high bluff country that millions of years ago was an ocean bed, the very rocks are part of the panorama of history. Some of them are so old in time that their age is beyond the imagination to conceive. One stands near the cliff, reaching up tentatively to explore the smooth strands of fossilized coral with fingertips. This delicate formation lived three hundred million years ago. To break one deliberately is like destroying a work of art.

The prehistoric Indian who drew his story on this cliffside so long ago had no other way to speak past his lifetime. He had no written language, no way to leave his story behind. This drawing was not only his art, it was his spark of life. We cannot precisely interpret most ancient pictures, but we do know that they were someone's striving to leave something behind, to communicate with those who would come later, perhaps the next day, the next week—the next lifetime.

They tell of simple, everyday things—births and deaths, successes and sometimes failure. They are small personal stories painted on enduring canvases. The best way to grow closer to the story of ancient man is to stand still and observe. Rest a moment in his footsteps, place your hand against the warm stone where he placed his. Feel the sensation of his presence and listen to him. He speaks across time, across the wind, and in his small pictures is the infinite beauty of his life.

APPENDIX 1

SPECIAL SCIENTIFIC EXPEDITIONS

A new idea in research is the scientific expedition that takes along volunteers. Each member of the crew makes a tax-deductible contribution to the expedition, providing funds for important research while gaining a rare opportunity to join scientists in the field.

Several archaeological expeditions are offered each year by the **University Research Expeditions Program** sponsored by the University of California. No special qualifications are necessary to join most of these expeditions. Field directors look for people who are interested, want to learn, and are willing to work. The financial contribution varies, depending on the length of the expedition and the locale. For information, write:

University Research Expeditions Program
University of California
Berkeley, California 94720

Earthwatch is another unique organization that matches scientific projects with amateur volunteers. Earthwatch sponsors various scientific expeditions all over the world, many of them devoted to archaeology. Research teams are usually small, between four and twelve people, and volunteers range in age from sixteen to eighty. There is room for almost everyone. Crew members share the cost by making a tax-deductible contribution.

For a nominal fee, Earthwatch advises its members of expedition schedules throughout the year. For information, write:

Earthwatch
10 Juniper Road
Box 127
Belmont, Massachusetts 02178

An exciting departure in adventure travel is offered by a few organizations that now provide wilderness trips guided by professional scientists. Professionals in various fields are involved, including archaeologists, biologists, botanists, geologists, and ornithologists. When you request information about current schedules, always specify that you are interested in archaeology. Many times special trips are arranged if enough people are interested in a given subject.

The following travel organizations usually offer at least one archaeological expedition each year:

American River Touring Association
1307 Harrison Street
Oakland, California 94612

American Wilderness Alliance
4260 East Evans Avenue
Denver, Colorado 80222

Chihuahuan Desert Research Institute
P.O. Box 1334
Alpine, Texas 79830

In the Tracks of Fremont
P.O. Box 18346
Steamboat, Nevada 89546

Smithsonian Associates Travel Program
Smithsonian Institution
Washington, D.C. 20560

Southwest Safaris
P.O. Box 945
Santa Fe, New Mexico 87501

Wild & Scenic, Inc.
P.O. Box 2123
Marble Canyon, Arizona 86036

Wild River Expeditions
Box 110
Bluff, Utah 84512

APPENDIX 2

NATIONAL ORGANIZATIONS

The **Archaeological Institute of America** has many interesting services and programs for amateurs. Members receive one or both of the institute's journals—the popular *Archaeology* magazine or the *American Journal of Archaeology,* a scholarly publication.

The institute also publishes several pamphlets of interest to both students and archaeology buffs. *Fieldwork Opportunities,* an up-to-date list of volunteer and staff positions available on digs around the world, is brought out every year.

Members can also join tours to important archaeological sites. All of these jaunts are led by distinguished scholars and scientists in the field of archaeology. For membership information, write:

Archaeological Institute of America
100 Washington Square East
New York, New York 10003

Other national organizations that may be of interest to amateurs include:

American Anthropological Association
1703 New Hampshire Avenue NW
Washington, D.C. 20009
(Publication: *The American Anthropologist*)

American Society for Conservation Archaeology
Museum of Northern Arizona
Route 4, Box 720
Flagstaff, Arizona 86001
(Publication: *ASCA Newsletter*)

Northwestern Archaeology
Box 1499
Evanston, Illinois 60204
(Publication: *Early Man*)

Society for American Archaeology
1703 New Hampshire Avenue NW
Washington, D.C. 20009
(Publication: *American Antiquity*)

RECOMMENDED READING

Bass, G. F. *Archaeology Under Water.* New York: Praeger, 1966.
Chapman, C. H., and Chapman, E. F. *Indians and Archaeology of Missouri.* Missouri Handbook, No. 6. Columbia: University of Missouri Press, 1967.
Deetz, J. *Invitation to Archaeology.* Garden City, N.Y.: Doubleday, 1967.
Evans, J. G. *An Introduction to Environmental Archaeology.* Ithaca, N.Y.: Cornell University Press, 1979.
Feldman, M. *Archaeology for Everyone.* New York: Quadrangle/The New York Times Book Co., 1977.
Heizer, R. F. *The Archaeologist at Work.* Scranton, Penn.: Harper, 1959.
———, and Graham, J. A. *A Guide to Field Methods in Archaeology.* Palo Alto, Calif.: National Press Books, 1967.
Hole, F., and Heizer, R. F. *An Introduction to Prehistoric Archaeology.* New York: Holt, Rinehart & Winston, 1965.
Howells, W. W. *Back of History.* Garden City, N.Y.: Doubleday, 1954.
Jennings, J. D. *Prehistory of North America.* New York: McGraw-Hill, 1968.
Kellar, J. H. *An Introduction to the Prehistory of Indiana.* Indianapolis: Indiana Historical Society, 1973.
Kidder, A. V. *An Introduction to the Study of Southwestern Archaeology.* Rev. ed. New Haven, Conn.: Yale University Press, 1962.
Kirk, R., and Daugherty, R. D. *Exploring Washington Archaeology.* Seattle: University of Washington Press, 1978.
Lister, F. C., and Lister, R. D. *Earl Morris and Southwestern Archaeology.* Albuquerque: University of New Mexico Press, 1968.
Mallam, R. C. *The Iowa Effigy Mound Manifestation.* Report No. 9, Office of the State Archaeologist. Iowa City: University of Iowa, 1976.
McGimsey, C. R. III. *Indians of Arkansas.* Arkansas Archaeological Survey, Popular Series No. 1. Fayetteville: University of Arkansas Museum, 1969.
McHargue, G., and Roberts, M. *A Field Guide to Conservation Archaeology in North America.* Philadelphia: J. B. Lippincott Co., 1977.
McNitt, F., and Wetherill, R. *Anasazi.* Rev. ed. Albuquerque: University of New Mexico Press, 1966.
Morris, A. A. *Digging in the Southwest.* Garden City, N.Y.: Doubleday, 1933. Reprint. Santa Barbara: Peregrine Smith Inc., 1978.
Newcomb, W. W., Jr. *The Indians of Texas.* Austin: University of Texas Press, 1961.
New World Archaeology: Readings from Scientific American. San Francisco: W. H. Freeman & Co., 1974.
Potter, M. A. *Ohio's Prehistoric Peoples.* Columbus: Ohio Historical Society, 1968.
Rackl, H. W. *Diving into the Past: Archaeology Under Water.* New York: Scribner's, 1968.

Robbins, M., and Irving, M. B. *The Amateur Archaeologist's Handbook.* New York: Thomas Y. Crowell Co., 1965.

Silverberg, R. *Men Against Time: Salvage Archaeology in the United States.* New York: Macmillan, 1967.

______. *The Mound Builders of Ancient America: The Archaeology of a Myth.* Greenwich, Conn.: New York Graphic Society, 1968. Also New York: Ballantine, 1975.

South, S. A. *Indians of North Carolina.* Raleigh: Division of Archives and History, North Carolina Department of Cultural Resources, 1976.

Struever, S., and Holton, F. A. *Koster: Americans in Search of Their Prehistoric Past.* Garden City, N.Y.: Anchor Press/Doubleday, 1979.

Walthall, J. A. *Moundville: An Introduction to the Archaeology of a Mississippian Chiefdom.* University: Alabama Museum of Natural History, University of Alabama, 1977.

Watson, D. *Indians of the Mesa Verde.* Mesa Verde National Park, Colo.: Mesa Verde Museum Association, 1961.

Willey, G. R. *An Introduction to American Archaeology: Volume One, North and Middle America.* Englewood Cliffs, N.J.: Prentice-Hall, 1966.

______, and Sabloff, J. A. *A History of American Archaeology.* San Francisco: W. H. Freeman & Co., 1975.

Wormington, H. M. *Ancient Man in North America.* Denver: Denver Museum of Natural History, 1957.

______. *Prehistoric Indians of the Southwest.* Denver: Denver Museum of Natural History, 1947.

FOR YOUNG PEOPLE

Baldwin, G. C. *America's Buried Past.* New York: Putnam, 1962.

______. *The World of Prehistory.* New York: Putnam, 1962.

Elting, M., and Folsom, F. *The Story of Archeology in the Americas.* New York: Harvey House, 1960.

INDEX